Contents

INTRODUCTION

Paintball is for me!

Casablanca, released in 1942, is one of the greatest movies of all time. In it, Humphrey Bogart sees a very beautiful and youthful Ingrid Bergman, a former lover from his days in Paris, and mutters something like, "Of all the gin joints in all the cities in the world, she had to show up here."

Paintball was like that for me. Too old for skateboards and snowboards and a little weary of the archery game, I needed a change and a challenge. I ho-hummed into flinging field paint with rental stuff only to find out that I was having a huge time! I hadn't had that much fun since … well, I don't remember when.

Playing paintball burst onto the windshield of my spare time (and disposable income) like a big, fat bug. Splaat. Hello! "Houston, we've got a problem." Now, I have another hobby and, like Humphrey Bogart's character, Rick, in Casablanca, I have to figure out how to rearrange my life. I need to know where to put paintball in my already busy life … and how to pay for my new marker and mask and all the upgrades I want. Well, I just have to trust that it'll work out. Somehow.

Heck, just 25 years ago there wasn't any paintball. Zero. Zip. Nada. Then, a couple guys saw some paintball pistols in an agricultural catalog and thought, "Wouldn't it be fun to play a game where we could shoot at each other with those? We could call it the National Survival Game and could make a lot of money building up a sport from nothing." And so they did. Well, sort of.

A lot has changed in the world and in the world of paintball since those guys played their first game of "capture the flag" in 1981. That "evil empire," the Soviet Union, was pointing hundreds of nuclear weapons at good old America and free Europe, which in turn pointed hundreds of their own right back. It was all enough to blow everybody in the world to kingdom come. Of course, the Soviet Union kind of disintegrated and at the same time, paintball went from two or three guys chasing each other around in the New Hampshire woods to a solid sport with 10 million people involved in the billion-dollar industry supporting it.

The guys who started paintball certainly could not imagine what would become of it. Their ideas were almost 180 degrees away from what has actually happened as our game has struggled for recognition and acceptance. Today, paintball has professional team tournaments in cool places like southern California and Aruba and Toulouse, France. It has thousands of regulated fields in every state and Canadian province where kids and dads and moms can play recreationally. And we can get involved in superbly produced 24-hour scenario games with characters and scripts and special effects and a thousand of our closest friends. We're even on TeeVee.

Paintball today is huge!

Paintball is popular because running around and shooting at people with globs of paint – and dodging when they shoot back – is just a whole lot of FUN. Of course, there are quite a few people who don't like the idea of shooting at someone. Well, they probably never played, either.

Paintball isn't life or death although we sometimes play like it is. It isn't hunting, and we don't use guns. We use markers because we take paint and mark our opponents by stamping their butt with our seal of gotcha. Sure, it seems a little militaristic with all the running and gunning. But so what?

Frankly, the people who are against paintball – yes, there are some hardheads everywhere – come out of the same tradition as the people who just hate the fact that someone – anyone – anywhere is having fun. They're the ones banning skateboards and giving you a ticket if they catch you riding your bike without a helmet or a license. They're right out of the "Eat your vegetables. Sit up straight and don't speak until you are spoken to" era. To heck with 'em … although eating your veggies is probably a good

Girls love their daddies, even when they are raggedy old paint-ball players. Although she has to wait until she is 10 years old to play on an insured field, there is absolutely no reason this young lady cannot grow up to be the hottest, baddest pro player in the world.

THE COMPLETE GUIDE TO GAMES, GEAR & TACTICS

RICK SAPP

©2004 Krause Publications
Published by Krause Publications

krause publications
An imprint of F+W Publications, Inc.

700 East State Street • Iola, WI 54990-0001
715-445-2214 • 888-457-2873
www.krause.com

Our toll-free number to place an order or obtain
a free catalog is (800) 258-0929.

Library of Congress Catalog Number: 2004100735
ISBN: 0-87349-743-0

Edited by Joel Marvin
Designed by Brian Brogaard

Printed in United States of America

Paintball may not be safe for boys and girls younger than 10 years old, but this game is for everyone, no matter how old they become. Generally, you can show up at any field and rent goggles and a set-up marker that operates on CO$_2$. Most recreational fields, in fact, welcome new players. You will make friends and have a terrific time playing.

idea, especially if you top them off with a good 12-ounce New York Strip steak.

So, one or two reasons paintball is such fun: It's safe and the equipment has evolved (a lot!) since the time the first guys played.

Studies by insurance suits say paintball is right up there, safety-wise, with badminton! Go figure. That surprises everybody. Me, too. But the way you get hurt in paintball, other than some fluky sprained ankle or getting sunburned, is when you ignore three rules:

1. Keep your mask on all the time you are playing. If you are on or approaching the field, put your mask on. No exceptions.
2. When you're not playing, keep a barrel cover over the barrel of your marker or a plug inside the barrel. Always. And cover or plug your barrel the moment you come off the field. Again … always.
3. Never use your marker and paint for horsing around off a field. Don't use it to blast your buddies or their dogs and cats or their dates on Saturday night. Or to get even for someone soaping your windows on Halloween. Or "just for fun." Never use it off the field. Ever.

Paintball is growing around the world. The equipment is getting better, faster, quieter and more reliable. We can keep it growing by observing the three rules above.

So, now that we've gotten the serious stuff out in the open, let's go look at some equipment … and then start having some of that FUN we're talking about. And as far

as scheduling your time and your bucks, burn that candle at both ends. Get a second job. Then, get out there and kick some butt! You are only alive once.

After all, you needed a new passion.

A SPECIAL NOTE

Paintball Digest is a gear-and-gadget-oriented book rather than a book about tactics or strategy, even though we do talk about how to play and where to go. But mostly, we talk about markers and drop-forwards and high-pressure air. We talk about Teflon and 6061-T6 aluminum alloy. If you like to mess around with the gear used to play, tuning it yourself and accessorizing it, this book is definitely for you.

Each equipment chapter reviews some of the issues and some of the gear. For instance, we discuss the difference between powering markers with carbon dioxide (CO$_2$) and nitrogen or compressed, high-pressure air (HPA).

We don't talk about every issue or every company's gear, however. Not every hot marker or excellent high-tech company that produces sniper barrels is mentioned, but we do cover a whole lot of them! Yep, we tended to lean more heavily toward the companies that were helpful with information and high-quality photos. We thank them, because they made this first *Paintball Digest* possible and, most of the time, fun. We tried to ask everyone for pictures, but for one reason or another, not every company responded. So, for the companies that are not fully represented, we apologize and hope that you will help us remedy that in the second edition of *Paintball Digest*.

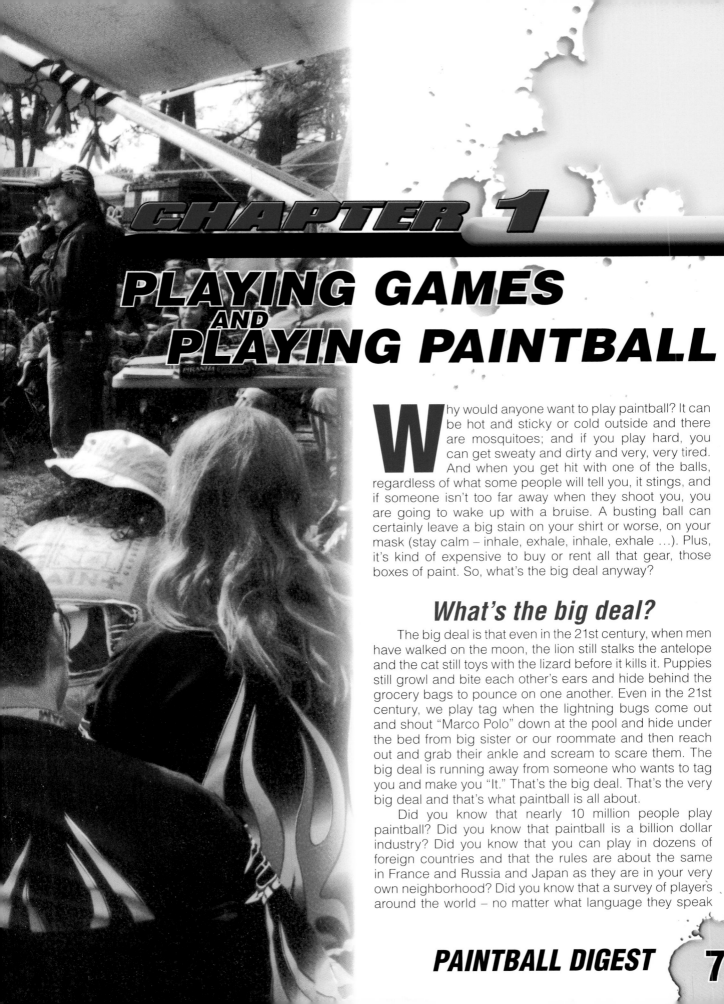

CHAPTER 1

PLAYING GAMES AND PLAYING PAINTBALL

Why would anyone want to play paintball? It can be hot and sticky or cold outside and there are mosquitoes; and if you play hard, you can get sweaty and dirty and very, very tired. And when you get hit with one of the balls, regardless of what some people will tell you, it stings, and if someone isn't too far away when they shoot you, you are going to wake up with a bruise. A busting ball can certainly leave a big stain on your shirt or worse, on your mask (stay calm – inhale, exhale, inhale, exhale …). Plus, it's kind of expensive to buy or rent all that gear, those boxes of paint. So, what's the big deal anyway?

What's the big deal?

The big deal is that even in the 21st century, when men have walked on the moon, the lion still stalks the antelope and the cat still toys with the lizard before it kills it. Puppies still growl and bite each other's ears and hide behind the grocery bags to pounce on one another. Even in the 21st century, we play tag when the lightning bugs come out and shout "Marco Polo" down at the pool and hide under the bed from big sister or our roommate and then reach out and grab their ankle and scream to scare them. The big deal is running away from someone who wants to tag you and make you "It." That's the big deal. That's the very big deal and that's what paintball is all about.

Did you know that nearly 10 million people play paintball? Did you know that paintball is a billion dollar industry? Did you know that you can play in dozens of foreign countries and that the rules are about the same in France and Russia and Japan as they are in your very own neighborhood? Did you know that a survey of players around the world – no matter what language they speak or what kind of job they have or how much money their family makes – reports that people play paintball for the very same reasons, because it's exciting and it's huge fun.

Now, some of this may not interest you, but it does mean that you are not alone and you're not weird because you may want to "splaat" someone. It means that you are part of a worldwide community of people who enjoy doing the same kind of things as you and for the same reasons.

"So what?" you may ask. "What does all this mean to me? All I like to do is run and throw paint and have a good time. I don't care about all that other stuff."

That's okay, too. Those are the same feelings that Egyptian players have, or Brazilian players. It means you are somebody and your feelings are important on a really global scale. It is like being part of a brotherhood in a way, or a sisterhood. This "paintball fever" sets you apart … in a good way. It isn't school, though. You don't have to care about the history of paintball or the National Professional Paintball League or even how your marker works. Go out. Have fun.

Paintball is not just fun, with the running and dodging and shooting at your buddies. Paintball is wonderful exercise. Paintball teaches teamwork and sportsmanship, competition and tactics; things you will need in business later in life. Every good team, whether it is a scenario team like Michael Hanse's Blue's Crew or a hot pro tournament favorite like the Brass Eagle All Stars, wins because they work together and respect the fact that whatever their personal financial, educational or employment circumstances, they can get out and play.

So, here's a thought. We expect to have a good time when we play. Are we sure it is okay for our dad or mom to have a good time like this though? And if it's okay for us or the parents, how about grandpa? Hey, why not!

Sometimes, the older that people become, the more they want to hide their enthusiasm, the simple joy of having fun and laughing out loud. It's supposedly "grown up" to be serious and more concerned about paying the bills and saving for college, or politics or hog futures or saving for your retirement. Well, all of those things are important, but religious leaders, philosophers, medical doctors, therapists and psychiatrists of all sorts tell us continually that putting "fun" as well as work and exercise into our daily drama is crucial to a long and healthy life.

Would you rather play a 24-hour scenario game with a huge new group of best friends (many of them dressed like it's Halloween) or would you rather run a 26-mile marathon? Either way it's 110 calories per mile, but one of them is actually fun.

Would you rather scream through a 5-man tournament with cash and prizes at the end or go to the gym and lift dumbbells? Either way, your muscles are going to get a huge workout.

While we're talking about what makes paintball

The Captain, our own William Shatner from the bridge of the Starship Enterprise, is a huge paintball promoter.

tick, let's talk teamwork. There's Worr Games Executive Director Sonny Lopez (certainly a responsible corporate position) screaming out movements and shooting like a mad dog for the top-ranked pro team Naughty Dogs in Huntington Beach. There go General Blue and his friends Mother and Pac Man leading a team through the woods to attack General Ben Torricelli's red team at the International Amateur Open's 8-hour scenario game.

Sure, paintball is competitive, and it is a whole lot better to observe the Golden Rule and give paint rather than receive it; but within the big world of competing alliances, backstabbing and cutthroat business practices, there is enormous cooperation. You could say that it is the cooperation and the teamwork that makes the competition possible. Otherwise, you're back in the woods 20 years ago playing the original survival game, alone with something like a Nelspot 007 single-shot marker powered by a 12-gram CO_2 cartridge and shooting oil-based paint. After the game, your clothes are going to be such a mess that you may throw them away rather than take them home. Long-time player Steve Davidson has said that in those days some of his clothes were so disgusting that burning them was the only way to safely get rid of them after a

You will see all kinds of gear and get-ups on a typical paintball field, from ninja to hand-me-downs. What every player has in common are goggles, markers, balls, barrel plugs and a smile that says, "Game on!"

game. And who likes that?

It is because they work together to accomplish a goal in a super-competitive environment that Team Dynasty is a winner and puts $20,000 in their pockets after winning an NPPL Tournament. If everyone went off on their own, they would be quickly eliminated by the other team, which has discussed and agreed on assignments to cover the field with fire and to keep paint rifling through approach lanes while their smallest, quickest member dashes for the flag.

Teamwork and competition. You're going to learn a lot about them in paintball because the more you dig it, the more fun you are going to have and the more successful you and your buddies will be. It's really a better gig than listening to your dad talk about how it was when he was a kid and had to walk to school.

And what about that other word, sportsmanship? What's that got to do with anything, much less paintball? Well … everything. There are rules in paintball just like in an English classroom or sitting in a jury box. There were rules in cave man society. There are rules everywhere human beings live, work or play, because believe it or not, it's the rules that we all observe that make

our games possible.

The first rule of sportsmanship is Play Safe. If you don't play safely, someone is going to get hurt, the game is going to stop, the refs are going to get angry and nobody is going to have a good time. So, never take your goggles off during a game or while you are on a playing field. Duh, dumb and dangerous. A paintball may not seem like much. It's light and squishy. But a hit in the eye can cause retinal detachment, which means you will have pain (a lot) and, at least in one eye, it will seem like you are dizzy and the world is dark and fuzzy for a very long time. You won't like that. And, of course, if you get hurt because you have ignored this primary rule, everyone else suffers, too. People yell at you. Your mother panics. The ride in the ambulance may be interesting, but you will be in too much pain to enjoy it. The field owner's insurance goes up. Bottom line: wear your mask.

The second rule of good sportsmanship is to Use Your Barrel Plug or Barrel Cover absolutely every moment you are not on the field playing. An accidental shot could blind someone and get you thrown off a playing field or a team … forever. Who needs that? And by the way, it's okay to remind someone that their barrel cover is not in

The player's party following the DraXxus International Amateur Open featured a boxed dinner, individual and team awards and dozens of free "door prizes" donated by paintball manufacturers. Debra Dion Krischke, who has been in the paintball business since the game's founders recruited her in the early '80s, promotes this popular annual and international event in Pennsylvania.

Another reason we like paintball.

place. If they don't like it, too bad. Here is a situation where everyone must do the right thing.

The third rule of sportsmanship is Honesty. Get hit? Get out. The paint didn't bust? Well, ask the ref for a paint check or just sit out for a while. In a big game, you'll be back on the field in a little while so use the time to rest, grab some water, squeegee your marker, load up with paint, check your air or eat a sandwich. In a tournament, you are going to see this rule bent to the breaking point (some people would say way beyond it) because money and pride and some pretty inflated egos are on the line. Tournament play

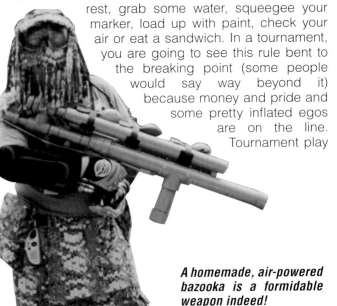

A homemade, air-powered bazooka is a formidable weapon indeed!

is very fast, and even with trained referees right on the spot, it is sometimes hard to decide who was hit first. In recreational play and scenario games, it's pretty rare to see anyone lose their mind. In tournament play, it happens all the time. You will hear a lot of talk about cheating in tournament competition. Don't be a cheater and don't accuse anyone else of cheating. Don't start shouting, "You're out! I hit you! You're out!" Get over yourself.

The fourth rule of sportsmanship is to Put Yourself in The Other Player's Position. This particularly applies to close shooting. The kid shot multiple times in the face at very close range at the 2003 International Amateur Open took one of the balls between his face and the edge of his mask with the ball traveling forward toward his eyes at a couple hundred feet per second (fps) or so. Very painful. It was most probably accidental because it happened very fast and with adrenaline levels very high. You don't want to get hit at ultra-close range; it's quite painful, it's not macho and it will leave a nasty little bruise. Give your opponent a chance to surrender before you stick the muzzle of your marker in their back and pull the trigger. Point and shout first, "You're out!" Give the person a chance to surrender and raise their marker over their head. If they turn and act like they would prefer to shoot it out with you at 10 feet when you've got the drop on them, well, what are you going to do? Let 'em have it!

CHAPTER 2
IN THE BEGINNING

Unlike horseback riding or archery or darts, we know precisely when paintball was invented. We know who did it, too, and even why. Or do we? Well-known attorneys who act in the public's interest, such as Mary O'Rourke of Florida, are schooled to understand that the testimony of eyewitnesses to a crime, for instance, will vary by a wide margin. They may even conflict, depending on their point of view or their interest in the outcome. Even the testimony of actual participants differs, and the further you are from the events themselves, the greater the participants' versions will diverge.

VERSION 1

In 1976, a 35-year-old guy named Hayes Noel went for a walk in the woods near Charlottesville, Virginia. The woods were on a farm that belonged to a buddy, because Hayes was from New York City.

Actually, Hayes may have been feeling a little bit insecure that day. He has said he was troubled by a philosophical question, but it may have been more personal than that. If the world went to hell in a hand-basket – as it showed every sign of doing in those days – was he tough enough, resourceful enough to survive?

Now, Hayes never went to Viet Nam. He was not a big-game hunter or a Harley rider. He was a New York City stockbroker! But wasn't making a living on the New York Stock Exchange practically as heart-pounding as stalking a wounded Cape buffalo in the long grass of Zimbabwe? Competition is competition, right? Cut-throat is cut-throat. If beetle-browed cold warrior Leonid Brezhnev touched off the Soviet Union's big nukes, and he wasn't killed in the initial blast, Hayes wondered if he could do whatever he had to do to survive. He really was not sure, but who could be if the unthinkable happened?

Hayes had a lot of friends. He eventually brought up his survival insecurities with George Butler and Charles Gaines. Charles was a writer and outdoorsman who lived in New Hampshire. Inside Hayes' circle, this survival debate grew with sides roughly forming around these two philosophical positions:

1. Country people would survive some kind of holocaust better than city people because people in the country grow up hunting, fishing and practicing skills that would help them adjust to a world that had suddenly turned hostile.

2. City people would cope better in emergency situations because they learn survival skills in places like the subway or even on the chaotic floor of the stock exchange – a rather intense example of cooperation and competition all mixed together – where country people, admittedly more attuned to nature's pace, would go bonkers.

So, Hayes invented paintball.

No, of course it wasn't quite that simple.

VERSION 2

While grilling king mackerel and drinking gin and tonics on the patio of a home on Jupiter Island, Florida, in 1977, Charles Gaines and Hayes Noel came up with the initial concepts of a survival game as a lark or just for fun. The practical problem was finding the right equipment and getting a place to give it a shot.

Their idea was to have a game that "might contain the childhood exhilaration of stalking and being stalked, might call on a hodgepodge of instincts and skills and might allow a variety of responses to this rich old question: 'How do I get from where I am now to where I want to be?'" They figured that if they could come up with a format, the game would appeal to kids and adults alike.

Then, Butler ran across a paint marker in an agricultural catalog. Sold by Nelson Paint in Michigan, it was called the Nelspot Marker and it looked like an unwieldy pistol with a clear plastic tube projecting out the back end. That tube was filled with round balls of oil-based paint encapsulated for Nelson by R.P. Scherer Paint Company. The marker relied on a replaceable 12-gram CO_2 cartridge in the handle for power, and the balls it shot were supposed to burst open when they hit. Farmers used the Nelspot to put spots on cows to designate those that, for instance, needed a vaccination. Timber cruisers used it in the woods or on construction sites to mark trees for cutting.

So, Butler and some of Hayes' friends ordered markers. Eventually, they had more fun than they ever believed was possible just running around and hiding and shooting at each other. In those days, shooting paintballs was kind of a random act and nobody bothered too much about wearing any kind of safety gear.

Hayes remembers the first time anyone got hit with a paintball … because it was him! He had taken a wild shot at Charles Gaines, the New Hampshire

The original paintball game was conceived of as a survival game. The best man wins. It was played in the woods in old clothes and some used camo. The markers were pump-action and the paint was real, oil-based goo that only came off with a liberal dose of turpentine.

Charles Gaines

outdoorsman, and when his buddy fired back, the ball hit Hayes squarely in the ass. It "raised a little welt," he has recalled.

These guys had so much fun they decided to have an organized contest. Maybe it was because Hayes was almost 40 years old that he felt he had to have a reason to have this kind of fun, running around and shooting at other guys like a kid at a pool with a water pistol. He was getting old. So, they mapped out a field and made up rules and got a lot of their other friends – almost all older guys, but from all over the country – to come and play.

The first organized game of paintball was held on Saturday, June 27, 1981, near Henniker, New Hampshire. Hayes and friends like Bob Gurnsey (who is still very much involved in paintball) used an 80-acre woodlot – which, after the day was over, they realized was way too big for

Debra Dion Krischke has been in paintball almost since Day 1. Today, she operates the popular International Amateur Open tournament and industry trade show held north of Pittsburgh each year.

just a dozen players – and placed flags at about the mid-point of the sides of the field. Each side of the field was represented by a different flag color. Hayes gave every player a rough map. The goal of this first game of "capture the flag" was to collect one of each color flag without getting hit by a paintball.

Here were the pioneers: Charles Gaines (writer), Hayes Noel (stock and options trader), Bob Gurnsey (sports products), Bob Jones (writer), Ronnie Simkins (farmer), Jerome Gary (film producer), Carl Sandquist (contracting estimator), Ritchie White (forester), Ken Barrett (venture capitalist), Joe Drinon (stockbroker), Bob Carlson (trauma surgeon) and Lionel Atwill (writer and author of the first "official" book about paintball).

So, who won the game … and how did it affect everyone's notions about who would survive?

The forester, Ritchie White, won the first game, which went on for several hours. Ritchie, who was a hunter and "lumber man," captured one flag of every color and was never shot, not even once. What is more interesting is that he never shot at anyone either!

For that first game, everyone was on their own. There were no teams. Consequently, each player used a different strategy. Some – those men eliminated quickly as it turns out – were aggressive and ran dodging and shooting after every flag. Hayes made up his mind to walk the perimeter and then go straight in toward the flags when he found them. He avoided firefights but was eventually eliminated when he got lost looking for the fourth and final flag.

So, the survival message was mixed. An outdoorsman, a forester, won the game, but his strategy was totally passive. Avoid other players and focus instead on the goal – capturing the flags without getting shot. (He may have won employing this non-interactive strategy, but one wonders if he had any fun this way.)

As a whole, the players in this first game said they had a terrific time. Hayes Noel has often been quoted as saying, "The illusion of danger was so real, it was the most exciting thing I had ever done. Every cell in my body was turned on."

The more Hayes Noel and Charles Gaines and Bob Gurnsey thought about it, the more they realized that

Paintball has come a long way since a couple guys shot at each other in the woods of New England. Representing the paintball industry, Debra Dion Krischke of TeamEffort Events, promoters of the International Amateur Open in Pittsburgh, presents its annual Lifetime Achievement Awards for 2003: (L-R) Debra Dion Krischke; former winner Laurent Hamet of France, a paintball promoter who was instrumental in developing inflatable bags for airball tournaments; Mike Ratko of ProCaps, who has dedicated years to develop ASTM standards to keep paintball safe and injuries down and who has developed the new X-Ball pro format; former winner Bud Orr, the popular president of Worr Games Products; and Dan Colby of Air America, who has pioneered player-friendly products since 1985.

shooting paintballs could become a game that people all over the U.S. would enjoy playing, and they soon decided they were just the people to develop it. Plus, it tied into their ongoing and unsettled survival debate. Well, these guys didn't just sit around dreaming, they got busy!

TURNING FUN TO PROFIT

In spite of growing governmental imposition at every level, one thing the homo sapiens species in the U.S. is blessed with is some old fashioned can-do entrepreneurial spirit. When Hayes Noel got "shot in the ass" that summer of 1981, apparently the first thing he thought of – other than "Ouch!" – was becoming the world's first paintball guru and starting a business. At that time, the whole paintball economy, worldwide, was squat. Zero. Zip. Nada. Today, it is in the neighborhood of a billion dollars. That's a one followed by nine zeros! It's truly, truly phenomenal, and it is based on one well-placed ball in the butt.

Not only that, but as many as ten million people play paintball games every year. And that's either a huge flash-in-the-pan sport or it's a phenomenon.

The inventors – Hayes and Charles and Bob – had so much fun shooting each other that they figured a whole lot more people would like doing it, too. So, some of these guys visited Nelson Paint in Michigan, and within a year or two, they were selling ten times as many markers

"Paintball is still in its infancy," says Ben Torricelli, owner of Millennium Paintball Productions and a specialist in producing 24-hour paintball scenario games. "It is going to continue to grow because it has everything. Action. High-tech tools. It's exciting and skill-based."

for paintball games as Nelson ever sold for agriculture and timber uses. (The Nelson Nelspot Marker was actually built by Daisy, of BB-gun fame.) The paintballs – of course, in those days they were real oil-based paint – were manufactured in a two-step process. Charles Nelson manufactured the paint and then shipped it to R.P. Scherer in Florida for ball encapsulation.

The founders got with the program right away and named their first marker the "Splatmaster." They figured they could sell the markers and paintballs in addition to licensing their game to playing fields around the U.S. They soon brought on Debra Dion Krischke, who now promotes the annual International Amateur Open north of Pittsburgh each year with DraxXus paintballs, as their public relations spokesperson.

Charles Gaines acknowledged the origins of paintball in his 1997 novel Survival Games (Atlantic Monthly Press) even though the names are changed and the ultimate action in the book is way, way out there.

For several years, the game Hayes and his business associates invented, the "National Survival Game," which was loosely based on their original "Capture the Flag" concept, grew slowly. They had trouble convincing the mainstream press, still reeling from the hang-over from the war in Viet Nam, that their survival game was fun, that no one got hurt and that it taught practical skills. But soon, of course, like any good idea,

Mike Ratko (left) from ProCaps in Canada has been a prime mover in the development of community standards for paintball. The ultimate result is safer play and a more widely accepted game by the general public. Dean Del Prete (right) is the President of Cousins Paintball stores and fields in New York, Connecticut and New Jersey. Cousins is one of the oldest and finest paintball operations in the world.

the original disciples found they had started something they couldn't control, something that quickly outgrew them. Survival became paintball.

Today, the original paintball entrepreneurs have pretty much gone on with their lives and only a couple of them are directly involved in the game or the business. The game grew in popularity and evolved, but their "National Survival Game," popular for half a dozen years or so in the early-to-middle 1980s, was essentially static, perhaps because their founding philosophical question – "Could I survive?" – dictated a very personal, individual approach to the sport. And times changed from the stress of an international nuclear standoff to a decade of prosperity in the U.S.

A game of survival is a thrilling concept, but in the U.S. it has a tendency to be viewed essentially as a

"Survivors will always live to tell of surviving by doing just the opposite of others who have survived. Medical experts have often told survivors that by all rights they should be dead. Instead of dying they had the WILL to live. YOU, TOO, MUST ENLIST THIS WILL, that sense of self-preservation, which starts with a deep breath and the determination not to give way at any cost."
— Anthony Greenbank, pg. xi, The Book of Survival *(Revised) Hatherleigh Press (WW Norton & Co.) 5-22 46th Ave. Suite 200, Long Island City, NY 11101*

solitary, individual game. The "I" is paramount. With some exceptions such as tennis or golf, most other sports played with a ball are team events: football, soccer, basketball, baseball … even polo and water polo. Founding a sport based on the ascendancy of a single individual, who physically eliminated his opponents, like in boxing, was bound to be confining. Even hunting and archery have met those invisible boundaries. Today, paintball is larger than its founders ever imagined. In the years since the first shot heard round the world, here is how the sport has evolved.

Style of Play: The early game was based on principles of individual initiative and individual decision-making: every man for himself. Today's game is all about team play, communication, coordination, mutual support,

"Never surrender ... unless you are completely surrounded."
Actor, author, crooner and paintball activist William Shatner of Star Trek.

and certainly, just like the very first firefight, straight shootin'.

Where to Play: The first recognized game in June 1981 was held in the woods on what would today be considered a "rogue field." Just 25 years ago, there were no fields and virtually no rules except the injunction to "be a good sport." Then, in April 1982, Caleb Strong opened the first outdoor playing field in Rochester, New York. Now, licensed outdoor paintball fields with strong insurance coverage and enforced rules for safety and play abound in the U.S. and can be found in dozens of foreign countries. There are even a significant number of indoor playing venues, tournaments and national championship events.

Marker: In the first games, players shot one ball at a time out of a see-through, gravity-fed tube that held 10 balls and stuck straight out of the back of the marker. Their Nelspot markers, such as the famous "007," were limited by the CO_2 power remaining in a replaceable 12-gram cartridge, which might deliver 30 to 40 good shots. This meant that accurate shots were more lucky rather than predictable. With one of today's markers, like a PMI Pro TS with electronic Storm frame equipped with

THE START OF THE ADDICTION: FIRST TIME
by Matthew Smith

Sweat pouring off your face, adrenaline pumping through your veins, diving into the mud without a single thought, hearing the sound of balls flying by your head, just like cowboys and Indians as a kid.

What is it that is so addictive about paintball you ask? If the pure thrill and adrenaline rush don't appeal to you, then you better keep your day job. For the rest of us, we'll keep our day jobs to support the paintball addiction!

What's the strategy? For those of us with only a few seconds to decide, we come up with a little game plan. The horn blows and it is war. Running through the woods, only thinking of one thing: get the other team before they get you. Getting the flag doesn't seem like an option until some of the opposing team members are eliminated.

I don't think I even remember hearing my heart beat, or feeling the condensation in my mask from my breathing. I didn't notice the mud that I was laying in until I looked at my clothes after victory was achieved. It was such a strange feeling, playing cowboys and Indians with rounds that were actually flying by my head. Not strong enough to seriously hurt you, but fast enough to sting and make you duck as far down as you can behind a tree stump.

Do I stick my head out and shoot or do I move to gain a better position?

The bunker is 60 feet away. I can barely see the four guys inside and I have no shot. I've already wasted 20 rounds from this spot. Pinned down by one guy behind a bunker 40 feet away. What do I do? Do I move and take a chance of getting hit or do I stay where I am. Well, I'm no good here.

I quit firing and wait, watching the opposing team take a dozen shots at a different member of my team. This is my chance to move. Gaining 10 yards on him, there's a small hole in his cover. Standing up with no cover, I fire as fast as I can, both at the tower and at this opponent in front of me. He is crouched down with his head almost between his knees.

I end up taking out two guys in the tower and the one in front of me, too. "They're out, let them off the field!" the ref shouts.

Ducking to cover, the two remaining opponents in the tower never see me. Here's my advantage. My other team members are drawing their fire and they'll never see me coming.

Being sneaky and cunning throughout the game is my personal strategy. I usually only take three to four shots from one spot and then I move if I can. In woods-style games, I always try to get close first and make sure I have a clear shot before firing. If I don't get my target by the third or fourth shot, I most likely wasn't going to get it from that position. I also know that once I shoot, my position is unsecured and I take on heavy fire.

The flag is to my left and the tower is straight ahead. What should I go for? Take out the tower or go for the flag and risk being shot? Better to take out the tower, I think.

As I head in, one of my team sprints for the flag and I take control of the building. A horn blows. Game over.

What an experience! I will never forget this and I suggest that everyone try it at least once in his or her life. If you don't fall in love with it, there has to be something wrong with you.

"That was the biggest rush I've had since basic training, 20 years ago," my dad, James Smith, said.

Courtesy of Matthew Smith and *www.warpig.com*

– used these first paintballs for marking trees. (Nelson still makes oil-based paintballs for timber cruisers.) With names like Chaos, Fury, Anarchy and Upheaval, today's water-based Nelson balls scrub off with soap and water. Unlike the early versions, these balls are almost perfectly round, and if stored properly, they stay that way.

Headgear: Early players might have worn baseball caps and maybe some protective goggles from the hardware store or just their own glasses. Today, no one – field owner, player, judge, photographer or observer – is allowed on an active field without complete face, ear and, if possible, neck protection. Today's players wear safety gear designed specifically for paintball, like Raven's NVX, an adjustable combo facemask, eyeshade and lens system.

Clothing: Blue jeans, tee shirts and tennis shoes or long sleeve tan work shirts and leather boots were the fashion on early fields. Old clothes were mixed with WW II army surplus woodland camo and tiger stripe from Viet Nam, feeding an early and unfavorable reaction to survival paintball games as militaristic, shabby and lower class. Certainly not a game for respectable families. Then, starting in the early 1980s, entrepreneurs like Jim Crumley (Trebark), Bill Jordan (Realtree and Advantage) and Toxey Haas (Mossy Oak) realized there was a men's market for boutique camo patterns, primarily in the hunting field. For its first decade, camo was the paintball garment standard. You still see old clothes and camo on the playing fields, but a whole new style has developed for paintball. Radical rap! These days, hot colors and bright, fun patterns are standard on playing fields. JT USA's Yellow Flame jersey and gloves, special all-purpose shoes with cleats, and black sock hats from Ronin Gear emphasize the development of merchandise for what has become a young person's market. Ain't no more shabby chic except at your local rec ball field.

PAINTBALL TIME CAPSULE

Paintball as an individual survival game was based in the socially and politically turbulent '70s, but this was also a time of extreme technological innovation. To understand the debate that is the foundation of our game, here is a quick look at some of the background events that shaped it and the men and women who developed it.

1970 Daisy builds first paintball marker for agriculture and forestry purposes.
"Cold War" pits U.S. against Soviet Union in nuclear standoff.
World Trade Center twin towers are completed in New York City.
1971 U.S. and South Viet Nam invade Laos.
The first microprocessor is available.
1972 U.S. begins withdrawal from Viet Nam.
Watergate scandal begins to overwhelm

First time!

a 68 cu/in Pure Energy 3000 psi carbon-wrapped bottle of nitrogen or compressed air, you can expect to get between 1400 and 1800 shots, all expelled with identical velocity and a high degree of accuracy out to possibly 40 or 50 yards. And the standard loader holds 200 or more paintballs ready to rip.

Paintballs: Yep. The founders played with the real thing, actual paint goop that took turpentine to dissolve. That's good for your soft skin and baby-face complexion! According to 64-year-old Nelson Paint, the original paintball supplier, Charles Nelson was the first person to develop a ball of paint that could be shot out of a CO_2 marker. Timber cruisers – men who surveyed woodlots and decided how much and what quality timber was available for cutting

President Richard Nixon.
Apollo 17's Eugene Cernan is last man to walk on to the moon.

1973 U.S. Supreme Court rules in the Roe vs. Wade case.
Vice President Spiro Agnew resigns.

1974 Richard Nixon resigns: Gerald Ford sworn in as president.
Hank Aaron beats Babe Ruth's home run record.
The first pocket calculators appear.

1975 Saigon falls to North Viet Nam.
The first home computer does not have a screen or printer.
Disposable razors are introduced.

1976 Jimmy Carter becomes president.
Apple Computers is launched.
VHS VCRs are introduced.

1977 U.S. turns Panama Canal over to Panama.

1978 In Jonestown, Guyana, 900 Americans commit suicide.
"Garfield the Cat" cartoon is syndicated.

1979 The Ayatollah Khomeini takes power in Iran.
The Soviet Union invades Afghanistan.

Paintball took off in popularity in the mid-1980s. Economically, those were boom times. The stock market got bullish and stayed that way. Money, happiness and prosperity seemed within the grasp of every citizen. And there was trouble in the Soviet Union's international worker's paradise because "The Wall" between East and West Berlin was going to fall this decade, something baby boomers, the children born in the decade immediately following World War II, never thought they would live to see. And almost immediately, our game began to change from an individual survival event to a team-oriented game of paintball.

1980 Ronald Reagan elected to the U.S. presidency.
Bill Gates licenses MS-DOS to IBM (for virtually nothing!).
The Empire Strikes Back is released.

1981 First paintball game with Bob Gurnsey, Hayes Noel and Charles Gaines.
The disease AIDS is first identified.
Ronald Reagan and Pope John Paul II wounded by assassins.
World population is estimated at 4.5 billion.

1982 Caleb Strong opens the first outdoor paintball field in Rochester, NY.
Hayes Noel markets paintball as the National Survival Game (NSG).
PMI (Pursuit Marketing, Inc.) becomes first paintball products distributor.
Barney Clark receives first artificial heart.

1983 First NSG National Championships have a $14,000 cash purse.

In America, the entrepreneurial spirit is still strong. When the founders of paintball decided to develop the National Survival Game, woodsy play became a business. Today, a strong business community is necessary to hold professional tournaments, develop safety standards and build expensive, high-tech equipment. Johnny Postorivo is chief operating officer of the world's largest paintball wholesaler, National Paintball Supply, and his second objective is to promote safe and reliable gear that is fast and efficient. His first objective, just like those founders of the game, is to make a profit for his company, because in America, nothing goes forward without a profit.

First Canadian paintball field opens in Toronto.
Sally Ride is first woman in space aboard Space Shuttle Challenger.
U.S. invades Caribbean island of Grenada.

1984 Called "Skirmish Games," paintball gets a start in Australia.
Caleb Strong opens the first indoor paintball field in Rochester, NY.
Paintball as "The Ultimate Challenge" takes hold in England.
Ronald Regan is re-elected U.S. president.

1985 Mikhail Gorbachev becomes leader of the Soviet Union.
Palestinian terrorists hijack Achille Lauro ocean liner.

1986 Space Shuttle Challenger explodes.
Halley's Comet is visible.
U.S. heavily involved in Nicaragua.

1987 Margaret Thatcher is Prime Minister in Great Britain.
Severe earthquake rocks Los Angeles.

1988 The IPPA (International Paintball Players Assn.) is founded to promote paintball.

1991 Paintball begins in France, Denmark and other European countries.

1992 NPPL, the National Paintball Player's League, is organized.

1996 Paintball fields and pro shops can be found in 25 countries.

Your Basic Paintball Marker

All paintball markers use air pressure from an air tank (or a 12-gram cartridge) to fire a paintball. The velocity of the paintball leaving the barrel is usually 250 to 300 fps, the maximum allowed at tournaments (290 fps is the maximum permitted on most playing fields). Air tanks come in different sizes. The bigger the tank, the longer you can play before requiring a refill. Sizes begin at 4 ounces and go up to 20 ounces.

1. Feeder (also called a hopper or loader): Paintballs drop one at a time from this refillable bulk feeder into the marker.

2. CO2 Tank: Air is pressurized at 750 to 1000 psi. Air leaves the tank through a valve into an airline. High-pressure air (HPA) is a non-CO2 system and requires a regulator. HPA tanks are pressurized to thousands of psi and are typically larger than CO2 tanks.

3. Air Line: Air travels up the line and into the chamber.

4. Trigger: Pulling the trigger activates the hammer. The hammer slides forward, pulling the bolt over the exhaust valve while pushing the exhaust valve forward to the chamber. Air shoots out of the chamber, through the exhaust valve and through the bolt.

5. Barrel: The released air leaves the bolt, forcing the paintball out of the barrel.

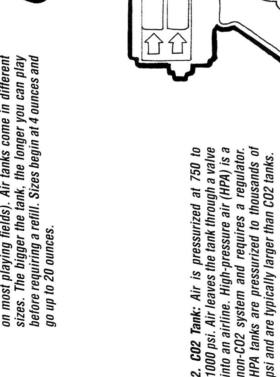

CHAPTER 3
RECREATIONAL PLAY

Paintball is a high-tech game of playing tag. The same philosophy applies: It is better to give than to receive. So, give all you've got.

Most of what you will read in magazines is about tournaments and airball fields and professionals. Now, 99 percent of us won't ever play competitive, cash-prize paintball and don't really care. Most of us just want to have fun. So, you can sum up all the tactics for playing recreational paintball in just ten words: you run, you shoot, you hide and you play fair. Nevertheless, here are some tips and essential playing skills for higher-level play.

TACTICAL TIPS

Use cover effectively. Whether you are hiding behind a big tree or a bunker, there are some specific practices that will help you keep an eye on the field without being hit every time you stick your head out.

First, remember those geometry classes you dozed through? Well, they could come in handy now. The closer you are to the bad guys, the less time you have to react and the tighter you want to lean into your cover. The farther you are away, the more time you will have to react and you can play a little fast and loose with the tree. It's a matter of angles, reaction time and the general inaccuracy of shooting on a rec field. Of course, the same principles apply to pro play as well.

When you lean out from the tree, present the lowest possible profile to see and to be seen. Keep your marker tight against the side and in the same angle as your face. Beginners often exhibit what is known as "lazy hopper syndrome," where they stick their marker and that big 200-count hopper out of cover … and get it blasted right away. You only need one eye to look for movement and targets.

Get a move on. Unlike that very first game of paintball back in '81 where the winner never shot a single ball and

Use cover effectively. This right-hander is switching to the left side of the bunker and shooting left-handed. He may not be quite as accurate, but this is good shooting technique to keep the opposition off guard.

Get a move on if you are charging over the top! Marker up, crouch and fire as you go.

only skulked from cover to cover in the woods, you've got to move if you're going to win in today's game. On the other hand, with the super high rates of fire most markers are capable of even on semi-auto mode (20+ balls per second), you do have to spend some time thinking about your moves before you jump out of cover. The important thing to keep in mind is that you can't freeze in the open. Do that and you are dead. Like a deer in the headlights. Practice your quick moves. Practice sliding legs first and head first. Sure, you can get scraped up. So?

Now, if you know anything about the field you are playing on, you can anticipate where the paint is going to be concentrated. After all, most fields today are tight and certainly the narrow airball fields have shooting lanes.

In rec ball, you will often go out without a team. Everybody who is a walk-on is kind of grouped into the player mix. Don't be shy. A good tactic is to recruit a buddy or, in a pick-up game, even somebody you don't know and become a team: one moves and one covers. At the end of the day, you will both wear less paint.

Shoot and shoot some more. That's what you are out there for. Face it. There are a lot of different styles of shooting your marker. You are going to find yourself in many different situations on the field whether it is rec play, a scenario game or a tournament, so why not practice for them? Practice being pinned down and needing to get

off a quick shot (called snap shooting) by putting a pie plate on a string 15 to 20 yards away. Then, from behind a wall or tree, practice leaning out and taking two or three fast shots. The more you try this, the better your hand-eye coordination will become. It's all about staying "alive."

Try shooting with both hands. Say 85 percent of us are right-handed. This means when your opponent leans out from behind the bunker, the chances are that he or she will lean out on their right side – the left side as you are looking for them. You can plan your shooting for this. People tend to exit the bunker running on that side, too.

In tournament play, the term "sweetspotting" or lane shooting is a very big consideration. We carry a lot of balls and we have high-rate-of-fire markers. Balls are cheap and we know the opposition has to move across "that lane" to run for the flag. So, fill it with paint. The clock is running and they have to move. So do you!

Finally, try shooting blind and shooting on the run. You are preparing to make a move. Slide your marker around the corner, keeping it level to slightly elevated and squeeze off a couple dozen shots. 'Course, if one of your guys has moved out in front you're going to waste 'em, but you can shoot accurately on the run can't you? If not, get some cheap paint and practice. Run and gun!

Talk to me! This means you have to communicate to your teammates on any paintball field. In competition, your team will have practiced giving signals on the field … and responding to them, too. In NPPL and PSP play, you cannot have anyone on the sidelines coaching or calling out positions or information. In the NXL and some

TEAMWORK

Battle Drills or Immediate Action Drills

When you are shooting from behind cover, present the smallest silhouette you can to look and fire. Lean out only long enough to get off your shots and then duck back. The next time you lean out to fire, choose a different spot to prevent your opponents from remembering that a right-hander will almost always lean out the right side to fire.

collegiate play, however, this is actually encouraged.

The problem with communication is adrenaline. It blocks your ability to hear, respond and react. It also blocks your ability to give directions. Everyone has seen the newbie hunkered in his bunker and just beyond there is an opponent approaching, intent on blasting him. The newbie's buddy, who is only 20 yards away but equally pinned down, yells at him again and again, but the newbie doesn't react. He has gone into a shell where nothing comes in and nothing goes out. It's adrenaline in its extreme form.

If you are on a team, practice giving and responding to signals. If you are not on a team and are playing as a walk-on with a group of players you don't know, you may want to pair off within the game for better attack and defense tactics and survivability.

You can play paintball forever on recreational fields and in scenario games. At some time in your life you may get tennis elbow from doing chin-ups or maybe bust a tendon in your foot from running road races, but attacking and defending, dodging and shooting paintballs is practically a lifetime sport.

What takes your play to the next level, however, is putting together or joining a team. In a team, you can really move around the U.S. in tournaments and perhaps – if you are good enough – pick up some sponsors and make a little money, too. Or maybe make a lot of money.

Working together in a scenario game makes for good team practice. Most generals are only too willing to have a good team on their side. It gives everyone confidence that at least part of a big group of players will work together.

According to Jon Harris, a retired U.S. Army NCO and specialist in small unit tactics (*www.tacticalmarkers.com*), small unit routines can mean the difference in staying alive and getting splattered in paint. In the military or on a SWAT team, where they use live ammo and a hit is much more serious than a washable mark, such drills are a regular part of combat readiness and preparation. "I can tell you from experience," Jon says, "these drills work. They are not hard, but coordination is the key. I remember practicing crossing the same road maybe 50 times in a day until I was satisfied that our squad had it right. Then, we did it again with everyone occupying a different position in the squad. Everyone had to know someone else's job."

Jon says an immediate action drill is used to rehearse reactions to contact with the opposition. Basically, they involve practicing your immediate reaction to a threat until it becomes an automatic response. In combat, you may only have seconds … if that.

Assume that the other team wants to catch you in an unfavorable tactical spot, an ambush, for instance. You will be tooling around with your buddies and suddenly, unless you are way out in the open, you will run into dozens of balls in the air heading right at you. You won't have a big chance to shout "Incoming!" and hit the dirt shooting. In an ambush, contact will be sudden, violent, close and at short range. If you react slowly or in a disorganized manner, everyone will "die" and you and your whole team will be sitting out for a half hour. Drills help you react right – RIGHT NOW!

According to Jon, this kind of organized practice (let's call it "practice," not "drill") is exactly the right answer to climbing the paintball ladder to top-level competitive play.

Here is one of Jon's immediate action scenarios. Remember that these tactics are proven and are actually practiced by military units in the real world.

Large inflatable bunkers are the rule on the professional tournament circuit. When the competition has you pinned down by laying paint on a lane or "sweetspotting," you can lean into these bunkers several inches to avoid flying goo. Be careful not to get comfortable, though, because the moment you do, somebody is going to lay paint on your back.

The Patrol

Your team is moving slowly and quietly along the side of a trail in the direction of the opposition. The team is staggered or alternated left and right by the trail. You know where the other team members are because you can see them.

Suddenly, your point man makes contact. He has to figure out if you have been seen, because that will determine your response. Figure you have been seen, so your point man shouts, "Contact, front!" to give direction, dives for cover and begins laying down fire.

The rest of the team echoes the point man's shout, "Contact, front!" and immediately moves forward into covering positions on either side. (Jon says it isn't necessarily important that the front person hit anyone, just that he makes people duck and hide while his team members leapfrog forward.) Alternating moving and shooting and remembering not to be in anyone else's line of fire, team members move gradually forward.

When they move, all team members shout, "Coming through!" to avoid being shot in the back. Paint is paint, but at short distance it can sting and how humiliating it is to be put out of the game by your own team member!

If a team member runs out of paint, he shouts, "Loading!" This alerts everyone as to why he is not shooting;

he doesn't want his teammates to think it's because he is taking a potty break in the middle of the action. Finished loading, he yells, "Up!" or "Ready!" Reloading under combat conditions while you are moving or scrunched up on the ground is tough and takes practice.

The team continues its leapfrog technique until the team leader realizes it is going to be overwhelmed or can take its objective. If it appears that the team is facing a superior force or one with superior firepower and cover, use the same leapfrog movement for a tactical retreat.

"Remember," Jon says, "you can never have too much firepower!"

TEN TIPS FOR BEGINNERS

Courtesy of Game Face

1. According to the folks at Game Face, communication is the key to all team sports. Use your teammates to find out exactly what your opposition is doing and where they are located on the field. This insures that everyone on your team is "on the same page." In a super-fast game of airball or hyper-ball, this is extremely important because seconds are crucial to survival. And in a scenario game, unless your team's general can communicate effectively with his troops, the game will rapidly degenerate into a

It's a team game, so talk to your teammates. "Here is how I'd do it," explains one teammate to another before their team takes the field at a tournament.

free-for-all. In that circumstance, everyone has less fun.

2. Make use of all available cover. On a field or in the woods, you must use everything from tree trunks to prepared bunkers. On a speedball field, the situation is different because you know in advance where every prepared element is located, where the flag is hung and what the lines of fire will be.

3. Wait for the right shot. In the beginning, a newbie will fling paint for the sake of seeing it fly. Accuracy is less important than the thrill of pulling the trigger. This stage of becoming a real paintball player doesn't last long though. After a few solid, stinging hits, even the dullest newbie learns pacing, spending as much time looking as shooting. Poorly thought-out shooting just gives away your position to more experienced players. When you find a target, take your time and wait for the good shot. Then fill the air with paint.

4. Listen for your opponent's firing. While you are playing, your ears can often be your best friends. Whether you are hunkered down breathing dirt behind the giant X in the middle of a grueling NXL game or ghosting through the woods in a Ghillie suit on the way to save the world from aliens, you need to listen for the sound of markers around you. Listen for people shouting directions. When people are re-grouping or confused is often the very best time for you to make a move.

5. Try snap-shooting. The term snap-shooting refers to exposing yourself from behind cover for only a brief period of time while you take a couple of shots. You immediately return to safety. You have a chance to look around, albeit quickly, and make a decision about your next move.

6. Look at the field from different perspectives. What seems open while you are standing may be completely different if you are kneeling or crawling. In a scenario game, slight undulations of the ground can often achieve maximum concealment. In a tournament, you will have a chance to walk the field and even make a map of the placement of the blow-up modules. Before the game, take every chance you can to figure out what your opponent is going to do, how he will approach, where she will hide a sniper.

7. Come out from behind cover with your marker ready. Whether you're on a recreational field or playing at the highest levels of international competition, expect the unexpected. When you leave cover, expect that you are going to be shot at and that you will find targets of opportunity to paint. Why miss a shot? Take it from the Boy Scouts and be prepared. If your gun is up and ready, you save several critical seconds.

8. Work with your teammates. It is much easier to move over the field if you coordinate and communicate with a squad or your team. You move; they cover you. They move; you cover. Or, in the real adrenaline rush,

Paintball players on patrol. "Are you covering my back?" Answer: "Yeah, are you scouting ahead or looking for nickels?"

Bunkering. A strong, sandbagged position on a hill combines effective cover and an advantageous slope.

Whether you win or lose, the most important part of paintball is learning how to play the game fairly and well.

your whole team charges the enemy camp, firing and screaming at the top of your lungs.(This usually doesn't work, but what a gas!)

9. Move around the field. It is much harder for your opponents to focus on you if you are continually changing positions. This also creates new angles on them while they are convinced that there are ten of you! Of course, in some situations, the more you move, the more you give away your position, direction and intent. So, be flexible and thoughtful.

10. Don't keep coming out of your bunker in the same spot. This really applies to rec ball and scenario games, because in a tournament, each player starts with the tip of their marker touching the "dead box." But only maybe five percent of all paintball is done in competition. The remainder is done for fun and to have the most fun you can possibly have, don't let your opponents realize that

you are coming out in the same area every time. If you do, sooner or later, they will be waiting for you with their gun up and balls in the air. By then, it's too late to switch sides.

WOMEN IN PAINTBALL

For *Paintball Digest*, the author had an opportunity to interview some of the girls, too! Here's what Blue's Crew "Press Wench" Amy "The Girl" Chantry says about playing, competing and kicking butt!

Paintball Digest: Amy, you're an avid paintball player and a member of a well-known amateur team with Michael "Blue" Hanse and EMR Paintball Park in Pennsylvania. I understand you're the official "Press Wench," so you must handle the publicity for Blue's Crew. Is that right?

Amy: Yes, I help out with press for the team and I'm also the mother of two beautiful little girls and, as you might imagine, I'm very involved in their lives. I volunteer at their elementary school, work with the Parent and Teacher's Association (PTA) and help out in the classroom, too. Plus, I cook and clean and play the big games when I can. I have a life, you know!

Paintball Digest: Anything involving children makes for one busy life. But don't you think playing paintball is kind of extreme for women and certainly for the mom of two little girls?

Amy: Well, it's like I told one of the paintball magazines a while ago, there ought to be a support group for us women paintball players, like Alcoholics Anonymous or Overeaters Anonymous, you know. "Hello, my name is Amy and I play paintball …" There aren't that many of us yet, and people are only slowly realizing that we can play as well as and have just as much fun as the guys.

It's when the other moms find out I play paintball that I hear, "Ah…. oh…really? Paintball? Doesn't that hurt?"

I remind them it's childbirth that hurts and we've done that! What the heck is a little paintball going to do to you unless you have an accident? Some tiny welt if you catch a ball in a soft spot isn't anything compared to the excitement of capturing a flag, or putting the opposing team's general out of the game or defending a castle. Now that's what I call fun. That or just sitting on the floor and playing with my little girls.

There's a double standard at work in sports like paintball and we need to change it. Paintball is not just a sport for men. Neither is skateboarding or snowboarding.

I see more women playing every time I go out. I hope it will continue to rise. I truly believe that paintball is for everyone. So, I say, ladies, if you have a desire to try paintball, try it! Don't let anyone tell you otherwise. You might just have the best day of your life. Hope to see you on the field!

Paintball Digest: So, as a woman player, how are you treated by the guys? After all, men are 90-something percent of the players.

Amy: My saying that we women need a support group probably makes you think I'm complaining about the guys, some kind of macho attitudes on the field, but I'm really not. That couldn't be further from the truth. When it comes to playing with the guys, I've never felt unwelcome on a field or felt like they were taking it easy on me because I was a girl. Actually, I've made some outstanding friends, maybe life-long friends, during the time I've been playing. I have always considered myself an equal on a playing field that's mostly men. When the mask goes on, we're all just players, and unless you know what your buddy is wearing, everyone is kind of anonymous.

Paintball Digest: So, being a woman on the field doesn't slow you down and it shouldn't be handicap for other women, either. Is that right? Attitudes are changing, and that's good for everybody.

Amy: Women love playing paintball as much as men. We girls want to tell people about it, share stories about stuff that happens on the field and encourage other people to give it a try. Nevertheless, when you're a girl, you sometimes get some odd reactions.

It starts right at home in your family. My mother, Patty Zewinski, was horrified by the thought that I was "taking up arms" and running around in the woods with a gun! She just couldn't (maybe she didn't want to) understand why I would put on camouflage and drive hundreds of

JT USA's promotional poster features their pin-up girl and spokesmodel Bon Bon.

The Airgun Designs spokes-model is more beautiful than her surroundings near the entrance to the Big Butler Fairgrounds north of Pittsburgh in July 2003.

Girls. Ladies. Gals. Women. Say what you will, women can play paintball as well as men. Before you take this tricked-out female paintball combatant for granted, you might want to check out her shooting iron, the sniper scope, the military camo, the sidearm and the gleam in her eye that says, "You slip up just once and you're dead meat." (Photo by Ted D'Ottavio.)

miles to play "that stupid kid's game." I tried to explain to her that paintball is fun. It's an exciting sport my husband and I can do together. I'm out there getting some aerobic exercise while I'm having fun, too. It's not like playing bridge or even pedaling a stationery bicycle in front of the television. And I can compete on an equal footing with the men, even guys who have been in the army and marines.

Still, mom kind of grouses about me playing paintball. Mind you, she never had a problem when my husband started playing. So, why the double standard? We're working on that, but it ain't done and gone yet. One day, maybe when my girls get to be my age, maybe.

Amy (again): Before we're done, I also would like to comment on the use of sexy girls in ads to sell equipment and such, but I didn't know if that would be mean spirited.

Paintball Digest: Hmm. Sort of a comment about the old advertising adage "sex sells," eh? From what you said, it sounds like you're against it, right? Well, fire away.

Amy: Now how did you know I would take the con side? Actually, I can see both sides, but here's what I think.

As a female player, it offends me to see manufacturers using sexy girls in their ads. That sends two messages. First, they are not considering me, the female player, as a consumer and are obviously targeting only the male demographic and that's wrong! Second, how good is their product really if they have to resort to sexy advertising? Got to get a hot babe to sell your marker? Your product probably can't hold up in quality!

Everybody knows that Tippmann, for instance, is a good quality marker and they have never (to my knowledge) used a cute, sexy girl or even a cartoon girl in a bikini to sell their product! (I gotta admit their spokes model is cute though.) And third, why can't manufacturers at least use girls who actually play paintball in those ads? You take one look at a lot of these girls and you know they have never been on a playing field!

I have male players tell me that they aren't influenced to buy by the girls in the ads. Most paintball players want to know all the ins and outs of their equipment and could care less who is holding it in the picture. If it's good quality, they will buy it.

So I don't feel that my position on this subject is completely because I am a girl. I'm against using sexy models to sell equipment because I am a serious player and want to be treated like one. Don't give me fluff. Tell me about your product!

The pro side of the kind of advertising we're talking about is that manufacturers are targeting that all-important 18-to-24-year-old male demographic and, let's face it, we always need new blood in the sport! Get them interested, and based on my experience, they'll get hooked!

There is a new paintball show on Fox Sports World called "Splatter Factor." The host is some bimbo with huge boobs who preens and pouts for the camera. At the end of one segment she said, and I quote, "When we come back [following a commercial] more of me dancing!"

What does that have to do with paintball? Nevertheless, the show is really good! They really give you the ins and outs of the game, the industry and the gear. So, I guess it's a trade-off. Hook the young guys who want to drool at the girl and maybe they will get interested in paintball in the process.

I hope that when paintball becomes a more mainstream sport they won't have to resort to tactics like this and we can start getting serious! Get rid of the bimbo dancing and show us more paintball!

Paintball Digest: Well, no one could accuse you of pulling your punches.

Amy: Thanks, but there is one more thing I want to comment on. When you [*Paintball Digest*] asked if men pee in the bushes while I'm around, well believe it or not, that actually has happened to me! I was out patrolling once with the general for our side in a big game. We were sweeping the field and such when he asked if I would look out for a second while he peed! I couldn't believe it! It was so weird, but on the other hand, some part of me doesn't view it as negative, but rather that he was treating me like an equal. I mean, he definitely would have asked a male player to watch out for him, so why not me, right? That told me he considered me just a player and not a girl on the field.

Paintball Digest: With almost eight million people playing paintball in the U.S. and Canada and the vast majority being men – maybe more than 90 percent – do you feel that this kind of thing keeps the women away from playing? Do you feel that a lot more women would get involved in paintball if using sexy girls to sell equipment were moderated?

Amy: That's right. Let's say there are 7-1/2 million men playing and half a million women. Doesn't it seem like there's a lot more room to grow the sport among women?

Paintball Digest: Since you specifically mentioned Tippmann, I ought to ask if Tippmann is one of your sponsors. Are they?

Amy: No, Tippmann is not one of my sponsors, but I have a special affinity for them because my first marker was a Tippmann Pro Am. It served me well those first years! I had to retire it when it became harder and harder to find replacement parts for the 'ole girl. It was a much older model (made of cast iron!) and I was swayed by the lightness of newer models. Being a member of (Michael Hanse's) Blue's Crew team, we mostly all play with the Generation E Matrix—electric blue ones of course!

* * * * * * * * * * * * * * * *

Another female player, Nancy Durham-Glynn is a member of the seven-woman, Tippmann-sponsored PaintGirls paintball team, all of whom are from Maine. "There are quite a few women who play paintball," she

Don't even imagine that girls can't play paintball, too!

said, "and some of them are as good or better than most men who are playing, so it's just about equal once you are out there on the field. I'm a member of an all-woman team and we're proud of our play and teamwork."

Nancy, who is in the unusual position of being a mother and a grandmother (although she looks about 25!), also owns the 202 Paintball pro shop and playing field in Manchester, Maine. She says there seems to be a difference in how women on the playing fields are treated depending on the age of the men playing. "Young men in their early 20s seem to pack a little attitude toward women," Nancy says. "They seem a little cocky at that age. Most other men on the field are a little protective, even the referees."

One thing that does concern Nancy is the use of young women, many of them teenagers, as sex objects in posters and in advertising, "It doesn't bother me so much personally or as a player. As a mom, though, I'm concerned about the message it sends to my 12-year-old daughter."

Right: A promotional poster by Ronn Stern.

CHAPTER 4

GAMES LARGE AND GAMES SMALL

The Big Game

Everyone has heard of "The Big Game." It's 24 hours of fun with field generals and objectives and tanks and land mines and sometimes a huge player party the night before the event kicks off. To end the game on Sunday, sponsors will sometimes organize one final mass battle. Just you and 1000 of your closest friends in a massive one-hour shoot off. Wow!

Often a Big Game is just that, a long game of capture-the-flag with some structural elements of a scenario game thrown in (a castle or fort, for example, is a popular theme). Lots of action. Lots of paint in the air. Lots of players and a simple, easy-to-follow plot line. "Keep it simple, keep it fun and keep it moving" is the motivating principle behind a Big Game.

Because Big Games bring hundreds of players together, they are often organized in approximately the same manner as a scenario game without space aliens or communist spies or magicians. In a well-organized game, teams are divided into companies and action squads. Assignments are called in to the team's commander or general and you win or lose depending on how many assignments your team accomplishes. Big Games are played over as much as 26 hours; people begin arriving on Friday, usually camp out Friday and Saturday nights (if they don't have a Saturday night mission), and then head home on Sunday afternoon.

Big Games use almost all of the formats of small capture-the-flag games with several interesting twists:

1. Elimination is not final. You simply go to a time out location or "dead zone" and wait for the buzzer to resurrect you and send you back in the game. Usually the buzzer gets this done every half hour, so you will not have to sit twiddling your thumbs for

Blue team's bunker is strategically placed to protect their headquarters in this big game. The red team will have to advance uphill on open ground in a firestorm of paint.

very long. After all, there's only so much goggle cleaning and gun squeegeeing you want to do when there's real action just out the door!

2. Everyone relies somewhat on an Honor System to make the game work. When your squad is ambushed at night or there is a frenzy of activity, the referee may not always know and be able to rule on who gets hit and who does not. Everyone relies on each other to fess up and count themselves out when they get hit. After all, you will only be on the bench for half an hour. It's not like you must sit out the rest of the game.

3. Typically, field owners will have hundreds or even thousands of dollars of door prizes to give away. At most scheduled breaks in the action – dinner and breakfast – there will be drawings and opportunities to win free stuff like shirts, paintballs and even donated markers.

4. The cost of a Big Game is twice what playing a day of recreational games normally runs. Figure you'll spend $50 for registration and maybe another $90 for a case of paint. That's expensive, but the field owner has certainly hired extra referees, solicited food vendors, purchased extra field insurance, bought a permit from the county and has medics (real medics, not role-players) on hand because some poor schmoe always gets his head banged or twists an ankle in the dark.

While The Big Game is the occasional star attraction, most playing fields regularly offer a variety of short, objective-based games. Having different types of games keeps you from becoming bored with doing the same thing time after time. Here is a sample of some of the games offered. It's natural that you are going to enjoy some of them more than others. If you get asked to defend the flag bunker and you just hate the fact you can't move around and be the aggressor, just hang on anyway and do your best. Games usually only last 10 minutes and there are probably players on your team who absolutely live to play a defensive game. Learn the techniques to win in every situation and you are well on your way to joining the elite ranks of paintball.

OPEN-FIELD GAMES

Let's talk about recreational paintball here, not professional or tournament play. Speedball and hyperball are sort of a cross between the most serious paintball play and simply filling the air with paint.

According to Steve Cranmer in New Jersey, who has played for practically 20 years and has an arsenal of paintball markers ("If we're ever attacked by paintball-playing space aliens," Steve says, "they're going to be in trouble at my place."), true speedball is played on a soccer-size field. Both halves are laid out with the exact same pattern of obstacles and bunkers. Team flags are placed at the opposite ends of the field, next to the starting

You will often see players with special powers or magical properties in big games. The rules will always be very clear about how they play the game and when you can shoot at them.

An open field game with a specific objective means it will be well defended. This newbie better get the lead out or he'll be painted like the Sunday comics.

gate for the opposition. The idea is that at the whistle, squads sprint from opposite ends and race to see who can bring their flag home the fastest. Obviously, this is a fast, aggressive game and it is a game for lithe legs and light, fast bodies. Probably not a game for the dads.

"In speedball," Steve says, "you get the proper angle on your opponent and lay down paint. Hyperball involves the same concept except with big field inflatables. In Hyperball, the proper angle sometimes lets you bounce balls off the inflatables and have them break on players hiding and shooting behind them."

Open-field games include mostly handheld flag games such as *Center Flag, Advance the Flag, Capture the Flag, Easter Egg Hunt, Speedball* and *Double/Triple Flag Relay*. These games involve players positioned in equal opposing starting positions, and movement on the field is basically unrestricted. When you play one of these games, you have the most freedom to decide when and how you are going to approach the objective. Each

player's personal tendencies of attack or defense dictate how the game progresses.

Open-field games usually have a specific objective to draw you and your buddies into contact at key points. Having an objective or two (as opposed to simple elimination games) increases the likelihood that everybody is going to get involved in the game and not feel that they are simply wandering around lost or assigned to a task that is not important or fun. An objective helps the referees keep track of how the game is progressing, too, so they won't accidentally end the game just before you make a break for the flag. An objective such as a flag makes

The safety briefing before every rec game. "Listen up, troops!" Whether you are a newbie or an experienced player, this is a time to really pay attention. Recall the rules and make sure you understand the boundaries and a field's special conditions if you have not had time to walk it.

it easier for referees to keep track of everyone because sooner or later you are going to gravitate toward it.

With the exception of speedball, these games usually run from 10 to 15 minutes, regardless of the number of people playing. This keeps players who are eliminated early from having to wait for a long time before they get to play again.

In *Center Flag*, a single flag is placed in the middle of the field. The object is for each team to capture this flag and advance it to the opponent's starting location. If you get shot while you have the flag in your hand, you must place the flag openly on a nearby bunker or tree. If time expires before the objective is completed, the team that captured the flag first wins. If neither team has touched the flag, the game is a draw.

When you play *Capture the Flag*, each team begins with a flag of the opponent's color hanging from in their starting location. The flag is hung or stood up by the referee (who is neutral) to ensure that it is plainly visible and accessible. The objective for each team is to attempt to shoot its way to the enemy's starting position, seize their flag and return it to their own home base. While this

is going on, your team members have to protect the flag at your base. If you get shot while holding a flag, you're out and that flag is placed in plain sight on a nearby bunker or tree. Players on the opposing team may not touch the flag they are defending at any time during the game.

Advance the Flag is similar to *Capture the Flag* except that each team begins with its own flag and has to advance it to the opponent's base. It's an important distinction! Players holding the flag are NOT required to keep it visible, but if you get shot while you are holding the flag, you must place it openly on a nearby bunker or tree. You can't touch the opposing team's flag at any time.

You might want to keep a referee in sight. It won't help your team if you plant the flag squarely in your enemy's camp and there is no referee there to signal victory!

A *Double Flag Relay* actually involves four flags, two of each team's color. One of each color flag is placed on central bunkers or at known locations. The objective is for your team to capture your own flags and return them to your base, but prevent the enemy team from doing likewise. Of course, you can't touch the enemy team's flags. (When the number of players exceeds 15 on each

Whatever game you play, the average recreational field will give you a lot of looks, bunkers in every shape and size and combination of materials. Maximize whatever cover they allow and watch for targets of opportunity.

The extra cost of a big game pays for special effects and structures. A lot of paint on the tower will make these defenders keep their heads down, but attackers will have to storm the fort at great risk to themselves.

side or everyone is playing particularly aggressively, the head referee can opt to put out a third set of flags to ensure a prolonged and hard-fought game.)

The *Easter Egg Hunt* involves placing three or four different colored flags on the field before the game. Each color is given a designated point value and placed according to its value. For instance, the more points a flag is worth, the closer it is usually placed to the center of the field, while lesser-value flags are place closer to the team bases for easier capture. For example, four blue flags worth one point are placed two-to-a-side near each base. Four red flags worth two points each are placed two-to-a-side, but closer to the center while two yellow flags worth three points each are placed on bunkers that are sure to be hotly contested near the center of the field.

If you capture a flag, you must return it to your base and place it visibly to be counted for points. Usually, the rules say you can only carry one flag at a time. Once a flag is captured, the player who picked it up is the one who has to return it. You can't hand off a flag to another player. If you get shot while you're holding a flag, that flag is out of play and you have to carry it off the field. And yes, you can capture flags from the enemy's base and return them to your own base, but only one at a time.

You get into a game of *Speedball* usually when a limited number of players is available, say seven or less to a team. Typically, it is a fairly basic hunt-and-shoot elimination game within specific boundaries, the object being to put paint on all your opponents before they put paint on you. It's fast and it's easy, and played every now and then, it's fun!

ATTACK-AND-DEFEND GAMES

Attack-and-Defend games include any game in which one team is confined to a limited defensive area and the other team must accomplish an offensive objective within that area. These games are lots of fun and help you learn teamwork, because each team has a clearly defined role and must adjust their play accordingly. Because there are only a limited number of games in this category – of course, you can switch roles, attacking one time and defending the next – you usually won't start a day with an Attack-and-Defend game.

Attack the Fort is a fun, simple game and a lot of paint flies through the air in 10 minutes. One team is on defense and enters the fort or a large bunker while the attacking team starts at a location out of sight of the fort and far enough away to allow for any "roamers" to disperse. One player on the attacking team is given a flag tied to a nerf-ball. The objective is for the attackers to work their way to the fort and get the flag into the tower section of the fort, while the defending team tries to prevent this from happening. Safety is a concern in this game, because a lot of close range action is to be expected toward the end of the game, especially if the attackers rush the fort. So, watch out with *Attack the Fort*. You're about to mix it up!

In *Attack the Fort*, the attacker's flag may be handed off to another player at any time. So, if you get shot holding the flag, you remain on the field as a neutral player, perhaps with your hand and the flag in the air (try that for 5 to 10 minutes if you think you have a lot of stamina), until one of your teammates can take it from you. (This is actually quite practical because it prevents your flag from being dropped and lost.)

Defenders begin the game in the fort and must remain there for the duration of the game with the exception of a few designated as "roamers," usually one or maybe two players each game. Roamers are the only players on the defending team allowed to move freely outside of the fort, although they too must begin the game inside the fort. If a roaming player is eliminated, that player may not be replaced. A roamer may return to the fort anytime though (as long as they are not hit), allowing another player to become a roamer.

In *The Bunny Game* the "bunny" is placed on the ground against the wall of a fort or bunker, plainly visible and not blocked. Neither team may touch or move the bunny during play, because the attacking team's goal is to assassinate the bunny by shooting it in the lens of its goggles. For 10 minutes, the defending team tries to prevent the attackers from killing the bunny. The defenders are restricted in their movements around the bunny while the attacking team begins at its base. Attackers may use the full range of the field, while the defenders must remain close to the bunny for the length of the game.

Of course, calling it *"The Bunny Game"* doesn't give it much of a macho image, but this game situation is very popular both among newbies and paintball veterans.

"Hit! Hit! I'm out!" When you're hit, raise your marker over your head, shout out that you are hit and head for the nearest exit. In a big game, you won't sit out very long.

MULTIPLE-LIFE GAMES

This category of games includes *Domination, Predator* and *President*, and they run in semi-open-field fashion but with each side being defined as either defending or attacking. Defenders are typically limited to an area inside which they must prevent the attacking team from accomplishing an objective (similar to *The Bunny Game*). Beyond normal field boundaries, the attacking team is not typically restricted in its movement.

In these games, attackers are granted an additional life. This means that when an attacking player is eliminated, he may return to base and then start again, but only one time. If the same player gets mushed again, then he's out of that game permanently. Defenders only get one life. Sorry.

The attacking team obviously has an advantage because its members have multiple lives (essentially giving them double the players), but they are playing against the clock as well as their opponent. If time expires and the attacking team has not accomplished their objective, the defenders win the game. So, shoot fast, stay low and run hard!

Domination operates on a big field with three flag stations set to the defending team's color. The attacking team has 10 minutes to capture all three flag stations around a field. To capture a flag station, the attacking team must lower the defender's flag and raise its own. The attacking team's flag must be at the top of the flagpole in order for the station to be considered captured. If a player is shot while raising the flag, the flag has to remain in the position it reached when the player was eliminated. Once a flag station is captured, the defending team may not recapture it. If eliminated, attacking players must return to their home base to tag up for their second life. If time expires and any flags are not completely captured, the defending team wins.

In playing *President*, one player on the attacking team is designated "the president" and is marked with a special armband. The defending team is restricted to a defensive zone less than half the size of the field and is allowed to set up within that area prior to the game. Attackers or aggressors begin out of range of the defenders. The objective is for the attackers to advance their president to a point within the defensive zone without the president being eliminated. The defending team must simply prevent this from happening in the allotted time.

For this game, just like in real life, the president only gets one life. If the president is eliminated, it's all over. If any other attacking player is eliminated, he may tag up at the starting base for a second life.

Predator is unlike other games of this category as time should not be a constraint. Essentially, *Predator* involves the bulk of the players as humans (with armbands) against a small group of elites known as predators. Predators are allowed to position themselves secretly on the field (under the supervision of a referee) prior to a game.

In this game, the predators have two lives. If a predator is shot, he must tag up at base before returning to play. When a human is shot, that player must return to a different designated area, but then may remove his armband and continue playing as a predator (basically they switch teams). The game continues until all the predators have been eliminated or all the humans have become predators. The game of *Predator* is typically allowed an extended time limit (15 to 20 minutes instead of 10) because all players have multiple lives.

(Attention predators. Get ready to catch paint. Usually,

The sniper rises silently from the bushes wearing his Ghillie suit from Rancho Safari. He has pre-chambered a round and removed his hopper to reduce his silhouette. He sights through his scope. All he needs is one killing shot, perhaps two in quick succession, to take out a high-value target before disappearing into the brush.

a lot of paint. So be sure to stay very cool. And if you are the last human surrounded by predators, get low and get invisible or get ready to go home a different color!)

THE PAINTBALL SNIPER

If paintball were only a fancy and expensive game of tag, it would not have wrapped so much of its personality into the sniper mystique. The one shot, one kill sniper. The lone gunman. The high plains drifter. Clint Eastwood, Tom Berenger watch out!

We believe that paintball is more than a game of tag. We believe that it is a way for players to expand their imagination to impossible situations and to become, for a brief time, more than they are in daily life as students and accountants, as kids with parents who boss them around or as parents with bills who boss them around. Maybe that is why the idea of being a sniper is so appealing.

One thing is certain. Wherever you go to play recreational paintball, whether it is to the famous EMR Paintball field's biggest scenario game or just to your local field for a Saturday afternoon butt-kicking with your buddies, everybody understands (in a general way) and accepts someone who is a sniper.

This is the "Sniper Creed" from *www.paintballzone.com*, one of the Internet's most informative sites about paintball snipers:

I am a Paintball Sniper

No paintball player is more professional than I. I am among the elite. I revel in the thrill of the game. I accept

The AM-4 Custom from Action Markers gives you the look and feel of a real military sniper with a low-profile 15-round feed tube and a collapsible butt stock.

nothing less than victory.

A single shot is all I need. I will strive to remain technically and tactically proficient in my craft. I will know paintball and I will make myself available to others to provide help or advice if needed.

No one is more dedicated to the game than I. I take great pride in my position and will at all times conduct myself to bring credit to my sport.

I will take no action to bring disgrace upon my sport of paintball. Never shall I wipe paint or turn a blind eye if another should do likewise.

I will never forget that I am a professional. That I am the best of the best. A predator among prey. I am a paintball sniper. I am an army … of one.

SNIPER TACTICS

A paintball sniper has to move in the shadows and off the beaten track, but why waste your time and energy until you are nearing the objective? Move quickly at first,

SNIPER SCHOOL

(By Carson "Squeegie" Jenkins and courtesy of www.paintballzone.com)

The flag hung from the pole slightly peppered with spray. The mad push to take the fort and the most valued prize had proved futile so far, costing many players and several hundred rounds. As their base security peered through the walls of the bunker, all seemed clear.

Inching my way through the thick palmettos that have concealed my movement, I bring my marker up to take a quick look around. I am careful not to angle the scope into the sun so that it glares, and I stay low in the shade of the jungle foliage. Nearly stepping on me, a ref makes his way through the tangled maze of palm fronds and knee high grass.

As I scan the surrounding area, a pair of eyes beaming through a set of goggles catches my attention. His attention is drawn to his two teammates running perimeter defense. TOTAL COVER. When the guy who was hit turns around to stare in your direction, you want him to see absolutely nothing.

then you may want to slide away from any action, any group and ease off to the side to look for an alternate path. There is certainly no need to crawl when you don't have to – getting down on your hands and knees isn't at all easy when you are older than an infant – but instead, move casually. Slump or crouch. Slouch! Forget what your mom said about standing up straight.

Even more important, though, is moving slowly without jerky head, hand and marker movements. Experienced LRPs (Long Range Patrols) from Viet Nam and big-game hunters know that you can get away with some movement if you are not directly in your quarry's field of view or if there are not a dozen people searching for you. Your movements need to be controlled, silky smooth and not exaggerated.

Most humans have forgotten how to move stealthily through the woods and over the fields, if indeed we ever knew it. Watch where you put your feet and what branches

The paintball sniper is a romantic figure. Stealthy. Alone. One shot, one kill.

and sticks are around you. Overhanging branches are a sure give-away. If you make an unexpected movement or a misstep, freeze. The chances are that if someone was watching and they notice movement, they will lose your spot if you don't reinforce their suspicions. Sink to the ground, wait and watch. After a minute or two, you can resume movement or look for a place that will cover you from enemy fire while you scope out the situation.

When you are ready to fire, the first rule actually is to wait. Be patient. That's not a misprint. Now you want to be even more patient than you have been moving into position. It is better to wait and take out a general or executive officer than it is one of the privates patrolling the boundary, because if you take out the leadership, the other side can become

The average rec player contrasted with a well-dressed sniper behind him. Soft, absorbent, multi-layer camo breaks up your outline and helps you blend into your surroundings. Plus, if you are discovered by the enemy, this three-dimensional camo helps absorb the sting of a thousand balls of paint that will immediately be sizzling toward you.

temporarily leaderless and directionless. Look for people giving instructions, the person on the phone or pointing and then find a firing position with a field of fire that is unobstructed. It only takes a tiny twig to deflect a paintball, and if all you have to shoot at is a narrow slit in some bunker, your chance of making the shot is questionable unless you have practiced and can shoot with confidence.

Finally, remember that the other team will have snipers, too, maybe several. If they are smart, they will have flanking defenders who are well concealed and are looking for you. The hunter becomes the hunted. A riddle wrapped in an enigma. As a sniper, you are only equipped to take on one other individual at a time. You are thinking "one shot, one kill," but they are going to light you up, fill the air with balls, and if that happens, you're toast. If there are three or four and you are in their way and you decide to take out the point man, you're toast. Shoot them in the back and you may take out several. Attack from the front and you will get one before you become … toast.

According to our friend Squeegee, firing your first round from a hidden position at the side or back of the competition takes a lot of discipline. You have to train your brain to fire only ONE SHOT. After that shot has landed, you want to reevaluate the area before you make the choice to fire again. With every round fired, you make it easier for the enemy to locate you. Take high percentage shots. Squeegee writes that you should fire only when you have a 90 percent chance of making a hit, but many experienced snipers talk about a 100 percent chance!

And you don't need to bunker players; they will bunker themselves. With the indiscriminate round coming in from a location no one can quite pinpoint, everyone thinks they are going to be the next target to be taken out. You are in their backyard. The little bunker that was keeping them safely in the game just minutes before suddenly becomes their coffin.

"All that fuss about one little paintball," Squeegee says.

The Sportsman's Guide offers a paintball Sniper Suit (YSPG2-68716) for just $69.97. This combat-ready suit comes fully assembled and covers your face, upper arms, head, chest and back for a whole lot of concealment for your money. The mesh area around your eyes allows you to wear it over your paintball goggles. This suit includes an extra pound of burlap in five colors so that you can tailor it to your exact environment and vegetation. Includes a fire retardant application and weighs just 3.5 pounds.

FREQUENTLY ASKED SNIPER QUESTIONS

Question: "Would an elevated firing position work for a sniper?"

Paintball Digest: According to our friends who are

Could this $600.00 MSRP Worr Games Flatline Auto-cocker be the ultimate sniper weapon? It's a closed-bolt, pneumatic system with the curved Tippmann Flatline barrel that puts backspin on the ball for stability in flight. WGP equips it with a shroud on top so that you can sight along a straight plane.

snipers, this works for a military sniper because he has a phenomenally accurate weapon and can shoot for hundreds of yards – maybe a mile – and for hunters because deer so rarely look up. But it isn't a good idea in paintball because the higher you get the less cover there typically is, and once you are spotted, getting down without being shot all to hell will be a bit of a problem.

Plus, even our very best markers just aren't all that accurate. To hit our targets, we need them to be close. Add in the problem of shooting down at an angle and the safety issue of falling and … well, most experienced snipers believe that being lower to the ground is infinitely better than being on top of something or even on a treestand (unless after one or two shots your objective is to be a human sacrifice).

Question: "Do they use snipers in tournaments or in competition?"

Paintball Digest: No. The emphasis in tournaments is to blast paint, run and gun. This runs 180 degrees opposite to the sniper philosophy of "one man, one shot." Plus, competition is timed and snipers need plenty of time to work out their shtick.

Question: "Do snipers ever operate in teams?"

Paintball Digest: Yes, and this helps put some of the teamwork and fun of working with people back in the game for a sniper. You and your sniper accomplice will want to practice working together, practice communicating with hand signals, practice the leapfrog approach and retreat, and practice covering each other. This is fun and can be a deadly tactic to use on the opposition, but a two-person team (even a three-man team) is two or three times as much movement and possibility for error, too.

Question: "I've heard that some snipers always carry grenades. What do you think?"

Paintball Digest: That's true, and it is an excellent idea. Tossing a grenade can help cover your escape after you shoot. Chances are that if you are on assignment in a scenario game, the target you are trying to take out will be of relatively greater game value than you are. Sorry, but it's true. Get close enough to shoot their general and the people around him (or her!) will be surprised and ticked. You should expect to be hit right away (and they will call you names, too), but just in case you are not hit, toss a

grenade to create maximum confusion and have your sniper partner (if any) distract the opposition with plenty of fire. You move out on your designated escape route.

Question: "Can I put a silencer on my marker?"

Paintball Digest: Yes, and we support almost any effort by a paintball sniper to remain silent and unobserved, but is not something we can advise you on since the US Bureau of Alcohol, Tobacco and Firearms regulates silencers rather severely. You can imagine why. Almost anything that will silence a paintball marker will have noise reduction abilities on regular firearms. As we recall, silencers worked best at very short range and with small-bore weapons like 22-caliber centerfire pistols.

Question: "I have heard snipers referred to as 'campers,' implying that they don't really do all that much. What's the truth?"

Paintball Digest: The people who are talking about snipers this way have either not met a real one or were just taken out by one! We think the difference is that a "camper" is a player who "camps out" at a bunker and really doesn't move much, just waits for the enemy to come to him to get involved in a shoot-out. A sniper is an active individual on the field who uses stealth and concealment to his advantage. A sniper is probably a very good paintball player who has found a role that he likes and finds challenging. A sniper is a person who has taken the "one shot, one kill" philosophy to heart rather than buying into the conventional wisdom that says the more paint you fling and the faster you shoot the better. In this sense, a sniper is to the average recreational player as a fly fisherman is to commercial fishermen or the bowhunter is to the rifleman. A bit more refined.

Right: Using a pod to load a hopper during the action.

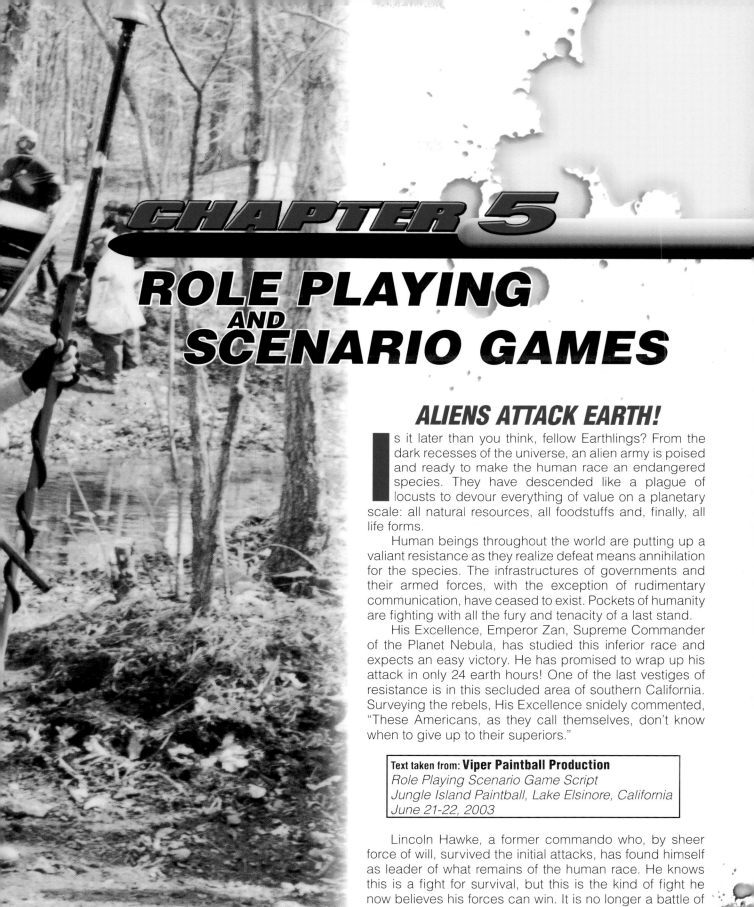

CHAPTER 5

ROLE PLAYING
AND
SCENARIO GAMES

ALIENS ATTACK EARTH!

Is it later than you think, fellow Earthlings? From the dark recesses of the universe, an alien army is poised and ready to make the human race an endangered species. They have descended like a plague of locusts to devour everything of value on a planetary scale: all natural resources, all foodstuffs and, finally, all life forms.

Human beings throughout the world are putting up a valiant resistance as they realize defeat means annihilation for the species. The infrastructures of governments and their armed forces, with the exception of rudimentary communication, have ceased to exist. Pockets of humanity are fighting with all the fury and tenacity of a last stand.

His Excellence, Emperor Zan, Supreme Commander of the Planet Nebula, has studied this inferior race and expects an easy victory. He has promised to wrap up his attack in only 24 earth hours! One of the last vestiges of resistance is in this secluded area of southern California. Surveying the rebels, His Excellence snidely commented, "These Americans, as they call themselves, don't know when to give up to their superiors."

Text taken from: **Viper Paintball Production**
Role Playing Scenario Game Script
Jungle Island Paintball, Lake Elsinore, California
June 21-22, 2003

Lincoln Hawke, a former commando who, by sheer force of will, survived the initial attacks, has found himself as leader of what remains of the human race. He knows this is a fight for survival, but this is the kind of fight he now believes his forces can win. It is no longer a battle of the big guns; it has become mano-a-mano, man-to-alien.

Watch for aliens! The portal to another universe is lighted at the lower right corner. A flare ignites the night sky over a scenario game in the U.S. Southwest. Looking directly at a flare can kill your night vision, but a flare can be extremely useful in re-orienting yourself and spotting the enemy in the dark.

The portal through which the aliens pass is lighted at night and leads to a new scenario dimension.

Players who raise their arms and markers during a game are hit and should not be shot at. Elimination in a scenario game usually lasts less than 30 minutes and can be a welcome break.

"Those swollen green brains of theirs look about as soft as the rest of their bodies," Hawk confidently told his troops.

Join the force of your choice in the battle to end all battles. Who shall be the victors and what is the future of planet earth? It all comes down to one final weekend, June 21 and 22, in the hills of California.

PLAYING THE GAMES

Role-playing scenario games got their start in the late '80s (as did most of the rest of paintball) and as they have developed, they have become extremely popular, mostly because they are extremely fun. If you have never played in a scenario game, you haven't experienced one of the most exciting things you can do in the outdoors.

Scenario games are fun because they stretch everything you normally do across a very large canvas. The difference in playing a 10-minute capture-the-flag game with a dozen buddies at your local hyperball field and a 24-hour assault on the king's castle with 700 of your closest friends is practically indescribable. And there are several other aspects to scenario play that you won't find at your average recreational game. These include the use of motorized tanks, mortars, bazookas, mines, night vision scopes, grenades, Ghillie suits, snipers, lasers, helicopters and special effects! The sky is the limit, but because of the suits and the charts and graphs running paintball insurance carriers, there are often very careful special rules about how, when and where such things as tanks, mortars and rockets can be employed.

Scenario games are often based on a story line, either historical or fictional. A historical story line, for example, could be a replay of the battle of Gettysburg in the U.S. War Between the States. A popular fictional storyline is the great castle assault that takes place in *The Two Towers*, book two in J.R.R. Tolkien's epic trilogy *Lord of the Rings*, or even a situation from a comic magazine (and movies) like the X-Men. Sometimes, the scenario director develops an all-new storyline that gives players great freedom to assume special characters and develop roles. A game based on a Vietnam situation or a terrorist incident may even incorporate air assaults, helicopters, booby traps, snipers and spies.

Now, all this doesn't come cheap, says New Jersey's Steve Cranmer, a member of the team Joint Fury. For a good 24-hour game, you can expect to pay $50 or more to register, he says. Paint is almost always "Field Paint Only" and, yes, field hosts do overcharge for the paint, sometimes as much as $90 for a case.

Sure, this is a lot more expensive than you can buy it at a local paintball retailer or over the Internet, but a 24-hour scenario game that draws hundreds of players is very expensive to produce. The field will have added more referees than normal and they have to work around the clock under pressure to enforce safety rules and

Allied armies storm ashore at Skirmish USA's D-Day re-creation and run for cover from the intense "German" fire, just like their parents from the "Greatest Generation." Plenty of referees dot the playing fields to make sure that all players keep their goggles on and that no markers exceed the 280-fps limit in a scenario game of this size.

make decisions they don't normally have to worry about. The field owners will have to add extra portable toilets, food concessions, extra rental markers and air/CO_2 fill stations. They will have to worry about zoning permits, noise ordinances, liability insurance, staff radios (dozens of replaceable batteries), game organizers, special game props, real medics on site and perhaps even off-duty police for traffic control. Then remember they need to make a profit, too, because without making a profit you won't have a scenario game to play in next year. It's the American way.

Nevertheless, whether you are a newbie or an experienced player, when you storm a Nazi bunker or are part of a gang holding up a train for the mine's payroll, you'll never forget the experience. A scenario game can't possibly be beat for getting you hooked on extending your paintball knowledge and experience.

Scenario games don't last just 10 minutes. If you get involved in one of these, expect to spend your whole weekend hustling and shooting. Actually, games can last from six to 26 hours. The event typically begins with a party and early check-in on Friday. Actual play begins on noon Saturday and ends around noon Sunday. There are scheduled breaks for dinner and A FEW hours of sleep at night. You will be tired, dirty and happy.

If you can, you certainly want to arrive at the field early on Friday, because the usual pre-game player party on Friday night will be one of the event's highlights. If the game organizers are at all on top of their game, they will make sure everyone has a chance to mix and meet each other, not just hang out in their own little groups. Anyway, you'll make dozens of new friends and meet the organizers and the specialized role players. Unless you are shy, you'll feel like you are a vital part of the event. Sometimes the party includes a barbecue, maybe a beer tent (if you are above the legal age) and possibly even a band.

After you register, you'll probably be given a packet that identifies who you will be in the scenario and what you must do for your side. Certainly, this varies with the scenario producer and by game, but a packet contains something like this:

1. A laminated badge for you to wear around your neck to show you have registered. It assigns your player number and attests that you have chronographed properly.
2. A "character card" that assigns you to a squad and gives you a particular role (a demolitions technician or a spy or a medic, for example) and lists any special gear you can carry. Your character card is the only proof of your game identity and your side affiliation. Without it, you may not be allowed to enter your home base, so keep it safe and on your person at all times.
3. Inside your packet will be a basic field or situation map that gives you an idea of the relative locations of objects on the field.

In a well-managed game, when the generals are really up to the task (and it can go both ways, unfortunately),

Skirmish USA Paintball Park in Jim Thorpe, Pennsylvania, hosts a D-Day Europe re-creation in July 2003, paintball style. At the horn, Allied players storm out of simulated Higgins boats and assault the German cliffs and trenches. With more than a thousand players involved, action is super hot and paint fills the air for more than 24 hours.

Before any scenario game, the field owners and producers brief players on safety, game rules, special effects and especially play at night when the rules often change.

players are divided into teams of several hundred people each. Each side or team has a headquarters or base of operations that consists of a command post and usually some other assorted buildings. Trenches, bunkers and special obstacles may surround these buildings.

Sides are organized into multiple task teams, five- to 10-player hit squads, each with a leader whose job is to communicate with the team's ultimate commander. The ultimate commander is conveniently referred to as "the general." Depending on the size of his force, the general will likely have a command staff to help motivate and direct the various squads. Typically the general will have an executive officer (XO) and several company commanders. Squad leaders receive their missions through this chain of command and then direct their squads as needed to accomplish assigned missions.

Most events begin Saturday by noon. So, Saturday morning you prep your gear, buy your paint and get ready to get your bang on! Just before the game officially kicks off, there is always a player briefing to review safety, game rules, and the game's theme. In addition, special role players are introduced and everyone is briefed on the powers these players have. At this last minute get-together, you will meet the opposing generals and referees, too. When the starting horn blares, it's Game On!

Play Begins

When a coded mission is called in to your general, get ready. A radio operator will decode the message before the general must begin making decisions. He consults with his staff, and if he accepts it or decides that it is feasible, he then assigns the mission to a squad. Given the nature of scenario play, you can assume that a squad of enemy players is probably being dispatched to attempt the same mission or even an intersecting mission, at about the same time. The scenario director, who is responsible for the unfolding plot line, calls in missions regularly throughout the game.

A mission can be as simple and straight-forward as sending all available players to storm the enemy base. Or, a mission can be as specific as giving Company A, Platoon C 30 minutes to capture Hill 66 and find the treasure that is buried there.

Missions are given point values and, ultimately, points are how the game is won or lost. Teams can only increase their points by accomplishing these assigned tasks. Obviously, the more missions you complete successfully, the better the chance that your side will win. Taking or successfully defending a bunker, for instance, may require at least 20 players to start and at least one of them must be at that location within 30 minutes. This mission could be assigned 10 or perhaps 100 points, depending on its strategic value in the game. If the mission is completed successfully, points are awarded to the aggressor team. The players who are most focused on accomplishing missions are usually the ones who win.

While missions are being run by both groups of players, any special characters are running missions of their own. These are also worth points. And spies for both sides are trying their best to add unexpected complexities to the game. Of course, both sides need to stay alert and

The general receives a mission from game control.

defend their prospective base camps from attack.

In scenario games, there is often a chance to capture another player. In fact, if that member of the enemy team is a spy, he could actually be setting you up so that he can plant false information. The "no shooting at close range" rule applies, and if you suddenly find yourself in position to shoot someone at close range, you can offer him the capture/shoot option and he must answer immediately. If he chooses "shoot," he is out until the next resurrection. (You do not actually pull the trigger on anyone at close range!) If he chooses "capture," he is out for 15 minutes. In a capture, he puts his gun on "safe" and follows you to your base for interrogation. Typically then, a referee will help you release your captive at a safe distance.

According to Wayne Dollack of Wayne's World Paintball in Ocala, Florida, the man often referred to as the "father of paintball scenario games," you may never physically touch a captive (or any other player) at any time.

The beauty of the scenario set-up is that both sides are "multi-tasking." Some squads are out on attack missions while others must be kept at hand for defense and special assignments. The task for the command staff is to keep track of everyone and manage the team's resources.

This may leave a hundred or more team players between missions. Use the time between missions to get paint off, fill the hopper, squeegee your barrel, check your gear or take a catnap. Some of the time, you will be in a defensive position somewhere on the periphery of your team's territory, because the other side will be trying to penetrate your team's defensive perimeter, put you out of the game and accomplish their goals, too.

Most events run until chow time. At five or six o'clock they take a one- to two-hour break for food and rest. There are usually prize giveaways and drawings at this time, but you should get off your feet and even take a catnap if you can, because you won't get much sleep during the night. And drink plenty of fluids.

Once night play begins after the dinner break, some of the rules change. Most events have you chronograph your markers down from the daytime 280 fps to 250 fps or even less. The reason is that at night, shooting action is often much closer than when you can see clearly during the day. On most fields, grenades or mortars are not allowed at night and most events count any hit, whether it breaks paint or not, as a valid elimination hit. Missions continue in the darkness along with the task of defending your command and protecting your general from assassination. These days, it is the rare event that continues play all the way through the night, though. Games generally suspend activity between midnight and at least 3:00 A.M. Most players have come to have a good time and by the early morning hours, everyone is worn out. It's time for players to return to their campsite and get some shuteye.

Night play is especially exciting, though. There are the standard dangers of falling on a poison punji stake and dying an agonizing death alone and in the dark (just kidding!) or getting whacked by a tree limb, but just distinguishing your team members from your opponents is the hard … and exciting … part. Someone in your squad will need a flashlight with good batteries.

Most teams devise secret passwords and responses for night missions or practice an audible but secret drill. "Pittsburgh!" someone will call out in the dark. The obvious answer can be "Pirates" or "Steelers." Answering correctly will mean the difference between a face full of paint and a welcoming pat on the back. Working with a partner makes this especially fun if one person does the challenging and the second person prepares to cut loose immediately if the response is wrong.

Regardless of whether the game was temporarily halted during the night due to lack of players on the field or even if some hard-core players continue the game until daybreak Sunday morning, most events schedule a breakfast break sometime around 7:00 A.M. At this time, some prizes are usually given away and the field commander or scenario director gives the players an update on how both groups fared the day before and on the respective point standings.

After breakfast, it's Game On! again! This is the final four to five hours, because most scenarios end at noon on Sunday. These final hours can be very fast paced because both groups are trying to make as many points on missions as possible.

About an hour before the game ends, Joint Fury's Steve Cranmer notes, many scenarios put on a final great battle. Both groups are "herded" to the center of the field and given an objective. Usually, it is to hold or seize a certain location or object on the field and teams are given the final hour to accomplish this. The final battle is often worth a large number of points, so a group that is behind in points can sometimes win the final battle and take the game.

When the final horn sounds and the game is over, everyone meets with the scenario promoter to hear the final point tally and receive player and team awards from their respective generals. At this time there is usually a final, grand prize drawing and it is frequently an expensive and desirable gear item donated by a paintball manufacturer, a new electronic marker, for instance.

Elimination

Eliminations in a scenario game don't have any effect on a team's score although they may affect your squad's ability to accomplish a mission. When a player is shot, he must check in at his team's "hospital" and await the next insertion window, which is usually every 30 minutes. This way, eliminated players only have to sit out for a maximum of 30 minutes at a time. When they go back into the game, they must enter through a "safe passage" entrance to their side's headquarters.

One of the roles most valued in scenario games that incorporate it into the script is that of "medic." If a medic tags an eliminated player within a certain amount of time from the moment of his hit—sometimes 90 seconds—the player is "cured" and may keep playing without leaving the field. Of course, the medic is vulnerable to being hit, too.

Elimination in a scenario game usually requires that players accept an honor system. With hundreds of players, numerous special "missions" taking place at any given time and play throughout the night, it is impossible for referees to rule on every hit. This may be a challenge for tournament players who often don't consider themselves "out" until they are flagged by a ref. But since "resurrection" normally takes place within half an hour, many experienced scenario game players don't mind taking a little time off the field to take their goggles off for a good cleaning, squeegee their marker and adopt the prone position briefly for some inner eyelid review.

Nevertheless, scenario events follow regular paintball rules of elimination. If you are hit anywhere on your body or equipment and the paint mark is the size of a quarter, or you accumulate a quarter's worth of paint splatter, you are eliminated. An eliminated player holds his marker high over his head, shouts that he is "hit" or "out" and walks off the field to a "dead zone" or the team hospital. But remember, in

Role players such as this Scottish warrior at Sherwood Forest Adventure Games, LaPorte, Indiana, in May 2002, have a special status in scenario games. This particular game, "The Quickening," was produced by Mackz Xtreme Sportz. (Photo by Ted D'Ottavio.)

a 24-hour scenario game you can get reinserted in about a half an hour. So, don't fret. You won't be out of action for long.

ROLE-PLAYING

In certain types of games, players take on popular roles from fiction or perhaps even from history and then compete to see who can accomplish objectives within the overall game. You might play Gandalf, Tolkien's wizard in the *Lord of the Rings*, or Robert E. Lee, the commander of the Confederate States' Army of Northern Virginia or even Ho Chi Minh in a Vietnam scenario. The possibilities, says Ben Torricelli, owner of Millennium Paintball Productions, are practically endless, but competition for the well-known roles is tough.

When you take part in a scenario game and especially when you accept a special role, play will not be predictable, certainly not as predictable as it is at your local field on an average Saturday afternoon. Expect surprises. Expect sudden air assaults. Expect espionage and even hostage-taking. Depending on the scenario director's inventiveness and the host field's capabilities, the sky is really the limit.

Look around at all the new faces. Scenario games welcome walk-ons and will usually rent all of the playing equipment you will need. The player meeting before any game, scenario production or a tournament, will orient you to the rules. This is the best time to begin psyching out your opponents!

Some Typical Scenario Roles

A Demolitions Technician (demo tech) is certified for missions or developing situations that require the placement and/or activation of demolition charges. Sometimes these charges will just be "Action Cards" that need to be placed, but they can also be physical objects resembling sticks of dynamite or satchel charges. Demo techs may be given simulated rockets to add realism to their roles.

Engineers are needed to help a team recover from the actions of demo techs. Engineers carry "Reconstruction Cards," enabling them to rebuild demolished structures. If the Mongol Horde, for example, demolishes a key bridge that the Teutonic knights need to accomplish a recon mission, the knights will fail unless they have their engineer play a Reconstruction Card to a referee and restore the bridge.

Each side has a few Medics who can heal non-lethal wounds in the field. The medic has a tablet on which he records the ID numbers of the victims he heals. Typically, a medic is given a limited number of healings, so this, too, is bound by an honor system. If a medic tags a wounded player within about 90 seconds of being hit, the wounded player can resume play right away. If a medic is eliminated, they can no longer heal others until they themselves are resurrected at the next player insertion.

Some character cards contain fascinating clues telling the player their role may include being a Spy, Secret Agent, Double Agent, Saboteur or even a Traitor. For example, look for a line that describes your character saying, "You have become disillusioned with the war effort and, given the right opportunity, you will be inclined to switch sides." Sometimes, only the double-agent with a special "License to Kill" card can take out the opposing team's general.

Game organizers will often recruit players to act out Special Fictional Roles. These help bring the unfolding scenario to life. You can see space aliens, wizards or historical figures roaming the field in full costume and acting out their parts. These roles are not for beginners, but can be a lot of fun when you have the opportunity to play something special.

And if you don't dress the part when you are asked to be The Gunslinger, you're not going to have all the fun you can. Here's your chance to strut!

Sometimes you can make up your own character. This is referred to as "going creative." But switching back and forth between characters in a single game is confusing. It won't endear you to your teammates and may not be appreciated by the scenario operator, either. You could

"Halt! And give me the password." A scenario team can't be too careful protecting their general and the headquarters.

know you personally, so if you don't like something, speak up! You are on the field to have fun, and if you're not having fun, do something about it. Don't be a pain, but don't be a pansy either.

Walk-ons, by the way, are welcome at all games including scenarios that are not filled to overflowing with people who have pre-registered. It is fun to go alone … and fun to go with your buddies, too. When you enter by yourself, you will get to meet a lot of interesting players and you will definitely learn some new tactics and make new friends. With a group of friends, you will feel less like an outsider and more at home playing with people you know and whose play you have learned. Beware, however, that as an individual walk-on, you may have to prove yourself to your team before they trust you completely because everyone is on the lookout for spies and saboteurs!

A SCENARIO EXAMPLE

The following is an example of a typical scenario game that was produced and hosted by some of paintball's greatest champions. While typical, the attention to detail and strong emphasis on a player-friendly environment make it non-typical, too. Nevertheless, this is what you may expect when you attend a first-class scenario game.

Scenario Game at EMR Paintball Park:
"Return to Wolf's Lair"
P.O. Box 728, New Milford, PA 18834
(570) 465-9622 www.emrpaintball.com
October 25-26, 2003
Produced by MXS and PMI

The Story

The Chronicler pauses in his address to the science and technology representatives. The auditorium is silent, as the members see their taskmaster hesitate. "It seems that your kind is obsessed with control at all cost," he continues. "The information you are soon to witness is scattered at best, but should be enough to aid you in your simulation research.

"Sometime in the 9th century AD, a Saxon prince by the name of Henry the Fowler – also called Heinrich – sought to separate from the Frankish dynasty and form his own Germanic power. During his conquests, Heinrich stumbled upon some ancient texts, much like how I retrieve data from the Ancients. Upon translation of the Eastern scripts, Heinrich convinced himself that his people were direct descendants of the Thule, a race of pure consciousness who were unknown to The Leaders, or myself, however. Heinrich was determined he could tap into the power of the Thule."

CHEN powers up to display a man chanting prayers. The image flashes to an army of human-looking creatures, but there is something wrong about them. "These beings are called zombies," CHEN reports.

end up with no one trusting you and, in that case, don't be surprised if you get shot in the back every now and then. (Shooting a disrespected officer or NCO in the back was called "fragging" in Viet Nam.) Some games allow you to bring your own props, like your homemade rocket launcher that shoots soft nerf balls, but you need to check with a referee or the scenario operator before you spring them on the field. Remember, if you are thinking about it, so are others; don't be surprised if some of the more experienced players try to go solo or operate outside of their assigned character.

Scenario Tips for Newbies

First, the huge crowds and the really experienced guys who have fancy equipment and who can talk the "in" paintball jargon can be intimidating. Sure, everything is new, but remember that every player starts at the beginning and generally knows little or nothing on their first day. Just think how much fun it will be when you eliminate that know-it-all.

Second, don't let yourself be forgotten out there guarding the perimeter, especially after dark. Make sure your squad leader knows where you are and you stay alert to any call-up to a mission. Your leader probably doesn't

The Sherwood Forest castle by day. The battlements are manned and defended. A definitive scenario set-up.

The zombie army destroys anything and everything that dares stand in its path. Suddenly, a man dressed in robes appears. He is resisting Heinrich's army of the undead. The scene erupts in chaos as the zombies attack the man who appears to be a monk. Blood and bodies fly from the epicenter of action. As the commotion settles, the monk is now carrying a limp Heinrich up the side of a mountain. The unconscious prince is being sealed into the mountainside tomb, guarded by many curses of foreboding.

The images change to Germany, many centuries later. CHEN explains the imagery: "Heinrich Himmler is a direct descendant of Henry the Fowler. Himmler is a high-ranking official in Adolf Hitler's Third Reich. He is an evil, soulless bureaucrat and the architect of some of the most horrible atrocities of the Nazi regime. He has founded the SS Paranormal Division, a collection of Germany's most ardent occult followers, dedicated to finding preternatural ways to further their country's war of conquest. Himmler has uncovered pieces and parts that, when brought together, could spell disaster for the free world and all mankind."

The scene moves to a hallway, then a closed door, upon it is a sign: Office of Secret Actions. CHEN explains: "The OSA is a joint venture between two countries, Great Britain and the United States, created to pursue clandestine operations behind the German lines during World War II. Information comes in from agents in the field and contacts within the resistance movements of German-occupied Europe."

The OSA verifies these reports to uncover Germany's plans. Now, the OSA has learned of Himmler's occult activities and has sent their best men and fighters to the village of Wulfburg to explore a structure called Castle Wolfenstein, The Wolf's Lair. It is here that rumors of occult activity and cruel experiments upon war prisoners are taking place.

The images change once more to show an American soldier sitting alone in a cell. He is repeating Standing Order #71 out loud. "If you are placed in a compromising position where you might divulge information regarding your mission or the OSA, take your own life by ingesting your cyanide tablet. As always the OSA will disavow …" Upon hearing footsteps approaching the door, the man crumples the paper in his hands. He holds his breath and waits. As the footsteps pass and fade, the soldier breathes again.

CHEN explains the imagery; "This is B. J. Blazkowicz, a top OSA agent and U.S. Army Ranger. During his recon of Kugelstadt, he was captured and thrown into a dungeon."

Blazkowicz stands and stretches, knocking his knuckles on the low ceiling. He makes his way to the single, tiny window that decorates his cell. Out the window, he can see Castle Wolfenstein across the lake. Screams of pain and terror there are not muffled. He turns to the dungeon's door, removes his combat knife from his boot and calls for the guard.

The images shift once more. "This is the lower keep of Castle Wolfenstein," CHEN explains. A Nazi scientist is putting a specimen – an allied prisoner – through a course of agonizing tests. The thing laying on the gurney is a severely malformed human. The Nazi can be heard chanting incantations as he hovers over the results of his twisted experiments. "This man is Heinrich Himmler," CHEN reports. The image stops suddenly leaving the council speechless.

Key Characters
OSA/Rangers

Name: The Director, Office of Secret Actions
Bio: Not much is known about this Englishman, other than he is a capable man who puts nothing past the Nazis. He will not dismiss a report out of hand just because it may seem outlandish. However strange it appears, he believes, the truth must be uncovered, or there could be a nasty surprise for Allied forces.

Name: Jack Stone, OSA
Bio: The Director's trusted assistant, Jack Stone is an American with a keen mind and a thorough knowledge of the workings of the German war machine. The highest officials heed his advice. He has been sent to the Malta office of the OSA and is responsible for collating much of the information as it comes in from the operatives.

Name: B. J. Blazkowicz, OSA/ U.S. Army Rangers
Bio: One of the top agents for the OSA, his talents are needed to investigate rumors of strange goings-on within the Third Reich. It is hoped that Blazkowicz can find out the truth behind reports of occult activity in the German hierarchy at The Wolf's Lair.

Name: Kessler, Kreisau Circle resistance group
Bio: You are the local contact for OSA operatives in the field. You have been successful in partially infiltrating the SS Paranormal Division's temporary headquarters and have valuable information regarding their activities. Finding and meeting with the OSA agents can be tricky, but you are determined to fight the Germans the best way you know how.

Nazis

Name: Heinrich Himmler, Founder of the SS Paranormal Division
Bio: An unusual interest in the occult, a little background research into the family tree and a temperament to make Hitler proud all pointed Himmler to his destiny. Gathering the most ardent occult followers and chasing down a myth—a tale from centuries past—has yielded a glimmer of light. His labs and dungeons are haunted by walking undead and monstrous creations and filled with screams from prisoners who know they will never be released from his horror.

Name: Wilhelm Strasse, high-ranking German scientist with the SS Paranormal Division

Taking the fortress means close-quarters shooting and house-to-house fighting. It's a scenario paintball game, not the streets of Baghdad, so there will be times when you need to offer an opponent the chance to surrender rather then get blasted at 10 feet. (Photo by Ted D'Ottavio)

Bio: Hi skull-like visage and twisted scientific research have earned him the nickname "Death's head." Strasse is close to Himmler, but does not subscribe to any of the man's occult beliefs. Strasse has two passions: science and machinery. He has spent years on his Projekt Uber Soldat, fusing metal and flesh with horrific results. His experiments have spawned creatures that are no longer human yet not fully mechanical. He gives credence only to that which is tangible and fights guns with guns.

Name: Marianna Blavatsky, Oberfuhrer, SS Paranormal Division
Bio: Madame Blavatsky has studied the black arts. She has established herself as the premier practitioner of the occult within the borders of Nazi Germany. As such, she has the ear of Himmler and vast power within the SS Paranormal Division. Blavatsky has mentored many in the occult. With patience and study, the Oberfuhrer has compiled information that could point the Nazis to a power greater than any yet known to the modern world.

We have a winner! National manufacturers like Tippmann Pneumatics will give away products as "door prizes" at big tournaments and well-attended scenario games.

Name: Helga von Bulow, SS Paranormal Division
Bio: This headstrong woman has studied under Marianna Blavatsky and does everything she can to help her teacher. Helga has become a leader in her own right, establishing the all-women Elite Guard to further the cause of the Division. While she has learned much from Oberfuhrer Blavatsky, von Bulow tends to be impetuous. She tries too hard sometimes, running headlong into situations where discretion may be necessary.

On-Site Information

To receive the discount for pre-registration, player entries must be postmarked by October 8th, 2003. The field will open after 9:00 AM on Friday to accommodate early camping, arrivals and recreational vehicles. Registration will be open on Friday from 4:00 PM to 6:00 PM and re-open at 7:00 AM Saturday morning.

A mandatory player orientation takes place at 10:00 AM Saturday. "Game on" is from noon Saturday until 2:00 PM Sunday. Event admission is $50 per player prior to pre-registration deadline and $60 after the per-registration deadline and on the day of the game.

Your admission includes: official embroidered series event patch; character ID card; laminated event badge; entry into the prize drawings; a BustNBalls "Free Money Instant Win" game card; and a 26-hour

event. Pre-registered-only players are guaranteed an event rocker; entry into the "Tippmann Reach Out and Tag Someone" drawing for a Tippmann Custom 98 and Flatline barrel system; entry into the Crossfire magazine FREE subscriptions giveaway and a chance to take home the "BustNBalls Mystery Grand Prize" at the end of the event!

The only paint will be PMI event paint. A 2000-round case is $80 on site.

Air fills: CO_2 is $4 each fill for any size bottle or three for $10. Compressed air is $18 for the weekend with unlimited fills.

Team Joint Fury will produce "HOLLOW of HORROR II" on Friday evening. Starting with an Octoberfest-style banquet from 5:00 to 7:00 PM, free for the first 200 registered players in line, compliments of Joint Fury. The Friday night fun will continue as players participate in the "Haunted Castle Arrrrgh" game, complete with ghouls, goblins, assorted lights, prizes and killer fog from 7:00 to 10:00 PM.

At 6:00 PM on Friday evening, there will be an Armotech Zeus "Top Gun One-On-One" competition for the first 20 registered MXS scenario players who sign up for it. The winner of this competition will take home a new Armotech Zeus semi-automatic pistol! Participants must sign up with MXS prior to the competition in order to compete.

The Scenario News Costume Contest on Friday night will begin at 9:00 PM. Prizes will be awarded to the winner of the costume contest by celebrity judges.

The traditional EMR Player Party will take place Friday night as well, with the Rec. Center open until midnight for ping-pong, pool, foosball and music. A volleyball net and horseshoes will be set-up during the day. E.M.R. will also have a bonfire on Friday and Saturday nights.

Tasty Tyme Caterers, owned and operated by Rich Barchock of Team Damage, Inc., will serve the player's lunch and dinner on Saturday and breakfast on Sunday!

Home away from home: There are 22 bunkhouses available free. They range from 12 to 21 bunks each. These must be reserved through EMR and bunk assignments are made on a first-register, first-get basis. Players must register a group of 15 people to get their own private bunkhouse. Otherwise they will be put with other players in a bunkhouse. The faster that players pre-register, the better bunkhouse they get. There is also free camping on-site.

Players are invited to cool their heels at the field and play some recreational ball on any of EMR's 24 fields after the awards ceremony Sunday afternoon until 6:00 PM, and are welcome to stay overnight on Sunday.

All participants need to know and/or to fill out: the story line, MXS Rules of Play, event registration forms and MXS Waivers, EMR Field Waiver, hotels/motels and directions to EMR Paintball Park. Please visit EMR's Internet site for additional information.

INTERVIEW: BLUE'S CREW

I asked Blue how he made his choices for teammates, writes Blue's Crew "Press Wench" Amy "The Girl" Chantry.

"Well, I was looking for a certain type of player," Blue replied. "I wanted this to be a team of aggressive players, not afraid to charge, real paintball warriors! But I know many excellent players out there and I couldn't choose all of them! Plus, I wanted to reward the players that have maintained their loyalty to EMR (my paintball park) all these years and helped my business grow. We really have a family here and when you get an opportunity to do something like this, you want your family with you."

Michael "Blue" Hanse says he has been in paintball practically since "day one," since the invention of the game. These days, he still plays the game, manages an internationally famous paintball scenario team called "Blue's Crew" – named in a way after himself – and, with his wife, Sue, operates the highly successful EMR Paintball Park in New Milford, Pennsylvania. (EMR stands for Endless Mountain Recreation.) During his paintball career, Blue has been involved in manufacturing markers and wholesaling gear. So, as far as paintball goes, Blue is about as well rounded as a 40-something married kind of guy can be.

Blue began playing paintball in 1983 when he bought four Splatmasters and chased friends around in the woods near his home in Chambersburg, Pennsylvania. Eventually he became a "suit," specializing in the office products and office design business. "I was smoking four packs of cigarettes a day," he remembers, "had an ulcer and never saw my family. I finally asked myself, 'Who needs this?'" Apparently, the answer was obvious.

"Today, at EMR, we're very player oriented," Blue says. "Whereas most of the fields in the U.S. cater to the part-time recreational player, to walk-ons, beginners and maybe bachelor parties or groups from the office, we have taken our fields in a different direction. We want the top five percent of players, the people who are serious, really love the game. We're open to anyone, though, and we try to help newbies feel comfortable and have a good time."

EMR holds Big Games and Scenarios on its 20 outdoor fields. Blue and crew have built a castle, villages and 35 bunkhouses. "We have 110 20-foot by 20-foot campsites and can sleep up to 600 people in the bunkhouses," he says. With 400 to 700 players showing up for a Big Game, EMR is obviously big-time paintball. "So far, 756 is tops, but we're still growing!"

For a typical Big Game event, players by the hundreds will show up and generals will be chosen for each side. "Tom Kaye, president of marker manufacturer Airgun Designs, was here as a general for our last game," Blue says.

"Twin Towers" was the most recent Big Game at EMR. "We kind of imitated [J.R.R.] Tolkien's book *The Two Towers*. We had castle attackers and defenders. It was a huge hoot. Obviously, with that many people, paint gets thick in the air, so if you get hit, you come out of the game, we chronograph your marker to keep you legal and then after 10 or 15 minutes, we reinsert you. This lets everyone get plenty of playing time. One of our Big Games can run from six to 26 hours, from noon on Saturday until two o'clock PM on Sunday."

Even though he is in his 40s, Michael still stays in shape, practices and will shoot up a case of balls when he gets a few hours to himself. "I used to hunt," Blue says, "but now I'm 100 percent paintball. A big difference in hunting and paintball is that the average hunter shoots a few times before the season to check his scope and then may get a couple shots during the season. Paintball is just the opposite. You can't get really good by conserving your ammo. When I was really into playing, I'd go out and run and shoot up maybe 4000 balls in a weekend. Try that hunting and you'll go through a dozen gun barrels."

Blue's wife, Sue, also plays. "That's another thing I like about paintball," Blue says. "When I got started maybe one half of one percent of all players were women. Now, they may make up five to 10 percent or even 10 to 15 percent of the total number of players. I imagine many women think they're going to go out and get bruised and muddy and have men run all over them, but paintball isn't like that. Size and strength really don't matter. Endurance matters and someone of smaller stature, someone who is agile and fast actually has a better chance than some 200-pounder. Paintball is an equalizer."

"Blue's Crew" represents Michael "Blue" Hanse's EMR Paintball Park at big games around the U.S. Blue says he organized his famous scenario team to "play hard and have fun!" (Photo by Ted D'Ottavio.)

So, how did Michael get nicknamed "Blue?" And how about "Blue's Crew?"

"Believe it or not, that all got started when I went to an event in Paw Paw, West Virginia in about 1989," Michael Hanse says. "Tippmann had just come out with the first really good functioning semi-auto, the 68-Special, and I went down there to try it out."

About 50 players showed up and Michael says 50 people was a real crowd in those days. On the way out the door, he grabbed a case of Nelson paintballs and when he got to Paw Paw, he realized he was not only the oldest player, but he was the only player not shooting bright red or orange balls. The Nelson balls were blue.

"That was 15 years ago," he says, "and I was running and shooting a lot then. I was pretty quick and a real good shot with that 68-Special. We ran game after game and … to make a long story short … at the end of the day, I had shot everyone at least one time and had shot some many times. So, there were 49 guys standing around covered with blue paint. To make matters worse – well, for them – they hadn't hit me one time. Not once all day! The guys began to give me a hard time in a joking kind of way and they nicknamed me 'Blue,' then and there."

Over the years, Blue has organized several well-known paintball teams, but his current team is named after himself, Blue's Crew. The 31 members and 12 associate members are fully sponsored by manufacturers for their clothing, equipment, game entry fees and even some of their travel expenses.

Imagine fighting your way through an Old West mining camp in a 24-hour scenario game. With practically a dozen years of producing role-playing scenarios and big games across the U.S., the producers have the games down to Safe and Fun! There is usually plenty of camping and a good time is had by all.

Wayne Dollack is considered the "Father of the Paintball Scenario Game" and a number of today's scenario producers (Diane and Patrick McKinnon of Mackz Xtreme Sportz, for instance) originally worked with him. Today, Wayne operates a paintball field called Wayne's World of Paintball in Ocala, Florida, and produces scenario games as well.

INTERVIEW: THE FATHER OF SCENARIO GAMES

Paintball Digest sat down with Wayne and Jackie Dollack at their playing field and pro shop "Wayne's World of Paintball" in Ocala, Florida. Wayne, who was 63 years old in 2003, laughed about his reputation as the "father of scenario games" because it made him sound soooooo ooold.

Paintball Digest: Wayne, I understand you had a colorful life long before you got to be the "father of paintball scenario games."

Wayne: I played my first game of paintball in 1983 after we moved to Ocala. Paintball was mostly rogue fields out in the woods in those days. Before that, I'd been a graphics artist specializing in advertising. But in the early'80s, artists began switching to computers to do all their art, and I figured that after 38 years it was time for a career change.

Paintball Digest: So, tell us about your first scenario games.

Wayne: It was back in 1986, I think, and the field was quite large. We called it "Operation CIA." We put in $2 each and buried the money in a cash box in a hidden tower we'd built in the middle of this field. The object was to find the money and keep from getting shot. If you found the money, you got to keep it. We had a ball.

The next year in "Operation Stealth," we built an airplane out of plywood that looked like a Stealth bomber and tried to get all 38 players in the mood. Then we looked up, and honest to God, we had police department helicopters circling overhead taking pictures. They were watching that black-painted Stealth bomber, I guess, because they never did contact us about it and we couldn't figure out what they wanted. Eventually they just flew off. What we didn't know was that the real Stealth bomber was about to be unveiled and it was real Top Secret stuff. How about that! Since then, we've had a lot of law enforcement people come out and play. That game, "Operation Stealth" in 1987, was our first role-playing scenario game.

Paintball Digest: So, your very first game drew a lot of attention, but it wasn't necessarily the kind of attention you wanted. How did the idea of playing roles in the game come up?

Wayne: I swear that story is true. But a buddy of mine, an army engineer who had been in Vietnam named Gaylan Lancaster, came up with the idea of character cards, and we got together and made up roles for some of the games. Gaylan, of course, wanted to be the "Game Operations Director" and called himself GOD for short. We soon discovered that the more you become your character, the more you get into it, the more you enjoy the experience and that's what it's all about.

Paintball Digest: Was that your first 24-hour game?

Wayne: Yes. In those days, a 24-hour game actually played for 24 hours. Today, most games shut down for dinner and then from about 2 to 7 on Sunday morning. Give everybody a break, including the referees. You get 300 people out on the field and with a 1:15 ref-to-player ratio, you've got a big staff to worry about, maybe 25 people.

Paintball Digest: How does a scenario game differ

Guards provide security for a shipment of gold in Nocer Productions' "Great Train Robbery" at First Strike Paintball in Newberry, Florida.

from tournament play?

Wayne: Tournaments are very fast and involve small teams that are sponsored by manufacturers. Team members are usually fast and athletic, so play can be much more aggressive. And with lots of money, often thousands of dollars, riding on the outcome of some 5-man shoot-out that barely lasts 5 minutes, tempers can get out of hand. The refs have to be on top of the play all the time. You almost never see somebody losing their temper on a scenario field. In scenario play, the emphasis is on sportsmanship and enjoying the game.

I mentioned that tournament teams are sponsored. That means manufacturers provide equipment, clothing or travel expenses to a high-profile team like Michael "Blue" Hanse's Blue's Crew or the Jacksonville Warriors from Jacksonville, Florida. The team gets its gear free, gets its picture in magazines, travels to tournaments or big, high profile games and sometimes even part of their expenses (meals or motels) will be reimbursed. A manufacturer gets visibility because the guys on the team wear the manufacturer's name on their clothes and let the manufacturer use their pictures and maybe do some PR stuff.

Paintball Digest: So where do you go from here?

Wayne: Jackie and I travel all over the country now putting on scenario games and there are a lot of other good groups doing it, too. We're headed up to Wasaga

Wayne Dollack (left) with his field and business manager Eddie Williamson at Wayne's World of Paintball in Ocala, Florida. Wayne says he never thought much about being called the "father of paintball scenario games." He just thought he was having fun and making a living.

Beach Paintball in Canada to help put on "Stars War" (didn't want to get in trouble with anyone in Tinsel Town) soon. Paul has a great operation. He gets 60,000 players a year at Skirmish and he's into white-water rafting, too. We did the only, or at least the first, 48-hour scenario game in the world at Skirmish. It was based on the movie "Blade Runner" and practically everybody had a great time. I had no idea that movie was such a hit.

Lying in wait!

People don't realize it, but planning a game and building props and scripting character cards and missions for 500 people takes from 4 to 6 weeks. Then you've got to haul everything to the field and hope for good weather. If the weather is great, you could have twice the turnout you expect and that leaves you scrambling for more Porta-Potties and referees. If it turns rotten, maybe nobody will show up and you can lose thousands of dollars.

But everything in paintball is changing fast. The equipment, especially. Paintball is on television now and then and lots of people out on the west coast are trying "air soft." It's like paintball, but you shoot little plastic pellets instead of breakable balls so, obviously, it is more of an honor-based game. You can't tell when someone else gets hit. But the air soft guns (they're not markers, because they don't actually mark anything) shoot faster and farther. Air soft hasn't caught on here in the east or the south, yet.

I'd say that even in regular paintball, though, the markers are much faster than they used to be. They shoot further and straighter, too.

Paintball Digest: How do you like being thought of as the "father" of scenario games?

Wayne: It's a compliment, really, but I never looked at it that way. I've always just had fun and my business is helping other people have fun and play this game the right way, with sportsmanship.

Paintball Digest: What are your favorite foods?

Wayne: I like a good cheesecake and there's a restaurant not far from here that serves a wonderful marinated octopus salad. [The noise in the background is Wayne's World field and business manager Eddie Williamson turning green.]

You can learn more about Wayne and Jackie Dollack's playing field and scenario games at *www.waynes-world. com*.

Packing paint and carrying a prize! If you don't carry extra paint with you, you may run out in an intense fire-fight and that can mean time off the scenario field.

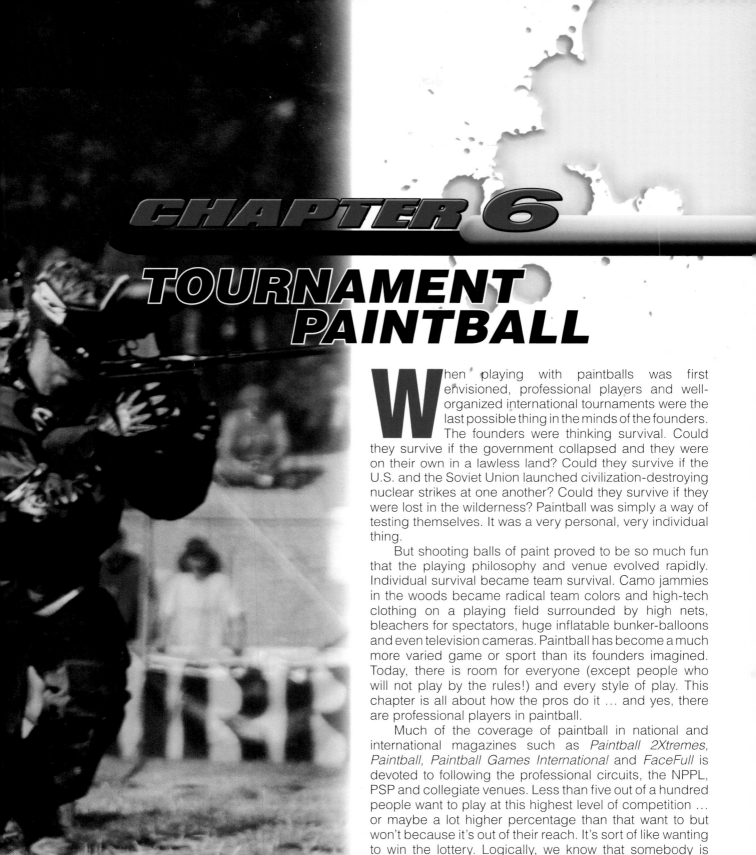

CHAPTER 6

TOURNAMENT PAINTBALL

When playing with paintballs was first envisioned, professional players and well-organized international tournaments were the last possible thing in the minds of the founders. The founders were thinking survival. Could they survive if the government collapsed and they were on their own in a lawless land? Could they survive if the U.S. and the Soviet Union launched civilization-destroying nuclear strikes at one another? Could they survive if they were lost in the wilderness? Paintball was simply a way of testing themselves. It was a very personal, very individual thing.

But shooting balls of paint proved to be so much fun that the playing philosophy and venue evolved rapidly. Individual survival became team survival. Camo jammies in the woods became radical team colors and high-tech clothing on a playing field surrounded by high nets, bleachers for spectators, huge inflatable bunker-balloons and even television cameras. Paintball has become a much more varied game or sport than its founders imagined. Today, there is room for everyone (except people who will not play by the rules!) and every style of play. This chapter is all about how the pros do it … and yes, there are professional players in paintball.

Much of the coverage of paintball in national and international magazines such as *Paintball 2Xtremes, Paintball, Paintball Games International* and *FaceFull* is devoted to following the professional circuits, the NPPL, PSP and collegiate venues. Less than five out of a hundred people want to play at this highest level of competition … or maybe a lot higher percentage than that want to but won't because it's out of their reach. It's sort of like wanting to win the lottery. Logically, we know that somebody is going to win, but let's be honest, it won't be us.

To the victor belong the spoils. JT USA's Team Dynasty takes the 2003 World Cup in Toulouse, France.

DO YOU HAVE WHAT IT TAKES?

Playing paintball at the highest level takes Personal Commitment. It takes something mental. Your mind first. Your body follows. Understand this. It ain't easy. Many are called, but few are chosen. Many begin on the path, but few go the distance. Can you go the distance?

To become a pro player, you need to find a way to make that goal #1 – numero uno – primero in your life. Everything else will need to take a back seat for a while. Girlfriend, school, job and even your family. Here are 12 "thoughtful spots" (yes, we ripped that off from Winnie the Pooh), places you can go mentally and physically to prepare for being a pro player once you have made the personal commitment. Six of these "thoughtful spots" are actions you can take and six are mental preparations. The mental side is the foundation for the action.

Six Actions

1. Read everything you can about paintball and playing paintball. You will learn about the equipment, other pro players and the pro competition circuits. Your sources will be magazines, books, company catalogs and the Internet.

2. Buy good gear. When you begin, you want good gear. It doesn't have to be the most expensive or the very best … yet. You want to be able to take your marker apart and learn to fix things. You want to make upgrades yourself. You want to learn your gear inside and out and that includes some screwing up.

3. Play. That's it. Play paintball every chance you get. Go to every rec field and scenario game you can possibly get to and check them out. Experience every situation. Immerse yourself in the paintball lifestyle and culture. Talk the talk. Walk the walk.

4. Get in shape physically. The best paintball players are fast, have extraordinary reflexes and good hand-eye coordination. Run. Swim. Lift. Dedicate your body to … well, not purity exactly, but health. No smokes. No chews. And if you drink … think moderation.

5. Travel to every event you can afford. Watch how today's pros play, how they study shooting lanes, map out the cover and work as a team. Watch how they act on the break, how they communicate and how they react when they are sent to the dead box. Since paintball is played around the world, if you learn to read and speak a foreign language like French or Spanish or German, you will become invaluable for other players and companies.

6. Get to know everyone in the game. Become a part of paintball. Get autographs. Meet the KAPP girls. Ask for Bud Orr's autograph. The more you belong, the faster you will approach your goal and the more you will hunger for it.

What does it take to play professionally? Well here is what is unnecessary and may actually not be helpful. Spouse. Kids. Wealth. A lot of time spent in school beyond high school. It doesn't take a steady job, either.

Great pro players come from all walks of life. You read their names in every magazine: Chris Lasoya, Rich Telford, Bob Long. Former greats include the likes of Oh Pawlak, Eric Felix and Shane Pestana. Oliver Lang, who plays professionally for Team Dynasty, says he loved skateboarding growing up as a California kid, but now he takes on the responsibility for getting his teammates pumped up before a game. He screams at them. He chants. He roughs them up … and they respond. They win. Not because they are in better shape or they want to win more or they have better equipment, but because, in the final analysis, Oliver says, it may be "all mental."

Six Challenges

7. Envision yourself as a pro player. Be a pro inside your head and your chosen path will appear. It's a "Build it and they will come" thing. Be very careful here, however, that it does not become an ego thing. No one was ever the fastest gunfighter in the West for very long. The real pro becomes a servant to the game rather than expecting the game to be his (or her) servant. It truly is a Zen thing.

8. Write everything down. Personal commitment is meaningless if you only keep it in your head. After all, think about how many thoughts move through your head every day. Thousands. Millions maybe. If you will only take the time to write down your goal, maybe make a poster for your bedroom, you are half the way to your goal.

9. Minimize other commitments. If you want to be the best, you have to give up things that get in the way of that goal, whatever they are in time or money.

10. Live inside your dream. Expect that many people will want to turn you aside from your goal, and they often have good reasons for what they say and do. Your parents will want you to get a good education. Your girlfriend will want to spend Saturday at the beach rather than at the rec field or your boyfriend will want to go to the movies and then out for a party before a tournament. Your buddies will want to play computer games rather than field-stripping and cleaning your marker. Expect pressure and prepare for it mentally. Don't get angry; get focused.

11. Decide what kind of pro player you want to be. Emotional or cool. What will you do to win? You will see some pro players lose their minds on the field. They argue with the refs and lose their temper. You will discover "that fine line" between what is right and what is wrong. Your job is to decide what side of the line you are going to walk.

12. The best pro player develops personal integrity. These are very basic principles of life and it takes some people, whether they are pros or not, a lifetime to learn them. Play fair. Be responsible for your actions. Treat other people the way you would want to be treated. Play with integrity and you will live with integrity. Live with integrity and you will discover that you have arrived.

When you have made the commitment and are ready to begin your path to becoming a professional paintball player, you will learn about today's dominant professional circuits, the NPPL and PSP, the apparently declining APL and the promising NXL. There is also a smaller, but growing, collegiate league and there are international leagues in Europe.

In America, the NPPL and PSP pro circuits are the heart of the hype, the excitement and the passion. They are like the American and National Leagues in baseball and football. In paintball, the venues of the two major leagues are slightly different, but they are strikingly similar in format, spectator appeal and playing styles. So, in the remaining part of this chapter, we are going to profile the basic structure, objectives and rules of the NPPL and the earlier APL, because they give us a format for understanding the game of paintball as it is played at the highest and most popular pro level.

THE NPPL AND PSP

The National Professional Paintball League (NPPL at *www.nppl.tv)* is the sole sanctioning body for all amateur and professional paintball players in North America. It is a league where player representatives formulate league rules, make business decisions and sanction and preside over all aspects of an NPPL event. It was founded in 1993 and is the oldest such organization in paintball.

The NPPL wants to become the worldwide governing body of the sport of paintball "to ensure safe competitive play for our members and teams, and to support our players and the paintball industry by showcasing paintball as a major sport with integrity and professionalism at the highest level."

NPPL Super 7

Since the NPPL considered sanctioning a new Seven-Man Series at the World Cup in Orlando, Florida, there has been some confusion and not a little speculation as to what this means to the teams and players who are currently part of the world's largest paintball league. Here's what the NPPL has written about its decision to part ways with the PSP and operate its own series:

"NPPL is a non-political governing body responsible for sanctioning quality paintball events and is committed to growing the sport at all levels. We are also dedicated to improving and maintaining the sport's integrity and professionalism.

"Our goal is to create a positive environment that encourages new players into the game and to provide all players and sponsors with a top quality flagship paintball series with sound infrastructure that delivers on its promises."

NPPL wants to legitimize tournament paintball by maintaining a body of independent pro referees to enforce rules and standards, referees who cannot be intimidated. Consequently, they must have the knowledge and authority to properly enforce the rules, specifically for cheating, foul language, physical altercations and threats, "which have not been properly addressed in the past." NPPL has developed a strict sanctioning program to make all event organizers adhere to high standards and work with the teams and industry.

The NPPL Super 7 tournament series was formatted to "globalize" the game and make it more presentable to

Some good reasons to get into competitive paintball: You travel to cool tournaments, you get to wear very rad uniforms and some of your gear is sponsored (that means you only pay part of its cost). It's exciting because you play some of the very best players. And you have cool tents and banners with your name on them. Jim Bergman of Troy, Ohio's BASE Paintball sponsors the traveling team Ohio Turmoil. His guys placed 14th out of 72 teams in their 5-Man division at the Team Event's 2003 International Amateur Open and won the Sportsmanship Award.

Big games attract big crowds. Most tournament formats do not allow spectators to coach from the bleachers. Whether they are 3-Man, 5-Man or 7-Man formats, rookie, novice or amateur level, games are short, fast and intense.

California's Team Dynasty, sponsored by JT USA, en route to winning the 7-man World Cup in Toulouse, France, in 2003. To win at this level of international play, player reactions and teamwork have to be near perfect and equipment has to be the very best.

You never want to run out of paint in the middle of a game. Carry plenty of paint ... and hitch a ride! Save your strength for the field.

Get ready. Get set. Tournament play at the International Amateur Open north of Pittsburgh in 2003.

television, outside sponsors and spectators. The 7-man is a "very strategic game, fun to watch and easy to follow. It fits most venue possibilities." The NPPL promised pro teams a minimum prize of $20,000 at each event, plus a $15,000 Champion's Prize. There were also cash prizes for amateur ($40,000), novice ($30,000) and rookie ($20,000) teams. Here is how the NPPL characterized its new Super 7 Series for 2003:

For 11 years, the National Professional Paintball League (NPPL) has brought teams from around the world to the U.S. to compete against the best players in the sport of tournament paintball. For 2003, NPPL introduced seven-man play (supplanting the 10-man and 5-man matches of former events). Each team had seven players on the field with one goal in mind: eliminating enough opponents to capture their flag and safely return it to their flag station. These matches are limited to 10 minutes until the semi-finals when game duration drops to seven minutes.

Teams are awarded the following points for each game out of a possible 100 points per game:

1. Three points per eliminated opponent. If any paintball breaks on a player or their equipment, that player is eliminated from the game immediately by a referee. If the player continues to play after being hit, the referee has the right to pull one or more of the player's teammates off the field as well.

2. One point per player who is not eliminated. Following the game, each non-eliminated player is inspected by a referee to ensure there is no paint on the player. For each "clean" player, that

One of the Tippmann teams prepares for the break.

3. **32 points for pulling the flag.** Each team has a flag hanging in the other team's flag station. If a clean player pulls their team's flag from the opponent's flag station, they are awarded 32 points.

4. **40 points for hanging the flag.** The first team to have a clean player retrieve their flag and hang it in their flag station is awarded 40 points.

There are numerous referees on each field who are each assigned zones to watch. If a player steps out of bounds or is hit by a paintball, the referee will eliminate the player by removing the player's armband.

The playoff system for all divisions (professional, amateur, novice and rookie) is as follows:

Preliminaries: 10-minute games with two minutes between games. Each team plays a minimum of eight games. The top eight teams from the professional and amateur division and the top 16 teams from the novice and rookie division go through to a quarter-finals.

Quarter-finals: 10-minute games with two minutes between games. Teams are seeded from points scored in the preliminaries, and the points are then cleared. The teams are split into divisions of four and play a round-robin format. The top team from novice and rookie divisions and the top two teams from professional and amateur go to the semi-finals.

Semi-finals: Seven-minute games with two minutes between games. Best of three format. Teams are seeded from points scored in the quarter-finals and the points are cleared. The first team plays the fourth team while the second and third teams play. The winning two teams go to the finals while the losers go to a playoff or consolation bracket.

Finals: Third and fourth playoff while first and second playoff. Best of three format in seven minute games. The first team plays the second team while the third team plays the fourth team.

Typical Prize Structure (Chicago NPPL Super 7 World Series 2003)

	Professional	Amateur	Novice	Rookie
1st place	$20,000	7 LCD TVs $800 Galyan's Retail Vouchers	7 Projectors $800 Galyan's Retail Vouchers	7 Film Scanners 7 Digital Cameras $800 Galyan's Retail Vouchers
2nd	$10,000	7 Film Scanners 7 DVD Combos 7 Digital Cameras $800 Galyan's Retail Vouchers	7 Film Scanners 7 Digital Cameras $800 Galyan's Retail Vouchers	7 Film Scanners 7 Digital Cameras $800 Galyan's Retail Vouchers
3rd	$ 5,000	7 DVD Combos 7 Digital Camera $800 Galyan's Retail Vouchers	7 DVD Combos 7 Digital Cameras $800 Galyan's Retail Vouchers	7 Digital Cameras $800 Galyan's Retail Vouchers
4th	$ 2,500	7 Digital Cameras $800 Galyan's Retail Vouchers	7 DVD Combos 7 Scanners $800 Galyan's Retail Vouchers	7 DVD Combos $800 Galyan's Retail Vouchers

THE APL TOURNAMENT SERIES

The American Paintball League (*www.paintball.apl. com* (800) 541-9169) was founded in Johnson City, Tennessee. The APL has sponsored an eight-tournament series and established appropriate rules and venues for its operation. National Paintball Supply is one of the major presenting sponsors of the series, so all games use supplied Diablo tournament paintballs as the exclusive field paint.

Bob McGuire, who founded the APL in 1991, has since branched out into field insurance, a Paintball Training Institute and the tournament series. "We have wanted carefully planned timing for our tournaments," Bob says, "so we schedule carefully, spend a whole lot of time coordinating tournament operations and make sure that all the prizes we advertise will actually be available. We are very player-friendly."

APL Player Classification

First, no player less than 10 years of age is allowed in an APL tournament. So, all players from 10-up in age must be able to prove their age at registration or when the team enters the field.

APL classifies individual players as rookies, novices, amateurs or professionals according to the number of seasons they have competed in tournament paintball. Recreational playing time (running around in the woods with your buddies or shooting up your local field) is not

Leaning into the shot.

In collegiate arena league paintball, teams compete in fully enclosed thunderdomes. Shouting, screaming and yelling encouragement and directions is part of this game!

included. But, after a player participates in his or her first tournament, their classification as an official APL "rookie" is established and it continues through December 31st of that year because typically, Bob McGuire says, paintball seasons – tournaments, point totals, standings – operate on a January 1 to December 31 calendar year.

A "professional" is anyone who has played in a tournament on a pro team during the previous 12 months. A pro player may move back to a lower division by not playing as a pro for 12 consecutive months.

An "amateur" is a player with three or more seasons of tournament experience who has not played as a pro during the previous 12 months.

A "novice" is a player with fewer than three seasons of tournament experience who has not played as a pro or amateur during the previous 12 months.

A "rookie" is a player with less than one season of tournament experience who has never played as a novice, amateur or professional.

Such a rigid classification is designed to keep experienced players and teams from "sandbagging" or dropping down into a less experienced division to give them a better chance of winning. All major tournament venues discourage such activity and may disqualify an individual or team that is discovered to engage in

sandbagging. With the exception of the pro level, a player in an APL venue may play at higher levels without losing their status. For example, a rookie could play on a novice or amateur team during a season without losing his rookie classification. As soon as he plays on a pro team however, his classification changes to pro for a minimum of 12 months.

APL Team Classification

Just as it certifies individuals into different classifications to make sure play is fair and all players have an opportunity, the APL classifies registering teams.

A "pro team" is a team in which any member has competed in a tournament registered in the pro division.

Interestingly, an "amateur team" is allowed to field a pro player, but it is limited to a seven-person roster with a maximum of five players allowed on the field during a game. No substitutions are allowed for any reason.

A "novice team" may field one amateur but is limited to a seven-person roster, and it, too, is limited to five players on the field with no substitutions allowed.

Referees are always on the spot during top-level airball or speedball play. Unlike in scenario games where play is strictly for fun, tempers can run hot when thousands of dollars in prizes and endorsements are on the line. Referees only have seconds to make the right call, which invariably is, "Did he or didn't he get hit?"

Finally, a "rookie team" may have one novice player but is limited to a three-person roster with three on the field at a time and no substitutions.

COLLEGIATE PAINTBALL

The National Collegiate Paintball Association, Inc. (NCPA at *www.college-paintball.com*) is an all-volunteer, non-profit 501(c)3 organization created by college player athletes to promote paintball at the interscholastic level. NCPA facilitates the creation and growth of college and high school paintball activity and coordinates competition among member clubs and teams.

The NCPA and its member clubs organize recruitment drives, informational meetings, recreational club outings, scenario and big games, charity events, intra-scholastic events for other university organizations and, of course, play in the national intercollegiate tournament league. NCPA members play a vital role in presenting paintball to the public in a positive manner through various volunteer and legislative efforts. The NCPA also provides various benefits for its members.

NCPA's nationwide college paintball league is designed to provide a friendly, quality and inexpensive way for players to try competitive paintball and improve their abilities. NCPA provides financial subsidies within its member leagues.

The first college paintball club was formed at the U.S. Military Academy (West Point) in 1986, followed within a few years by Penn State, Michigan and Purdue. In May 1994, the first intercollegiate tournament was held at Sherwood Forest in LaPorte, Indiana.

INTERVIEW: AND THE CAPTAIN IS....

Eric Garbers was just 18 years old in 1988 when he made his first 12-inch replaceable machined-aluminum barrel for a Splatmaster. That quality of work in itself was pretty amazing, but Eric, being the entrepreneur he has turned out to be, soon had a local machine shop tooling specialty barrels for him to sell. Then he began collecting and selling paintball stuff and eventually he opened a real bank account and got into debt and rented a building and went into business. Now, Toledo Indoor Paintball (www.toledoindoorpaintball.com) is big.

And somehow, in his mid-30s, Eric still finds time to manage and train one of the Tippmann Pneumatics (www.tippmann.com) top teams, the Tippmann Effect. And they're darn good. In 2002, they won the Draxxus International Amateur Open seven-man team event in Pittsburgh. And they placed second in the five-man event. Not too shabby!

Now that he's in his mid-30s, though, Eric himself doesn't necessarily play every game, even though he's the captain. Tippmann Effect travels with nine guys, he says, so depending on the event, the kind of game and the size of the field, he can send out the mix of Effect competitors that has the best chance to win.

Certainly, since he got started in the '80s, players have become more athletic. "You don't see too many big guys out there any more. Those guys hang out at the rec fields. Tournament competitors are young and fast and athletic. They're serious players."

Eric organized his team into Front, Middle and Back players. The more aggressive Front and Middle players take some direction by hand signals, but mostly by just yelling at each other. Of course, front players are most quickly eliminated, but they eliminate the most enemy team members, too. When Front players go down, Middle players move up in their place. On a team like Effect that has worked and practiced together, it becomes almost automatic. Middle players are Eric's tactical reserve.

The Back players on Tippmann Effect are what Eric calls "the backbone of the team." They stay on their feet, yelling directions and helping spot threats … until the action gets too hot and close. Then they do whatever they have to do to stay in the game and help their team win.

Before a tournament, Eric walks each field and makes a map of it. The team discusses strategy in advance so everyone knows what his responsibility will be, and then they try to figure out how the other team will play it. Will they be aggressive and come at them in a rush? Will they hang back and run the clock down, thinking the Tippmann guys will get nervous? Will they push heavy on one side or the other, perhaps in some spot where there's a little bit of extra cover?

So, how do the yelling back and forth and the finger pointing and arm waving and frantic hand signals work in the pressure of an actual tournament, one they've paid maybe $6,000 to $10,000 to attend? Well, the team is good. In their fourth season, they are nationally ranked in the "Amateur Novice" category. Eric's team isn't a bunch of pros, but maybe if they were, that would take some of the fun out of it, Eric wonders.

Eric gets his team together for practice at least once a week, sometimes twice. They practice teamwork, learn to take direction, learn where they fit in and how they will be expected to support the team in order to field a winning group.

"It's a blast going to a paintball event," the captain says. "I enjoy seeing the people, hanging out, meeting friends in the industry and players on other teams we compete against. I'm glad to see 'em."

And we'll bet they are glad to see you too.

Eric Garbers, The Captain.

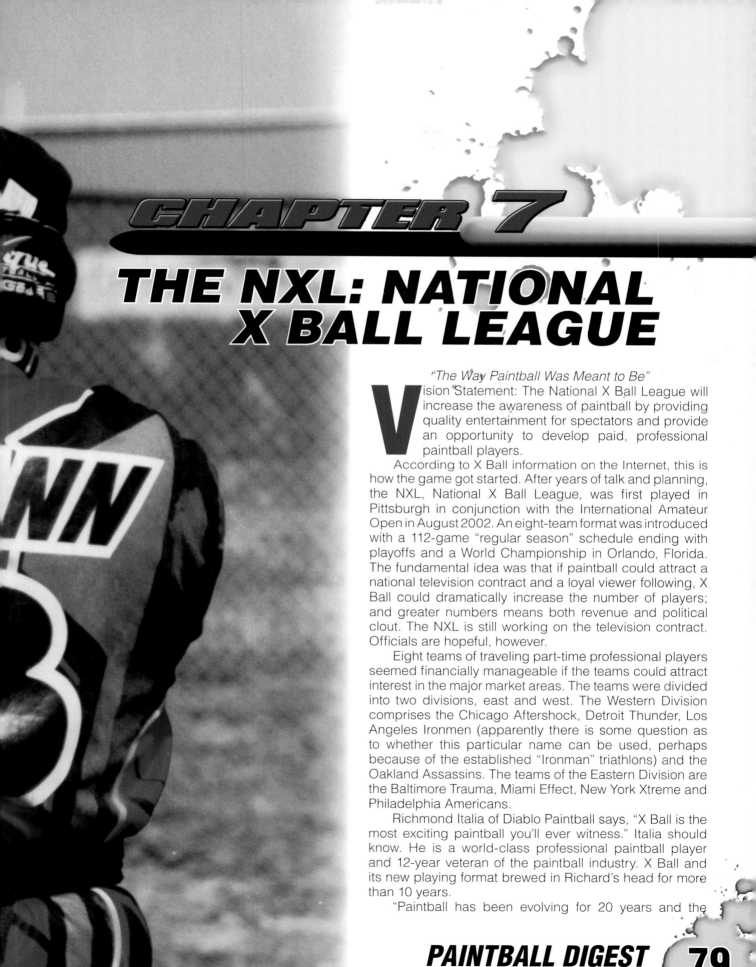

CHAPTER 7

THE NXL: NATIONAL X BALL LEAGUE

"The Way Paintball Was Meant to Be"

Vision Statement: The National X Ball League will increase the awareness of paintball by providing quality entertainment for spectators and provide an opportunity to develop paid, professional paintball players.

According to X Ball information on the Internet, this is how the game got started. After years of talk and planning, the NXL, National X Ball League, was first played in Pittsburgh in conjunction with the International Amateur Open in August 2002. An eight-team format was introduced with a 112-game "regular season" schedule ending with playoffs and a World Championship in Orlando, Florida. The fundamental idea was that if paintball could attract a national television contract and a loyal viewer following, X Ball could dramatically increase the number of players; and greater numbers means both revenue and political clout. The NXL is still working on the television contract. Officials are hopeful, however.

Eight teams of traveling part-time professional players seemed financially manageable if the teams could attract interest in the major market areas. The teams were divided into two divisions, east and west. The Western Division comprises the Chicago Aftershock, Detroit Thunder, Los Angeles Ironmen (apparently there is some question as to whether this particular name can be used, perhaps because of the established "Ironman" triathlons) and the Oakland Assassins. The teams of the Eastern Division are the Baltimore Trauma, Miami Effect, New York Xtreme and Philadelphia Americans.

Richmond Italia of Diablo Paintball says, "X Ball is the most exciting paintball you'll ever witness." Italia should know. He is a world-class professional paintball player and 12-year veteran of the paintball industry. X Ball and its new playing format brewed in Richard's head for more than 10 years.

"Paintball has been evolving for 20 years and the

The symbol of the rising National X Ball League is a giant, inflatable X bunker in the middle of the field.

audiences are getting bigger all the time," Italia says. "X Ball takes the game of paintball and adds exciting twists borrowed from hockey, soccer, football and even basketball, to make the game a lot faster, way more dramatic, and much more fun to watch. With X Ball, spectators see extreme paintball games, formatted more like team sports played in the Olympics and on prime-time television extravaganzas. X Ball is still essentially paintball as we know it, but with a giant dose of steady action and continual excitement. Think of paintball in the Mad Max ThunderDome and you've got X Ball."

Mike Ratko, Commissioner

c/o Procaps Softgel Encapsulation, Inc.
6000 Kieran, St. Laurent, QC H4S 2B5
(514) 337-1779 x 209
info@nxlpaintball.com
www.pspevents.com
www.xballpaintball.com

X BALL GAME FORMAT

Multi-Game Matches

Similar to American football, X Ball matches are played in four 10-minute quarters. Teams are motivated to hang the flag as many times as possible before the buzzer marks the end of each quarter. Every flag-hang marks the end of the game, the beginning of a three-minute pit stop, and then, a new game. The same teams face each other hang after hang, game after game, quarter after quarter, until the match is over.

Between games, players can be substituted, like football, basketball and hockey. X Ball was designed for a five-player team format, but any number of players can be used (five-player teams will be used throughout this explanation).

Teams are allowed one two-minute time-out each game.

Player Substitutions

Teams can dress up to 10 players. This allows substitutions as required during the course of the match. After every flag-hang, during the three-minute "pit stop," coaches decide which five players will return to the field.

A coach's decision may be based upon the score, time remaining, team strategy, individual player strengths and talent, possible injuries and remaining player stamina.

As in most team sports, you will see coaches communicating (often vigorously) with the players, calling last-minute strategy changes and "plays," and occasionally throwing coaching tantrums!

Elimination: A ball must break on a player or his equipment to be grounds for elimination.

An X Ball "game" is not a one-shot proposition. Teams play multiple games and there is usually a clear winner ... at least for today. Tournaments attract thousands of spectators.

Field

The field consists of a custom-designed airball field with optimum bunker positions for rapid advancement of players and maximum action in a spectator-friendly format. Capping the ends of each field are "the pits." Pits are team staging areas and are usually a frenzy of action, all by themselves! A regulation-size field of 125-feet by 150-feet is recommended.

The Pits

With only three minutes to recover and regroup for the next game, you will see teams and their pit crews scrambling to assist their players between games. Pit crews are teams of three individuals who must get players ready for every re-start and back on the field as fast as physically possible. In just three minutes, the pit crew must: clean off the paint hits, top off the air tanks, refill the ball packs, squeegee the barrels, quench a player's thirst, clean the goggle lenses and then stuff the players through the nets just in time for the re-start. If a player is late, the game begins and his team plays that game without him.

Scoring

The often complex scoring of a paintball game has been replaced by simply awarding a team one point for each successful flag-hang. The team with the most points at the end of regulation time is the winner. Matches that end in a tie are decided by a sudden-death playoff game.

Penalties

Players who commit infractions normally resulting in elimination, penalty points or one-for-one penalties can be sent to a penalty box. Like hockey, the team that has a player penalized plays short-handed during that player's penalty. Assessed penalty times are based on the severity of the infraction: minor – two minutes, major – five minutes and misconduct – ten minutes.

On-Field Chronograph

The entire crowd knows instantly when a chronograph judge nails a speed violator. X Ball takes a strong stand for safe playing conditions. On-field speed violations are one of the infractions that result in an immediate penalty.

Game Face's Detroit Thunder flings some heavy war paint.

Judges periodically conduct random on-field chronograph checks and the results are instantly sent via radio frequency transmitters to the X Ball scoreboard. Three hundred fps is the typical playing speed and a serious violation is a ball clocked at 25 fps above that speed.

Equipment Notes

Double-action triggers (trigger actions that depart from the one-pull, one-shot rule) and on-field communications devices are specifically prohibited.

Commentator's Command Tower

The game official's Command Tower is a mainstay feature in every legitimate professional sport, from soccer to hockey, from baseball to football, and now, paintball, too. From a high vantage point in the tower, officials can communicate freely with field judges for critical on-field calls and updates. All essential information can be calculated and immediately entered into the command center's computer. This way, viewers in every part of a stadium, arena, or game field can look to the scoreboard for information about and statistics relating to the game in play. A digital X Ball scoreboard mounted high atop the commentator's command tower will be visible to the players and spectators. It will display the score, remaining game time, reset time status, remaining penalty minutes and chronograph speeds from on-field radio-frequency chronograph transmitters.

In late 2003, the NXL signed a partnership with Dick Clark Productions to put paintball, by way of the X Ball League, on network television. Dick Clark is going to cooperate with the NXL to develop the game for exciting television viewing. "We think our paintball productions are going to be very popular," said a senior spokesman for Dick Clark Productions. Over the next few months, the NXL will work closely with Dick Clark Productions to tailor the presentation of the NXL and the game for television.

In a related move, Bill and Adam Gardner of Gardner & Gardner Productions and Smart Parts are currently talking to several major movie producers for a paintball-based movie and perhaps a celebrity challenge series as well. Paintball is indeed "on the radar screen" in Hollywood, Bill Gardner says. "Mr. Clark and his team are very enthusiastic about the long term prospects for paintball on television."

INTERVIEW: THE INSERT PLAYER

At only 27 years old, Sonny Lopez is a youthful Director at Worr Game Products. He has a bachelor's degree in psychology with an emphasis in industrial psychology

Covering a lane with paint is called "sweetspotting." If they are going to take the flag, they have to go through the lane you are covering and, running or crouching, you've got 'em … unless they get you first.

Sonny Lopez is the Naughty Dogs bad boy and marketing director at Worr Games Products.

business applications from California State – Fullerton. Sonny is also a player on the highly regarded professional paintball team Naughty Dogs. How he manages to be a full time director at a major paintball manufacturer and a top-level player at the same time was one of the first things we asked him about.

Paintball Digest: How do you juggle your time, Sonny? Your job at Worr Games is demanding, but finding the time to be a contributing player on a top-ranked pro team must be real demanding, too.

Sonny: Both are full-time jobs. In addition to managing the advertising and marketing, I also work with sponsorships and our other sponsored paintball teams. I've been off and on at Worr for eight years now with five years being part time and three years full time. I guess I just gradually worked my way to the point of total involvement in the sport and the business. Bud Orr, owner and founder of Worr Games, wanted me to finish college and then go to work for him full time when I completed my degree. Bud is CEO and his wife, Kathy, is CFO. Jeff and Robb Orr are both Bud's sons and are vice presidents.

It is a great work environment at Worr and because it is a family-run business, in some ways, it is really laid back. You are expected to get your job done and do it right, but at the same time we all get to have laughs and do what we love to do. It really doesn't feel like work most of the time. I just do my best at what needs to get done. So, juggling time is more of "Oh, my God, it's lunch time!" Then, hours later, "Whoa, it's seven P.M.! I got to finish all this work and try to get an hour or two of practice in at Adrenaline Park!"

Scott is smokin'! Notice that he finds he gets faster groups of shots off if he uses two fingers on the trigger—his middle and "lazy" fingers. Or does he?

Paintball Digest: Still … the time required to be a pro player and a company director must not leave you much time for a life.

Sonny: Well, I'm not married and don't have any children. I got mean fish! Really mean fish …

I don't try to manage everything in life. I just let it happen. My main focus right now is Worr Games and helping paintball go mainstream. This sport is blowing up so huge that, honestly, time is just flying by right now.

I do a lot of traveling, seeing paintball friends around the world and making new friends all the time. They say time travels fast when you're busy and having fun. Well, that's for sure.

I am dating Kat from the team Fallen Angels. She is captain of our all-girls team and is also a fully sponsored paintball player. Her team shoots WGP 'Cockers and travels around to select competitions. They also do promotions at the WGP booth here and there. Girls playing against boys …and beating them! Now, that is some cool stuff.

Paintball Digest: When did you begin playing paintball?

Sonny: I started playing paintball in 1989 when I was 13 years old and began working at the paintball park, SC Village, in 1994 and then Worr Games in 1995.

Paintball Digest: Tell me a little about your pro team Naughty Dogs.

Sonny: Naughty Dogs is owned and managed by Rocky Knuth from Oregon. He runs it from his field in Oregon called Albany Outdoor Paintball. The team has 14 members and our major sponsor is Worr Games, so we all shoot high-quality Auto-Cocker markers. We are also sponsored by DraXxus Paintballs, NPS, JT USA, Planet Eclipse, XS Sports, AOP and Viewloader. Most of the guys are from Portland, but we also have a couple of players from California, Utah and Washington. It's true when they say that the difference between us and a lot of other teams is that we go to tournaments to win, not to just have a good time. We are true competitors who try to represent our sponsors the best way possible, with WINS!

I can't give up all the good stuff because then other teams will just copy Rocky's formula. [Rocky Knuth is also team captain.] The Dogs train hard, play hard and compete to win. We walk every field together before games and go over the plan and our little doggy secrets. It's kind of like a game of chess that you play with people instead of little plastic pieces. We shoot out the positions of the competition and we move on them.

Last month [July 2003], we won $15,000 as a PSP X-Ball team and so far this year, we've won more than $60,000. I have to give a shot out to Sherry and Lee

Posting up close to an inflatable bunker on an airball field. They're soft. They give. But you can get smeared with somebody else's paint, too, so watch out.

Ingram, the true backbone of the team. We all love you guys! They do everything for the team and take care of a lot of stuff so the players can focus on blasting people who are standing in the way of more cash prizes.

Paintball Digest: What position do you play on the Naughty Dogs?

Sonny: I'm an "insert player." I hold back at the break and try to lay down a lot of paint. I'm one of the team's centrally located communicators. I yell a whole bunch, calling out positions and movements. I look for the "sweet spots" on the field, places where you can get clean lines of fire. Then, as people begin to be eliminated, I go where I'm needed to mount either a counter-attack or to help the push to win.

I also have to give all my Dogs a shout, so Wassup! to our captain Rocky Knuth and to the other dogs, Raymond "Green" Knuty, Trevor "T-Dogg" Hocking, Mapp "Crazy Cambodian" Chimm, Brian "Big B" Meggison, Troy "White Man" Kessel, the twins Cory and Kasey Field, Erik "Head" Hunter, "Bad" Brad Russon, the "White Ninja" Mark Kolek, Mike "Asian Sensation" Lew and of course, BW and Karen!

Paintball Digest: What 'Cocker do you shoot and why?

Sonny: I shoot an E-Class Orracle and a Black Magic mechanical 'Cocker. Bud's markers shoot straighter than anything else on the market. They're all designed and produced here in Southern California, except the Eclipse Blade frames on my electronic Orracles that come from England and are made by a company called Planet Eclipse. So, my Eblade markers are made in the USA with some English love added to it. Jeff Orr himself built my Black Magic. I have a couple of his limited edition markers, and they are the pride and joy of my collection. His work is flawless and unmatched in quality. He has designed so many paintball products over the years it's amazing! He doesn't want to be in the spotlight, but he should be because his ideas are revolutionary and he comes up with new stuff all the time. These markers give me the speed and accuracy that no other markers can match.

Paintball Digest: What is the most critical position on a team?

Sonny: It is a team sport so every position is important. I guess you have to start from the top. The captain must be on top of things at all times. The captain must be looked up to and respected by all to get everybody to do their job right. So, I guess if I had to choose the most critical position it would be captain.

Paintball Digest: What does "practice" involve? Just to get your team together for a practice would involve major travel, wouldn't it?

Sonny: Most of the guys are in Portland, so some of us need to jump on a plane and get up there to play some hardball. Rocky makes us play seven-on-seven or five-on-five. Sometimes, we get a lot of people up there and it turns into old school 10-on-10 games. If I can't make it up to Portland, I practice at Adrenaline, Tombstone or SC Village, because all are in the Riverside area.

Paintball Digest: What was your best win as a team?

Sonny: I think the very last 10-man pro event from the PSP series had to be it. It was in Pomona [California] early in 2003 and we played Bushwhackers and Dynasty in the finals. We beat the Bushwhackers after a hard-fought game. They played great and attacked us harder than any other team at that event. Then, it all came down to us and Dynasty. Everybody expected Dynasty to kick us off the field. We came out hard and everybody played their spot correctly. We beat them off the field in about four minutes and only lost one guy! Our "snake player," Bad Brad, was the Most Valuable Player of the game. I just happened to be the first one down the field to get Dynasty's flag and return it. That was an amazing game and a great tournament.

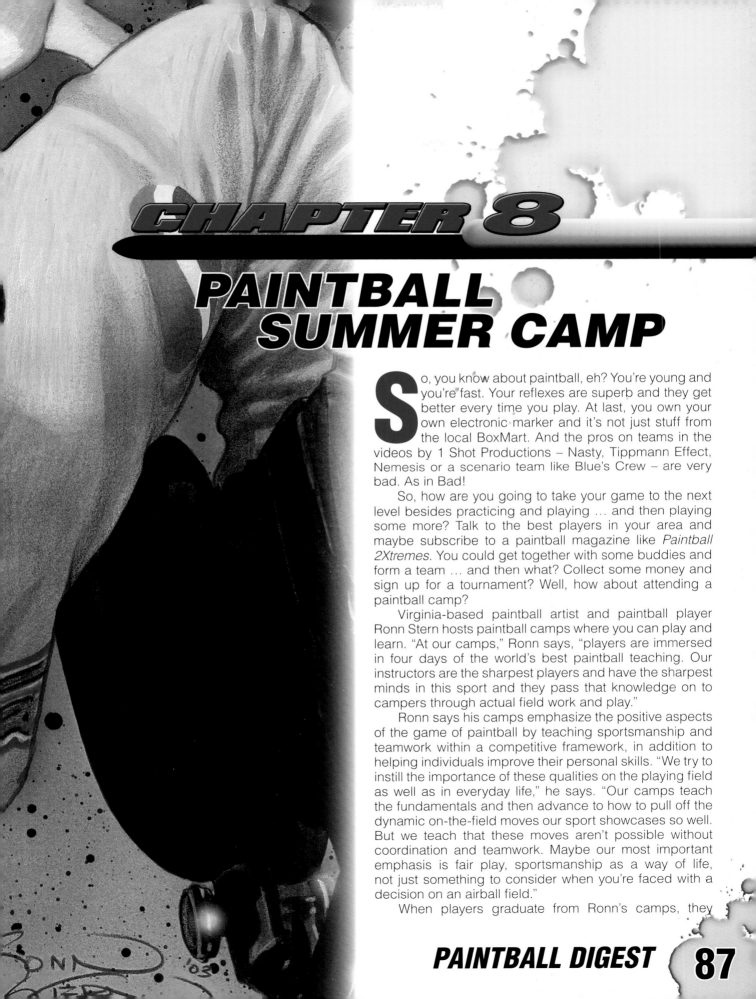

CHAPTER 8

PAINTBALL SUMMER CAMP

So, you know about paintball, eh? You're young and you're fast. Your reflexes are superb and they get better every time you play. At last, you own your own electronic marker and it's not just stuff from the local BoxMart. And the pros on teams in the videos by 1 Shot Productions – Nasty, Tippmann Effect, Nemesis or a scenario team like Blue's Crew – are very bad. As in Bad!

So, how are you going to take your game to the next level besides practicing and playing … and then playing some more? Talk to the best players in your area and maybe subscribe to a paintball magazine like *Paintball 2Xtremes*. You could get together with some buddies and form a team … and then what? Collect some money and sign up for a tournament? Well, how about attending a paintball camp?

Virginia-based paintball artist and paintball player Ronn Stern hosts paintball camps where you can play and learn. "At our camps," Ronn says, "players are immersed in four days of the world's best paintball teaching. Our instructors are the sharpest players and have the sharpest minds in this sport and they pass that knowledge on to campers through actual field work and play."

Ronn says his camps emphasize the positive aspects of the game of paintball by teaching sportsmanship and teamwork within a competitive framework, in addition to helping individuals improve their personal skills. "We try to instill the importance of these qualities on the playing field as well as in everyday life," he says. "Our camps teach the fundamentals and then advance to how to pull off the dynamic on-the-field moves our sport showcases so well. But we teach that these moves aren't possible without coordination and teamwork. Maybe our most important emphasis is fair play, sportsmanship as a way of life, not just something to consider when you're faced with a decision on an airball field."

When players graduate from Ronn's camps, they

Detroit Thunder's Jason Trosen takes aim. Attend a paintball camp and you will get personal instruction from top pro players like Jason.

have not only improved their personal playing skills and increased their knowledge of how their gear works, but they will have met a number of well-known people in the industry and will take home some super memories, too. "We have fun," Ronn says, "but we do take safety seriously. Our staff and instructors enforce a very strict goggles-on-for-safety policy and all campers have to adhere to it."

According to Ronn, at paintball camp, you learn the winning skills used by top tournament players and a great deal about how your equipment works, too. "Our teaching provides a solid foundation and advances quickly to the skill set needed to win at the super-competitive national level. For instance, in our first year, one of the world's best front players, Rocky Cagnoni, taught how to get to your bunker and be effective up front. Jonathan Call demonstrated how to become skilled at snap shooting, and one of America's finest women players, Bea Youngs, showed how to look for the sweet spots in your opponent's running lanes. Players walked the fields with top-ranked player Shannon Mahone and learned how to identify the must-make bunkers. Finally, our own Ronn Stern Gear staff and recognized industry experts like Tom Kaye from Airgun Designs and Josh Silverman from *Paintball 2Xtremes Magazine* shared technical and practical

knowledge about the game and the gear."

Ronn Stern Gear Paintball Camps are limited to ages 10 and over, both male and female, and the instructor-to-student ratio is relatively low. "This gives each camper a personal experience with our instructors," Ronn says. As a session ends, campers participate in a tournament and the winning team plays against the instructors for the title of camp champions. Ronn's camps are sponsored and endorsed by Pepsi-Cola, National Paintball Supply (NPS), Airgun Designs, *PB2X Magazine*, DraXXus Paintballs, Warpig.com and many others.

Admission to a camp is "first come, first served," Ronn says, but each camping session is limited to 45 students.

Resident Campers: Camp normally begins at 5:00 PM on the Sunday of camp week and runs until 4:00 PM on Thursday. Owned by SplatBrothers Paintball, the large, well-equipped playing fields are located in Hopewell, Virginia. Resident players share a suite with a fellow camper of the same gender and age group at the nearby AmeriSuites. All meals are included as are two cases of paintball and air. Rental equipment is available if needed. In the evening, separate classes taught by recognized industry experts may be available. The current cost, if a

At camp you learn to walk the field before a game or tournament and study shot angles; then, work out team assignments and plan your moves before the game.

student registers more than 45 days in advance, is $899. Otherwise, the cost is $949.

Day Campers: For individuals who live close enough to drive to the fields each day, camp dates and hours are the same, but only lunch is included in the camp price. The 45-days-in-advance registration is $699; later registration is $749.

For additional information on these one-of-a-kind paintball player's camps, visit *www.paintballcamps.com* or call Ronn Stern Paintball Gear toll free at (866) 321-CAMP. For 2004, Ronn's camps have an expanded schedule and will be held in California, North Carolina, Ohio, Texas and Virginia. "Paintball is the world's greatest sport," Ronn says. "It allows everyone to play on an even field. Male and female, young and old can pick up a marker and compete. No other sport provides the excitement that paintball delivers while emphasizing the need for teamwork and safety."

CHAPTER 9

ALL ABOUT PLAYING AND REFEREES

Y ou just want to run and shoot and hide and shoot. And yell at your buddies and shoot and shoot. You don't want anything to go wrong or anybody to get hurt. You don't want any hassles. You don't mind paying for the privilege. You just want to play. Am I right or am I right?

Well, if it seems like everything runs smoothly and successfully when you go out to your favorite field or maybe enter a tournament with a bunch of buddies or even travel to play a scenario game, it is because a tremendous amount of work has been done before you arrive.

Here is a quick look at how a recreational field and its referees are organized ... just for fun ... and long before your carload of hotshot party animals gets there.

ALL THE RULES FIT TO PRINT!

By Matt Stephenson
First Strike Paintball, Newberry, Florida

Safety Rules

1. Any person on the field during the hours of operation must wear an ASTM certified paintball goggle/mask at all times whether a game is being played or not. All markers connected to an air system must have a barrel plug or barrel cozy. A barrel swab or squeegee is not acceptable as a barrel plug.

2. Players may not "blind fire." They must be able to clearly identify their target and its immediate surroundings.

3. A player within 25 feet of an opponent who has an unobstructed shot should extend an offer of surrender. At this distance, the opponent has the option to refuse. Within 15 feet, there is no option to refuse. If two players are on opposite sides of a bunker, the first player to hit the bunker eliminates his opponent. A tie always

A good referee is a vital part of any paintball game. In scenario games, referees are called on more to keep players out of trouble, but in competition, referees have to keep unscrupulous players from cheating by wiping off paint and playing on after they have been hit.

goes to the aggressor. A player who shoots within five feet of someone at anytime must be removed from the game.

Player Rules

1. A player is eliminated if hit by a paintball on any part of the body or on any of his equipment and the paintball breaks. The paintball must hit the player directly. Splatter from a tree or bunker is not considered a hit.
2. A player is eliminated if he calls himself out and he shouts "Hit!" or "Out!" or raises his marker in the air. Once a player is out of the game, that player may not return. If a player calls himself "Hit" and then realizes the ball did not break, he may not return to the game.
3. If a player runs out of paintballs, CO_2 or compressed air or their marker malfunctions, they are not required to call themselves out, but that player may not leave the field and then return.
4. Once a player is eliminated, he must leave the field. To leave the field, a player should raise his marker above his head and should shout the word "Hit!" repeatedly. Referees should inform "live" players that a hit player is coming through so they do not shoot

them accidentally. Hit players should proceed to the nearest exit, keeping their markers in the air so as not to be mistaken for a live player.

REFEREE DUTIES

1. Before going onto the field, referees must have a two-way radio. It is also a good idea for a referee to carry a rag, a handheld chronograph and a squeegee for cleaning jammed barrels.
2. It is important to stay in contact with other referees so everyone is informed about the progression of the game. Keep the head referee informed if an objective is about to be completed so the game can end promptly thereafter.
3. Every referee is responsible for knowing and enforcing Field Rules and conducting a pre-game safety briefing. Referees are responsible for the safety of every player. Mask or barrel plug violations should be reported immediately following a game. One referee should be positioned next to the field entrance before a game begins to remind players to keep their masks on. At the conclusion of a game, they should return to the general field exit immediately to check for barrel plugs.

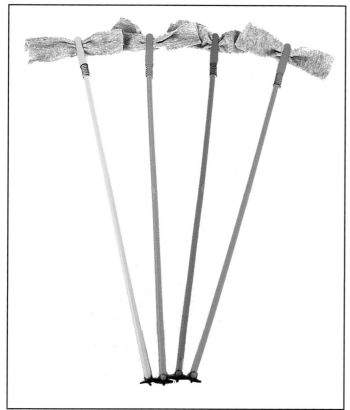

A ref won't stop play because your marker jams, so always carry a couple squeegees or cleaning rods like these push-through rods from Allen with you. They are cheap and effective at removing paint and paint shell obstacles from your barrels.

4. Referees are responsible for maintaining fair play. If a player is hit, the referee ensures that the player leaves the field immediately. Aid players in leaving the field by alerting "live" players. Referees will conduct paint checks at a player's request. Any player caught cheating will be removed from the field and warned of potential suspension from future games if such behavior continues.

5. Referees maintain field equipment. Equipment should be prepared before players arrive. Referees help with returning, cleaning and storing equipment. Damaged equipment must be labeled and set aside. Referees aid players on the field with malfunctions of rental markers. If a piece of equipment is not repairable on the field, the player should be sent to the front desk for repair or for a new marker.

6. Referees are not responsible for a player's personal equipment. If a player loses an item on the field, a referee should accompany that player to the field to help search for it between games.

7. Referees must ensure that markers are chronographed and kept within the legal limit [260 fps at First Strike]. A marker chronographed between 260 and 270 fps must be adjusted and retested prior to the next game. Players chronographed on the field over 270 fps will be removed from the game. Any player chronographed over 290 must be removed and referred to the front desk.

8. Between games, referees prepare for the next game. If no work on the field needs to be done, the referees should make sure that new players get a safety briefing or else should be preparing equipment, cleaning masks, filling tanks or cleaning markers.

The Head Referee

In addition to normal referee duties, the head referee organizes the games and runs the fields. There is only one head referee per field.

1. The head referee decides what games to play and on which fields. He is responsible for explaining the rules and making sure every player understands them. The head referee makes sure all other referees know what game is next so they can prepare the field. Games should be explained loudly and clearly and questions answered before entering the field.

2. The head referee organizes players and ensures that teams are as even as possible. He ensures that games run regularly and that players do not feel too much time is spent off the field. Unless there are not enough players, breaks between games are 10 minutes. It should be made clear that games will not wait for a handful of players who are not ready. It is a good idea to announce that the next game will be starting shortly. This gives players ample opportunity to prepare. Head referees are responsible for the integration of new players onto teams and being sure that they receive a safety briefing.

3. Head referees start and end games with either a whistle or an air horn. The head referee also keeps the time for each game, announcing time remaining to all players at the 5, 3, 1 minute and the 30-second mark. Games should run no longer than 10 minutes (with the exception of the final game of the day) so that players who have been eliminated are not forced to wait overly long. The head referee should also be sure that support referees are aware of the game time.

Support Referee(s)

In addition to normal referee duties, support referees help keep games running smoothly.

1. Make sure fields are ready for the next game. If flags must be placed or stations repaired, support referees ensure this is done before players walk onto the field.

2. Help the head referee gather players, organize teams and identify players (usually with an arm band) properly. Check that players have wiped off paint from previous games.

3. Chronograph a new player's marker.

CHAPTER 10

BUY THE BEST GEAR AND GET THE BIGGEST BANG FOR YOUR BUCK

Your buddies have their gear already, so now you just can't wait. After all, the rental stuff is okay … sometimes, but it's kind of beat up and pretty inaccurate and the goggles have been worn by half the players in the state, right? So, you gotta have your own stuff – right now! Here is a checklist that will guide you in making buying decisions. If you just take a few minutes asking yourself some questions … and answering them honestly … you'll end up with gear that's just right, not too expensive for what you want and not too cheap to perform so you aren't embarrassed.

YOUR MARKER

How good are you?

Beginners and Casual Players: You're going to hear people suggest you begin with a marker that isn't too expensive. After all, if you like it, you can always upgrade to an electronic gun with a drop-forward tank and sniper barrel, and if you really get hooked, you will have to. Pay $250 for a durable non-electronic marker. Do not buy anything plastic. A marker that is made in an Oriental country – okay, in China or Sri Lanka or Myanmar or someplace – can be just fine, certainly at this level.

But probably, the best advice is to decide if you really like this game before you spend, like you were buying a car. So, ask yourself if you have the time and interest to play. Get to know the game some before you plunk down your life savings, because in the long run you will be happier.

At this stage, it is important to buy a good, solid marker. Guys, visual creatures that they are, tend to be impulsive and ask for the first thing that looks good or that the in-crowd is using. They often want to buy what their

When you are ready to move up from an introductory marker or perhaps your first pump, several paintball manufacturers offer fast, reliable markers at a reasonable cost. The 2003 WGP Vertical Feed Cocker was on sale at www.xtremz.com on 10-7-03 for $349.00 and you have a choice of red, green, black or blue.

Almost any version of the Kingman Spyder, such as their Victor Illusion, will be an excellent introductory semi-auto. It's relatively inexpensive, easy to maintain and reliable.

When you are ready for a more advanced design, the Minimag from Airgun Designs is described as a blow-forward, open-bolt semi-automatic.

buddy is shooting. Girls, talkative and meditative animals, will research the question to death and end up, after a year or so, going back and buying the first marker they liked. Whatever your strategy, give yourself a time frame of say a month, do the research, and then get going. You just can't learn or progress in paintball without your own gear. An example of fine markers at this stage are Kingman Spyders, Tippmann 98 Customs and PMI Piranhas.

Serious Recreational Player: This is the first step to upgrading your play and your gear. Now, 99 percent of all paintball players play at this level for a few years ... or a few minutes. And how about spending $50 on some new Mossy Oak camo down at the local BoxMart instead of those old clothes? Players will take you more seriously.

At this stage, you need a very good semi-auto, perhaps stepping up to an Evil Omen, a Worr Games Outkast or a Viking from AKA. A lot is going to depend on your own ability to service a more complex marker or what kind of support there is for your choice in your neighborhood. As markers become more sophisticated, they naturally take a little more care and maintenance to keep in top shape. Serious players pay $600 to $800 and there is still plenty of time to upgrade to a force-feed hopper or perhaps an electronic operation. Enjoy the playing, because if you decide to try for the next level, paintball will either become the joy of your life or just plain work. And who needs to turn play into work? There will be enough of that later; count on it.

Tournament and Team Player: You will want to buy a marker that meets the demands of the position you play

on a team: front line, covering fire, sniper, or utility player. Of course, if the team is good, it may land an endorsement contract and everyone will shoot WdP Angels or AGD X-Mags. This may mean purchasing multiple barrels, unless you get a barrel sponsor like Hammerhead. Well, you're looking at maybe $1500 for the marker and another $500 to $1000 for upgrades, travel gear and clothes. At this level, you won't want to wear camo. For advanced or tournament or professional players, camo is for newbies.

How much are you going to use your marker?

The second factor in selecting or upgrading your marker and its accessories is how you want to play the game. This is serious, because as you get better, as you begin to learn how to win at different types of games, you will want different kinds of equipment. If you play as part of a team or as you develop your own feel for the game, three positional players will stand out: front, middle and utility. How you play will have as much effect on making an intelligent choice about a new marker as how often you play.

A "front player" is the first person to try to bust into the enemy camp, spray paint and cause havoc. The front guy is a brash player who, because of his speed, size and agility, is able to draw the fire and attention of the enemy players. Then some days, front players will do more running, watching and dodging than shooting. Whatever. It's an active position, a burn calories job, but front players usually prefer lightweight markers, as the difference between a five-pound set-up and a three-pound set-up is noticeable after a couple hours of running and dodging.

Would you prefer to mount your air supply on your marker or carry it on your back? Your air bottle may be more comfortable on your back and this configuration may give a front player greater ability to move with freedom. However, there is an air hose from the remote on your back to your marker. It's something you should definitely try out a few times before even considering purchasing.

When a front player shoots, he needs to be accurate because he may be shooting on the fly and often won't get a second chance. Up front, paint can be on you fast. If you select an air supply directly attached to your marker, you want a durable set-up and a secure fitting so you can use it essentially like a gunstock. Like a tripod, it is a point of support and stability.

A "cover (or middle) player" has the job of laying down paint so that front and utility players can move around on the field and threaten the enemy home base or enemy-held objective. So, you want a large air supply, perhaps a remote system, and you want a large, dependable force-feed hopper and spare bottles designed to let you refill and shoot rapidly. When you are not flinging paint at the bunkers and trees the enemy is hiding behind, your team is in danger. And for a marker, you will want one that is capable of putting out a lot of paint fast and accurate when you identify a target. For a mid-player, 600 rounds per minute is a whole lot preferable to 300 rounds per minute. Your team will appreciate it. If you have very tall or overweight persons on your side, the middle positions should be tailor-made for their abilities.

The "utility player" needs mobility and capacity. A sleek marker-hopper-air supply system that is manageable in your hands is the best choice. (Lefties need to remember that paintball markers aren't like off-the-shelf shotguns. There's no hot, spent casing ejected out the side to hit you in the face.) A utility player's job will be to move and hide, slip and slide in the shadows, perhaps lay down covering fire for a front player threatening the objective or protect the flanks of a cover player. This position varies, but you must choose a marker and accessories that support your team's objectives, so think durability and reliability before you rush out to buy the hottest and sometimes most delicate marker you can afford.

What's the right pressure or power delivery system for you?

The most common pressure system is CO_2, carbon dioxide, because it is the least expensive system for recreational fields to install and maintain. For most rec players, a CO_2 system is safe and reliable enough. But

Filling the air tank before the call, "Game on!"

once your bottle is filled, CO_2 can be a liquid, a gas or both at the same time depending on the temperature, especially if you are playing a cold-weather game and the outside temperature is around or below 50 degrees Fahrenheit. Extreme cold or heat will cause fluctuations in CO_2 pressure and ball velocity. This will cause your shooting accuracy to fluctuate. When you find yourself in this unfortunate pickle, more paint on target may be better than less paint selectively placed!

The other option for power delivery is compressed air (or nitrogen). Compressed air always operates as a gas, so your marker doesn't fall prey to changing temperatures and fluctuating velocities. Properly regulated, your accuracy will be better under all conditions and you will therefore get to play longer and … let's face it, you'll win more. HPA is trickier to handle and a little more expensive usually – there had to be a catch – but if you are serious about paintball, as you move from weekend warrior to veteran scenario wizard or tournament hot shot, you have to consider this option even though some playing fields won't be able to fill your power needs. As always, call and check BEFORE you go to a game and certainly before you buy something new. On the other hand, many markers these days are designed so that they can shoot either CO_2

Call it a hopper or a loader, its purpose is to carry a couple hundred balls and feed them smoothly into your marker. This is a camouflaged hopper from Allen.

or compressed air effectively.

Of course, the size of the tank is what essentially determines the number of rounds you will be able to shoot before you need to leave the field for an air refill. Larger (greater volume in cubic inches) tanks equal more shots.

YOUR LOADER

A hopper (also called a loader) is a plastic, inverted bottle that holds your paintballs on top of your marker. On your typical inexpensive markers, the removable hopper uses gravity to feed – let balls drop, actually – through the feed tube into the receiver. Of course, once you get hooked on the need for speed, you will want to add an electronic feed system to your marker. A $5 no-name 200-count gravity-operated hopper was fine when Thag and his cave-man buddies invented the game of paintball, but on today's hot markers, Mother Nature just doesn't cut it. She needs help. Take that $5 hopper off and throw it away. A motorized hopper will ensure that you almost never have a ball crushed in the receiver because gravity is feeding balls too slowly for a high rate of shots per second.

Hoppers come in a variety of shapes and sizes and hold from 40 to 300 paintballs. The older, stick-style tubes held 10 balls in-line and can still be found today on old markers and some side-arms, useful if your semi-automatic gunks-up or breaks and you just can't leave the game to fix it.

So, what kind of hopper (and don't forget the feed elbow so you can see) should you add to your marker? Mobility and weight are a factor in selecting the hopper for you. A 300-round hopper on the top of your gun creates torque when you are moving and shooting, which sometimes causes you to miss what you are shooting at, especially when the hopper is full of balls. If you are the running-and-gunning type and carry a couple spare tubes of balls on your belt, then a smaller hopper might be best. If your team assignment is to stay in one place and lay down fire on an objective or to draw attention away from teammates sneaking around the side, you probably want the largest hopper you can buy.

What happens if you buy the wrong hopper? Well,

unless you get an electronic motorized unit, hoppers are cheap. It may be best to have a spare anyway. At *www.ontoppaintball.com* (6-3-03) a basic, gravity-fed 200-round hopper cost $3.75. On the other hand, the eVLution II in clear or black from Viewloader holds 195 balls and costs $77. The difference is that the eVLution II offers a clean feed rate of 17 balls per second with a coated, 6-blade flexible propeller, an LED low-battery indicator and an IR sensor that controls ON/OFF propeller actuation.

YOUR AIR SUPPLY

Most players mount their power tank on their marker so that it gives them a steadying point against their shoulder or arm. This is important for shooting accuracy. Tanks come in several sizes, shapes and strengths depending on the power (CO_2 or compressed air).

Some players prefer to mount their air supply on their belt or on their back. This is called a remote set-up. The gas runs through a coiled flexible hose from the tank to the marker. This decreases the weight in your hands and some players feel it increases their mobility. The other point of view, however, is that for someone who is running and dodging and moving, that hose is going to get hung up on a branch or the edge of a bunker and then there's going to be trouble. You will see a number of remotes in a gang of scenario players, but remotes are not common in higher-level tournament play.

So, the pros and cons of a remote mounting system have to be studied before you buy into the system. Besides your tank, you need a coiled tournament remote with a slide valve to prevent the tank from exploding if the hose is severed and gas can flow without restraint and this costs $39.99 (*www.paintball-discounters.com* 6-4-03).

What is common among more experienced players is a drop-forward set-up that repositions the tank (and its weight) forward by six inches or so. This moves your marker's center of gravity forward, which makes it easier to handle, to move quickly and to acquire your target. A couple hundred bucks will get you a good volumizer, flexible braided steel hose, regulator, micro-gauge and drop-forward bracket.

A refillable 20-ounce aluminum CO_2 tank from Game Face.

Viewloader's heavy-duty Cordura nylon loader pouch with adjustable web belt includes two 100-round tubes.

A red dot sight such as the Bushnell Trophy (pictured with mounting brackets) may be the answer to steadying your aim, especially if you are a back player who is responsible for throwing a lot of cover paint at the opponents or for a sniper or for someone who has trouble with hand/eye coordination.

YOUR HARNESS SYSTEM

So, you went out for a 15-minute game with a hundred rounds and within five minutes you blew your load. You aren't having fun and you have let your team down. The answer, of course, is to carry extra ammo in a harness system. You gotta hold on to your balls.

Actually, you need a good belt pack whether you carry extra ammo or not … and you probably should carry extra tubes of ammo. Where do you put your car keys and your spare change or wallet when you are on the field? If you put these things in your pockets, the first time you slide or throw yourself over a log you can easily lose them. Better to keep your valuables locked in your car and put your car keys under the front wheel on the driver's side. Nobody ever thought to look there …

Harness systems are cheap and easy to carry, but they vary in quality of manufacture, the number and size of tubes and the number of accessory items. At *www. paintball-discounters.com* (6-4-03) a 2+1+1 32-Degrees Rhino camo pack holds two 140-round tubes of balls, a water bottle and a pouch for stuff like your wallet and car keys. Heck, it only costs $19.99. On the other hand, the Redz 5.4 Dimension Pack costs $46.99 and requires the Comfort Belt at $21.99, but it holds up to nine 150-round pods! Before you buy any belt, check to see if the tubes are included or not. If they cost extra, don't worry. They're cheap.

THE SQUEEGEE

"Oh, get real! Now you are going to tell me that I need shoes and a handkerchief and underwear." Well, a squeegee is for real … and it's such a small thing.

You gotta have a squeegee to keep your barrel clean. Balls break. Literally, with cheap balls or when there is no electronic feed system. When this happens, the dye and gunk left in the gun dries and gums up your barrel. You either can't shoot or if your marker will shoot, it won't be accurate.

There are two kinds of squeegee, push-through or pull-through. Both work fine, but just make sure the one you buy works on your marker's barrel and receiver. You can put a coiled (or wadded up) squeegee in your pocket or in your belt pack. Keep it with you, because the barrel always plugs up when the action is hottest. You may be able to hunker down in a safe position and quickly pull it through your barrel and get right back in the action.

You'll pay five or six bucks for a squeegee, but it will be an excellent investment.

SIGHTS AND SCOPES

The whole idea of laying down paint is to tag the enemy, put him out of the game. Typically, under the "you get what you pay for" heading, more expensive markers have qualities that make them more accurate and there are special barrels and accessories you can buy for more precise shooting. One of those accessories is a sight or a scope.

A sight mounted on your marker helps you verify your shot angle by giving you extra points of reference that, when brought into proper alignment, help you place paint squarely on your target.

Sights – and certainly optical scopes – handy to a point. That point is that paintball is a fun run-and-gun game. Most shooting is done at fairly close range. It isn't like you are really a sniper, taking out a target a half-mile away with one carefully controlled bullet. A paintball sniper shoots a couple hundred feet, max.

Think about those old World War II movies – and, of course, they are a mix of a lot of fiction and a little bit of fact – before you buy a sight. A paintball marker is more like the submachine gun than a precise, high-powered sniper rifle. The guy with the submachine gun or semi-automatic handgun walks on camera and sprays bullets everywhere, hoping he'll hit somebody or something. Your marker and your game are like that.

Nevertheless, a sight will give you a slight advantage in some situations, and they fasten to the built-in sight rail on the top of your marker (not all markers have one). Nevertheless, take the Dye Red Dot Sight ($49.77 from *www.xpaintball.com* on 6-4-03), which is available with a black or polished silver body. There are less expensive sights as well. When you look through it, you see a red dot that you can put on your target – if you have time – before you pull the trigger. Look for a red dot sight with variable intensity, because the brightness of the day will determine how bright you want the dot to be. In fog or early evening,

JT USA's signature two-piece screw-together barrels are made with hard anodized aluminum tips in black, red or blue and stainless steel and polished aluminum backs.

you won't need much of a dot, and in fact, a very bright dot will obscure the target. In the middle of the day, however, you want to turn the rheostat up bright for quick target acquisition.

BARRELS

Markers come with "stock" barrels and most are pretty good, designed for the marker. So, why change? Well, several reasons. First, low-pressure systems can make effective use of longer barrels and this will almost certainly increase your accuracy. Don't forget to make sure the barrel insert you are considering is matched to the diameter paint balls you are shooting: small, medium or large. Most markers and barrels are machined for .68-inch diameter balls, but there is really a lot of operational difference between .680 and .693. Finally, the length and thickness of different barrels provide a weight-in-the-hand difference, and there is some question of mobility around the field. If you are an action kind of guy, then perhaps a shorter barrel is best for you. If you are a hunt-and-stalk player, a sniper or somebody in the middle laying down tons of paint, then the most accurate shooting system you can put together is the way to go and this usually means a longer barrel.

Barrels are expensive and you may or may not see a

change in your shooting after you fit one to your marker. For instance, the micro-ported, aircraft-grade, machined-aluminum 6061 T-6 Armson Stealth Barrel costs $79.95 (*www.proteamdirect.com* 6-4-03). This barrel is ported to cut the noise of a shot but still put the most energy possible into a ball. It is also rifled (spiral grooves are cut along its length, inside the barrel) and this is supposed to give the ball spin and, hence, stability and, hence once more, increased accuracy. For this particular Armson barrel, you have a choice of lengths, but you must fit it specifically to your marker.

PROTECTIVE GEAR

Vests/Chest Protectors

Vests are recommended for paintball, but people don't mean just any traditional style vest with goose-down padding. JT USA offers a flexible, vented and puncture-resistant eMotion Chest Protector ($42.00 at *www.paintball-discounters.com* 6-4-03), which will make you look like Bat Man. It's sculptured to give you biceps and a 6-pack. The idea of a vest is that it needs to provide protection in the critically sensitive areas of your chest, including your kidneys, heart and back. Well, a vest protects some of your critically sensitive areas. For a man, a cup protects the rest.

Frankly, not many people wear a vest unless it's like a tee shirt with the sleeves cut off and that's just to look cool. Most people do wear a couple layers, though, because unless you are really out of bounds, you are not going to get hit hard enough or often enough to wear something that's going to be hot and in the way when you are runnin' and gunnin'. So, layer appropriately. One way is to wear your most durable cotton tee shirt and a good long-sleeve paintball shirt that reflects a company you support, or if you are good enough, one that supports you!

Let's say you wear two layers for most games with a sweatshirt for afterwards on a cool venue. A long-sleeve 100-percent-cotton jersey over a tee would be ideal. Figure $23.77 for a black Raven Flames long-sleeve tee (*www.xpaintball.com* 6-4-03) or, for a Redz paintball jersey and pants, $39.99 and $59.99 (*www.paintballdiscounters.com* 6-4-03).

Whatever you choose, you just don't want balls busting on your bare skin. The "play paintball naked" movement is way overrated.

Pads and Gloves

Protect and preserve the areas of your body that get roughed up when you're sliding, crawling, falling or getting hit in sensitive areas. Pads are hot in the summer or when you're running and sometimes they are uncomfortable, but consider them an investment in keeping the bod in good working order. Renegade kneepads are $39.95 on *www.paintballgear.com* (6-4-03). They are foam-molded poly-cotton spandex with adjustable stretch Velcro straps to hold them in place. Raven's black neoprene elbow

Ain't no girl gonna love somebody dressed like a bum!

Even on the economical end of JT USA's goggle system, a mask like the nVader is available with a single or thermal lens.

pads are $19.95.

A good pair of gloves now, that's the ticket. Wear gloves. You will forever be glad you did because if you are active and in pursuit of the flag, your hands take a beating just brushing up against stuff and banging around. The $34.99 Surgrip blue gloves from Paintball Junkies are breathable with padded knuckles and super gripping material on the palms and the palm side of the fingers. These kinds of sticky gloves sometimes make it a little hard to shift and slide the marker around in your hands 'cause they stick to it, and if you don't like this, you can find some other types for about five bucks less from Paintball Junkies.

Head, Neck, Face and Eye Protection

Nobody will let you out to play unless you have up-to-snuff goggles. Industry-standard ASTM-approved goggles are NOT an option. They are required. No sunglasses. No ski masks. Not your daddy's goggles from Home Depot left in the toolbox in the shed. Not your contact lenses. Spend. Sssspend. Protect your face 'cause ain't no

girl or guy gonna love you if you look like you took a trip down the freeway on your face. The paintball industry has invested a lot of money and time developing excellent criteria to protect you from the impact of a hundred-mile-an-hour paintball so that when you're teaching your kids how to play, you will still be able to actually see and hear them. Rule of thumb. Buy the best paintball goggles you can afford and remember: you get what you pay for.

Paintball goggles will protect you and help increase your peripheral vision, too. This means you will have a wider field of view or, put another way, you can more easily detect those guys sneaking up on your sides. Goggles come with face shields and eye armor and cover the forehead, ears and jaw. Who wants to scrimp and then eat paint?

Goggles are like cars or computers. You can go basic or you can go high end. The basic green V-Force Armour goggles are about $17.99 on *www.paintballgear.com* (6-4-03) and they do the basic job of protecting you. At the high end, the V-Force Morph-Mirror with gold lens and green mask is $89.99. Whatever you buy, a good thing to do is keep your goggles in a bag to keep the lenses from getting scratched and miscellaneous grime from getting inside. And don't forget the cool stickers and different lenses for different playing conditions, such as double-layer thermal lenses with anti-fog, anti-scratch coatings.

PAINT

Ingredients: Back in the '70s, paintballs were oil-based and that meant players had to scrub with turpentine to get the paint off after they shot it out with each other. The paint ruined your clothes. Now, they still have these balls for farmers and foresters, but you don't want to shoot these. Today's paintballs are water-based, biodegradable and non-toxic. The paint is supposed to wash out of your clothes, but it'll still leave stains on cotton if you let it dry for a couple days before you wash up.

Diameter: Paintballs actually come in several bore sizes, which are designated as a caliber (there are 100 calibers to the inch) – 50, 62, 63, 68 and 78 – and this does not even consider air soft shooting, but, of course, those aren't balls of paint. The whole object of this is just to confuse you. Well no, not really.

Paintball gear evolves, changes. Like the game itself. Like everything. Paintball has moved in the direction of standardized 68-caliber balls and it has essentially arrived. Go to your local retailer or a BoxMart and you will invariably buy 68-caliber balls. But will they be .681 or .689. It matters; it really does. Yes, the game and the business have gotten sophisticated down to the thousandths.

You have to match your barrel to your ball diameter. Remember "thousandths" later when we spend more time talking about barrels and ball sizes.

Color: So, what color do you want? Paintballs come in a variety of bright colors on the outside and the inside – and white and black, too, although the problem with basic colors is that sometimes electronic eyes that help position balls in the chamber for firing will not "see" a dark, solid-color ball. Thus, balls are neon, marbleized, multi-colored, banded and swirled. Balls have insults printed on them. Is it just a girl thing or is it okay to have a team color? Áhh, it's okay. Try a Nelson Chaos for example: blue with yellow-neon fill. Shop around online and you can get a box of 2000 for about $50, about 2-1/2 cents per shot plus shipping.

It is said that the color and consistency of the "fill" (the goo inside the ball) you select should be determined by your playing conditions. For instance, you may want a bright color in densely wooded areas so you can see where your paintballs are hitting. There are even fluorescent balls for night play.

Freshness: Age and humidity are the two biggest enemies of paintballs (and paintball players). Keep a fresh supply and store them in a cool, dry place like under the bed or in the back of the closet. Do not, however – and this is important – use dirty balls. Nobody likes 'em and they can harm the barrel or prematurely explode and clog it up.

Storage: According to Viewloader, for best performance, store your paintballs between 59 and 86 degrees Fahrenheit (that's 15 to 30 degrees Centigrade) and 40 to 50 percent relative humidity. Protect your balls from freezing and prolonged exposure to direct sunlight or heating vents.

Nelson says if the balls are stored right, they can be expected to last for several months, so buy only what you are going to use within a month or so. As we mentioned above, store them in a cool, dry place and keep them in a tightly sealed bag using twist ties or some other means of isolating them from humidity. Never leave your paintballs in the trunk of a car or behind the back seat of your pickup because the heat can be fierce and cause them to quickly deteriorate.

There are times, especially in colder climates, that paintballs have signs of dimpling. "In most cases," Nelson says, "you can open the bag of paintballs and as you allow them to warm up to room temperature and re-hydrate, the dimples will disappear." After the dimples disappear, reseal the ball bag.

ZAP SKYBALL 6

The Largest 5 Player Tournament
In The World!

CHAPTER 11

PAINTBALL MARKERS

I n *Paintball Digest*, we use the term "marker" for that clunky gizmo that fires a paintball out of its barrel. It looks like a gun, but we call it a marker. Is this just being politically correct or is there some really good reason not to call it a "paintball gun?"

Under "gun," *Webster's American Dictionary College Edition* talks about everything from (#1) a weapon shooting projectiles with an explosion to (#8) gunning (revving-up) your engine to (#12) someone under pressure as in "under the gun." Their fourth usage does specifically mention paint: "any device for shooting or ejecting something under pressure, as staples or paint."

In the same dictionary, "marker" is defined as (#1) "a person or thing that marks." If we accept the proposition that in paintball, all we want to do is mark our opponent in a playful and non-lethal manner, we ought to be comfortable using the term marker.

So, it's true. We are putting a little distance here between the firearms community and ourselves. Paintball is a non-lethal activity and firearms have gotten a great deal of negative press lately. Calling our markers "guns" may appeal to some of the youngest or most macho brothers and sisters in our neighborhood, but we are going to take the safer route in this situation. Actually, a casual review of a couple dozen Internet sites suggests that the paintball industry itself is divided about whether it should use "gun" or "marker."

YOUR FIRST MARKER

The majority of markers, and chances are, the kind you will probably buy first, are called "blowback" semi-autos. Blowback refers to the method the manufacturer uses to shoot paint; each time you fire a ball, some of the air pressure released is vented backward in the marker to push the marker's bolt back in preparation for the next

A good reason to attend any major paintball tournament or trade show is to see the new gear and meet the inventors in person. Here, a potential customer tries out Jack Rice's new Alien marker. The event was the 2003 International Amateur Open at the Big Butler Fairgrounds north of Pittsburgh.

ball to drop. So, at the same time one ball is flying down and out the barrel, your marker's metal and plastic internal parts (called the "action") are moving at lightning speed to get ready to shoot again.

Some individuals (and some manufacturers who make other types of marker actions) claim that accuracy with a blowback versus a blow-forward type of marker is more difficult for two reasons. First, not all of the pressure released is used to shoot the ball, and second, a blowback design causes the marker to move slightly when firing. For these two reasons, some individuals claim that a blowback just can't shoot straight on a consistent basis. Baloney. Overall, blowback markers offer excellent value, an excellent price vs. performance ratio, and very good performance characteristics.

"Mechanical" markers such as standard blowback semi-autos dominate the entry-level price range. Mechanical suggests that the markers are without electronics, batteries, multi-mode firing, LCD screens, game timers, shot counters, text messaging and marker-to-marker programming. These days, however, it is relatively inexpensive to retrofit or upgrade your basic blowback with an electronic trigger frame and add exotic multiple features including an electronic, programmable hopper.

If you get hooked on paintball, you will soon want to replace the simple mechanics of your standard mechanical trigger with an adjustable electronic trigger. An electronic trigger will let you shoot much faster and more accurately. The switch to electronics makes the feel of your trigger comparable to the mouse click of your computer. Because of the ease of pulling an electronic, response-style trigger, especially a double trigger that is designed to be pulled with two fingers, balls can be fired much faster. With the proper electronic setup, your rate of fire is limited only by how nimble your fingers are. The negative implications to electronics are that batteries, typically housed in the "grip frame" of the marker, are required for electronic power. Also, an inexpensive gravity-feed loader may not be able to drop balls into the marker as fast as you can pull the trigger, and finally, hot, humid weather and rain can be a factor in smooth electronic operation.

CLOSED BOLT vs. OPEN BOLT

Your first marker will probably be a garden-variety closed-bolt blowback peashooter, but you may eventually want to experiment with a different style because two types of operating actions are available—open bolt and closed bolt. Is this just to confuse us? The terms refer to the position of the marker's bolt when you are not shooting it, when it is in its "at rest" position.

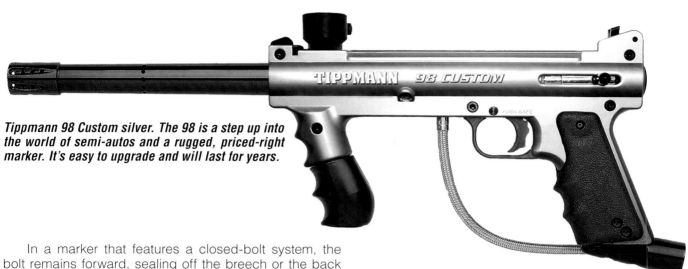

Tippmann 98 Custom silver. The 98 is a step up into the world of semi-autos and a rugged, priced-right marker. It's easy to upgrade and will last for years.

In a marker that features a closed-bolt system, the bolt remains forward, sealing off the breech or the back section of your barrel until you pull the trigger. After you pull the trigger, the bolt opens, a new ball drops in, the bolt slides forward and you are once again ready to fire. Some examples of closed-bolt markers are the WGP Autococker, Kingman Hammer and PMI Tracer.

If your marker has an open-bolt action, the bolt remains "open" or at the back of the breech until you pull the trigger. When you pull the trigger, the bolt slams forward to shoot the paintball and then pops back to the back of the breech, allowing another ball to fall into the chamber. Now, it's ready to fire again. Some examples of open-bolt markers are the WdP Angel, AGD Automag and PMI Piranha.

Which style is better? It's totally a matter of personal preference and logical arguments are made for both. Some players claim that closed-bolt markers are faster because in an open-bolt system the ball may roll around slightly in that fraction of a second before you shoot, and since the bolt may begin opening again before the ball actually exits the barrel (when you are shooting as fast as you can, for instance), an open-bolt marker cannot

Close-up of WGP's VF Tactical Autococker showing the vertical feed tube and the matte-black, non-reflective finish. This marker was $699.99 at www.xtremz.com on 10-7-03. The closed-bolt marker was designed with the scenario-recreational player in mind.

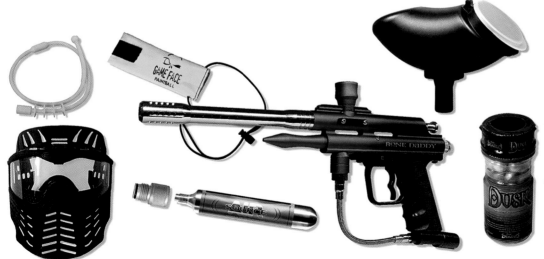

The Bone Daddy Ready-2-Play Kit from Game Face is an excellent way to begin in paintball: marker, mask, gloves, air bottle, squeegee, barrel cover and hopper. Everything but the paint!

possibly shoot with the same speed and accuracy as a more stable closed-bolt system.

Recently, the folks at WarPig.com (www.warpig.com) set out to prove the following proposition: A closed-bolt marker is inherently more accurate than an open-bolt marker.

WarPig.com set up an objective test, firing at a 28-inch-square powder-coated metal target at a distance of 25 yards, which, they believe, is an appropriate "engagement distance" for paintball players.

The tests were independent. WarPig.com says they had no interest in the results, only curiosity. They used Nelson Challenger paintballs, first discarding any that were obviously out-of-round. They bolted their marker into a stand and outfitted it with an Adco Square Shooter sight. Regarding the use of a sight, WarPig.com commented that they were testing the marker's capabilities, not their own shooting abilities.

For the test marker, they chose a Stingray because they wanted to be able to fire both open bolt and closed bolt with one marker. This would keep many variables, like barrel length and porting, the same. The conversion took some work in their shop, even though they modestly say that it was "relatively simple." Otherwise, everything about the marker was identical: same barrel, same bolt and same CO_2 supply. WarPig.com justified the conversions because the test was "not about the performance of a modified Stingray, but a difference in the performance related only to the way the bolt operated."

During the testing, the average velocity was 267 fps. The technicians made allowance for any changes in CO_2 pressure during the firing process.

Here's what WarPig.com concluded under their controlled circumstances: "Firing our marker as an open-bolt, blowback-operated semi-automatic, we found the same level of accuracy as when firing as a manually operated closed-bolt marker. Our conclusion – the great inherent accuracy of closed-bolt markers over open-bolt markers is a myth."

PUMPS AND AUTOMATICS

Today, there are basically two types of paintball markers available: pumps and automatics. Pump-action markers have a manual pump mechanism similar to a pump shotgun that loads a paintball into your marker's receiver while re-cocking the marker at the same time. A player must pump the marker armature after every shot, and often, the tube with the balls for pumps will only hold 10 balls. Some pumps are powered by 12-gram cartridges and others by tanks of CO_2.

Automatics have a ball loaded into the marker after every shot. Balls are fed into the marker from a plastic ball-holder called a loader or hopper. These refillable loaders hold around 200 balls, and they rely on either the force of gravity or a more expensive electronic feed arrangement to load balls into the marker's receiver. A

When a ref hangs one of these hand-held paintball RadarChrons from Sports Sensors on your barrel, he's going to ask you to pull the trigger a few times to measure your marker's speed.

tuned-up automatic shot in the semi-auto mode shoots balls as fast as you can pull the trigger. If the marker has an electronic-powered action, it can often shoot in full-auto mode and just watch the paint fly then! The full-automatic mode is not allowed in tournaments, scenario games or even normal recreational play.

PAINTBALL SPEED

You need to know your marker speed, and it's fun to learn what it is. The velocity of the ball leaving the barrel of your marker is normally between 250 and 300 feet per second (fps), which is about 200 mph! Depending on your marker and air power setup, balls can go much faster, but faster speeds are not normally allowed because even though paintballs are small and soft, they can hurt like the dickens if they hit an unprotected part of your anatomy. Tournaments allow 300 fps, but most venues, including the popular 24-hour scenario games, regulate marker velocities to about 280 fps for the safety of players. At night, because players who aren't catching some Zs usually shoot at each other from much closer distances, scenario producers require an even slower speed of 250 fps.

The speed (velocity) of a paintball is checked with a chronograph, which uses a small Doppler radar. The paintball is fired over the machine and the radar tracks the distance it covers in a specific time. This is converted electronically to feet per second (fps) and displayed on

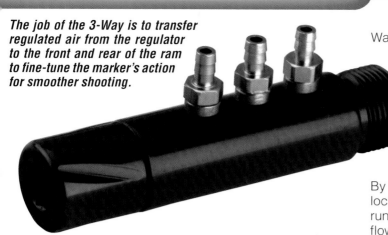

a digital read-out. Earlier model chronographs used a different measuring system. A paintball was shot through two separated beams of light and the time it took to travel the distance was measured. Because the distance between the beams of light was fixed, the measurement easily converted into fps.

AIR POWER!

All paintball markers use air pressure from a tank filled with compressed air, nitrogen or CO_2 to fire a paintball. Usually, the tank is attached directly underneath the marker. The larger the tank, the more it holds and the longer a player can run and gun without having to stop for a refill.

For CO_2, power is weighed in tank sizes that begin at about four ounces and go up to 20 ounces. An inert gas, CO_2 is pressurized between 750 and 1000 pounds per square inch (psi), and it evaporates into a gas at 70 degrees, producing roughly 850 psi of pressure. Actually, the very small, disposable tanks in some beginner or pump markers hold only 12-gram cartridges of CO_2.

Compressed air and nitrogen are called high pressure air systems and the abbreviation is HPA (or N for the much less frequently used nitrogen). Tanks of air are measured by volume in cubic inches and pressurized by volume in pounds per square inch. Air America's Armageddon, for instance, is an 88-cu/in 4500-psi tank. That's a big, tough tank of air.

So, how does your marker actually use the power of the compressed CO_2 or HPA? When you pull the trigger, a regulated amount of gas is released from the tank. It zooms from the air hose and into what is called the chamber. Pulling the trigger releases the hammer in the trigger assembly, which slides forward, pulling the bolt over the exhaust valve while pushing the exhaust valve forward into the chamber. Air shoots out of the chamber, through the exhaust valve and through the bolt. The released air leaves the bolt, forcing the paintball out of the barrel.

ABOUT THE 3-WAY

Usually, an entry-level marker does not have a sophisticated 3-Way. If your marker does have a 3-

Way, though, its job is to transfer regulated air from the regulator to the front and rear of the ram to fine-tune the marker's action.

The position of the O-rings on the shaft in relation to the hose fittings on the body is what determines to which end of the ram the air will travel. An actuating rod connects the trigger to the 3-Way. With the trigger in the forward position, the flow of air is being routed to the back of the ram, keeping the bolt in the forward or closed position. By pulling the trigger and holding it back, you change the location of the shaft O-rings in relation to the air hoses running to the ram. This movement is what transfers the flow of air through the 3-Way from the back of the ram to the front of the ram. As long as the trigger is held back, the bolt will stay in the back or open position.

There are two types of 3-Ways and they work exactly opposite one another. Most (WGP, KAPP, ANS, Palmer and ACI, for example) are designed with two O-rings on the shaft. A few (Dye and Shocktech) have three O-rings on the shaft. The air hoses must be run according to the travel of the air, determined by the type of 3-Way you have.

Trigger pull and release is what cycles the cocking system, and there are two types of trigger systems: the slide trigger and the hinge or swing trigger. These work in opposite manners. When a slide trigger is pulled back, the actuating rod and 3-Way are also pulled back. When a hinge trigger is pulled back, the actuating rod and 3-Way are pushed forward. Depending on whether the 3-Way is pulled or pushed determines the configuration of the hoses.

With a hinge-frame trigger and two-O-ring 3-Way or a slide frame and three-O-ring 3-Way, the hose connections are as follows: front of 3-Way to front of ram, back of 3-Way to back of ram and middle of 3-Way to the regulator.

With a hinge frame and three-O-ring 3-Way or a slide frame and two-O-ring 3-Way, the connections are as follows: front of 3-Way to back of ram, back of 3-Way to front of ram and middle of 3-Way to the regulator.

TIMING

According to Dye, timing is the time interval between the firing of your marker and the re-cocking. You can adjust the timing on a hinge-trigger marker by changing the amount of overlap between the hammer lug and the sear with an Allen wrench through the timing hole in the main body. The trick with timing is to have your marker's recharge rate slightly faster than you can pull the trigger. This is the most efficient setting.

On a Dye marker like the Ultralite, turn the wrench clockwise to close the timing. This moves the firing and re-cocking events closer together. Be careful, however, because timing too close can cause excessive blowback in the feed tube, chopped balls, no firing at all and low velocities.

Turn the wrench clockwise in the timing hole to

open the timing. This moves the firing and re-cocking events farther apart. Timing too far apart, however, may cause your marker not to cock and may cause velocity fluctuations.

CLEANING AND CARE

And you thought you were too young to join the army. Well, it isn't just GI's who field strip and clean their M-16s … and occasionally the ciggy butts around their barracks. It's us paintballers, too!

Field stripping allows you to really get to know your equipment and how it all works together. Its complexity will probably amaze you. Plus, field stripping lets you give your marker a thorough cleaning, which is recommended periodically but certainly after heavy use like a 24-hour scenario game. After all, if you think the dirt and paint and general field grime are only attracted to your body, use a clean white cotton cloth and a little bit of a very lightweight oil (oil specifically designed for markers or firearms, please!) when you clean your marker and you'll be amazed at the gunk that comes out.

For this book, we have selected the Field Stripping Guide that Tippmann publishes for their A-5 as an example, but every state-of-the-art semi-automatic marker works in essentially the same manner – with some important variations. So, check your owner's manual and your manufacturer's Internet site before taking your marker apart.

The first time you field strip your marker, you should lay out a diagram and make sure you can identify the parts, maybe going so far as to make a list of the order in which they suddenly appeared in your hand … or on the floor.

1. CAUTION: Before doing any marker disassembly, remove the CO_2 cylinder and unload your marker. Put the marker in the un-cocked position before beginning to field strip it. If your marker is cocked, hold the bolt's cocking handle back, pull the trigger and release the cocking handle forward. This will un-cock the marker.
2. Adjust the front grip by loosening the screw inside the front grip and sliding it forward or backward. Then re-tighten the screw to lock it in place.
3. Remove the barrel by twisting counterclockwise.
4. Remove the front sight by removing the screw below it and sliding it upward.
5. Remove the rear sight by pulling it up and out.
6. To remove the gas cylinder line from the upper receiver, remove the pushpin in front of the gas line plug on the upper receiver, release the "Tombstone Latch" and the gas line will pull out.
7. To detach the grip and lower receiver, remove the two designated pushpins and the lower receiver will detach.
8. Remove the trigger assembly from the grip by

pushing the safety out the left side of the lower receiver and pulling up on the trigger assembly.

9. To access trigger parts, pull the left plate off the trigger assembly, but DO NOT remove the six long pins from the right plate.
10. To remove the drive assembly (front bolt, power tube, valve, rear bolt, linkage arm, drive pin guide,

drive spring and end cap assembly), first screw the velocity screw in past the receiver. Next, remove the last pushpin holding the end cap in place. Finally, pull the end cap out and tilt the marker up. Drive assembly parts should slide out the back.

11. After cleaning the inside of the upper receiver and the removed parts, it is time to reassemble your marker.

   a. Insert valve into power tube with receiver gas line plug cutout aligned down to match the power tube cutout. Insert the Tombstone adapter to check the fit.

   b. Insert the reassembled parts (front bolt, power tube/valve, rear bolt with linkage arm facing up) until Tombstone adapter can be inserted, pushpin can be replaced and velocity screw can be accessed. (You may need to jiggle the marker while sliding the parts in.)

   c. Insert drive spring and drive pin, end cap unit and replace upper end cap pin.

   d. Reinstall trigger group into grip, insert safety, reconnect lower to upper receiver and install last two pushpins.

   e. NOTE: It is only necessary to disassemble the upper receiver halves to access six parts: ball latch, front grip nut, cocking handle spring, Tombstone latch and Tombstone latch spring.

LUBRICATING YOUR MARKER

To clean your paintball marker, Tippmann recommends you use a damp towel with water to wipe off paint, oil and debris from the outside. A premium gun oil such as Hoppe's #9 will help maintain markers in good working order. To oil all internal parts, put two or three drops of oil in the tank adapter, then install the CO_2 tank and fire the marker. They also recommend using white lithium grease on the barrel O-ring, safety O-ring and tank O-ring. DO NOT use any cleaning solvents as this can damage the finish.

Before doing any maintenance or cleaning, Tippmann says you must definitely remove the CO_2 cylinder and unload the marker.

   A. Unloading the marker: First remove the hopper. Then, point the marker in a safe direction and fire several times to be sure there are no balls left in the feeder or lodged in the chamber.

   B. Removing the tank: To remove a charged CO_2 cylinder, turn the cylinder approximately 3/4-turn counterclockwise or out. This allows the tank pin valve to close so that no CO_2 will enter the marker. Point the marker in a safe direction and fire the remaining CO_2 in the marker by pulling the trigger until the marker stops firing. (This may take four to five shots.)

If your marker keeps firing after you have turned the tank 3/4-turn, the tank pin valve has not closed yet and you may have to turn the tank counterclockwise a little further.

If you turn the tank 3/4-turn and it begins to leak before you pull the trigger, you have turned it too far and may have damaged the tank O-ring.

Because of the variances in tank valve parts, each tank varies slightly on exactly how far it should be turned. (If this process does not work, the tank valve pin could be too long.)

MARKER STORAGE

Store your marker in a dry area after making sure it is cleaned and lightly oiled so that it will not rust. Store your marker with the bolt in the forward position. Always empty and remove the CO_2 tank before putting your marker in storage. If your marker is going to be in storage for a long time, you will want to dust and re-oil it before using it again.

MEET THE MARKER MANUFACTURERS

32 DEGREES (NPS)

Players who have known the Rebel markers from 32 Degrees by way of National Paintball Supply (NPS) will now find a new name on the 32 Degree list, the Icon. The 68-caliber Icon is available in manual (Icon Z) or electronic (Icon e) formats. In either variety, the Icon has a custom sight rail with beavertail, double-trigger setup, 45 frame, low-pressure chamber, quick disconnect, vertical feed port, custom anodizing and milling, fore grip with expansion chamber, drop forward, new style ball detents, rear velocity adjuster with lock and a one-year warranty. You can expect to shoot up to 13 bps and the electronic marker has an adjustable dip-switch panel with four modes of fire: semi-auto, 3-shot and 6-shot burst and full-auto. The Icon e was on sale on *www.paintball-discounters. com* on 9-29-03 for $119.99.

The venerable Rebel comes in many versions, including the newest Rebel 02 Xtreme in manual ($119.99) and electronic ($149.99). Both have the 45 frame, drop forward and a double trigger. In the electronic mode, look for the full function LCD in the grip for four rates of fire: semi-auto, full-auto, burst and reactive.

The PT Xtreme sidearm or back-up pistol ($109.99) holds 10 rounds and operates on a conventional 12-gram CO_2 cartridge that powers this marker's spring-loading action.

ACTION

Action Markers builds the Sentinel in various configurations, but the body of the new TS Pro is made from aircraft-grade aluminum and has dual ball retainers, a Vari-Grip threaded feed tube, Hogue Grips, Delrin upper

This is the Sentinel TS Pro from Action Markers. Because the TS Pro's pre-set regulator is designed for compressed air, it will increase air efficiency by regulating airflow down to optimal shooting levels.

Action Markers makes the William Shatner Limited Edition Illusion Marker (pump or CO2). It's gold plated and very hot.

bolt and, Action Markers says, it can be field stripped in just three seconds. Action Markers offers a two-piece barrel with a .689 back bore and 12-inch overall length. The fully adjustable trigger lets you find your own sweet spot. In red to black fade the TS Pro costs $325.00 from Action Markers.

Because the Sentinel's pre-set regulator is designed for compressed air, it will increase air efficiency by regulating airflow down to optimal levels. Most high-pressure air systems regulate pressure output to around 800 psi, Action Markers says, but markers actually use far less than that. By further regulation of pressure, bringing it down to the optimal level for your marker, you can achieve greater consistency in ball speed, which translates directly and immediately into more accurate shooting.

The TS Pro's Advanced Drop has several features for flexibility and convenience such as a dovetail connection to the tank adapter that allows you to slide your tank forward or backward, depending on your comfort position. The Drop also features three receiving slots for the tank adapter for offset left, offset right and underneath tank positions. The tank adapter itself has three air-line ports so you can add your bottom-line anywhere you like. You can also add an extra gauge. The AM Advanced Drop also features an on-off valve for air conservation.

The standard Sentinel has an interesting feature that Action Markers says answers the question, "Where do I put my other hand?" The Sentinel Gas Thru is not an expansion chamber, volumizer or regulator and does not improve gas efficiency while using CO_2. It is a "cheap, simple, good-looking way to incorporate a fore-grip into your paintball marker." All Action paintball marker Gas Thrus are ASA compatible for in-line use.

The Illusion Pro from Action Markers is a professional-quality pump-action marker. It was created with the advanced and pro-stock-class player in mind and features dual pump rods for smooth action and a light return spring to bring the pump block and bolt back to the forward position. This Pro is anodized with popular black-to-red satin finish. Threaded feed tubes make switching to stock feed simple and quick. It also features Hogue grips and an easy-to-pull quick-release pin for fast field stripping. This model includes the Vigilante Regulator, factory installed and adjusted, for maximum performance and the CP two-piece barrel system. MSRP is $460.00.

The AM-P Illusion is Action Markers' signature pump marker created with the beginning player and the advanced stock-class player in mind. It features dual pump rods for smooth action and a light return spring to return the pump block and bolt to the forward position. It includes a 10-round feed tube, a quick-release 12-ounce air adapter for true stock-class play, Hogue grips and an easy-pull quick-release pin for simple and fast field stripping. The MSRP is $274.95.

Action Markers also makes the William Shatner Limited Edition Illusion Pump Marker. Only 25 of these markers are being made with real 24-karat gold-plated body and chrome accents. This sweet marker comes in a handsome hardwood case for display. William Shatner's signature is engraved on the side, and he has personally signed the Certificate of Authenticity. The cost is only $2150.00 from Action Markers!

The AM-4 Scenario Series marker is designed for rugged woods play and is created to bring you the feeling of military training equipment. The AM-4 Custom features a collapsible, three-position butt stock, a long sniper-style barrel and a CNC machined-aluminum barrel shroud to complete "the look." The AM-4 Custom also features an angled feed neck to allow the addition of a scope or a sight. With an extended drop-forward, the AM-4 Custom is precisely balanced to limit wrist and arm fatigue. This marker also includes a gas-through fore-grip. It is anodized in a flat-black finish to limit glare and blends in almost anywhere. This sniper has a 15-round feed tube to reduce profile and a $355.00 MSRP.

AIRGUN DESIGNS (AGD)

Tom Kaye's Airgun Designs (AGD) has an excellent reputation for marker design and performance. Its markers are usually called "Automags" and have a brand following similar to Bud Orr's "Autocockers."

Tom's 68-caliber blow-forward semi-auto, the Automag Classic ($229.99 standard and $289.99 with power feed at *www.xtremz.com* on 7-03-03), will operate on CO_2, nitrogen or compressed air. AGD says you will get a 26 bps rate of fire with the AGD Reactive Trigger and X-Valve. This marker measures 8.5 inches long (w/standard barrel and no tank) and weighs less than 2 pounds without a tank.

AGD promotes and sells the body of a paintball marker that it calls the Automag Classic because, according to them, "The first thing every player wants to do is customize his marker. It didn't make sense to force you to buy stuff you were going to get rid of anyway when you upgrade. The Classic allows you to get exactly the barrel you want, find that perfect front grip and set up a drop-forward so it's super tight! It is good for guys on a budget who want a strong, reliable marker that will take a beating and keep on ticking."

The 68-caliber blow-forward semi-auto Minimag ($279.99 to $479.99 depending on the upgrades at *www.paintballgear.com* 7-03-03) uses CO_2, nitrogen or compressed air to give you a marker capable of shooting more than 20 bps if you set it up with the AGD Reactive Trigger and X-Valve. The 13.5-inch marker comes with an 8-inch barrel and weighs about 2.5 pounds.

AGD says the Minimag is a player favorite because it is very tightly packaged. The vertical ASA adapter keeps liquid CO_2 out of the valve, so CO_2 users really enjoy this marker. To change to a high-pressure system, just bolt on

Airgun Designs sells its Automag as the basis for a customized kit. You select the barrel, power attachment and ball-loading accessories of your choice.

a bottom line and run a hose to the vertical ASA. Many upgrade possibilities include barrels, double triggers on the AGD Intelliframe, front grips and Warp Feed. It comes with rubber grips, stainless hose and quick disconnect.

The 68-caliber Automag RT Pro is $539.75 on *www.paintballgear.com* (7-03-03). This blow-forward semi-auto operates on compressed air or nitrogen and shoots at more than 20 balls per second (bps) with the Reactive Trigger and X-Valve. It is 16.5 inches long and comes with an 11-inch Autococker-threaded barrel. The weight is just over 3 pounds.

The Automag RT Pro is a top-of-the-line mechanical marker for people who play hard and can't afford failure. It features the tough Reactive Trigger valve system that recharges faster than you can pull the trigger. The Pro is also equipped with the double-trigger, aluminum Intelliframe, which gives you the ability to run your electronic hopper or Warp Feed every time you pull the trigger.

Tom Kaye's 68-caliber E-Mag was $779.95 to $999.95 depending on accessories and upgrades on *www.paintballgear.com* on 7-03-03. The E-Mag is an open-bolt blow-forward semi-automatic and it operates on HPA with an input pressure of 600 to 1000 psi. A nickel-metal-hydride rechargeable battery is rated to about 20,000

The Automag RT in the "pro" version from Airgun Designs.

The new X-mag from Airgun Designs. Hot!

shots. You can expect to achieve 20 bps with the Reactive Trigger and X-Valve without shoot down. The E-Mag has an 11-inch barrel with Autococker threads. Overall, this electronic marker weighs almost 4 pounds and is 17 inches long with the barrel.

"Here is our offering to the electro-marker world," AGD says. "The E-Mag is our flagship marker, at least until the new X-Mag is out. An onboard microprocessor gives you perfect trigger timing so you never 'short stroke' or get 'shoot-down.' You can set the speed limiter with the side-mounted display and never outshoot your hopper, too. All stainless body construction. The Advanced Integrated Regulator means you don't have to upgrade to a regulated front grip and the RT valve system, which allows up to 26 bps shooting, is standard."

Trigger tension and stroke are independently adjustable. The secret is magnets. Add more to increase tension or take some away to reduce tension. AGD uses a second magnet to activate a magnetic sensor in the grip to fire the marker.

The E-Mag features a 45 grip and an LED display for the countdown timer, shot counter and other functions. (CO_2 is not allowed in this system. Compressed air only.) The E-Mag Extreem has an aluminum main body with an interchangeable breech for the AGD Warp or standard vertical feed systems.

The E-Mag's most unique feature is the Manual Override Switch just behind the trigger, which lets you completely bypass the electronics and fire the marker in "Manual Mode" with a flick of your thumb. The front grip houses the removable nickel-metal-hydride battery pack that can power you through 20,000 shots before it needs to be recharged. You can use the included charger to "juice up" the battery using your car's accessory outlet (cigarette lighter).

The newest 68-caliber, open-bolt blow-forward marker from AGD is the X-Mag. Look for this paint shooter to cost around $1000 depending on accessories and upgrades. It is powered by HPA and an 18-volt nickel-metal-hydride rechargeable battery runs the electronics. Expect as much as 26-bps shooting with an X-Mag equipped with the Reactive Trigger and X-Valve. It weighs around 3 pounds with its 11-inch Autococker-threaded barrel and is 17 inches long.

This upgraded E-Mag incorporates all of AGD President Tom Kaye's innovative ideas. It begins with the ultra-lightweight, precision-machined ULE aluminum body and Level 10 Superbolt II with power tube tip. It has a removable breech and manual override. The X-Mag is a fully adjustable semi-auto with an unbreakable on/off switch.

AKA

AKA's 68-caliber open-bolt semi-auto Viking is $775.00 (www.akalmp.com 7-03-03). It will use CO_2, nitrogen or compressed air and cycles 13 balls per second. It comes with an Autococker-threaded Javelin barrel. The 3-pound Viking is 18.125 inches long, 8.17 inches high

and 1.75 inches wide. It operates on one 9-volt battery.

This is AKA's newest marker and it was designed for budget-minded players. AKA says you can get more than 1000 shots on a 68-cu/in, 3000-psi tank. The Viking is equipped with AKA's adjustable low-pressure system and a cartridge-based component system for quick repairs. Its low-pressure, high-efficiency Tornado Valve, Delrin Lightning bolt, quick-release pin, 45 grip, adjustable double or single triggers, ball detent, built-in vertical mount, Sidewinder vertical pressure regulator and adjustable rate of fire make the Viking a contender! The AKA circuit board accepts ball breech sensors. A barrel sock and carrying case are included.

At the upper end of the AKA line is the 68-caliber closed-bolt, semi-automatic Excalibur. Use CO_2, nitrogen or compressed air to power this 13-bps shooter. It comes with a 'Cocker-friendly Javelin barrel and measures 18.125 inches long, 8.17 inches high and 1.75 inches wide. The Excalibur weighs 3 pounds without tank, barrel or 9-volt operational battery.

AKA lists the operating pressure for the Excalibur as 140 to 180 psi depending on the type of paint and says you can get more than 1000 shots on a 68-cu/in, 3000-psi tank. The Excalibur is equipped with AKA's adjustable low-pressure system and a cartridge-based component system for quick repairs. Look for the low-pressure, high-efficiency Tornado Valve, Delrin Lightning bolt with quick-release pin, 45 grip, three-point adjustable double or single triggers, ball detent, built-in vertical mount, Sidewinder vertical pressure regulator, pull-through cleaning and adjustable rate of fire. The AKA circuit board accepts ball breech sensors. A barrel sock and carrying case are included.

ALIEN

The Alien is new from the company of the same name. Alien's ET (Electric Tournament) had an $895.00 MSRP at www.alienpb.com on 8-28-03. Jack Rice, owner of Alien, says his electro-pneumatic marker is "super fast, low pressure and amazingly accurate. I want it to be a premier tournament marker." It includes an LCD, high and low constant-pressure regulators and a barrel. Their "Sweet Touch" trigger frame lets players lower their hand position for better trigger alignment and allows an LCD to be placed above the thumb for easy viewing. The new Alien ET is available in green, blue, red, orange, silver and gold.

There are several available options for the Alien if money is a little tight. The $775.00 Alien Skeleton has a low trigger profile and is not equipped with an LCD, high-pressure regulator or barrel. Two models that are still on the drawing boards are the Alien B blowback, an economy Alien marker, and the Alien E, a blowback Alien with an electronic trigger.

Wicked Air Sportz (www.wickedairsportz.com), the "rocket scientists of paintball," build the electronic Equalizer Boards for the Alien ET. Jack Rice claims these boards give this marker the ability to cycle more than 50 bps! "We have had to include an electronic eye to slow the Alien's light speed operation down to what a hopper can feed," he says. While most markers operate "in-line" with a bolt or spindle pushing the ball forward and sealing the chamber, the Alien works "off-axis," from the side, with a "hatch cover" pivoting from the side to seal the chamber. The hatch cover gives the marker closed-bolt accuracy and excellent efficiency. It widens the profile by about an inch, but this is more than made up with a shorter marker. This shorter, more compact marker is possible because all previous barrels have attached to the front of the marker. A 12-inch barrel would give you a 20- or 21-inch marker. The Alien moves the barrel to the back, so that with a 12-inch barrel, you have about a 15-inch marker. The Alien is the only marker we know of that seals from the side.

Two other interesting features are the Alien's "Sweet Touch" trigger frame and Mayday barrel system. With about a 5-degree angle, the Sweet Touch places your palm lower so that your fingers line up correctly. "You see players rotating their trigger hand down or sometimes shooting with their second and third fingers," says Jack Rice. The "Sweet Touch" is identified by the lower position of the thumb. It puts the top of your thumb and your middle finger at the same height, the index finger being higher.

Alien's new Mayday barrels will have distinctive porting and an ultra-honed finish, but they are just entering the final design phase. They will have a "Cocker threading" attachment style and are designed to lower standing pressure in the barrel as the ball is fired.

The Alien will weigh about 2 pounds without a barrel, drop or tank. The operating pressure is a low 85 pounds and it takes less than 300 pounds firing pressure to achieve 300 fps. An Alien marker measures less than 1.5 inches wide at the rails, 2.5 inches wide at the top plate and it is about 7 inches tall.

ARMOTECH

Armotech has developed three distinct marker styles. The Speedball Series is a conventional marker style for rec play and competition. The WG-65 Series is based on an AR-16-styled body for specialty play or training scenarios. The Zeus Series is a pistol style for use as a back-up or a sidearm in paintball games and training situations.

The $249.99 (MSRP) Mars EVO is an electronic 68-caliber semi-auto that gives you the options of switching from semi-auto to burst mode or even full automatic. Switch the safety to "on" and Armotech says the Mars EVO can fire up to 13 balls per second, but is nevertheless "highly reliable and virtually maintenance free." This stylish marker operates on CO_2 or compressed air and includes a quick-strip pin that lets you take the guts out for cleaning. It comes with a bottom-line setup, pressure gauge, regulator, low-pressure chamber and drop-forward. Velocity is easily adjustable and the sight-rail is built on to the body of the marker. It also includes a ported 14-inch barrel and LED display.

The $499.99 (MSRP) WG-65 looks like an AR-16,

Young paintball player with an Armotech AR-16 look-alike and a remote setup that allows him to pack air on his back. The other black strap on the marker is a sling.

which is the civilian styling for the military M-16. It was originally designed for police and military training scenarios because it looks and, in many ways, feels like the real thing. This 68-caliber semi-auto uses either compressed air or CO_2. Because of its use as a training tool, Armotech says it is built "extremely rugged and durable, requiring minimal maintenance."

Mechanically, the WG-65 has a collapsible telescoping stock, fully-adjustable military-style sights and a sling loop. The push-button safety and rear velocity adjuster

make the "65" excellent for rec play or scenario games. According to Armotech, the action and recoil emulates the military's "real thing" version of this marker: "The vertical adapter accepts standard paintball tanks, but this marker is best suited for a remote line to get the full effect."

Before you purchase a WG-65 for knocking around in the woods near your house, consider this note from Armotech: "The WG65-M4 is NOT A TOY and is virtually an exact replica of the real thing. Do not carry this marker in public or in the passenger compartment of your vehicle."

A fully loaded WG-65 with laser mounted sight, sniper scope and heavy-duty sight rail costs $579.99 from the factory.

Armotech's third marker style is the Zeus sidearm. With several different versions available, the aluminum Zeus is basically a 10-shot CO_2 powered pistol with a rear cocking knob, removable magazine, tournament-style rear velocity adjuster, quick-change 12-gram CO_2 compartment, sight rail and contoured rubber grip. This unique pistol can be upgraded for use with a bottom line and constant air source. With the Zeus G2, Armotech includes an extra barrel and bore sizer insert. Ball velocity is adjustable between 200 and 350 feet per second and the safety is a pushpin style.

BOB LONG

Talk about "Timmys" and everybody will know you are shooting one of Bob Long's 68-caliber Intimidators. Like top Autocockers, Automags or Angels, at more than $1000, these well-known markers can empty your

For newcomers to the paintball game or people who live in areas where service and support is not high, a paintball kit may be the way to go at first. Brass Eagle offers a relatively inexpensive starter kit built on their Afterburner marker, the JT USA Sentry goggle system and all the accessories you need (except air in your tank!) to get started.

wallet. On the other hand, they are open-bolt, electro-pneumatic-operated, low-pressure nitrogen or compressed air machines milled to frightening perfection with built-in regulators and a 300-psi gauge. These markers only have a semi-auto shot mode, but Bob Long says they are capable of shooting 25 balls per second and each is equipped with an anti-chop electronic eye. Timmys are available in numerous colors and color combinations.

Here is a run-down on some of the current models and costs (on 9-15-03 from *www.paintballgateway.com*):

Alien Species: The newest Timmy costs $1494.88. Its Equalizer Board programs a shot counter, game timer and anti-chop eye custom front regulator, but curiously, there is no LCD screen. It weighs 2.6 pounds, is 22.5 inches long and 8.625 inches high.

ECX: You will lay out $1050.00 for this 2.5-pound, 19.875-inch long and 8.625-inch high marker. Its electronics are powered by an S.O.B. Board (shot counter, game timer, anti-chop eye), but like the Alien Species, it is not equipped with an LCD screen.

Texas Storm: You can purchase this tournament-grade Timmy for $1150.00. It weighs 2.85 pounds and is 19.875 inches long and 8.625 inches high. Its Equalizer Board (shot counter, game timer, anti-chop eye) comes with an LCD Screen.

Lasoya: For $1294.77, you can own this Timmy, named for top tournament competitor Chris Lasoya. It weighs 2.85 pounds, is 22.5 inches long and 8.625 inches high. Its

Equalizer Board
(shot counter, game timer,
anti-chop eye) comes with an LCD screen.

Additional Intimidator models include: Dragon ($1294.88), Ironmen ($1200.00), 2002 Intimidator ($994.88), GZ ($994.88) and the Z ($949.95).

BRASS EAGLE

For years, Brass Eagle has been known as the low-cost provider of Chinese paintball markers to the BoxMarts of the world. They still are and as a consequence, they sell more markers than any other company in the world. Still, they have begun to upgrade their marker line with a range of 68-caliber semi-autos like the Afterburner, which sells online at *www.paintballgear.com* (5-21-03) for just $99.99. This 18-inch, 2-pound aluminum marker with a ported and fluted barrel will shoot 300 rounds per minute or about five balls per second. For major league markers, this is just above pump rate.

Brass Eagle says the Afterburner is the "third entry in Brass Eagle's Aegis Series of tournament and field-grade markers, designed for high performance and durability." It has a newly redesigned field-strip pin, a self-locking velocity adjustment, vertical feed, two-panel grip, double-finger trigger, laser engraving and newly redesigned top cocking bolt. The Afterburner's Player's Kit includes a 200-count hopper, game flag, barrel plug, squeegee, 9-ounce CO_2 cylinder, two spare ball tubes, goggles and a marker oil packet.

The 68-caliber, open-bolt, blowback semi-auto Marauder uses CO_2 or HPA and costs $48.84 (*www. walmart.com* 5-21-03). Brass Eagle says this modest performer shoots five balls per second, and its polished aluminum barrel is ported and fluted. It is 19 inches long with the barrel, and without the tank, weighs less than 2 pounds.

The Marauder belongs in Brass Eagle's Aegis Series of tournament and field-grade markers for performance and durability. The receiver is a lightweight molded composite and has a 45 grip. It has a quick-pull field-strip pin for easy maintenance and metal internal parts plus self-locking velocity adjustment, right-hand feed, custom-designed trigger guard, double-finger trigger, newly redesigned side-cocking knob and bottom-line adaptor.

The Marauder Player's Kit includes a 200-count hopper, barrel plug, squeegee, goggles, paper targets, Brass Eagle stickers and CD-ROM.

WalMart sells the Talon Ghost, which Brass Eagle says is made in the U.S., for $39.99 (*www.walmart.com* 5-21-03). It is a 68-caliber pump powered by a replaceable, non-refillable 12-gram cartridge. The Talon Ghost comes with a 10-count tube and can be fitted with an optional hopper. The receiver is made from impact-resistant, smoke-colored polymer. The 7.25-inch barrel is fixed

The Brass Eagle Marauder semi-automatic marker has a high-impact polymer frame.

and non-removable. The TalonGhost is 13.75 inches long and weighs less than 1.5 pounds. The Player's Kit includes a 10-count feed tube, barrel plug and Brass Eagle stickers. Brass Eagle says this little marker is perfect for newbies.

Brass Eagle's entry-level 68-caliber pump Blade 02 costs $24.99 at *www.paintball-adventures.com* (5-21-03). The Blade 02 is powered by a 12-gram CO_2 cartridge. It is 17.5 inches long without the CO_2 adapter or tank, and with its lightweight high-impact polymer frame, weighs about 1.5 pounds. The Player's Kit includes a 50-count hopper, barrel plug and Brass Eagle stickers.

DYE

Dye's 2003 Autocockers are machined from the basic WGP Bud Orr Autococker frame. After that is done, Dye adds its own parts. One of the results is the Reflex for $799.96 (MSRP) and the Ultralite for $899.96 (MSRP). These sharp-looking markers with black and silver Dye Ultralight barrels come in a number of fade colors: black to blue or red, or clear to cobalt or orange. They feature a 45 frame with sticky grips, the Dye front end kit with 3-Way and an in-line regulator. The Ultralite has the same features as the Reflex, but is machined to take out every possible ounce of extra weight. As a result, it is 20 percent lighter. The Ultralite comes with a machined dovetail sight mount for the Dye Izon sight, which is included.

EVIL (PMI)

The Evil 68-caliber semi-automatic Omen is a true closed-bolt action, pneumatic-re-cock marker with electromechanical, independent hammer, re-cock piston and external re-cock regulation. It weighs 2.7 ounces and measures 19.7 inches long and 8 inches high. The one-piece barrel is 12 inches long with a .690 ID for the first stage (six inches) and a .700 second stage. It attaches to the marker with Autococker threading.

It features a 45 grip, an adjustable, electronic double trigger and an electronic on/off switch. The cam-operated force-feed has an anti-doubler arm to prevent ball-jam. An adjustable re-cock, independent re-cock/reload assembly, vertical regulator for velocity control and low-pressure operation are also featured. A 9-volt rechargeable battery with AC and DC charger is included. Tournament-legal tail, Venturi-style Delrin bolt, "Evil"-style Delrin valve stem, stainless steel body and the on/off bottom line are all standard. The feed tube threads the same as the 2k3 Piranha, Impulse, Shocker and Bushmaster markers. The Evil Omen will operate on either CO_2 or HPA. Operating pressure is 250 to 500 psi. Inlet to the regulator is 1000 psi. (Use a scale for CO_2 and a pressure gauge for HPA to prevent overfilling.) $449.00 is the MSRP at *www.evil-paintball.com*.

FREE-FLOW

You will recognize the Matrix Trauma because the Free-Flow and Trauma logos are milled into the sides of this marker. Both air chambers open inside the marker body to allow for four times more air to the bolt, Free-Flow says. This marker comes with a custom-milled Trinity Regulator and Free-Flow Bolt Kit that increases shot count dramatically. It has either Centerflag or new Crossfire in-line regulators. Clamping low rise and high rise are included. Expect the Free-Flow trigger, breech knob and front regulator adjuster to also be included. Single- or double-trigger versions are available. You will find an adjustable LCD trigger frame with all on-board options and custom programming. This marker is ABS enabled and available in dust black or silver and glossy yellow or dark gray for a MSRP of $1199.

Free-Flow says the basic Smart Parts Impulse is the best electro-pneumatic marker available for under $500.00. It comes standard with a progressive barrel and vertical Max-Flo regulator and costs $424.99 (MSRP). Step it up with the Vision Eye to eliminate chopping paint by only allowing the marker to fire when a paintball is in the breech—even if the gun is tilted to the side—for $599.00

Step it up again as the Detroit Thunder Impulse and it will include: a new up-front Max Flow LPR, brass hammer, titanium hammer piston, titanium bolt pin, LP bolt, the Vision Eye, Freak Barrel, dust anodizing, reverse polarity magnetic trigger, vertical Max Flow, custom Twister feed tube and a new milling design! Each Detroit Thunder Impulse sold at *www.4freeflow.com* is set up and tuned by Mitch Karn from the NXL pro team and it comes with an exclusive Lifetime Warranty for just $999.99 (MSRP).

GAME FACE

The Thunder Vision Impulse is made in the U.S. by Smart Parts. Although the manufacturer suggests $1199.00 (*www.gamefacepaintball.com* 7-28-03), you can find this 68-caliber electronic semi-automatic marker online for $974.99 to $1049.99 depending on the marker's

Custom shops like Jeff Sabatini's Ditto Paintball in Redlands, California, abound in paintball. They can take your common out-of-the-box marker and really dress it up.

paint job (7-28-03 *www.paintballgear.com*). It uses CO_2, nitrogen or compressed air and comes with a 14-inch two-part ported Freak barrel.

This is a new marker designed for Game Face by their professional NXL team, the Detroit Thunder. It offers a custom-milled body and all the essential upgrades that make it perfect for top-level tournament play. The lightweight, custom "Vision" firing system allows the Impulse to fire only when a ball is centered in the breech. This makes it virtually impossible to chop a ball, even when the marker is tilted straight on its side, Game Face says. It has a vertical regulator to the bottom-line setup and a low-pressure kit with Tapeworm valve system to control output pressure for controlled firing. The lightweight, low-maintenance Delrin plastic bolt does not require oil to prevent scratching. Titanium pull pin, magnetic blade trigger and an extra vertical handle for upgrading to the Max-Flo 4500 air system are included.

The non-electronic version, the Game Face Thunder Impulse from Smart Parts, carries a suggested retail price of $799.00 from Game Face ($675-$699.99 on *www.paintballgear.com* 7-28-03) and includes a 14-inch ported and fluted Tear Drop barrel. It includes the Twister feed port that doubles as a feeder-locking device. The body is custom milled and designed to be used with these included features: a vertical regulator to bottom line setup, lightweight Delrin bolt, magnetic blade trigger and titanium pull pin.

For an entry-level marker, the E-Rex Pro is a solid, 68-caliber electronic multi-mode shooter (semi-auto, burst and full-auto). This Taiwanese marker operates on CO_2,

The Thunder Impulse with 14-inch Tear Drop Barrel from Game Face in red, blue, black and silver.

nitrogen or compressed air and retails online for $189.99 *(www.paintballgear.com* 7-28-03), which is not bad for your first 20 bps hunter. It weighs 3.36 pounds and measures 20.1 inches with a 12-inch two-piece barrel.

Engineered with a custom body and sporting an engraved ACL barrel and M92 aluminum grip frame, this electronic marker reliably withstands rough rec use. The two-finger aluminum trigger and drop-forward make it comfortable to carry and handle while the low-pressure chamber with a thumb velocity adjuster keeps the paint flying. An LCD full-function trigger board display lets you choose between semi-auto, burst (up to 10 bps) and full-auto. The LCD display also gives you a shot counter, game timer and battery status. Look for a vertical ball feed, expansion chamber, mini-gauge, regulator, drop-forward, sight rail, rear cocking pin and volumizer.

A stripped-down version of the E-Rex Pro, the Elite, was available for just $169.99 from *www.fogdog.com* on 7-28-03. It offers firing in semi-auto and full-auto modes.

The made-in-Taiwan Bone Daddy Ready-2-Play Kit costs $89.99 at *www.pyramydair.com* (7-29-03). It is everything you need to get out on the field – right out of the box—including a Game Face Skul Mask, 200-count hopper, a 100-count pod of paint, air source, flexible squeegee and barrel glove. The 68-caliber semi-auto open-bolt blowback marker is powered by CO_2, nitrogen or compressed air. It weighs 3.1 pounds and measures 17.7 inches long with a 9.5-inch anodized ported barrel. This marker shoots seven bps.

The Bone Daddy BL power-feed marker features a lightweight aluminum receiver, rear cocking pin and double trigger on a 45 frame with rubber wrap-around grip, velocity adjuster, vertical ASA connector and low-pressure volumizer chamber. A bottom-line adapter is standard.

Game Face inherited the 68-caliber closed-bolt Sheridan PGP2 pump, which many players still find a value at $72.95 on *www.paintballgear.com* (7-28-03). A 12-gram CO_2 cartridge is all you need to make this pump go bang and no matter how much you love your semi-auto, you can always use a backup. The rugged, 10-shot PGP2 has proven its value on rec and scenario fields for years. It also features a solid-brass 6.5-inch barrel, dual fiber optic sights, a field-strippable bolt, rear velocity adjuster and self-lubricating synthetic pump forearm.

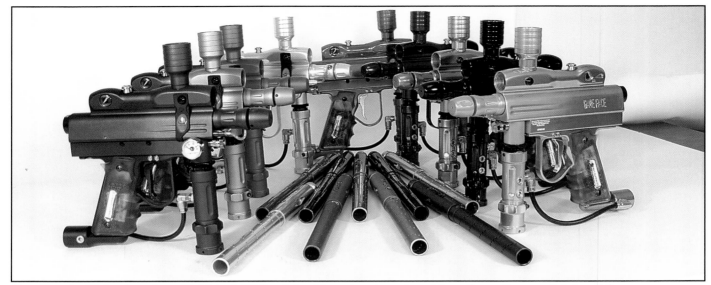

New Thunder Vision Impulse with 14-inch AA Freak front barrel and one insert from Game Face, a division of Crosman.

INDIAN CREEK DESIGN (ICD)

ICD's lightweight 2-pound 10-ounce BushMaster is legendary. The BushMaster is actually a series of markers that range in price from $299.00 to $629.00 or more, but they all come with a quick-disconnect pin on the input side of the regulator to allow quick cleaning or replacement of the entire bolt assembly. No tools are required. The body is machined from aircraft-grade aluminum and is then hard anodized. Look for the following mechanical features: vertical feed, fore-grip, double-finger trigger and a removable 12-inch spiral-ported muzzle-brake step barrel that is mirror honed. These markers are available in red, green, blue, black, silver, gold or purple. They accept all loaders with 1.05-inch outside diameter feed tubes.

The BushMaster is set up as a low-pressure marker for a nitrogen or compressed-air system. It comes with two internal regulators and a viewable pressure gauge. The first regulator drops the pressure to between 225 and 275 psi and the second knocks it down a bit further to between 85 and 95 psi!

While CO_2 can be used as a propellant, ICD says, it is not recommended for the BushMaster. If you use CO_2, "your results may not always be as expected," ICD says. Consult the place where you purchased your BushMaster, or a competent airsmith, for instruction in the safe handling of compressed-air cylinders before purchasing or connecting one to your BushMaster.

The electronics are powered by one 9-volt battery located in a compartment or "tray" in the right side of the marker frame above the trigger and the on/off switch. The BushMaster does not have a separate manual safety.

The BushMaster series is an electronic solenoid-actuated computer-controlled marker. Its electronics offer precise velocity control, game timer, shot counter and multiple firing modes including full-auto on the B2K2 version's LCD screen. The LCD readout screen is located on the back of the B2K2 only. That's really in your face!

The software and on-board connector for the IR sensors (anti-chop eye) are already built into the board so that upgrades will always be easy.

Rate of fire is dependent on the mode and settings of the DIP switches on the circuit board. For the B2K and B2K2, they are: semi-auto, 2-shot/3-shot/6-shot burst modes, auto response (fires on the pull and the release), zip and full-auto. Rate selection will give you between 4 and 13 balls per second.

ICD has an interesting safety note in its BushMaster instructions, but it really applies to all high-end markers: Before pressurizing your BushMaster series, check to make sure that you have a barrel plug in place and that there is no paint in the marker. The on-off switch should be off. Air can now be applied to the marker and it will become pressurized.

The manufacturer suggested retail price (MSRP) of markers in the BushMaster series depend on their capabilities:

1. The $299.00 BKO is ICD's entry-level electro-pneumatic (not electro-mechanical, ICD says) marker.
2. The B2K-PDS is $599.00 and includes all of the features of the standard B2K, plus the PDS (Paintball Detection System) system with an external on/off switch to turn the sensors on and off.
3. The $529.00 B2K is all new, from the new grip frame to the regulators and adapters to electronics. The grip frame features a four-way adjustable.
4. The $629.00 B2K Flame-Custom is a custom-milled version of the popular B2K. It features a radical flame design and sleeved bolt.
5. The GS-Custom B2K is $629.00. It is a custom version of the popular Bushmaster B2K that is designed by Greg Schutte and Hawk Dobbins of ICD.

JT USA

JT's 68-caliber Excellerator series is numbered or indexed and the higher the number, the more loaded it is with features.

The Excellerator 6.0, for instance, cost $199.75 online at www.paintballgear.com (5-23-03). This electronic semi-auto operates on CO_2, nitrogen or compressed air. It is a little heavy, but its standard polished-aluminum barrel is ported and fluted. The backlit display features alerts and messages including a greeting (12-character message of your choice), game time remaining, balls fired, life counter (number of balls fired, including dry fires, by marker during its entire life), remaining game time alerts in audio and vibrating mode (the audio provides a voice alert which calls out the remaining game time), a visual low-battery alert, battery-level indicator and initial game time with settings from one to 60 in one-minute increments.

This marker "will cane your Muppet ass!" JT says. It has a double-touch trigger, quick-strip pin, CA adapter/volumizer, vertical feed port, low-pressure mini-gauge, regulator, integrated sight rail and custom aluminum grip frame. Included are a drop-forward with bottom line, rear-cocking bolt, Venturi bolt and high-impact polymer grips. (An electronic loader is also recommended by many users.)

Stepping slightly down, the electronic semi-auto Excellerator 5.0 costs $168.77 online (*www.xpaintball.com* 5-23-03). You can use CO_2, nitrogen or compressed air to power it. The Excellerator 5.0 with electronic double trigger and LCD Information Center is designed for intermediate players. This semi-auto has a quick-strip pin, vertical feed port, CA adapter/volumizer, expansion chamber, integrated sight rail, die-cast aluminum grip frame, rear-cocking bolt, custom drop-forward, bottom line, polished aluminum, and a ported and fluted barrel.

The $199.99 semi-auto Excellerator 3.5/3.5E (*www.paintballgear.com* 5-23-03) is available with or without electronics. It is also available as a kit with goggles, tank, loader, barrel plug and a squeegee. You can shoot the 3.5 with CO_2, nitrogen or compressed air.

The Excellerator 3.5 manual and E-Grip have been built for the beginner paintball enthusiast, but JT USA says it can be used successfully on any venue. Every 3.5 semi-automatic has a double trigger, quick-strip pin, vertical feed-port, volumizer, expansion chamber, integrated sight rail, polished-aluminum barrel and die-cast-aluminum grip frame.

KAPP

KAPP stands for Kick Ass Paintball Products. KAPP is known for their sensuous models and for their aftermarket products, but they also sell a couple of fine semi-automatic, closed-bolt markers.

KAPP's Reflex Autococker bodies are the only factory Worr Games bodies with a built-in feed port. The rest, KAPP says, have press-in ports. Each body is machined with

JT USA markers feature the company's celebrated banana logo.

This JT USA Excellerator 3.5 has a quick-strip pin.

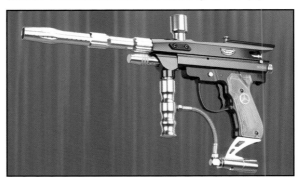

Shown here is a JT USA Excellerator 5.0 semi-auto.

perfection and anodized in multiple color options. KAPP has added every Autococker accessory KAPP produces, including their Tear Drop V2.0 drop-forward, F.A.T. Ram and KXS barrel; and all of this for $749.00 (MSRP). Reflex Autocockers are timed and ready to air up right out of the box with CO_2 or compressed air. Kapp says you just add your tank, fill the hopper and go play some ball!

The Kapp Reflex Autococker also includes a Hogue wrap-around grip and Torpedo in-line regulator.

KINGMAN

If it's a Spyder, it is a Kingman. This California company has named its entire line Spyders – Spyder Victor, Spyder Sport, Spyder Xtra and so on. These markers range from simple but solid paint flingers like the $79.95 (MSRP)

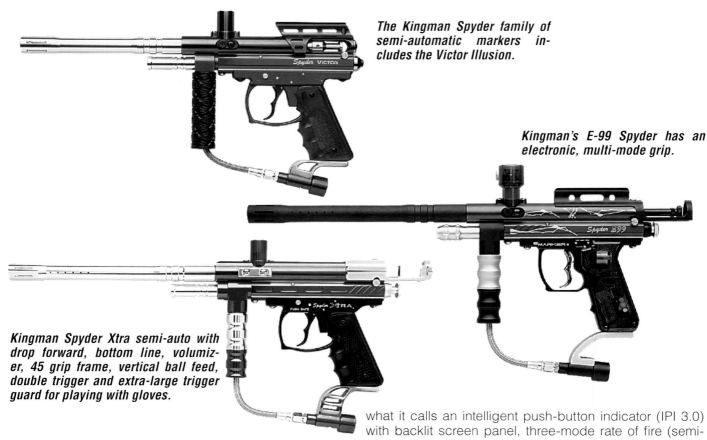

The Kingman Spyder family of semi-automatic markers includes the Victor Illusion.

Kingman's E-99 Spyder has an electronic, multi-mode grip.

Kingman Spyder Xtra semi-auto with drop forward, bottom line, volumizer, 45 grip frame, vertical ball feed, double trigger and extra-large trigger guard for playing with gloves.

Spyder Victor to well-proportioned electronic markers with digital LEDs. Kingman's specialty is "outsourcing" their markers to the Orient where high-quality markers can be built relatively inexpensively.

For instance, the Spyder Electra Digital LED has a large-format display, one-touch mode adjustment and battery-power indicator. The reactive response, double trigger, velocity and rate of fire (semi-auto, 3-round or 6-round burst and full auto) are all adjustable and the safety is illuminated. You can recharge the battery with this marker's external port.

Mechanically, all of the Electras have an anti-double-feed system, in-line expansion chamber with fore-grip, matte-finish anodizing, drop-forward with bottom-line setup and a steel braided air hose. In addition, look for a low-pressure chamber, deluxe sight rail, vertical ball feed and quick-disconnect pin.

The Electra DX (MSRP of $329.95) comes with a two-piece, 14-inch tournament-grade barrel and in-line regulator with gauge. A Java 9.6-volt rechargeable battery, battery charger and spare parts are included. Kingman says the battery can be recharged as many as 700 times before it needs to be replaced. Spyder Electra Digital LED markers operate on CO_2 or compressed air.

Kingman's new Spyder E99 Avant ratchets the price of an electronic marker down even further, and it is available in black or green. Kingman's electronics are based on

what it calls an intelligent push-button indicator (IPI 3.0) with backlit screen panel, three-mode rate of fire (semi-auto, burst and full-auto), low battery indicator, Java 9.6 battery and charger.

Additional features include push-button take-down pin, tear-drop extended drop-forward, low-pressure chamber see-through, vertical adjustable ball feed, matte-finish barrel and receiver, external battery charging port, reactive trigger response, double trigger, fore grip with expansion chamber, adjustable velocities with a maximum 14 bps rate of fire, steel-braided bottom line air supply and 45 grip. It is a lot of electronic marker for the MSRP of $249.95.

The $349.95 (MSRP) AMG has a multi-mode electronic LCD trigger frame with tournament lock, the standard four firing modes (semi-auto, full-auto, 3-shot burst and 6-shot burst), adjustable aluminum reactive double-trigger response, smooth in-line expansion chamber, regulator with mini-gauge, vertical ball feed, deluxe sight rail, drop-forward, quick-disconnect system, velocity adjuster, new anti-double feed and a Java 9.6-volt rechargeable battery with recharging unit.

Most of the markers Kingman sells, of course, are non-electronic. A quality marker such as the Compact SE (Special Edition) retails for $269.95 (MSRP) and comes with a rubber-covered 45 grip, deluxe sight rail, turbulence-dispelling Venturi bolt, dual air source, anti-double feed, two-finger trigger with extra-light pull, power feed, hard-line hose, velocity adjuster and muzzle-brake barrel. This marker is splash-anodized green.

Aaron, Larry and Eileen Alexander are the heart of AKA, the "Low Pressure Experts." You can find them busily making repairs, servicing their customers and upgrading markers at most major tournaments.

PALMERS PURSUIT SHOP

Glenn and Craig Palmer specialize in building interesting, custom markers and paintball accessories. Craig notes that his father built the first functional gravity-fed semi-automatic marker ever made for paintball, which Glenn named "Camille." Today, markers like the fascinating all-brass double-barrel "Nasty" Typhoon set a standard for innovation and interest that is truly out there on the cutting edge of hand-built gaming products. The Blazer and the Houndstooth give us a feeling for the custom potential in a marker.

The Palmer Blazer ($430.00 with a vertical ball feed and about $800.00 fully tricked out with Palmer upgrades) is a closed-bolt, pneumatic, auto-cocking semi-auto. All-internal gas channels eliminate external hoses. It is 100 percent made in the U.S. from aircraft-grade aluminum with stainless steel and brass internals for corrosion resistance. Its black receiver is hard anodized for maximum durability. The compact Blazer weighs 2 pounds and measures 15.5 inches with its 10.5-inch barrel. With what Palmer calls "maximum performance valving," the company says you can achieve 80 shots per ounce of CO_2 and it also runs very efficiently on high-pressure air.

The brass barrel for the Blazer is a slip-fit into the receiver, with a tight, virtually seamless fit, rather than being screwed or clip-locked in place. A small set-screw clamps the barrel down securely. Craig Palmer says the "rotatable barrel allows for true barrel matching and the threadless design allows for perfect barrel matching." The ridges of this "wedgit" system stop "rollout" and eliminate the need for changing barrels to accommodate different size paintballs.

The Blazer's cycling system is familiar to players who know the Autococker and Palmer's Typhoon. Nevertheless, the Blazer's all-internal design requires a unique arrangement. The trigger has two separate functional stages. The first part of the pull lowers the sear and releases the hammer. The spring-loaded hammer strikes, opening an exhaust valve and allowing CO_2 or compressed air to flow through the bolt and fire the paintball. The second half of the trigger pull switches a 4-Way valve to redirect low-pressure (regulated down by the pressure regulator) gas from the back to the front of a pneumatic cylinder (the "ram"), which draws back the bolt and hammer to start the cycle over again.

Velocity adjustment is simple. As with most markers, it is achieved by increasing or decreasing tension on the mainspring behind the hammer. An Allen screw in the plug at the back of the lower receiver adjusts tension on this spring.

Palmer says that the speed of the marker depends on speed of your finger on the swing trigger, but that it is "blazing fast." The Blazer operates on CO_2 or HPA (compressed air). It features a sight rail, easy-dial speed adjuster and vertical ASA.

The Palmer Houndstooth is a custom-built pump gun that is designed to operate on CO2. It features a brass Palmer barrel (spiral venting is an option), and for only $250, you can order this wall-banger in a double-barrel configuration. On the Internet, one reviewer liked the light, crisp trigger pull, but felt that the pump stroke was a bit stiff, perhaps because his marker was new and he was not totally familiar with it or perhaps because of the thick O-rings placed around the bolt that prevented any hint of air escape … which is good. But in a hot shoot-out, such uncorrected stiffness could cause some inaccuracy and slower shooting, and if you did not fully cycle or push the pump arm forward, you could get a lower velocity ball. When told of that reported pump stroke stiffness, Craig Palmer commented that the new marker might only have needed some lubrication!

PMI

Founded in 1982 by Jeff Perlmutter and David Freeman, Pursuit Marketing Inc. (PMI) is one of the world's top distributors of paintball gear and the exclusive distributor of balls from R.P. Scherer. They also market a line of widely popular markers in their Piranha family. We have selected a high-end Piranha electronic marker, the Pro E, a mid-range non-electronic marker, the EXT Pro G3,

The tournament photo team from Pocono Whitewater Photos was there from the beginning, l-r: Jesse Rhyden, Cleo Fogal and Tom Lesisko. "I began doing whitewater rafting photography for my family's outfitting business in 1982," Cleo Fogal says. "When we added a paintball field, Skirmish USA in 1983, we added paintball photos. I am extremely lucky to be able to make a living doing something as creative, challenging and active as paintball photography. The big trick is to keep paint off the camera."

Paintball photographer Cleo Fogal (front and center) and "some of my main shooters" from Skirmish USA paintball park in Jim Thorpe, Pennsylvania. Don't even think you can't play paintball after you are old enough to drive alone! Front (l-r): Jesse Rhyder, Lee Conklin, Cleo Fogal, Paul Fogal, Patty Fisher and Tom Lesisko. Rear: Bernie Mack, Brian Back, Bob Ford and Doug Edwards.

and one of their entry-level semi-autos, the Black Maxx, to show the range of their lineup.

First, PMI currently considers the Piranha Pro E 2k3 ($319.95 MSRP) semi-auto, a pneumatic re-cock tournament-grade electronic marker, as the "flagship" of the Piranha line. It has multi-mode settings: semi-auto, a burst of 3, 6 or 9 shots and full-auto. This Piranha comes with a 12-inch interchangeable, threaded aluminum barrel with spiral porting and Piranha/Spyder compatible threading. The marker body is made from corrosion-resistant aerospace-grade aluminum, and it is coated with a wear-resistant Teflon finish on all internal parts. The 2k3 is named after the CNC-milled body.

Besides enabling multiple shooting modes, the electronics package has multiple alarm settings, a timer, shot counter and LCD display. It features an electro-mechanical multi-mode aluminum double-trigger frame with an on/off switch, powered by one 9-volt rechargeable battery. This trigger allows up to 12 shots per second.

The DSR in-line adjustable regulator and micro-gauge work together to make an efficient low-pressure marker. The bottom-line adapter is designed for Pure Air energy gas systems and the Piranha Pro E operates on CO_2 or compressed air. Pure Energy vertical regulator, drop-forward and low-pressure internals are also features of this marker, which has an overall length of 21 inches and a weight of 3 pounds.

The non-electronic version of the Pro E is the EXT Pro G3 ($249.95 MSRP), which also weighs in at about 3 pounds. The EXT Pro G3 is a semi-automatic blowback that operates on either CO_2 or compressed air. Its 11-inch barrel is compatible with Piranha/Spyder threading. Overall, the EXT Pro G3 measures 21 inches and it is available in silver, red, blue or green fade.

PMI says its $74.95 (MSRP) Black Maxx semi-auto

blowback is an excellent entry-level marker. It operates on either CO_2 or compressed air. Its 9-inch removable barrel comes with Piranha/Spyder compatible threading. With the included flush cocking system and removable Venturi-style bolt, adjustable sight, instant field-strip pin, bottom-line setup and double trigger, it measures 17 1/8 inches long with the stock barrel. The Black Maxx weighs about 2 pounds.

POWERLYTE

The patent-pending Powerlyte Hybrid P is a low-pressure, closed-bolt, pneumatic marker with a machined timing plate for ultra-fine tuning, high-end pneumatics, micro-honed bolt and hammer chambers, a Delrin-sleeved stainless steel hammer, Delrin bolt with quick pin, a balanced valve and an upgraded internal ram system. Powerlyte President Paul Fernandez says this internal system places the ram inside the body and connects it directly to the back block, eliminating the need for a front block and pump rod.

You can purchase the Hybrid P in black, blue or red for $599.95 from Powerlyte. Each marker comes standard with an Axis hinge frame that is designed for smooth, fast trigger pull, adjustable forward and rearward trigger stops, interchangeable trigger styles and a flush mount safety. According to the Powerlyte Internet site at www.powerlyte.com, the Axis gives you dependable, near-electro-pneumatic speeds of 15 to 17 balls per second. Independently as an upgrade, the Axis costs $99.95 or $109.95 with sticky grips. A 12-inch one-piece Speedline barrel, also made by Powerlyte, is standard.

PSYCHOBALLISTICS (NPS)

Psychoballistics builds a classic pump-action marker and an inexpensive electronic semi-auto. The Delta 68 pump "assault pistol" (about $150.00) is available in black, blue or silver. It holds 10 rounds and is powered by traditional 12-gram CO_2 cartridges. It has a 45-grip frame with sticky grips and the aluminum frame is bead-blast finished.

The electronic Silver Bullet semi-auto is also available in blue, black or silver. Capable of a 13-bps rate of fire, the electronics are housed in the 45-style custom trigger frame. It has three button-controlled firing modes: semi-auto, 3-ball burst and full-auto. The Silver Bullet comes with a fore grip with regulator, custom sight rail, Delrin bolt, low-pressure chamber, quick-disconnect pin, vertical feed port and all-new-style ball detents. The velocity is adjusted at the rear and can be locked in place. Psychoballistics gives a two-year warranty with the purchase of this $169.95 marker (9-18-03 on *www.888paintball.com*), which, for $30.00, can be upgraded to include an LCD readout.

SMART PARTS

Few companies have the reputation for quality and precision on an international scale that Smart Parts enjoys. Their 2003 Shocker is considerably lighter and smaller than earlier versions. The Shocker is an open-bolt, seal-forward marker. Seal Forward Technology (SFT) is unique to the 2003 Shocker and allows the open-bolt operation while still having the breech seal a split second before the ball is fired, like a closed-bolt marker. By sealing the breech before the ball is fired, Smart Parts claims, the Shocker is able to have the accuracy and trajectory of a traditional closed-bolt setup, but also the rates of fire and simplicity of an open bolt. Rate of fire and air efficiency have been improved also.

The Shocker 2003 is 8 inches long without a barrel and 6 inches high. It weighs about 2 pounds without a barrel or tank. Operating pressure is 180 to 220 psi and it operates on CO_2 or compressed air. Smart Parts says the Shocker

2003 is capable of a 20 bps rate of fire or 1200 balls per minute, but the mode of fire is strictly semi-automatic, tournament-legal only. The power source is a common 9-volt battery for the Shocker's Vision Eye in Vision mode. The trigger is fully adjustable.

SYSTEM X

One of the larger, but quieter companies, System X has recently upgraded its AutoCocker-style marker line of the X8, Vengeance Type X ($649.95 MSRP), Attitude and Vengeance Pro 2.0 to include the new Xonik Electronic Marker. The Base System X Vengeance was $399.99 on *www.paintball-discounters.com* on 9-18-03.

The new System X Xonik electronic-frame 68-caliber semi-auto is based on the success of its predecessor, the Vengeance Pro 2.0. In several fade color combinations with a two-piece barrel and an in-line regulator, it is governed by the electronic Xonik board in the trigger frame. Included as a stock item on the Xonik marker, the electronics by the same name will allow a 16-round rate of fire and they are available as an upgrade kit on any AutoCocker. The Xonik features an LED and adjustable trigger that allows classic or semi-auto firing modes. The Xonik (and the upgrade kit) comes with an anti-chop sensor eye that is adjustable for sensitivity. An eye cover and battery are included.

TIPPMANN

Tippmann markers are considered rugged and capable. The A-5 is their new 68-caliber, open-bolt blowback semi-auto factory equipped with Tippmann's patented, automatic Cyclone Feed System that increases your firepower without a battery because it is powered by your air system. The faster you shoot, the faster it feeds, whether your power source is CO_2, nitrogen or compressed air. The A-5's base

Here is Tippmann's top-of-the-line A-5 semi-auto (with hopper).

Tippmann's 98 Custom rigged for long-range, precision shooting, perhaps for a sniper.

This is a Tippmann Pro/Carbine.

cycle rate is about 13 bps, but the Cyclone is capable of a firing rate beyond that when combined with a Response Trigger and E-Bolt Electronic system. These upgrades allow the A-5 to fire faster than gravity can feed balls to the chamber, but the Cyclone pre-chambers balls in its star-shaped feed sprocket, which is linked to the air system. When you fire, the sprocket automatically chambers the next ball. Because the sprocket is linked to the firing cycle, the faster you fire, the faster the Cyclone feeds. And, since the balls are pre-chambered, you virtually eliminate chopping balls at high rates of fire.

The A-5 also features the high performance CVX Valve, a built-in vertical tank adapter, adjustable front grip, ultra-light trigger, MP5-style adjustable rear sight, braided stainless steel gas line, internal linkage arm and external velocity adjustment. The A-5 will accept the E-Grip electronic kit, Response Trigger kit, Comp-Air kit and Double Trigger kit. The front cocking knob allows for a fully enclosed receiver to protect it from the elements. With a "no-tool" field-strip feature, the A-5 is easy to clean and maintain. The 8.5-inch micro-honed barrel is removable, and the overall length is 20 inches without a tank. The A-5 weighs 3.5 pounds, and although Tippmann suggests a base price of $369.00, you can buy it in black at *www. paintball-discounters.com* (5-16-03) for $219.75 or

$269.99 if you equip it with the Response Trigger.

The A-5 can also be purchased as a kit that includes a hopper, spare tank O-ring, cleaning cable, Allen wrenches, marker lube, barrel plug and owner's manual. The 9-ounce tank is optional.

The 98 Custom is Tippmann's bread and butter CO_2 marker. It is a 68-caliber open-bolt blowback semi-auto that can retail anywhere from $119.77 for the base model in black (*www.xpaintball.com* 5-16-03) to as much as $445.95 when upgrades like the Response Trigger, Flatline Barrel and Electronic kits are added.

The 98 Custom has a rep as a very reliable first-timer's marker with its 660 rounds per minute rate of fire. The 98 is 19.63 inches long (with the standard barrel, but no tank) and weighs about 3 pounds. Tippmann includes a hopper, spare tank O-ring, cleaning cable, Allen wrenches, marker lube, barrel plug and owner's manual. A 9-ounce tank is optional.

Tippmann says the 98's large, high-performance CVX Valve gives maximum output in varied weather conditions. The Hyper Shot Trigger System has a 3-pound trigger pull. The rear sight is adjustable.

The 98 Custom has a vertical grip for comfort and stability. The forearm grip is also removable to accept vertical mounts for expansion chambers for a vertical tank. Other features include a 45-grip frame with custom rubber grips, a quick-release feed elbow for easy cleaning, braided stainless steel gas line, internal linkage arm, external velocity adjustment screw and a quick-thread, micro-honed barrel.

The older Pro/Carbine is a 68-caliber open-bolt blowback semi-automatic powered by CO_2 that cycles about 7 balls per second. It's 10.5-inch micro-honed, ported barrel is threaded and removable and its overall length is less than 21 inches. Without a tank, it weighs about 2.5 pounds. Online at *www.paintballgear.com* (5-17-03) the Pro/Carbine cost $144.75. With your purchase, Tippmann includes a hopper, spare tank O-ring, cleaning cable, Allen wrenches, marker lube, barrel plug and owner's manual.

Built off the 68-Carbine line, the Pro/Carbine maintains the more consistent CVX Valve for changing weather conditions and the 45 grip gives you the ability to customize. The receiver is also modifiable to convert to a vertical gas line setup or expansion chamber. The forearm grip from the earlier Pro-Lite makes cleaning easy. Also, the forearm has more strength to accommodate larger hoppers. The Pro/Carbine comes with a braided stainless steel gas line, quick-release, rear sight, velocity-adjustment screw and bright dip finish.

Tippmann's 68-caliber slide-action CO_2 pump is the SL-68 II. It has an 11-inch barrel and measures 17.25 inches. At a little over 2 pounds without a tank, the SL-68 costs $109.99 (*www.paintball-discounters.com* 5-17-03) online despite Tippmann's $195.00 suggested retail price. Tippmann includes a spare tank O-ring, Allen wrenches and owner's manual.

The SL-68 II is made of solid-cast aluminum with non-corrosive internals and the valve's cup seal is guaranteed for life. The breech is incorporated into the receiver for easy barrel cleaning and the velocity-adjustment screw is accessible by the front bolt for quick adjustments. Other features include a short pump stroke, micro-honed barrel and a built-in rear sight.

VIEWLOADER

Viewloader is now part of the Brass Eagle paintball family. Their 68-caliber Genesis Surge df II is an open-bolt blowback semi-automatic marker with a field-strip pin

Viewloader Genesis Surge df II custom-grade semi-auto with regulated drop-forward bottom-line adapter.

A Viewloader Prodigy E-Grip semi-auto.

The Viewloader Genesis II semi-auto paints the opposition at a max of 5 balls/ second. The field-strip pin on top allows one-step, easy-pull, field-strip cleaning.

for easy cleaning and maintenance, an aerospace-grade aluminum alloy receiver with custom surge-green pattern, a self-locking velocity adjustment, direct feed, two-panel contour grip, double-

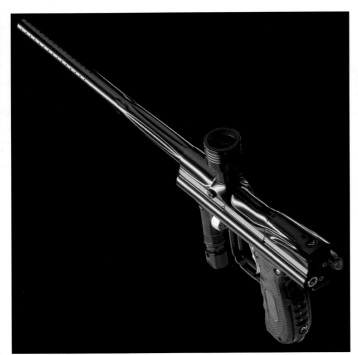

The Angel from England's WdP is the most expensive marker available in the world right out of the box; its reputation for accuracy, speed and reliability support the price.

Looking for the halo! Close-up of the fore-end of an Angel.

WdP ANGEL MARKERS

When you talk about paintball markers that retail for more than $1000, markers that most users agree are actually worth that much money, the Angel line of WdP markers from England has to be on top of the list. WdP has a reputation for not only high-quality marker performance, but for treating its customers well. That's good because today's tricked-out Angels are edging up toward $2000 – each!

The Angel Speed was offered for $999.99 on *www.paintball-discounters.com* in September 2003. For this amount of dough, you should – and you do – get a pretty good loaf. This electronic marker operates on a 4.8-volt metal-hydride rechargeable battery that WdP claims is good for 100,000 shots. A new Angel Speed includes a battery charger. The included software has five rate-of-fire settings in semi-automatic and other indicators including the Angel Sensi Load Detection System. WdP says you can achieve a rate of fire of 30 bps if you work the electronics just right, but in actuality, 20 bps is as fast as you will get … and that's plenty fast enough.

The Angel Speed is a low-pressure operator and WdP says the current model uses a third of the gas of previous Angels. That means one-third less force is applied by the bolt to the ball, which, experiencing less dynamic stress, should have a cleaner, faster and more accurate flight. This reduced-gas operating system is more efficient and WdP says will not affect rate of fire. The working pressure is 180 to 350 psi while increased porting delivers double the previous gas flow to the bolt. The new bolt is 20 percent more efficient and this typically raises velocity by 40 fps at the same working pressure.

Out of its nicely padded box, WdP says, you can expect to achieve up to 1450 shots at 290 fps from a 68-cu/in, 4500-psi tank.

Introduced originally in 2002, the Angel IR3 costs $1450 (MSRP for black or silver), but is $1399.99 at *www.paintball-discounters.com* (9-03-03). This 68-caliber semi-auto low-pressure shooter with its trademarked 90-degree space frame is really packed with features. Indeed, it has been called a "true Freestyle machine" for die-hard

finger trigger, laser engraving and micro gauge. An expansion chamber and volumizer are built in.

Viewloader's Onyx Regulated Drop Forward design improves balance, increases cylinder clearance and enhances the marker's compact profile. It contains an adjustable regulator and micro-gauge. The Player's Kit includes a 200-count hopper, 9-ounce tank, squeegee and cable, barrel plug and goggle system.

This made-in-Taiwan marker operates on CO_2, nitrogen or compressed air and will shoot a safe 5 bps. The barrel is 10 inches long, factory ported and fluted, making the marker 18.5 inches in length and under 3 pounds in weight. Online at *www.cnejs-hunting-fishing.com* (5-21-03), the Viewloader Genesis Surge df II costs $153.99.

The new, electronic Prodigy E-Grip semi-auto has stepped up the rate of fire to 420 bps and is a little shorter and lighter. The Player's Kit includes an electronic 12-volt 200-count loader, 9-ounce tank, squeegee and cable, barrel plug and goggle system. Viewloader says this E-Grip marker is "value-priced," but includes a field-strip pin for easy cleaning and maintenance, a lightweight aerospace-grade aluminum-alloy receiver, a self-locking velocity adjustment, welded vertical feed port, two-panel electronic grip, double-finger trigger, laser engraving and redesigned top-cocking bolt.

The VL Prodigy E-Grip features a bottom-line constant-air cylinder adapter and its custom-contoured electronic grip has an LED on/off indicator. The E-Grip requires one 9-volt battery, which is not included.

paintball players because of its adjustable mechanics to match individual shooting styles and fully programmable electronic options. WdP says the IR3 is "smaller, lighter and faster."

When you get your IR3 home, you are going to be impressed. The 44-page, four-color glossy manual is well illustrated with exploded diagrams and reference charts. (The charts for converting things like gas and pressure from metric to the old English foot-pound system of weights and measures we still use in the U.S. are especially helpful!) Your new purchase also includes the ported WdP .690-inch (inside diameter) Infinity barrel, vertical regulator, spare seals and feed gate, a container of WdP Love Juice lubricant, a sock-style barrel cover and your air hose and fittings. If you purchase the Angel Air system, all fittings, mounts and screws are included, too. Here is a list of important IR3 features:

1. Between the grip frame and the receiver, WdP's COPS (Crystal Operated Paint Sensor) is designed to prevent dry fires. The IR3 is designed to shoot any color (or multi-color) paintball. It is unaffected by sunlight or weather and has an anti-double-ball feed. This small piezoelectric strip rests below a plastic pin that barely extends into the bottom of the breech. When a paintball drops into the IR3, the impact of the ball on the pin transfers the energy to the sensor, which converts it to a tiny electric current that is fed by wires into the circuit board. Thus, the IR3 can be set up to not fire until a ball is fully in the breech. This prevents misfires and balls that are chopped from firing when they are partially fed.

2. No external components or wiring.

3. Lightweight Delrin bolt.

4. The trigger can be positioned in three different pivot points, but it comes shipped in the rearmost mounting hole. You get to choose what feels best for you. Both forward and rearward trigger movements are easily adjustable with the two setscrews already installed. Thus, you can change from the approximately 5-mm pull to something much shorter if desired, the old "hair trigger" trick. The latest model of the IR3 has an opti-mechanical trigger. When you pull the trigger, you don't trip a mechanical switch. Instead, you break the beam of a tiny infrared circuit to fire the marker.

5. A vertical grip and not the conventional 45 grip found on most markers and, indeed, on earlier Angels. WdP figures most individuals will shoot the IR3 with an air tank resting against their shoulder, and in this position, a vertical grip is actually much easier to handle and more effective to operate than the 45 style, which slants back toward the shooter. With the grip rounded at the bottom, Angel users have actually found this to be an excellent and practical factory upgrade.

6. The Space Frame is contoured for best palm-to-frame contact and fitted with a knobby "Skin Grip"

that has an ultra-high coefficient of friction (it won't slip out of your hot, sweaty hands). Delivers improved ambidextrous firing ergonomics.

7. The patent-pending Gated Feed offers unidirectional ball feed for resistance-free entry into the feed tube. It prevents ball re-entry from the receiver back into the feed neck when the marker is inverted (or when you are lying on your side) with a tiny plastic ring and three arms that will only bend to let balls down, not back up. (Safety Note: Up to three balls are held secure in a ready to fire position by this armature system, even when the loader is removed. Consequently, the barrel must be checked and blocked or plugged when not in play.)

8. The LCD screen allows scrolling messages including a maintenance advice system.

9. This part is very cool. The IR3 permits multi-level marker-to-marker communication for wireless programming, servicing and software upgrades. You can customize IR3 settings using your palm pilot or even download settings and program them to your IR3.

10. It comes with a rechargeable metal-hydride 6-volt battery and charging unit.

11. The rate of fire is adjustable to 20 bps. Most of the 26 advertised modes of fire are actually disabled although WdP does not advertise this: "ASTM Approved semi-auto firing modes (Extra Firing Modes Activated Where Permitted)."

12. Features a dual-menu computer interface. Simple external setup and adjustment of non-critical control parameters is achieved via three color-coded buttons on the frame.

13. The IR3 circuit board is encapsulated in a plastic anti-tamper shell inside the grip. The IR3 programs are protected by "rolling encryption" technology, which makes hacking the settings very difficult.

14. The non-adjustable electronic total-shot counter is critical to the IR3's service announcement system. It tells you when it's time for recommended maintenance. After 8000 shots, for example, the first time the IR3 is set to SAFE the display scrolls the message "OIL SERVICE" to remind you it's time to oil the seals. The IR3 also displays a greeting to its new owner the first time it is used. Following the counters is the ID number of the circuit board (also not adjustable).

15. Adjustable electronic activation of the hopper motor.

16. The included fast charger plugs into a car's cigarette lighter and into the back of the grip frame. When the power switch is activated, the IR3's LCD indicates that it is charging the internal, high-capacity nickel-metal-hydride battery.

17. The infrared emitter is used to send and receive data with other IR3s. On a team using all IR3s, the captain can set timer values for specific plays

and then beam the settings to the rest of the team. This way, everyone gets a synchronized signal to make their move!

18. The firing-mode menu features 26 total options, but the only one available in the U.S. is ASTM mode, "SEMI" or semi-automatic with a maximum rate of fire of 20 balls per second. ROF is adjustable from 2 to 20 bps, useful for game handicapping, for example, or to keep from outpacing a hopper that does not feed at higher rates.

The advanced Angel IR3 C+C (Coloured and Carved) silver sold for $1750 (red, blue, green, champagne – dust or fade) or $1499.99 depending on your options on *www.paintball-discounters.com* in September 2003. The C&C version of the IR3 includes an Intellifeed port on the sight rail (less for mounting a sight than to provide access inside), which can be used for communication between the marker and hopper.

WORR GAMES

Bud Orr's company Worr Games Products (WGP) is an institution and his trademarked Autocockers or 'Cockers are much imitated. The 68-caliber Orr-acle Autococker can be found online for $849.75 in manual or $1249.00 in electronic mode (on *www.paintball-discounters.com* on 8-7-03). The Orr-acle is a closed-bolt semi-automatic marker that operates only on HPA, although its operating pressure is 230 psi. It will cycle at 16 bps. The standard barrel is a 14-inch two-piece .689 autococker-threaded Kaner, which gives the 2.5-pound marker an overall length of 20.5 inches. It features a threaded vertical feed and both high-rise and low-rise feed tubes are included as are a Black Magic in-line regulator, STO Ram, and Orr-acle CT 3-way.

As an electronic marker, the Orr-acle frame holds the electronics, battery and sear-release mechanism. The 9-volt battery should be good, WGP says, for 20,000 shots. Up front, a manifold holds the electro-pneumatic solenoid valve that controls the ram. The timing of both is controlled electronically from the PCB. All parameters of the timing are adjustable. To get the highest rate of fire with least risk of chopped balls, WGP recommends fitting the E-Class marker with the small, reflective sensor eye that comes free with the frame.

The E-Blade frame allows you to adjust trigger travel and the magnetic strength of trigger return. The magnetic action can be set very snappy or very light.

The E-Blade comes fitted with custom rubber wrap-around grips. Every parameter of the electronic firing cycle is adjustable on the Orr-acle via the heads-up LED display: eye sensitivity, breach open and close time, sear-release time, over-lap times, cycle modes and so on. There is also provision for PC-upgradeable software installation and parameter adjustment via an optional Com-Cable.

The Black Magic Autococker is a closed-bolt pneumatic semi-automatic that will operate on CO_2, nitrogen or compressed air. It cost $699.00 at *www.*

iisports.com (8-8-03). It is an 18.5-inch marker with an 11-inch, two-stage stainless/aluminum barrel. The Black Magic weighs slightly over 3 pounds without a tank. Its features include a threaded feed port, lightened body, Orr-acle CT 3-way, Tickler regulator, STO Ram, enlarged valve system, Venturi bolt, 3-D flame drop-forward, Hinge frame with gem grips, 15-degree ASA and more.

WGP notes that CO_2 will power a pneumatic Autococker. Properly filled, a CO_2 tank is about 68 percent liquid. With a bottom-line setup, even if the marker is level, liquid CO_2 will flow into the marker, causing it to freeze and the velocity to spike up and down. CO_2 is generally not as clean as compressed air (or nitrogen) so it can cause more wear and tear on some of the marker's parts, especially in the in-line regulator and the cup seal. The worst that can happen as a result of CO_2 use is that the cup seal could develop a leak or the in-line regulator may begin to leak or spike. Problems from CO_2 use are usually easy fixes, though. In most cases, CO_2 will get the paintball job done, but if you want to tweak the most performance possible out of your 'Cocker, then compressed air is definitely the way to go.

The Outkast is a $489.95 (*www.paintballgear.com* on 8-7-03) 68-caliber pneumatic closed-bolt semi-automatic that operates on CO_2, nitrogen or compressed air. With modern machining cuts and a lightweight body, WGP says the Outkast is performance-oriented, but still affordable. It includes a vertical feed, hinge-frame trigger with 45 Gem grip, STO Ram, 3-Way and Black Magic adjustable front regulator. This marker is considered by many to be WGP's best deal for an excellent marker at a good price. A 12-inch two-piece autococker-threaded barrel is standard.

WGP's newest member of the Outkast Series is the Nightkast Autococker, a Worrblade-modified version of the Outkast. It debuts an innovative new style of anodizing, a half-gloss, half-matte finish. The Nightkast is available in black, blue and red. The STO Ram, Outkast adjustable front regulator and two-piece barrel are standard, as is the Ergo regulator, which delivers consistent pressure so you never have to worry about shoot down. The Worrblade includes a redesigned double-finger curved trigger and a large trigger guard for players who wear gloves. The Worrblade also features an integrated dovetail rail, universal with most rail-based air systems and air system adapters. With a vertical feed design, closed-bolt operation and reliable electronic rates of fire, the Nightkast is accurate and fast. It carries a MSRP of $1025.00.

The $499.99 (*www.xtremz.com* on 8-7-03) 68-caliber Flatliner is another pneumatic closed-bolt semi-automatic that operates on CO_2, nitrogen or compressed air. Its standard barrel is a Tippmann Flatliner with Flatline barrel mounting for backspin, extra in-flight stability and greater distance and accuracy. The Flatliner Autococker weighs 3.5 pounds. The Flatliner features a vertical-feed design with hinge-frame trigger, 45 grip, in-line regulator and one-piece 3-Way. Velocity adjuster included.

Designed by Jeff Orr, the new 68-caliber VF Tactical 'Cocker (expect to pay about $675) was made with the

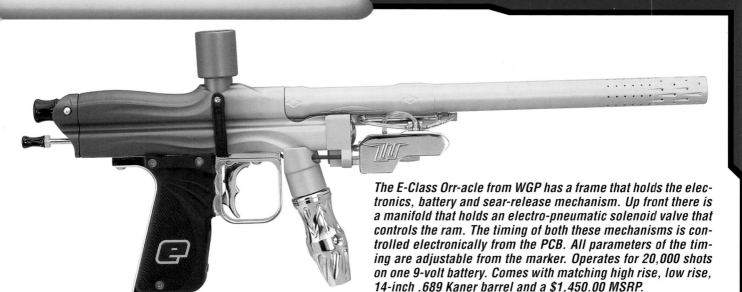

The E-Class Orr-acle from WGP has a frame that holds the electronics, battery and sear-release mechanism. Up front there is a manifold that holds an electro-pneumatic solenoid valve that controls the ram. The timing of both these mechanisms is controlled electronically from the PCB. All parameters of the timing are adjustable from the marker. Operates for 20,000 shots on one 9-volt battery. Comes with matching high rise, low rise, 14-inch .689 Kaner barrel and a $1,450.00 MSRP.

scenario game and recreational player in mind. It features the same closed-bolt system found on all WGP 'Cockers and includes the new VF-T front block, ergonomically designed for better hand placement, and the VF Tactical Shroud with rail system. Additional accessory rails are available, but with the standard rail, you can add an optional M-3 Tactical Illuminator by Streamlight. Or, with the optional rails, you can add a laser sight and infrared lighting system. Features include: custom milling, all-Delrin bolt with O-rings, WGP curved trigger, Outkast adjustable front regulator, Black Magic Barrel and pull pin.

Special WGP Marker Note: If you continuously break paint in any Autococker, check to see where the ball is breaking. If there is little or no paint in the bolt or breech area, chances are that the paint is too large for the barrel. There is nothing wrong with your Autococker; the paint just doesn't fit the barrel. Remove the barrel from the marker body and insert a ball into the rear of the barrel after cleaning it thoroughly. Try to blow the ball out of the front of the barrel. If you can't do this, there is probably nothing wrong with the marker … or with you! You just need to change either your barrel or your paint. If paint is breaking in the bolt or breech area, you need to adjust your feed system.

ZAP MARKERS

Zap offers some pretty hot paintballs and two lines of markers, electronic and semi-automatic. It also has a 12-gram pump marker. (All prices listed are from *www.paintballgear.com* on 8-19-03.)

Zap's five electronic markers all feature vertical loading. The competition/tournament-grade Reactor ($159.75) has an electronic double-trigger frame with double trigger and LCD display with mode options (semi-automatic, multi, nitro and automatic), shot counter, game timer and battery status. Rates of fire are adjustable with the top being about 11 bps. An expansion chamber with mini-gauge, drop-forward, volumizer, two-piece custom barrel, sight rail and adjustable sear are included.

The Zap Generator ($128.75) and Transformer ($99.75) markers are stepped-down versions of the top-of-the-line Reactor. (The new electronic aluminum-frame Zap-600 is about $250 online.)

In the non-electronic mode, the upper-end Zap offering is the top-loading semi-automatic blowback ZXS-500. It features an all-aluminum frame and barrel, volumizer, double trigger, fore-grip, drop-forward, wrap-around gel grip and will spit out balls at a rate of 8 per second. The ZXS-500 Kit includes a marker, goggle system, 200-round hopper and elbow, squeegee, dual holster with paint tubes, barrel plug and 9-ounce CO_2 cylinder. The new ZXS-555 also features a keyless velocity adjuster. The ZXS-555 Kit costs $189.99.

Zap's other semi-autos offer fewer features as you go down the line in price and some, like the ZXS-444, are built on a polymer frame.

The Zap ZXS-200 pump-action marker has an all-polymer frame and operates on a 12-gram cartridge in the grip. The ZXS-200 Kit ($59.99) includes the marker, goggles, squeegee, barrel plug and a small, 48-round hopper.

CHAPTER 12

MARKER UPGRADES AND ACCESSORIES FOR SPEED, ACCURACY AND COMFORT

L ike the $6-million-man, we can make you better. We can make you faster. We can make you more accurate. With upgrades!

Upgrades are after-market add-ons that make your marker better. Almost every part of your marker can be changed and improved, from the barrel to the bolt. You can add an electronics package and even pack up your gear and send it off for bright, flashy and personalized anodizing or have your name laser etched in the body. (And you thought they would never name a paintball marker after you!) Speaking of bodies, many high-end companies sell their markers as bodies only— without barrels, for instance—knowing that if you have enough moxie to buy one of their markers, you are smart enough to want specialty upgrades.

Here are a few of the many paintball companies that specialize in upgrades. Some are high-quality marker manufacturers and some are specialty manufacturers that only design and built regulators, for instance. So, enjoy and upgrade, upgrade, upgrade!

MANUFACTURER UPGRADES
AIRGUN DESIGNS (AGD)

In 2003, Airgun Designs released its new, all-aluminum main body called the ULE for UltraLight Engineering. Compatible with Automag, Minimag, RT Pro and E-Mag markers, the ULE main body was initially available in vertical-feed-only although AGD has planned to release a Warp Feed version. The $145.00 cost gives you a 54 percent savings in weight, by moving from stainless to

Scenario games feature 24-hour action, such as this lighted castle by night in Sherwood Forest (LaPorte, Indiana). You will see every kind of upgrade at a big game. Study them all and try them out if the owner is willing. This gives you a good basis for evaluating your own hard gear needs.

aluminum, and a variety of colors: black, red, pewter, purple and blue. The ULE main body's vertical-feed neck and ball detents are Angel-threaded, which allows you to select from a wide variety of aftermarket accessories, and the barrel interface uses popular Autococker threading.

Airgun Designs describes its aluminum X-Valve as a "hyper-fast recharging integrated regulator with Reactive Trigger technology." AGD says that because it fully recharges in .04 seconds, shootdown is a thing of the past and the achievable 26-rounds-per-second rate of fire is faster than you can pull the trigger!

The Reactive Trigger actually pushes your finger back after firing each shot, enabling you to easily reach much higher rates of fire as compared to the standard Mag valve. Consistent pressures inside the valve give you consistent velocities. The X-Valve system comes with the AGD Level 10 Superbolt upgrade. You need to remember that this system only operates on compressed air/nitrogen. This upgrade requires fine-tuning, and when first installed, you will need to turn up the ball velocity. It costs $225.00 from AGD if you turn in your complete old valve system and $325.00 if you do not.

The AGD "Level 10" replaces the stock bolt and power tube tip with a new 1.16-ounce stainless Superbolt II and power tube tip. With this kit, your Automag bolt should

bounce right off brittle tournament paint. The kits work on all AGD markers. The bolt operates through two phases, slow at first and then fast. The slow (four to six fps), low-pressure initial phase prevents chopping balls and it will not crack or bobble a ball waiting to enter the chamber. As the bolt starts initial travel, the vent in the piston moves past the power tube O-ring. The hole lets a miniscule amount of air through the power tube tip. If a ball is only partially in the breech, the slow-moving bolt stops on the ball, rather than chopping it and the power piston vent allows pressurized gas in the chamber to escape. Once enough air pressure escapes, the bolt spring pushes the bolt back to re-cock and the ball drops into the breech. The marker is once again set to fire. During acceleration, the end of the power piston moves completely past the power tube O-ring. This lets pressurized air flow into the power tube where it pushes against the larger diameter section in the middle of the power piston. The bolt accelerates to full speed (about 15 fps) and the valve goes to full power, loading the ball in the barrel, firing, and retracting the bolt. The faster acceleration stage allows the Superbolt II to maintain a high firing rate. This upgrade is just $85.00 from AGD's pro shop.

AGD says its Warp Feed was the world's first force-feed or pressure-feed system. Instead of relying on gravity

Airgun Designs (AGD) has a new, all-aluminum main body called ULE for UltraLight Engineering. Compatible with Automag, Minimag, RT Pro and E-Mag markers, the ULE main body was initially available in vertical feed only although AGD planned to release a Warp Feed version. ULE recognizes a 54 percent savings in weight by moving from stainless to aluminum. The ULE main body's vertical feed neck and ball detents are Angel-threaded, which allows you to select from a wide variety of aftermarket accessories, and the barrel interface uses popular Autococker threading.

to feed paint, the soft urethane wheels of the friction drive grip balls to gently push them from your loader into the marker's breech. A reduction gear allows balls to slip when finished feeding so a ball can't jam or crush. The Warp will feed paint faster than you can pull the trigger, more than 20 bps with 12-volt input, says AGD, and with an adjustable, flexible hose, you can position it and your loader away from the top to the side … or even the bottom of your marker. This feature can dramatically reduce your silhouette! The Warp is 6 inches long, weighs 15 ounces and operates on a 9-volt battery. Priced at $175, it is designed for the AGD E-Mag, but adapters are available from Pro Team Products for most markers.

A switch in AGD's Intelliframe intelligent electronic grip allows you to mount a roller micro-switch that activates with every trigger pull. This switch easily wires into your hopper so it agitates and feeds every time, too. In fact, it can run your AGD Warp Feed. AGD says it's "double trigger speed" for just $115.00. It requires a 9-volt battery.

The "Level 10" replaces the stock bolt and power tube tip with AGD's new 1.16-ounce stainless Superbolt II and power tube tip. With this kit, your Automag bolt should bounce right off brittle tournament paint. A slow, low-pressure initial phase prevents chopping or cracking balls. During acceleration, the end of the power piston moves past the power tube O-ring to let pressurized air flow into the power tube where it pushes against the larger diameter section in the middle of the power piston. The bolt accelerates and the valve goes to full power, loading the ball, firing and retracting the bolt. The faster acceleration stage allows the Superbolt II to maintain a high firing rate.

Airgun Design describes its aluminum X-Valve as a "hyperfast recharging integrated regulator with Reactive Trigger technology." Because it fully recharges in .04 seconds, shootdown is a thing of the past. Consistent pressures inside the valve give you consistent velocities.

The electronic Intelliframe grip from Airgun Designs can double your trigger finger's effectiveness for just $115.

AKA

"Are you tired of running out of air?" AKA's Aaron K. Alexander asks. With its low-pressure input of 150 to 250 psi, the AKA Tornado valve increases marker efficiency on the order of 2000+ shots per 20-ounce CO_2 tank. It can be used on CO_2, nitrogen or compressed air (must use a regulator). It is manufactured from high-quality, heat-treated stainless steel and comes with a lifetime warranty.

Many upgrades to paintball gear – electronic triggers, hoppers, special game timers – require batteries and it is a very good idea to take a fresh set to every game and to replace them occasionally, even if they seem to have power before you leave home.

The Lightning Bolt drastically increases focused airflow so your average ball velocity increase is 30 to 70 fps! It also allows for a reduction in operating pressures. It is offered in hard-anodized, nickel-plated aluminum or self-lubricating Delrin.

The AKA Mitey Max ensures that you have the air capacity needed to operate a low-pressure system (lower pressure, higher volume) by increasing air capacity more than 50 percent on 1997-style Autocockers. Easy installation replaces the front mounting block bolt. It is manufactured from heat-treated stainless steel for strength and safety and is available in bare or nickel-plated steel.

One of the keys to efficient low-pressure operation is a free-flowing, consistent air supply. The adjustable (zero to 700 psi with a top input pressure of 800 psi) Sidewinder regulator is designed for low-pressure operation and features a 360-degree, swiveling bottom cap. This allows the regulator to be set up in virtually any configuration. The Sidewinder also features three sizes of top caps and it works with CO_2 or HPA. This small regulator is 3.875 inches long and 1.125 inches in diameter with the swivel sleeve.

ALLEN

It is not necessary to let liquid CO_2 leak into the chamber of your marker to cut your shooting performance. Allen builds several expansion chambers, designed to give CO_2 the space and time to change from its liquid to its gaseous state. Its Force-Flow is designed with a seven-chamber internal system. The grip is cool, polished chrome, but comes with a removable rubber sleeve for a no-slip grip. The cost from Allen is $39.95. With a bottom-line adapter and fittings, expect to pay $54.95. A "multi-chamber" economy version is available for $27.95.

CENTERFLAG

CenterFlag manufactures an electronic grip called the HyperFrame. It is designed to replace the existing grip on popular Spyder, Piranha and AutoMag markers. These E-grip frames give you an extremely light trigger pull for a faster rate of fire so you can keep up with the other electronic markers on the field … without purchasing a whole new marker! Using an electronic grip with a light trigger pull also enhances your off-hand shooting technique (If you are right handed, your left hand is your off–hand.) and stops dreaded short-stroke from occurring when the battle heats up.

The HyperFrame operates on one 9-volt battery and features three modes of fire:

Semi: Currently the most common mode allowed in tournaments and during open-game play, the semi-auto mode allows you to shoot one paintball for each pull of the trigger. It can be programmed to shoot at a rate from one to 13 bps.

Burst: Allows you to shoot a string of three, four or five balls for each trigger pull. The rate at which this group is fired can also be programmed from one to 10 bps. If the trigger is released in mid-string, the marker stops shooting immediately.

Hyper: This unique mode allows the equivalent of full-automatic firing as long as the trigger is continuously pulled at a rate of five to six bps. It is adjustable from three to five shots per trigger pull at a rate from one to 10 bps.

The HyperFrame also has a countdown game timer and shot counter. The timer is easy to set from 10 seconds (Have you ever played a game that felt like it only took that long?) to 99 minutes and 59 seconds for scenario games. The timer starts without having to shoot a paintball simply by pulling the trigger with the safety on. When the timer is at zero or the game ends before time runs out, the timer can be started over again by pressing the Mode Set button, which will reset it to the last time that was programmed. The Shot Counter tells you how many times you have pulled the trigger. This function helps indicate expected battery life. The counter resets to zero when the battery is replaced, but it could (theoretically) go as high as 99,999! A standard 9-volt battery should allow about 15,000 shots.

The HyperFrame regulated solenoid pushes the sear to release the bolt. The amount of energy required to

This 3.5-pound Vertical Feed Autococker from Worr Games Products is equipped with a shroud to protect its delicate 3-Way air routing system. It is a closed-bolt semi-auto with a 12-inch barrel that will operate on CO_2 or HPA.

push the sear will vary from one marker to the next. When less energy is required to push the sear, battery power is conserved, giving you more shots per battery cell. To increase or decrease the amount of energy going to the solenoid, use the Service Mode and set it to the shortest charge time that will release the bolt. Note: Battery life can vary depending on your bolt-to-sear match-up, battery cell shelf life, O-rings in the on/off assembly and your Service Mode settings. If the battery is disconnected for 15 minutes, settings reset to zero.

The safety on/off is located behind the plastic grips. This mechanical safety button locks the sear, but does not disable the electronics. The on/off safety button is designed to prevent the marker from discharging in the event that the trigger is inadvertently pulled or the unit is bumped, dropped or slammed down. Note: Purchasers of HyperFrames, or those from other manufacturers, need to know that no manufacturer will accept responsibility or liability if the safety on/off is modified or changed in any way outside the factory.

CenterFlag says that if you have been "itching for a new electronic marker, but don't want to give up your current marker, or can't afford a new, overpriced E-marker," they offer a low cost alternative ($500.00 from CenterFlag).

Worr's VF Tactical in black looks like a futuristic weapon out of "Star Wars" and can be equipped with an under-the-barrel flashlight like the M-3 Tactical Illuminator from Streamlight for scenario-game operations at night.

DARK HORIZON

Dark Horizon (*www.darkhorizoncorp.com*) machines aftermarket titanium hammers for paintball markers. Their replacement hammer for Spyder and Java markers costs $39.95 from Dark Horizon, which says it is 56 percent of the weight of a stock steel hammer. No extra drilling or machining is required to make the upgrade, either. "The strength of steel at about half the weight!"

But why replace the stock hammer? Dark Horizon says a polished titanium surface is almost as slick as the surface of a non-stick Teflon skillet. This lightweight hammer weight reduces cycle noise and kick while at the same time increasing gas efficiency and conservation, accuracy and cycle rate. "Our hammer," says Dark Horizon, "costs less and weighs less than competitive stainless hammers. The surface is slicker and more resistant to rust

than plated stainless steel replacement hammers."

Titanium, notes Dark Horizon, is the 22nd element in the periodic table and the fourth most abundant metal in the earth's crust. Its alloys have strengths comparable with alloy steels while the weight is only 56 percent that of steel. In addition, the corrosion resistance of titanium alloys is far superior to aluminum or even stainless steel. Titanium's additional properties include: low weight and density, high fatigue strength, non-magnetic, non-toxic, non-allergenic and, of course, it is fully bio-compatible.

According to Dark Horizon, the most frequently asked question is: Will I be able to shoot 13 bps more accurately if I replace my stock bolt with a titanium bolt?

"We don't make a lot of claims about the increase in speed our lighter hammer will allow," the technical folks at Dark Horizon write, "because there are so many

Kingman's E-99 Spyder has an electronic, multi-mode grip. The electronics in this marker are a factory-installed upgrade to a popular top-of-the-line Spyder semi-auto.

other factors that come into play, but our calculations of the physics of the mass reduction alone would indicate your speeds would be about one-third faster. But, that is not the biggest advantage of the Dark Horizon titanium hammer. The marker operates smoother, quieter and doesn't bounce around nearly as much. That allows you to put more paint where you want it. Less bounce is a result of much less mass being slammed back and forth in the marker for each shot. The better the hammer, the bigger the improvement by going to titanium."

INDIAN CREEK (ICD)

The 2003 Grip Frame is a $98.00 (MSRP) upgrade with BushMaster-specific four-way adjustment. The trigger has three swing selections and the length of pull, actuation and spring tension are completely adjustable.

For $64.00 (MSRP), ICD's Complete Drop Forward System comes with both short and long extensions. The pinch-type adapter tightens on dovetail-mount regulators and the screw-in type allows you to adapt all other types of tank adapters and regulators that are not dovetail type.

For $79.95 (MSRP), you get a complete drop-forward system with an on/off ASA (tank adapter) including a gauge, so you can know what your pre-set tank is outputting for pressure, an elbow and macro-line hose.

KINGMAN

Kingman offers two styles of electronic trigger upgrades for its markers: the Sprint and the ESP. In black or chrome, the ESP is compatible with any Kingman semi-automatic marker with a Kingman #18A or #18B striker. The two styles of ESP are the Classic (multi-mode dip switch board with window) and Deluxe (multi-mode dip switch board with window and LCD). The ESP features three shooting modes (semi-auto, full-auto, 3-round burst and 6-round burst), reactive two-finger trigger response and adjustable pull, car charger, 9.6-volt rechargeable battery, external recharge and ESP striker bolt.

The lightweight Sprint polycarbonate electronic trigger frame is powered by the patented ESP system. Rate of fire is up to 13 shots per second and it is available in silver, red, blue, black and green. Markers equipped with the Sprint electronic trigger upgrade operate effectively on CO_2 or HPA.

Kingman marker upgrades include Regulator Kits

such as the $79.95 (MSRP) Compact. The kit includes a drop-forward, regulator, braided stainless steel hose line, tools and screws.

PALMER

The Pro-Touch Trigger custom trigger with inclusion of a two-finger trigger shoe involves fine-tuning the stock trigger on the Blazer and costs about $120.00, but it has led reviewers to swear that the shorter, lighter trigger pull that is then achieved is well worth the cost.

Palmer's Elliptically-Honed Barrel is a custom, 12-inch, spiral-ported match-honed Palmer barrel. The $72.00 (MSRP) upgraded brass barrel is nickel-plated on the outside. Palmer uses an elliptical tight-loose-tight honing pattern in the barrel to control, accelerate and again control the paintball before releasing it.

The Stabilizer in-line pressure regulator threads into the vertical ASA. It is essentially a Palmer Rock pressure regulator "beefed up" to put out a higher flow and handle higher pressures. The $95.00 (MSRP) Stabilizer ($105.00 with the quick disconnect) is known for its consistency and for keeping liquid CO_2 from spilling into the feed line. An anti-siphon tube is recommended for best results. It is available in several models to accommodate a wide variety of setup preferences.

TIPPMANN

The Double Trigger kit is a drop-in that replaces the single trigger and trigger guard on popular Tippmann markers. It includes a double trigger and a tournament-legal trigger guard. "Now," the Tippmann catalog says, "you can shoot all day long without fatigue." Tippmann suggests a price of $24.95 for the 98 Custom Double-Trigger Kit and $29.95 for the A-5 Kit. It's $15.95 for either at *www.ontopmarkers.com* (5-17-03).

Expansion chambers work well for markers using CO_2, Tippmann says, because by giving the liquid CO_2 from the tank extra space, chambers allow it to expand into a gas before it enters your marker. In this way, an expansion chamber fights inconsistency in velocity. No more drop-off of speed in cold weather or "velocity spikes" when it's hot. A good expansion chamber keeps your marker from freezing. The marker uses its propellant more efficiently and the internal O-rings and seals last longer. Tippmann's Vertical Expansion Chamber Kit is $59.95, but at *www.paintballgear.com* (5-17-03) the cost was only $32.95.

The Response Trigger System Kit increases trigger speed by resetting the trigger and sear with some of the excess gas during the firing sequence. This gas operates a cylinder behind the trigger, which does the resetting. The pressure of your finger on the trigger pulls it back to fire the next shot. Ball speed and the upper limit on rate of fire are determined by the amount of flow through the knurled adjuster on the side. At a suggested price of $99.95, the Response Trigger System is available for the 98 Custom, the A-5 and can be retro-fitted to the older Model 98. It is $79.97 for the older Model 98 at *www.paintballgear.com* (5-17-03).

The electronic WorrBlade from WGP.

Tippmann's E-Grip system for the A-5 marker uses an electronic control board to activate a solenoid to disengage the sear and fire the marker. A 9-volt battery concealed inside the grip powers the system. All electronic components are also contained inside the grip, which allows you to quickly and easily change grips. The trigger assembly, electronic components and grip frame are included. Firing modes are semi-auto (one shot for each trigger pull), auto-response (one shot each trigger pull and release), full-auto (fires repeatedly as long as the trigger is held from four to 13 bps), three-shot burst and turbo (one shot for every trigger pull and then one shot for every trigger pull and release if the time between trigger pulls is less than one-quarter second). Suggested price is $150.00, but it was only $124.99 at *www.xtremz.com* (5-18-03).

The Tippmann E-Bolt electro-pneumatic conversion kit for the 98 Custom uses an electronic control board with a solenoid valve. The solenoid operates a pneumatic hammer that opens and closes the power valve. The E-Bolt uses a standard 8-volt battery and has an average life of 500,000 shots per battery. This kit is easy to drop into a 98 Custom. Suggested price is $295.00. Firing modes are semi-auto, auto-response, three-shot or six-shot burst, full-auto and turbo.

A growing demand for compressed air systems has caused Tippmann to develop an after-market kit that offers increased efficiency at a set low pressure. Although a stock 98 Custom marker will operate on HPA without the kit, there is little advantage over CO_2 because the internals

are not designed for a high-pressure system.

Markers that operate on CO_2 have to accommodate a wide pressure range, from an empty bottle up to 3000 psi, at which point the rupture disc fails. CO_2 changes pressure as the temperature changes—the higher the temperature, the higher the pressure.

To cover the entire pressure range is not realistic, Tippmann says, so they shot for the most common operating pressures, 300 to 2000 psi. To have a marker function through this pressure range without large velocity variations, some efficiency and shooting comfort had to be sacrificed. With a high-pressure (HPA) system, you work with a preset operating pressure. Tippmann believes the most efficient pressure is between 300 and 400 psi. By changing the configuration of the valve and rear bolt, they obtained better efficiency, less recoil, and a more consistent shot-to-shot velocity.

The new HPA kit consists of a lighter rear bolt, new rear cocking assembly, lighter drive spring, new valve assembly, new vertical adapter and a low-pressure chamber. With the operating pressure around 350 psi, the valve opens much easier, but also requires a larger amount of gas flow to maintain ball velocity. Along

Upgrading the internals is always on the mind of top players. Experimenting with parts to find the perfect 3-Way or bolt for your marker is part of the game. The WGP Outkast Bolt has a redesigned single internal ball detent and two-O-ring design with an open-face front for $35.00.

with valve modifications, the low-pressure chamber supports these flow and volume demands. A nitrogen bottle and secondary regulator are not included in this kit, but they are required. At a suggested price of $119.00, the kit is currently available for the 98 Custom and Model 98 and will be available soon for the A-5.

WORR

Worr Games says its electronic Worrblade kit upgrade "gives recreational and tournament players unprecedented firepower." This electronic frame is a joint project between WGP and Planet Eclipse. It uses the same internals as its predecessor, the Eclipse E-Blade, except that Worr modified the frame to include a redesigned double-finger curved trigger and a larger trigger guard for playing with gloves. The kit includes an integrated dovetail rail (universal with most rail-based air systems and air system adapters) and an all-Delrin bolt (with O-rings included to create a tight seal and reduce blowback). The lockdown

The outside of the WGP Sledgehammer regulator does not give a clue about the complexities of the valves and pistons inside. Regulators are required on HPA systems.

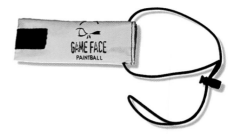

A barrel glove or barrel plug is required at fields, pro shops, tournaments and scenario games whenever you are not actively engaged in playing.

hammer with nylon insert prevents the lug from slipping during high rates of fire. Nickel-plated or anodized black, it is $475.00 (MSRP).

WGP 3-Ways are available in black, nickel, blue, green, red and purple. The $25.00 Worr STO 3-Way has a one-piece body with a super-smooth stroke. The $45.00 Worr CT-3 is adjustable by using a 3/16 Allen wrench in the front end. It works best with a Worr hinge frame and a Cam-Adjuster. The $60.00 (MSRP) Orr-acle is a CT 3-Way with a spooler valve preinstalled.

WGP Note: Like any number of quality manufacturers, WGP has useful questions and answers posted on their Internet site at *www.budorr.com*. For instance: "A 3-Way controls the re-cocking of a marker. If it is not properly adjusted, it can leak or perform poorly. On an Autococker that has either a hinge frame or a slide-style frame with a properly adjusted 3-Way, you should be able to look down inside the front hole, check the adjustment visually and make a manual adjustment. If your 3-Way leaks, it is probably because the two O-rings are dirty. Clean and lubricate with Vaseline or replace them to fix the leak. (For the details of making these operations, check the WGP Internet site or *www.wpgchat.com*.)

WGP's $35.00 STO Sledge Hammer is a low-pressure regulator available in nickel, blue, black, green and purple. The Orr-acle Tickler is a compact, high-flow regulator. The $60.00 Tickler is externally adjustable with the twist of its front knob. The Outkast Sledge Hammer ($55.00) is fully adjustable with a 3/16 Allen wrench.

Worr's $25.00 (MSRP) STO Rams are precision polished inside to provide a smooth stroke. The STO has always been easily re-buildable and is standard on the Black Magic and Orr-acle.

WGP also builds a series of replacement bolts. The Outkast has a two-O-ring design with an open-face front and a new single internal ball detent for $35.00 (MSRP). The Black Magic is a Venturi design to help distribute air flow evenly around the ball. It includes the new internal ball detent for $45.00 (MSRP). The all-Delrin WGP bolt is self-lubricating so it does not require O-rings or oil. It is available for Autocockers made since 2000 for $40.00 (MSRP). The Worr Blade features low-friction Delrin operation and is very light to reduce mass. Its O-ring design eliminates up to 80 percent of blowback for its MSRP of $45.00. The Orr-acle Delrin allows maximum air-

per-shot consistency. It includes the new single internal ball detent for $60.00 (MSRP).

ACCESSORIES
BARREL PLUGS AND COVERS

When your marker and hopper are loaded and you are not actively in-play, there is no question that you must always use a barrel plug (about $2.50) or cover. Shooting someone accidentally between games is a horrendous *faux pas* that is serious enough for you to be asked to leave many fields and not come back. Viewloader and many other companies offer a variety of plastic plugs that are designed to fit snugly inside any barrel. These days, barrel covers (also called socks or condoms) are increasingly in vogue. They are held in place by an elastic cord that loops around the loader or the back of the marker.

SQUEEGEES

You really ought to have several squeegees with you when you play, just in case one breaks, gets lost or your buddy doesn't return it. The one-piece Viewloader Proflex pull-through squeegee is made from injection-molded rubber. ($2.99 on 6-5-03 at *www.paintballgear.com*)

SIGHTS

You are familiar with the idea of a sight on a barrel from lots of movies and television shows. For a firearm, a sight is practically mandatory to hit a specific target at more than 25 yards. Sights and optical scopes mount on top of the barrel and may replace or substitute for the "iron sights," the built-in unmovable sights that most guns come with and which have to be brought into and kept in alignment to hit your target. That's tough under pressure. Ask any cop.

Sights can magnify the target … or not. If you are shooting in difficult weather conditions or at distances greater than 100 yards, magnifying lenses make excellent sense. At smaller distances, a non-magnifying red dot sight (or a sight with very low magnification like the 2x - 4x scopes used on many pistols and shotguns) may serve you better.

Paintball shooting is done at short range with markers

Brass Eagle's Electronic Point Sight puts you on target quickly with just the flip of a switch. Battery is included.

that do not incorporate fixed or "iron sights," and because the balls are not precisely accurate at any speed, the kind of sight used on an open-bore shotgun may be perfect, if one is needed at all, and that is debatable. Hence, the relative popularity of inexpensive red dot sights in paintball among the small percentage of players who use sights.

Certainly, most paintball players – recreational players and seasoned competitors – do not use sights of any kind. In airball tournaments at any competitive level, the games are simply too fast, the distances too close and the players' markers are too sophisticated with upgrades for sights to be of any practical value. You can watch the flight of your paintballs, so it is easy to adjust your point of aim and impact.

Some recreational players enjoy using sights and their use can be of value. In a scenario game, using a red dot sight can help you get on target faster if you have zeroed your sight for customary shooting distances of about 30 to 40 yards. Most players do not use sights in part because a sight adds bulk and the play can be fast, but you might want to be the player who changes that trend on your local rec field. Anyway, it is fun to try out new gear, but always try before you buy.

ADCO builds a couple of sights that will fit on most paintball markers that have a sight rail. These sights are okay for some of the fast-action, close-quarter work that paintball warriors are required to do. The ADCO Sure Shot is a black, non-magnifying red dot sight – not a laser, as it does not project the dot onto your target – that carried a price of $29.50 on *www.paintballgear.com* on 8-24-03. It does not magnify, either, so all you have to do is put the red dot on your target and open fire. Adjusting for elevation is up to you.

ADCO's Red Dot Imp sight has an open, low-profile design in front but the non-magnifying eye-piece is protected from dirt and flying paint. It's easy to adjust elevation with the thumb-screw. Since paintballs are so light and aerodynamically inefficient, gravity and friction cause them to begin to drop significantly after only a couple dozen yards. So, the ability to redial quickly for various ranges is important if you are interested in using a sight. Windage (left-to-right) adjustments must be done with a screwdriver (or a knife-edge if you are in a hurry). No brightness or contrast controls are available, just that one on/off switch for the red dot centered in the lens. A watch-style wafer battery that can be replaced by most discount or drug stores powers the Imp.

Better than the Imp, even though the design is about the same, ADCO's HotShot Sight has a larger reflective lens. This gives you a greater field of view and means faster target acquisition. Plus, this ADCO sight has on/off and a high/low brightness switches, sturdier mounting

brackets and a much better warranty than earlier sight versions. According to the company, for $8.00 shipping and handling, they will pretty much fix whatever is wrong or replace the HotShot with a new or reconditioned sight … no questions asked. You can't beat that! The HotShot was $24.99 on *www.paintball-discounters.com* on 8-25-03.

The Dye Izon, $59.99 on www.paintball-online.com on 8-25-03, is a different style red dot scope. Unlike the ADCO scopes, the Izon is an "occluded eye" sight. You don't actually see through it! Instead, you keep both eyes open and your brain superimposes the image of the dot from one eye over the target image to the other eye. This style sight takes some practice, but once you get used to it, you will most certainly learn to acquire your target more quickly. And, since your eye does not actually see through it, it is not affected by a marker's feed neck and hopper, which are usually mounted in the way on top. The Izon has windage and elevation adjustments.

The Izon has a mounting style that fits over and around the marker's sight rail. To hold it in place, you tighten four hex screws into the marker's anodized sight rail. The housing is aluminum and the Izon is available in silver or black. The rear lens is well protected while the front cover over the optical fiber is a durable, clear plastic.

Dye's Izon uses a short fiber optic cable to capture light and bring it to your eye. No batteries are needed. On the other hand, as light grows dim, so does the pinpoint of red light on your target. Still, the optical fiber is a specialty cable designed to carry light beams (waves? rays?), so it will almost always be brighter than your surroundings in the morning and evening.

The Tasco EZ dot sight has a two-position switch that lets you select a red or a green dot. Depending on your playing conditions, whether it is bright or dark, foggy or maybe late evening, one color will be better than the other for your particular eyes, and yes, eyes really are different. That isn't just marketing – well, not all of it.

The EZ sighting tube is an inch in diameter. It is set up to mount on a standard 3/8-inch sight rail and has thumbscrew adjustment knobs for fast adjustment of both windage and elevation. A single watch-style battery powers this sight.

A completely different style of sight is offered by North Pass, a sight manufacturer for the firearms industry. They offer a "light pipe," a cylinder of translucent plastic that takes ambient or even artificial light in from all sides and re-directs it to brightly illuminate the ends. The ends glow brightly, like a tiny neon bulb in whatever color from which the plastic is molded, usually either red or green.

As with a shotgun, the HiViz is essentially a pointing aid. Its snap-on mount wraps securely around the barrel and places the light pipe dot near the muzzle.

HiViz paintball tubes come in two sizes: APG-S for .710- to .840-inch outside diameter barrels and APG-L for .841- to 1.000-inch barrels. Each sight package includes four light pipes in orange and green. Dot sizes are .135 and .175 inches. Selecting the correct bright neon contrasting

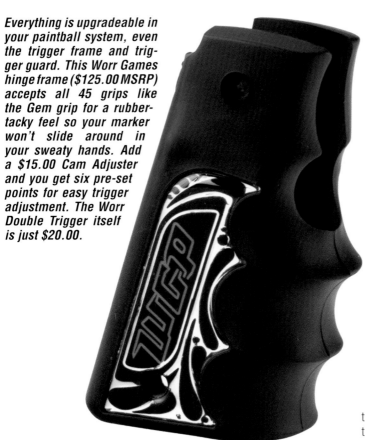

Everything is upgradeable in your paintball system, even the trigger frame and trigger guard. This Worr Games hinge frame ($125.00 MSRP) accepts all 45 grips like the Gem grip for a rubber-tacky feel so your marker won't slide around in your sweaty hands. Add a $15.00 Cam Adjuster and you get six pre-set points for easy trigger adjustment. The Worr Double Trigger itself is just $20.00.

dot color depends on your eyes' ability to make rapid color discriminations, where you are playing, the time of year and perhaps the weather.

If you are considering this type sight, it would be good to take a look at the fore-end of your barrel before you buy. Not all barrels, especially those that are the coolest and most stylized, will readily accept the HiViz mounting bracket.

COLLAPSIBLE STOCK

Tippmann offers several shoulder stocks for its A-5, 98 Custom and Model 98 markers. For $51.15, you can get the Lapco Drop Forward with an adjustable skeleton bar stock. The 3-position Pro Team Products (PTP) Collapsible Stock will mount on the 98 Custom ($79.95) or the A-5 ($82.95) by replacing the end cap. PTP also has a solid stock for your A-5 ($79.95). Several other companies build custom shoulder stocks for paintball markers.

Why add the weight and bulk of a stock to a paintball marker? Tippmann says a stock gives your marker a "unique look and excellent support." There is some truth to what they claim. A stock pressing against your shoulder with a good view down the sight rail or through a sight is the surest way to acquire a target and put paint on it.

Imagine how a chair or stool acquires stability. Two legs, not good. Three legs, better, and four, better still. Two solid points of support and one point of support

that is variable (e.g. two hands holding a marker with a tank loosely touching or tucked in between your arm and chest) are not nearly as good as two hands plus a stock that is firmly planted against your shoulder. The greater the stability, the better the shot. For a sniper, for example, a stock is something he has to consider for his marker. A sniper is playing for one shot, maybe two. He has to make them accurate and on target or he's going to get wasted.

A stock changes the look of your marker, too. Lots of experienced players will tell you that if you are assigned a team job to hang back of the rushing front line, a stock is going to help lay down an accurate base of supporting fire. Accurate shooting makes the enemy keep its head down because your paint is finding the cracks in their bunkers.

On the other hand, if you are running and gunning, rushing forward in the front line and shooting from the hip on 3-shot burst mode, a stock will be in the way. Some players find that a stock helps them stabilize the marker between their elbow and waist. Obviously, it is your choice, but the way a stock feels to you and your role on a team has a lot to do with whether you want this add-on or not.

The Viewloader Lug Case is a soft-exterior carrying case for markers, barrels and accessories. It features an open-cell foam interior with a hook-and-loop fastening system to securely hold contents.

"Run, run as fast as you can; you can't catch me 'cause I'm a Game Face man."

PADDED CARRIER

Viewloader's Lug Case is a soft-exterior, black carrying case for your marker, specialty barrels and paintball field accessories. It has an open-cell foam interior with a Velcro fastening system to securely hold the contents. A handle and zipper closure add convenience ($19.99 on 6-5-03 at *www.paintballgear.com*). (You will find additional cases in the Protective Gear chapter.)

TIMERS

Viewloader has a new timer that gives critical game time voice warnings, but has a mute option for stealthy play. The Talkin' Timer also has a memory key for quick clock reset and game-end auto shut-off to extend battery life. It is designed so that it can attach directly to the rear of the Viewloader 9-volt and 12-volt Revolution feed loaders for true in-your-face—and ear, since this one talks—game play. It comes with batteries, mounting screws and a lanyard ($24.99 on *www.paintballgear.com* on 6-5-03).

Battery life is 400 hours with silver oxide cells sold at most electronics stores.

HOPPE'S #9

Hoppe's #9 Powder Solvent is probably the most universally recognized and accepted solvent for cleaning firearms, and if it is good enough to remove primer, powder, lead and metal fowling from high-power rifles, it should be good enough for your paintball semi-auto. It also helps prevent rust. Hoppe's #9 is available at most hardware stores, at the BigMarts and certainly at hunting and shooting retail stores in your area. At *www.precisionreloading.com* (6-2-03), a 4-ounce bottle cost $4.79 and a 32-ounce bottle cost $14.99.

Hoppe's also manufactures several gun cloths that paintball fanatics will like because they are effective at removing grime, oily fingerprints and corrosive epidermal oils without making a big mess. The 4-ounce flannel silicone cloth or the standard gun cloth cost $2.99 and will fit in your back pocket for a quick wipe-down in the field.

THE ULTIMATE CUSTOMIZER

In an interview with Glenn Palmer, founder of Palmer's Pursuit Custom Shop, in July 2003, *Paintball News* Managing Editor Rene Boucher discovered the truth behind the development of the only double-barrel paintball marker and an interesting story about paintball ambassadors around the world.

Paintball News: Glenn you have introduced quite a few "new markers" to paintball players around the world. What are some stories on those?

Glenn: Well, when I first introduced the Doubles as a 12-gram pump gun in June of 1988, almost everyone that picked it up would say one of two things—either "Holy shit!" or "This is nasty!" Since I couldn't name it the former, we dubbed it "Nasty."

Everything I've brought to the game was pretty much a matter of solving problems and overcoming limitations in my own equipment that could keep me from playing my best game. Very early on, it became quite evident that a player was most vulnerable when out of air. Paint could be added to the gun quite quickly, but changing CO_2 cartridges could take 30 seconds and had to be done about every 10 to 12 shots. Therefore, the first order of business was to make the gun more efficient and speed up the process of changing cartridges to reduce vulnerability.

It wasn't real difficult to double the efficiency of the guns of the time as the valves were all designed to shoot small BBs or pellets, but an effective quick change was also needed. About that same time, some airsmiths had gone to bulk tanks (CA or constant air) to compensate for the inefficiency of the equipment. But I didn't want to pack all that hardware around on my gun so I worked from the inside out to maximize efficiency. What I came up with was the first available cartridge quick-change system, called the QuikSilver. It made changing cartridges so fast – 1.5 to 3 seconds – that constant air had no advantage. Besides, CA was not allowed in the tournaments at that time.

So, by mid-1987, I was sporting a Sheridan/PMI-based paintgun that would get 30-plus shots out of a 12-gram cartridge, and I could change it out in the wink of an eye. Couple that with the development of an elliptically shaped barrel, an effective muzzle brake and the inherent benefit to accuracy that efficiency brings, and I was set for everything since.

Then one day early in '88 at a local tournament, I got in a position in a game where it was one on one, but the other guy had the better cover, a huge tree. We traded shots for several minutes, during which time I picked up his rhythm, but I'd shoot to one side of the tree and he would look out the other. I was telling myself that if I could put a ball by both sides of the tree at the same time, I'd have had him quicker. Before that one confrontation was over, I had decided to build a double-barreled gun to solve that problem, and about three weeks later, I went back to that same field with the first of the doubles. It was a K-series, rifle-based gun with a pair of 14-inch barrels with adjustable shot spread and independently adjustable velocity. I put a little spreader between the barrels that I could adjust with a thumbscrew to set the shot pattern to the size of the tree that the opponent was behind. It also worked well for covering two sides of a fort building at the same time, or adjusting the barrels to shoot through two windows at the same time. Such adjustments made for a lot of fun in some circumstances, but are a bit impractical, so they aren't a part of currently built doubles called the Nasty.

Paintball News: Where are some of the places you have been and will you tell me about some of the folks, (odd and fun) that you have run into over the years?

Glenn: Paintball has taken me all over the world, mostly as a member of the *Green Machine*, International Training and Demonstration Paintball team. We used to go someplace in the world at least once a year and hook up with the locals to organize a tournament, American style, in areas where paintball was just getting started. As a "Machiner" I have been to Australia, all over western Europe and England, Russia, Brazil, Venezuela, Canada and numerous locations throughout the U.S. I've also done quite a bit of traveling outside of my connection with the Green Machine that has gained me acquaintances in paintball throughout most of southeast Asia, the Philippines and Malaysia.

Probably, the most memorable individual that I've met throughout my travels was a fellow named Victor in Moscow, Russia, in May 1995. He was the trainer for the Russian national soccer team, so we got to meet the team and even showed them a bit about paintball. The whole team got to shoot one of my markers and when we used the soccer ball as the target, it got painted quite severely and bounced all over the practice field.

Anyway, Victor was a very intelligent man and even though quite small of stature, he walked the legs off Jim Lively and me during numerous sightseeing excursions around Moscow. Jim and I thought we were champion walkers when it came to getting to know the places that we traveled, and we did our "walk-about" early every morning. We would often cover more than 10 miles before breakfast, but after a few days with Victor as our guide, 10 miles was just a warm up and we both conceded to Victor's endurance. That man just flat wore us out, but we sure had fun and learned a lot in the process.

A funny thing is that the nature of paintball players is pretty much the same all over the world and a paintballer never has problems making friends with other paintballers even without a common spoken language.

NOTE: Juvy and Rene Boucher's informative newspaper *Paintball News* (see their web site at *www.paintballnews.com*) is published 26 times a year. The Bouchers are tireless paintball promoters and are present at large and small gatherings of players and manufacturers worldwide. "The Ultimate Customizer" is used with permission.

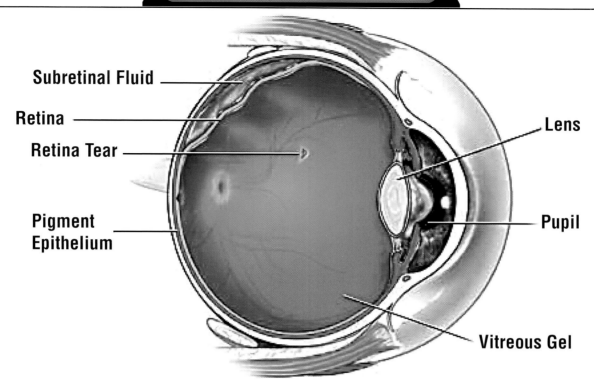

Subretinal Fluid

Retina

Retina Tear

Pigment Epithelium

Lens

Pupil

Vitreous Gel

A paintball traveling in the neighborhood of 200 mph will sting when it hits, but it will cause serious and perhaps permanent damage to an unprotected eyeball. Never shoot a paintball marker or even play paintball in the back yard without wearing approved protective goggles.

Preventing Serious Eye Injuries

Retinal Detachment: What Actually Happens

If you get hit in the eye, retinal detachment can progress quickly. First, the retina of your eye actually stops working when it loses contact with the tissue beneath it. This usually begins on the side (your peripheral vision goes first) and spreads to the center and you can literally go blind for a while or maybe forever. A concussion to the eye causes a tear and the liquid in the eye (the vitreous gel) leaks out behind your retina. Reattaching the retina and restoring vision requires surgery.

Choosing and wearing approved protective gear – especially people who wear contact lenses – is absolutely essential to protect your eyes, writes Paul F. Vinger, MD, a clinical professor of ophthalmology at Tufts University School of Medicine in Boston.

First and foremost, Vinger says, outer lenses should be made of three-millimeter thick polycarbonate. Polycarbonate is the strongest and most durable lens material available. Make sure your lenses are treated for scratch-resistance and will absorb ultraviolet (UV) light. The sun's ultraviolet rays can be excessively harmful to the eyes.

"The most critical part of goggles is the eye protection lenses," says ProCaps' Mike Ratko, who has worked for years to help the paintball industry develop acceptable engineering standards for safety equipment.

Sports goggles should carry a seal from the Protective Eyewear Certification Council and an ASTM rating indicating they are approved for paintball. Contact lenses or even your regular eyeglasses, by the way, offer no protection at all.

What's Polycarbonate?

According to Chuck Cooley, vice president and lens designer at Feather Visions, lenses are available in four materials: polycarbonate, optical plastic, composites and crown quality or optical quality glass.

Although polycarbonate has been around since the '50s, its use in high-quality lenses is relatively recent. Polycarbonate has a 90 percent light transmission rate and a 1.59 index of refraction. The relatively high 1.59 refractive index means that light bends very little as it passes through the lens (the greater the curve, the lower the RI index number). Because it takes less polycarbonate material to make a lens for any given prescription, Chuck says, polycarbonate lenses are thinner and lighter than other materials.

For a paintball madman or woman who is depending on a polycarbonate lens for a clear picture of the target, this can present a problem around the edges in the early morning or late evening. Still, polycarbonate is impact resistant and the optics industry as a whole recommends it for "active people" … and paintballers are, by and large, active people – real active.

And there is more good news. Polycarbonate naturally blocks 99 percent of the sun's ultra-violet rays, both UVA and UVB, too.

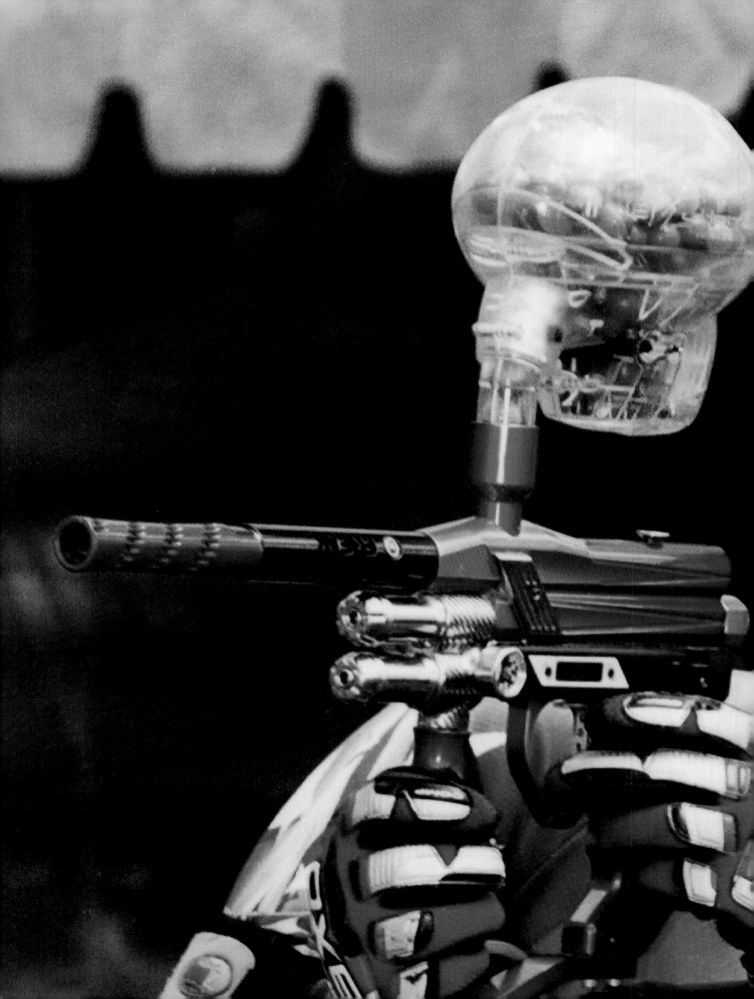

CHAPTER 13

BARRELS

As a paintball player, you will occasionally hear or read the term "aftermarket." Right now, while we are thinking about marker barrels, is the perfect time to let you in on the secret of this fascinating bit of jargon. Actually, it isn't so secret or all that fascinating, because you can hear it used to refer to car stuff and camera stuff and lots of whatever purchases. Aftermarket means "add-ons," things you install to replace the things that originally came with your marker or things better than original components to help you shoot faster, more accurately and more consistently.

When you buy a paintball marker new, chances are it will perform well right out of the box or the pro shop. Then, after you play for a few months, you will discover there are people out there who can still shoot faster and more accurately and who are troubled less with chopped balls, people who spend less time tuning and cleaning than you do. This could be because they have replaced critical parts of their original marker with specialty aftermarket parts that are most certainly more expensive but also perhaps better designed and manufactured. In paintball, aftermarket parts are normally called "upgrades" as opposed to add-ons. Of course, if you replace something that works okay with something that works lousy, it's really a "downgrade," but you are smart enough not to do that. Aren't you?

Marker barrels are one of the first aftermarket upgrades to think about, perhaps after an electronic hopper, maybe because they are so easily replaceable or because they are so in your face. Consequently, there are two opposing schools of thought about barrel replacement:

1. Marker manufacturers are primarily interested in developing the guts of the marker, the mechanics of the air-bolt-ball shooting system. They consider the barrel just a nuisance tube (a bore!) on the front of the marker that is there more for balance and good looks than for anything even remotely related to shooting well.

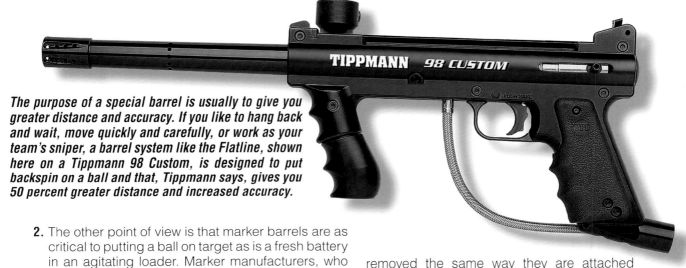

The purpose of a special barrel is usually to give you greater distance and accuracy. If you like to hang back and wait, move quickly and carefully, or work as your team's sniper, a barrel system like the Flatline, shown here on a Tippmann 98 Custom, is designed to put backspin on a ball and that, Tippmann says, gives you 50 percent greater distance and increased accuracy.

2. The other point of view is that marker barrels are as critical to putting a ball on target as is a fresh battery in an agitating loader. Marker manufacturers, who are bright folks and who are almost always paintball players too, certainly understand this and would not ignore the dynamics of a ball spinning down the barrel at close to 300 fps. With some obvious exceptions, the "stock" barrel (the one that originally comes with the marker) is just fine.

So, which view is correct? Well, opinions are divided. Most manufacturers provide a barrel when you buy one of their markers. On the other hand, some markers are sold with so-called "name" barrels, in which case they seem to recognize the superiority of or just the general name-recognition value of specialty aftermarket barrels like "The Freak."

Perhaps the best thing to do is buy your marker and shoot it for a while. If you are happy with its speed or accuracy or the general way it shoots and looks, well … be happy! If you are not happy, begin searching (and saving) for upgrades. The first upgrade, the one most experienced paintball players say will make an immediate difference, is a specialty barrel.

Pro players typically claim the barrel is the most important upgrade you can make to a marker and to advance to their exalted ranks, you might have to buy-in to their philosophy. Their motto is that virtually any specialty barrel is better than any stock barrel. So, what makes a good barrel and who makes the best?

Before you buy an expensive name-brand barrel on an impulse, you need to check the attaching mechanism to the body of your marker. We mentioned earlier that barrels screw off. Well, that's only generally true. Some barrels do not come off at all, but this is only common on relatively inexpensive and starter markers. With a cheap marker, a high-end barrel would cost more than the marker itself. That would be like dressing a pig in a prom gown. So, before you go shopping, figure out how your barrel attaches. Some stay put when you push them into the marker body, held in place by friction and gaskets. Most barrels attach either by screwing them into place or by snapping them onto the receiver with a twist and lock motion. They are

removed the same way they are attached (except in reverse!).

Two other considerations regarding barrels are whether they attach to a marker of the open-bolt or closed-bolt variety and whether you are shooting with a high-pressure or low-pressure system:

1. An open bolt starts back, away from the ball. When you pull the trigger, the bolt is propelled forward, striking the ball and sending it out the barrel. Open bolt systems need retainers or detents to keep the ball in place, and in this case, larger bores are usually acceptable.

2. A closed bolt snaps forward and remains in contact with the ball when the marker is at rest. When you pull the trigger, it is drawn back against a powerful spring before being released. In this case, a smaller bore, one that can hold the ball in place, is fine.

High-pressure or low-pressure systems behind the ball make a difference, too:

1. High pressure uses a smaller volume of air in a smaller chamber under greater pressure. This air hits the ball hard, causing its shape to distort. If you could see a ball being hit, flying down the barrel and then out with super-high-speed photography, your ball would look like "flubber," and you would be amazed that it would either hold together or actually fly to the point you aimed it. With high-pressure systems, a smaller barrel works best.

2. Low pressure relies on a larger volume of CO_2 in a larger chamber under less pressure. This air hits the ball with less initial force of impact and therefore distorts it less. There is less distortion and consequently less friction when it is in flight, too. Because low pressure requires a larger volume of air, a larger inside diameter barrel is usually recommended.

This young paintball player is chronographing his marker for speed. The marker is equipped with a curved Tippmann Flatline barrel.

Here are the things you will learn about when you begin thinking about upgrading your barrel: length, diameter, thickness, material, coating, rifling, porting, air pressure and whether it looks good or not. Not much more than a college degree or two in physics, chemistry, aerodynamics and fashion is required!

But isn't paintball a 68-caliber sport? Doesn't everything pretty much conform to those exacting tolerances? And what is caliber anyway?

First, caliber is an old method for trying to be precise with our rather imprecise English Standard of weights and measures. The measurement called "caliber" and, indeed the entire English Standard, evolved in an era when people based their fair value exchanges on things like how far down a grain of wheat, for instance, pushed a hand-made brass scale or how loud a dog barked or how far away they could spot a witch riding her broom across the face of the moon. Yeah, well, dealing with explosives like gunpowder, those measures were lethal to practically everybody, especially the shooter and the shootee! As a result, they put decimal points around stuff and divided it by hundreds and … when they applied this to feet and inches, they came up with something totally new, but not totally better, and therefore, something like 0.68-inch became 68 caliber. In other words, there are 100 calibers to the inch.

The other confusing problem is that sometimes caliber is expressed in thousandths (like for paint) rather than

hundredths (like for markers) of an inch. Does 68 caliber mean .681 or .689 or even .68709? Most paint is marked to the third decimal point, but some is not marked at all. Assume it is .68-something. Anyway, since aftermarket barrels are sized across a specific range by their inner or inside diameter (ID: basically, the size of the hole), you will discover that one size does not fit all. Some barrels work better with some paints than with others. That is one reason why experienced, dedicated players own a variety of barrels, and before a money match or a big game, they will test the field paint against their selection of barrels.

Barrels are made for perfectly round paintballs, but the balls vary ever so slightly in size and shape. This variability is barely enough to be noticeable, but significant enough to matter. Frankly, it's hard to keep something so soft and squishy to stay perfectly round, especially if balls have been in a storage container for very long or the weather is cool and dry.

You would like your balls to be perfectly round, though, not "pretty much round" or "almost perfectly round." Look at a bunch of field paint under an average magnifying glass, and you will be surprised at their condition, shape and the surface texture. This is why barrels are something of a science.

Balls are sized by diameter or by "bore." Imagine the inner diameter of a barrel. It circumscribes a hollow space, kind of a tube of air. That's the bore. Balls range from small bore size (.65 to .67) to large bore (.68 to .70).

These are JT USA's Predator Paintballs. The ball needs a secure fit in the chamber, but if it is too tight, it will jam, and if it is too loose, it could roll out the barrel and your marker will not use its air efficiently. Balls vary in size very, very slightly from manufacturer to manufacturer.

You can wad up one of these pull-through squeegees from Allen and stuff it in your pocket or backpack. It's a good idea because one pull through your barrel typically removes paint and broken ball husks. Get down behind a good bunker and you won't even have to leave the field.

How much barrel do you need? The general rule of thumb is that the farther you shoot the longer the barrel you need.

But you want your barrel to fit the ball perfectly.

On the day of the big game, unscrew your barrel and put a ball in the chamber end of the barrel you intend to use. You want to see if you can blow it out the other end. You won't look weird … much. You are trying to make sure the size of the game ball matches your barrel diameter. Now, put your mouth over the end of the barrel where the ball is and try to blow (don't inhale!) the ball out of the barrel. If it shoots right out, your match is probably correct. If you can't blow it out or the ball barely moves, try other barrels to find out which one works best because the bore you are holding in your hand (and mouth) is probably too small for the paintball … or the ball is too big for the barrel. If the ball just rolls out, the barrel is certainly too large. Weather conditions affect the ball and to a lesser extent the barrel. Temperature. Humidity. Different materials react differently, but they all react. Unless you're just out at a local rec field tossing paint with a couple buddies, it matters, and even then, you don't want to play like a sap.

"Well," you might argue, "why don't they just get one doggone standard and make everyone do the same thing? Wouldn't this be better?"

At 68 caliber – sixty-eight-hundredths – manufacturers are dealing with extraordinarily fine (as in very small) tolerances. Something the thickness of a hair or a sheet of onion skin paper can throw the whole manufacturing operation out of whack.

Unfortunately, too, it is hard for paintball manufacturers to share information with each other. With the cost of a paintball at about 2.5 cents, the business is very competitive. Information has value and no one wants to lose one's competitive edge. And there are usually several different ways to make the same thing. For instance, we are reminded when we change a nut with a socket wrench that there are two systems—English and metric—for how things are measured. So, it's easy to imagine how much more complicated everything is at a big manufacturer like

RP Scherer (paintballs) or Brass Eagle (markers). The manufacturing process is fluid, dynamic. Machine parts change. Operators come and go. And, we do still live in a free country, so making people conform is, well, as the English would say, "just not done."

How much barrel do you need? Barrels come in different lengths. Some aftermarket barrels are almost 2

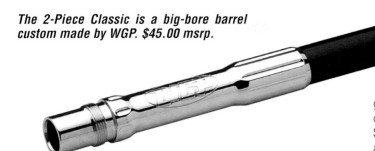

The 2-Piece Classic is a big-bore barrel custom made by WGP. $45.00 msrp.

feet long. For argument, though, it is safe to assume that an 8-inch barrel is the absolute minimum necessary to get a ball to fly properly, and many people would argue that a 12-inch barrel is the minimum length. What we are saying is it is necessary to have a barrel that long to give the ball time to stabilize and fly out in the best shape possible. We may also be saying that a particular marker's operation uses the propellant gas most efficiently when it works within a barrel that long. In general, figure low pressure needs longer barrels. High pressure will do okay with shorter barrels.

Although the dynamics are different, the model is the same with a shotgun barrel. Short barrels with wide open chokes means a wider shot pattern or greater dispersal of the BBs. Longer barrels or barrels choked down tight at their ends give you greater distance and tighter shot patterns.

Your position on a team or your style of play may have a lot to do with determining what length barrel you prefer. Up-front players, the "rush-the-competition" crowd, may benefit from shorter, lighter, more maneuverable barrels. Think of this as the "Tommy gun" or the "shotgun" approach to close-range shooting. Accuracy per shot is not as important as filling the air with balls, surprising and confusing the other side. You will get some hits simply because you are throwing out so much paint.

Players in mid-field and back-line players, who spend less time rushing blind from bunker to bunker or who provide cover for the up-front guys, want a longer barrel on the assumption they can place paint right on the edge of the bunker where the enemy is going to appear to shoot back rather than splashing the whole bunker randomly with paint.

The "sniper" marker is usually coupled with a longer barrel, often as long as 18 to 20 inches. Snipers want to sneak up on their opponents without being seen, shoot greater distances from hiding (a lot of snipers wear shapeless Ghillie suits) and put their balls on target immediately without giving away their position. Unlike in the movies (or maybe in real life, who knows?), this is tough in paintball. After all, what's a long shot in paintball? Maybe 200 feet. Nevertheless, longer barrels are marketed specifically for this purpose.

And what about weight? You want a lightweight marker if you are going to carry it all day and night in a scenario game or are running and gunning like crazy in a fast-action tournament game. Barrels can be heavy, and in general, the longer they are, the heavier they can be. Of course, different materials have different specific weights. Stainless steel is usually heaviest. Brass is also heavy, aluminum is somewhere in the middle of the weight range and the new composite (carbon/fiberglass) barrels are the lightest. This said, everything really depends on barrel thickness and length, and perhaps a smaller air tank – even though you may have to fill it more often – will make more difference than the barrel material or its length.

As far as what happens to the ball as it travels down the barrel, polished or "micro-honed" metals are smoother than the typical composite barrel, which means a ball encounters less friction. A coating with DuPont's Teflon (the slickest material known to man) to reduce the drag or friction is the cure-all though for most rough surfaces.

Regardless of what you have heard, with barrels, longer does not necessarily mean more accurate. A 12-inch barrel usually has very similar shooting characteristics to a 16-inch barrel of the same design or by the same manufacturer. The difference you expect and usually find when you equip your marker with a longer or specialty barrel is YOU, the player. Most people, whether or not they realize it, sight by the tip of their barrel. In archery, it is called point-of-aim when people use the tip of a drawn arrow for the same purpose. The longer the barrel, the more "on target" it will be when you point your marker, and this can give you the illusion that the longer barrel is more accurate.

When it comes to a consideration of rifling and porting, the record is no clearer for paintball than that for barrel length. Your decision on a purchase can't be faulted if your only consideration is whether the barrel "looks cool" on your marker. Indeed, the majority of stock barrels do not come with rifling at all and you can play successfully without a rifled barrel.

The idea behind a rifled barrel as opposed to a smooth bore is that the "lands and grooves," the high parts and the valleys where the barrel is cut away, are supposed to help the ball fly in a more stable and consistent manner. This is because the rifling causes the ball to spin before it leaves the barrel and the balance between the forces on the ball, centrifugal and centripetal, give the ball stability. With solid bullets in firearms, this is demonstrable. High-speed film confirms the effects when a rifle is fired at a target. All things being equal, the pattern closes dramatically when the bullet is fired from a rifled rather than from a non-rifled barrel. Hence the superiority at distance of the rifle over the smoothbore.

A paintball, however, is round and squishy, so barrel

Worr Games says the Triple Threat is a great two-piece "starter barrel kit." You get a .689 nickel-plated back end and three tips creating lengths of 10, 12 and 14 inches for $95.00 (MSRP).

makers have had to study the dynamics of the ball and barrel to come up with some of the rifling options we discuss later in the chapter.

Those of us who grew up on James Bond, Secret Agent 007 movies think of the fat thing on the end of a barrel as a silencer. With just a little knowledge of firearms, it becomes apparent the muzzle brake is a flash suppressor that is important in night combat. Maybe this is true on Bond's Beretta, but the primary purpose for a muzzle break on the barrel of a paintball gun is to look good. It is part of a "dress-for-success" philosophy.

Even on higher-end airguns, such as those from GAMO USA, the company acknowledges the muzzle brake on the end of its 1000-fps 177-caliber Stutzen is included to give you something to hold while you are cocking it.

Some people claim that a ported muzzle brake helps the paintball make the transition from the close confines of the barrel to the open air by releasing some of the accuracy-draining turbulence, but this has not yet been proved to have scientific validity.

Muzzle porting has a different effect than a muzzle brake. Think of a paintball sitting quietly in the receiver waiting to be fired. One instant, the pressure on all sides (except for the slight pressure of a ball detent that keeps it from rolling out the end) is equal to whatever the air pressure happens to be on the day you are playing. Suddenly, you pull the trigger and that paintball's life changes. An extreme blast hits it from behind, and it is suddenly propelled forward through the bore of the barrel. But there is still air pressure in front of the ball. That doesn't change just because you have pulled the trigger. The air in front of the ball essentially has to get out of the way, but it is slow to do so and so the ball is squeezed between the higher pressure behind it and the lower pressure in front of it. Squeezing distorts the ball and distortion causes

erratic flight. It also slows the ball down and prevents it from achieving its peak velocity.

As a rule of thumb, conventional wisdom claims that a ported barrel is better than a non-ported barrel. This much is clear, as just about every manufacturer ports their specialty barrels and many stock barrels, too. Porting, as we have said, allows the air resistance in front of the ball to be relieved by forcing air out holes or slots in the barrel. Facing less opposition, the ball theoretically flies faster, straighter and with less distortion. Ports can be holes or even slots. Any pattern basically does the same thing.

Because the paintball does not make a perfect match with the barrel, some gas escapes before the paintball flies out. This effect creates additional turbulence that the ball is forced to fly through. Non-ported barrels can send a paintball flying off at weird angles. Here is where porting becomes a dynamic function in straight flight. Porting vents excess and turbulent gases out as the ball accelerates down the barrel and helps control the effects of turbulence. An added bonus is that porting makes the shot a lot quieter.

BARREL BUYING

Multi-size barrel kits or individual barrels of different inside diameters (IDs) are available from many manufacturers: ACI, Armson, Custom Products, Dye, Empire, J&J, Lapco, PMI, Smart Parts and 32 Degrees. If you are conservative or working on a budget (and who isn't!), you may want to add one additional barrel at a time. Just remember that some manufacturers offer multi-barrel kits that, when purchased as a kit rather than individual barrels, are very value-oriented. Here is a suggestion from DraXxus on the order in which to purchase a new barrel or set of barrels:

1. Most markers come with .689-inch ID barrels, except Tippmann, which is more in the .692-inch ID range.
2. First, consider a .686-inch or .687-inch barrel to handle the widest array of performance paints.
3. Next, go smaller with a .684-inch barrel for serious small-bore use.
4. Then, go big caliber for hot, humid days when shells absorb water or the ingredients inside expand, and look for a .692-inch to .694-inch barrel.
5. Finally, get a barrel for super-small balls, a barrel that will cope with paint in the .679-inch to .682-inch diameter range.

Once a new or used barrel is purchased, you should take care of it properly in order to keep it in fine working order and shooting straight. To keep your barrels shooting as accurately as possible, be sure it is absolutely clean and free of gelatin buildup. Swab or squeegee any paint residue from your barrel and use a gelatin build-up remover like Pro-Team Products' "Pro-Clean" to remove built-up gelatin residue. A squeegee will not remove accumulated and dried gelatin. This residue builds up fast, it's almost

With the Kaner barrel system, Worr Games says you get to select three front tips for overall length (10, 12 or 14 inches) and a back end bore dimension for perfect fit (.684, .687, .689 and .691). The system is $199.00 (MSRP).

invisible and it will temporarily ruin the performance of a perfectly good barrel – and you won't even know why! Finally, check for burrs, scratches or sharp snags in the breech and barrel that could cause balls to break or tear. Any sharp edges have to be repaired right away.

With a super-clean barrel, you will notice that your shot groups will tighten considerably and your velocity will pick up.

MEET THE MANUFACTURERS
32 Degrees

The Whisper is available finished in chrome, blue, green silver and black and in 12-, 14- and 16-inch lengths. All sizes feature 7 inches of non-ported back section with unique, small-to-large in-line porting holes from the middle to the end of the barrel. Because of all the heavy porting, the Whisper is a pain to clean if you break a ball inside, but its quiet shooting is a nice feature indeed.

32 Degrees' Ice Cold in 12- and 14-inch lengths is made from polished aluminum and is then nickel-plated. The fore end of the barrel is spiral ported while the back 4 to 5 inches are stylishly scalloped so you can get a grip when removing it.

32 Degrees has put a very nice looking ported carbon barrel in play. Carbon, they say, is eight times stronger and two times stiffer than aluminum but still 15 times lighter!

The barrel is available with an aluminum or stainless steel base in lengths of 12, 14 or 16 inches.

Allen

Allen says their lightweight machined-aluminum Air Control barrels are made with "precision position porting to minimize ball distortion" when you shoot.

The 12-inch Firestick comes in red, blue or gray with straight ($54.95) porting or spiral ($59.95) porting. The 12-inch Widowmaker is honed to .690-inch in the same porting schemes, colors and prices.

The two-piece, spiral-ported Firestick II is available in 12-inch ($74.95) or 14-inch ($79.95) lengths, but in red or blue only. Allen says its barrels are micro-honed to

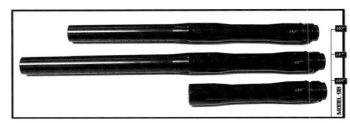

A multiple barrel set like this one from Allen Paintball Products are often the first upgrades a serious paintball player will make to his marker.

Now THIS is a barrel!

.692-inch diameter before they are mirror-polished. The Widowmaker II is also offered in a two-piece set.

Empire

Exclusively distributed by National Paintball Supply, Empire is new on the paintball scene. Their 14-inch 4-Piece Barrel Kit, a starter kit or a kit for recreational players, has three backs and one front for $99.95. Their new 7-Piece Barrel Kit cost $159.95 on *www.paintballgear.com* on 8-17-03. The Kit contains a case, one front and six backs (.681, .684, .687, .690, .693 and .696) for a 14-inch barrel upgrade. Empire's 10-Piece Barrel Kit costs $189.50. It has five polished nickel-aluminum backs and five fore ends for 10, 12-, 14-, 16- and 18-inch lengths.

Evil

Exclusively distributed by Pursuit Marketing International, Evil barrels are not sold consumer-direct. Their PIPE screw-in barrel system is extrusion pressed, arbor honed, anodized and plating enhanced. The porting system has a cool name, too – gaseo dynamic porting. Sexy. Of course, these barrels are precision machined, and they are available individually or in a five-pack carrying kit. Evil has five front tips (10-, 12-, 14-, 16- and 18-inch) and five back sizes (.683, .686, .689, .692 and .695). Check 'em out at *www.evil-paintball.com*. Evil offers a magnificent 10-piece barrel kit with five

different barrel lengths, five different bore sizes and, in all, Evil says, 25 different configurations. The brightly polished barrel bores are: .687, .689, .691, .695 and .698. Coupled with the shiny black anodized barrels, the overall lengths (bore plus barrel extension) are: 10, 12, 14, 16 and 18 inches. This barrel kit comes in a semi-hard-sided black case.

JJ Performance

JJ offers a number of barrels and accessories. Its 12- and 14-inch ceramic barrels ($34.99 on *www.paintball-discounters.com* on 8-16-03) are actually 6061 T-6 aluminum with a ceramic coating that is Teflon impregnated for a very smooth "flight line" for your paintball. JJ suggests that its ceramic barrels are "self cleaning." The Edge Barrel Set, one color anodized fore end and four black backs (.685, .688, .691 and .693), is available in 10-, 12- and 14-inch lengths ($114.99) and comes with a padded carrying case. Full Tilt two-piece barrels, including the Full Tilt Ceramic, are available in lengths from 10 to 16 inches. The JJ Pro 1 ($49.99) is ported down its length of either 12 inches for black or 14 inches in red, green or black.

JT USA

JT offers a set of screw-together Excelleration barrels (and one fluted, ported 14-inch single-piece black aluminum barrel called the Spyder for $39.99). The

The custom 12-inch ported barrel from Brass Eagle fits their Stingray II and Stingray II Ice semi-autos. They are made of custom clear-coated anodized aluminum.

aluminum fore-end or tip is anodized in metallic black, red or blue while the stainless steel butt end is polished, engraved and clear coated silver. They are round-hole ported at the tip and in a line along the fore-end. These barrels are available in bore sizes of .690, .688 and .686 in lengths from 10 to 16 inches. With their Intra-Lock alignment system, JT advertises "a perfect flight center through your barrel. Any size, any length, any time! Why get stuck with a barrel that's glued, when you can get screwed!" Wow. Backs cost $56.50 for stainless steel or $51.50 for aluminum, while, regardless of the length or color, the fluted, ported front sections cost $56.50 (*www.paintballgear.com* on 6-6-03).

Powerlyte

The Scepter Five Insert Barrel System offers a set of five mirror-honed bore kits (.684, .686, .688, .690 and .692) in stainless steel ($209.95 MSRP) or aluminum ($199.95 MSRP) with your choice of 12-, 14- or 16-inch muzzle lengths. Powerlyte says their barrel's "front load compression-lock sleeve eliminates any chance of the sleeve turning or shifting while firing, a self-align system which precisely aligns the bore of the sleeve with the bore of the muzzle providing a perfectly straight flight line for the ball to travel." In addition, the insert sleeves are color coded, to help you match any size paint quickly.

Powerlyte also offers a set of mirror-honed Speedline barrels with .0005-inch tolerances and what it calls its patented "side-by-side porting." These are offered as one-piece or two-piece barrel upgrades for other markers. (The one-piece Speedline barrel is standard on the Powerlyte Hybrid.) The aluminum two-piece in 12-, 14- or 16-inch lengths is $89.95 (stainless is ten bucks more) while the aluminum one-piece Speedline barrel (12-inch aluminum only) is $59.95.

PMI

International paintball distributor PMI is known for its Piranha markers, but it also sells a line of Razzor Multi-Metal Barrel upgrades. Designed for its own Piranha and the popular Spyder markers, Razzor barrels come in titanium, red, blue and black, but their primary characteristic is their highly stylized chrome overlays. The 12-inch barrel is honed and spiral-ported. The 14-inch length is roller burnished inside the spiral-ported aluminum barrel and sells for $39.77(MSRP). Perhaps the most interesting (at least to look at) of the PMI barrels is called the Clear Prism, which is a transparent, ported, polycarbonate barrel tube within a polished chrome cage.

Ronin Gear

The Katana is a mid-level adjustable-bore barrel from Ronin Gear with some pretty interesting characteristics. Without using inserts or screw-together fronts and backs, the Katana has a variable-bore rear section. The outside of the back section rotates through five notched positions. The internal bore of the back section has a long slit running down its length, and as the outer sleeve rotates, it allows the internal sleeve to open or close. This makes the bore bigger or smaller. The Katana has laser-etched bore values and a marker arrow that allows you to quickly set the size from .675 to .692.

Because so many players enjoy personalizing and upgrading their markers and attached shooting gear, most manufacturers make parts and pieces available separately. These are different color Orr-acle bodies from Worr Games Products.

Smart Parts

Four-barrel sets are offered by Smart Parts. The Freak is a remarkable three-part barrel. Smart Parts says to choose the back (in aluminum or stainless) that attaches to your marker, then the inserts based on the bore sizes you need and finally select a Freak Front or an All American Front (the difference is in the style of machined spiral porting) in the color and length you want. Freak fronts are available in 10-, 12-, 14-, 16- and 18-inch lengths, while the slightly less-expensive All American fronts come in 12, 14-, 16- and 18-inch lengths. If you have more than one marker, the inserts and fronts work with all of the backs, no matter how they attach to the receiver. Freak barrels feature spiral porting. A Freak barrel—one back, insert and front—carries a suggested retail price of $109.00, and a Total Freak package (one back, one front, eight inserts and a case) is $199.00 or $179.95 on *www.paintballgear.com* on 8-18-03.

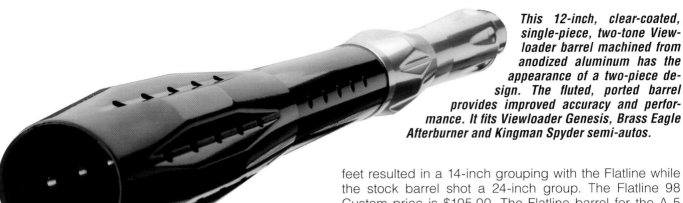

This 12-inch, clear-coated, single-piece, two-tone View-loader barrel machined from anodized aluminum has the appearance of a two-piece design. The fluted, ported barrel provides improved accuracy and performance. It fits Viewloader Genesis, Brass Eagle Afterburner and Kingman Spyder semi-autos.

Smart Parts also builds single-piece barrels that, they claim, shoot like a Freak. Spiral porting allows the single-piece Tear Drop barrel to retail for $49.95 and the Progressive to retail for $39.95. These barrels are available in five colors, a standard bore size and 12- or 14-inch lengths.

Tippmann

The curiously curved Flatline barrel system puts backspin on the ball for greater accuracy and 50 percent greater distance, Tippmann says, without sacrificing breaks on impact. Tippmann calls it a "system" because the Flatline is actually a three-part device made up of the shroud in the front, the barrel itself and the adapter. The kit or system comes assembled for Tippmann's suggested price of $149.95.

Tippmann also makes 12- and 14-inch "Sniper" barrels with a suggested retail price of $44.50 each.

Online, www.ontoppaintball.com (5-17-03) said the 3-pound Flatline barrel increases your effective range by 140 feet (Tippmann only claimed 100 feet.) at 280 fps. The Flatline registered "little or no arc" at 180 feet while the stock barrel on the 98 Custom required 7 feet of arc to hit the same target. Shooting to zero the marker at 50 feet resulted in a 14-inch grouping with the Flatline while the stock barrel shot a 24-inch group. The Flatline 98 Custom price is $105.00. The Flatline barrel for the A-5 cost $119.95, but MSRP was $149.95.

Viewloader

The 12-inch VL aluminum barrel is clear-coated and two-tone, polished black and silver. The two colors give this barrel the appearance of having two sections, but nope … sorry, just one. The mouth of the barrel is fluted and the entire length of the black fore-section is ported for "improved accuracy and performance." It cost $49.99 (6-5-03 at www.dickssportinggoods.com).

Worr Games

The WGP 2-Piece Classic is a fixed, big-bore custom-made barrel for $45.00 with rows of round-hole porting on the color-anodized fore end.

With the Kaner Barrel System, you can pick the front length (10-, 12- or 14-inch), the back-end bore dimension (.684, .697, .689 or .691) and the color. The front and rear pieces simply thread into each other. WGP says the fully ported aluminum Kaner is the most accurate barrel it has ever made. In black or chrome, the Kaner Barrel System includes three ported tips and four backs for $199.00. A single Kaner Barrel is $85.00 or you may buy a single tip for $45.00 and back for $45.00.

The WGP Triple-Threat is a great starter barrel kit. It includes a .689-inch nickel-plated back end and three tips to create barrel lengths of 10, 12 and 14 inches for $95.00.

Protecting Your Eyes

First, if you wear certified and approved head protection, there is never a reason that you should get hit in the eye. On the other hand, there are always going to be accidents, weird circumstances, people bumping a hair-trigger when they are trying to duck and fill their hopper at the same time, or a newbie fumbling around, getting familiar with all his new stuff under fire.

Get hit at ultra-close range by any marker and it's gonna sting and leave a bruise. Get hit in the eye with a paintball and you are going to experience a whole new world of pain. Even a scratch from a tree branch is so painful that you won't soon forget it. You could lose vision in the eye because the nerve bundles there are real screechers. Even putting in a pair of soft contact lenses can be irritating if they are the least bit folded on the edge or scratched. Like running your fingernails down a blackboard.

And your eyes are Out There! They are wet organs exposed to the elements. They itch and become irritated by pollen and pollution and we jam our big fingers in there and scratch and rub around. Just imagine if your brain or your stomach were uncovered and hung in a bag on the outside of your body. Wow!

You gotta protect the eyes 'cause if you don't, you can't play paintball or drive a sports car or see if the person you're smooching is really as good looking as the roommate says.

What if you do get something in your eye? According to Kim Rutherford, MD, NYPH Weill-Cornell Medical Center, New York, treat minor eye irritations by flushing the eye … after you wash your hands with soap. "Flushing" means splashing and pouring and gently squirting lots of clean water in your eye and blinking and rolling your eye around and hoping whatever it is gets washed out. Medical folks say not to get impatient. Flushing may take as long as 10 or 15 minutes.

If you try to remove an irritation with a handkerchief or your finger or the corner of your sleeve, you may scratch the surface of your eyeball. That would mean blurred vision and irritation (pain) for some time. Anything more serious – like getting hit squarely in the eye by a paintball – is probably going to require medical attention. So, play hard, but be careful!

Let's say you are running along from cover to cover without a mask for some stupid reason and – Bingo! – you get a stick in the eye. After you pull the stick out, carefully cover your eye and either have someone drive you to a hospital emergency room or call for emergency medical help. (Chances are that during this time, the field owner and the refs, all of whom have harangued you continually about keeping your head protection on, will be kicking your butt, so by the time you get to the emergency room, your eye may not be your biggest problem!) To save your vision, you will have to react immediately.

Now, a paintball (or the proverbial stick) in or around the eye will also give you a black eye, a so-called "minor injury" that can just ache like the dickens. It should begin to disappear, along with the swelling, in about 48 hours, but if it persists, you will want to see a doctor.

On the spot, however, put a cold compress over your eye and leave it on for five to 10 minutes and then take it off for 10 to 15 minutes. If there's no ice available, a cold soda can will do to start with or even a cloth soaked in cool water. If you use ice, make sure it is covered with a towel or sock to protect the delicate skin of the eyelid from an ice burn.

Use cold compresses for 24 to 48 hours and then switch to warm compresses. This helps your body reabsorb the leakage of blood and may help reduce swelling and discoloration. A couple acetaminophen (not aspirin or ibuprofen, which can increase bleeding) may then help to reduce any throbbing. As we have said, if what appears to be a simple black eye doesn't get better pretty fast, make a doctor's appointment.

Gogged! And hence the need for a high-quality set of paintball goggles and replaceable lenses.

12 GRAM

eagle air
rass eagle

5 ct. CO2 CYLINDERS

FLATLINE REGULATOR 1500 PSI

0 2 4 6 8 10 12
psi x 100
Airgun Designs Inc.

0 1 2 3 4 5
psi x 1000

DOT-E11194 4500PSI M4927
TC-SU 5303   310 BAR   04-C-0
6151-59202 REE   15.4CC

CHAPTER 14

AIR POWER

According to the "father of scenario games," Wayne Dollack, in paintball, nitrogen (nitro), high pressure and compressed air all refer to essentially the same power source and it is NOT CO_2. CO_2 is a liquid, Wayne says, that expands at different rates depending on the temperature and volume of the tank. CO_2 is usually cheaper and easier, but it is NOT the best power system and it is gradually fading in importance on fields around the world.

High-pressure bottles such as the AGD Flatline 4500 come in different capacities and maximum filling pressures. The capacity is stated in cubic inches (cu/in) and the maximum filling pressure in pounds per square inch (psi). The higher the capacity, the more shots you will get from a bottle.

Because of the high pressures the bottle must contain, the most common bottles are made of steel. In an effort to make the bottle lighter but retain the strength, there are bottles made of aluminum wrapped with high-strength carbon fiber. The wrapped bottles are lighter, but more expensive than steel bottles.

Two types of valves are used on HP bottles:

1. The standard regulator allows the player to adjust the pressure into the paintball gun. These regulators require a cradle as a means to attach to the paintball gun and a combination of hoses, elbows and a quick disconnect/slide check valve.
2. High-pressure pin valves act in the same way as the pin valve on a CO_2 bottle; therefore, this type attaches to the paintball marker just like a CO_2 bottle. This type of valve doesn't require extra hardware. The pin valve style typically has the output pressure preset by the manufacturer to the range required by most paintball guns. There are some HP pin valves that also have an adjustable feature.

A box of 12-gram CO_2 bottles for light use in markers and air-guns from Crosman and Game Face. This is where your paintball game started. Expect about 30 good-quality shots per disposable 12-gram bottle.

Is preset or adjustable better? Preset HPA bottles are less expensive than adjustable models. Typically, most markers have a preset input pressure that maximizes its performance. For markers whose operating pressure matches the preset output of the HP bottle, preset bottles are fine. In certain markers like the Autococker, for instance, the operating pressure can be adjusted. For those types of markers, adjustable bottles (although not necessary) may increase the marker's performance.

HIGH PRESSURE vs. LOW PRESSURE

Interestingly, tournament players were the first paintballers to experience the benefits of high-pressure air systems, as they needed improved gun velocity consistency to minimize penalties for "hot guns" and they wanted better cold weather performance. CO_2 markers typically "freeze up" below 40 degrees, and it is virtually impossible to keep your air "hot" by snuggling the tank against your body. That will freeze you rather than warming the air.

Making the move from low to high pressure, from CO_2 to compressed air, means that you will have extra weeks or even months, depending on the year, of playing time in the fall and early winter. Bottled nitrogen is available as a CO_2 substitute, but it is expensive. After field owners and operators discovered that air was virtually free after they purchased the compressors and bottles, the move was on to do away with CO_2. And, of course, if in the midst of a hectic tournament you believe that your marker is running short of power, you can get a quick recharge. The compressor is never going to run out and a refill is fast, unlike CO_2.

Although most tournament markers are attached to bottles filled with 3000 to 4500 psi, there are systems available that operate with 1800-psi tanks and which use

Many entry level and older style pump markers use 12-gram CO_2 cartridges as their power source.

conventional 20-ounce bottles, the same as CO_2. Such a bottle will usually hold enough compressed air for more than 350 shots. That's plenty for a recreational game but on the edge for tournament play.

THE REGULATOR AND WHY IT IS IMPORTANT

Your marker cannot use the full pressure direct from your tank. Slam 4500 psi into the chamber of a marker and something would have to give. It wouldn't be pretty.

So, a "regulator" – a device about the size of your thumb – is used to step down the pressure of the air in your tank to the marker or actually to a flexible metal-weave hose that is attached to the marker. By "step down," we, of course, mean lower the pressure.

Think of the regulator as a tube with a piston at one end, a valve at the other and a hole somewhere in the middle. Inside, between the piston and the valve is an empty chamber. (Well, not empty, exactly. It is filled with air.) Air enters the chamber from the tank and through the valve, is regulated or adjusted at the piston end and goes out to your marker through the hole. Simple, right? Well, only in theory.

On the piston end of a typical regulator is an adjustable screw that tightens or loosens a big spring pack inside the regulating end. This lets you increase or decrease the volume of air and air pressure inside the chamber. Tighten the screw down for less air inside and loosen it for a greater volume of air. When pressure inside the chamber is just right, this spring pack holds the piston steady and effectively prevents more air from flowing in through the valve.

The 4500-psi Worr Games Peanut is preset for 800 psi output. These are lightweight tanks. The 70-cu. in. tank and regulator weighs 2 pounds, 12 ounces. Output pressure is adjustable from zero to 1500 psi. Worr tanks have a 5-year hydrostatic retest date.

The CT 3-Way from Worr Games Products adjusts by using a 3/16-inch Allen wrench in the front end ($45.00 MSRP). With a Spooler Valve installed to smoothly distribute airflow, this 3-Way is called the Orr-acle and retails for $60.00. With the Spooler Valve installed, the 3-Way is hand adjustable or adjustable with your Allen wrench.

At the opposite end of the chamber is a small valve that operates in response to the piston. As we have said, how much air it lets in from the tank is governed by the tension on the adjustable spring on the other end and how great the pressure is in the tank.

Somewhere around the middle of the regulator chamber is a hole or port that leads to the marker. Now, all the air in the hose between the regulator and the marker is at the same pressure (unless there is some other "downstream" regulator). This air is at the same pressure because pressure seeks equilibrium or balance. Therefore, the air pressure is the same at the beginning of the feed line as it is at the end, or the same at one end of your bedroom, for example, as the other end. The only way this balance can be upset is if you are firing faster than your air source can deliver power through the system.

So, air enters the regulator by flowing through a valve into the chamber. In the chamber, the air pressure exerts force against the piston and this piston is supported by a spring pack. The pressure in the chamber causes the spring pack to compress, moving the piston a distance proportional to the pressure in the chamber. When the spring pack compresses to the correct or preset pressure, it moves just enough to allow the valve to close completely. This shuts off the supply of air from the air source.

Most regulators have adjustable output pressure. You only have to turn a screw in or out. This works much like the velocity adjustment on most markers. When you

turn the screw, you shift the distance of the base position of the spring pack in relation to the valve and air must compress the spring pack a different distance in order to close the valve. So, the air pressure must change in order to compress the spring pack this new distance.

A regulator also adjusts pressure by using the adjusting screw to move the valve. This does the same thing as adjusting the spring pack except that it changes the position of the valve in relation to the spring pack.

When adjusting a regulator, you may see some velocity fluctuations directly after an adjustment is made. Fire a string of shots, though, and the fluctuations should settle down. This happens because the regulator's springs do a better job if they are in a set pattern of movement. When you make an adjustment, the pressure in the chamber is different than it will be after normal firing and the springs bounce a little different. So, the regulator needs to cycle a few times before it begins to regulate properly again.

Most regulators have a pressure relief in case the pressure in the chamber becomes too high. This prevents extremely high-pressure air from entering your marker. The pressure relief is a small hole (or some other system) that is designed to allow air to escape from the regulator body. It is placed so that if enough pressure compresses the spring pack, the seal on the piston will clear the small hole and vent gas out of the regulator.

A regulator is a great marker upgrade, but if dirt gets inside, it can cause the valve to leak. This will cause most of the problems that are encountered with regulators. When the valve leaks, air will continue to flow into the chamber because it is attempting to go to equilibrium. If the regulator's valve leaks, the regulator will not be able to stop the high-pressure air from entering the chamber. You will suddenly have a "control issue." Since most markers that use regulators run at a lower operating pressure than the air source (low pressure, high volume), your marker will shoot with too much air and this will cause hot shots. You may find yourself in trouble at the chrono table. If the

The Flatline fiber-wrapped tank is available in two capacities (4500 and 3000 psi) and two sizes (47 cu. in. and 68 cu. in.) from Airgun Designs.

leak is really small, you will probably not notice a problem until you chronograph after you have waited a while since your last shot. After a long wait, you will take a shot and the marker will kick harder than normal.

A leaking valve can also cause the regulator to vent air out of the pressure relief if your air source has a high enough pressure. A pressure relief leak can also mean the seal on the metal that supports the spring pack is bad. This is probably the case if you have made sure the valve seal is not leaking and your pressure relief is still venting air.

HOW TO REPAIR TANK LEAKS

The most common CO_2 leak is caused by a faulty O-ring says Tippmann Pneumatics. This O-ring, which is located on the tip of your tank valve, should be replaced with a new one if it is found to be faulty. The best tank O-rings are made of urethane because high CO_2 pressures do not affect them.

MEET THE MANUFACTURERS
Airgun Designs

The Flatline from Airgun Designs is a 4500-psi (or 3000-psi) maximum compressed air system. Either 68- or 45-cu/in fiber-wrapped tanks are available with the following features:

1. EZ Turn on/off valve (only 1/4-turn)
2. High- and low-pressure mini gauges (1200 psi and 5000 psi)
3. Hardened Q-D male output and fill port with back check valve
4. Adjusts from zero to 1200 psi (best between 700 to 1200)
5. Includes dovetail mount that fits most standard drop-forwards
6. Anodized aluminum construction in various colors
7. Crossfire blow-off disc assembly
8. Easy-to-adjust Airgun Designs style regulator nut with lock ring

Airgun Designs suggests $480.00 for a 4500-psi 68-cu/in tank, but at *www.exoticsportz.com* (7-2-03) the

Air System FAQs:

Q: How many shots can I expect out of my 68-cu/in 4500-psi air system?

A: The amount of air used will be determined by many factors, most of which are not relative to the air system or the regulator. Conditions such as ambient air temperature, moisture content of the fill, conditions of the paintball, the match between your barrel and the paint and modifications to the marker are a few of the many variables that determine overall air efficiency.

Q: Will Brand X regulator give me more shots than Brand Y?

A: This is strictly BS and sales hype. See the above answer!

Q: What is a dual regulator?

A: In the common reference, a dual regulator first regulates storage air pressure in the regulating chamber and then lowers that pressure to a regulated output pressure.

Q: What is the difference between an adjustable regulator and a preset regulator?

A: A HECK of a lot more than just "lip service" and sales hype!

Q: Why make the transition from CO_2 to high-pressure air or nitrogen?

A: HPA is the propellant for all weather and temperature conditions. It is safer, less expensive to refill and is more player-friendly than CO_2.

A drop-forward mount such as this from WGP is required to mount your tank forward of the typical position when you take it out of the box. Many players find that a drop forward makes the marker more comfortable to shoot and more accurate.

3000-psi Flatline was offered for $229.00 (47 cu/in) and $329.00 (68 cu/in). At *www.paintballgear.com* the 4500-psi tank was $340.99 (45 cu/in) and $379.99 (68 cu/in).

Air America Regulator/Bottle Combinations

The Reg ($189.99) has all stainless steel internals, not chrome-plated brass. Its externals are lightweight aluminum alloy that have been hard-coat anodized for extended life under the most severe conditions. High-side AND low-side safeties to watch your back are provided. All fittings are rated at 4500-psi working pressure. The Reg is wrapped up tight on top of a current-dated 68-cu/in fiber-wrapped, 5-year rehydro tank. A limited lifetime warranty is included.

The Armageddon 88-cu/in 4500-psi nitrogen system sells for $349.95 from Air America. Armageddon is a single-stage regulator that is micro-precision machined in stainless steel and high-strength, tempered-alloy aluminum. It is designed to accept input working pressures up to 4500 psi. With an adjustable 200-to-1100-psi output pressure range, Armageddon is compatible with virtually all of the markers currently used in paintball. Composite-wrapped Armageddon bottles deliver unmatched tournament-level performance, high- and low-side pressure safeties, ambidextrous input/output hose and gauge positioning, fractional on-gun slide mounting rail adjustment, and precision input/output gauges.

Air America's $374.95 Apocalypse 2K is a single-stage regulator that is micro-precision machined from a solid block of the toughest aircraft-grade aluminum and backed up with a Limited Lifetime Warranty. It accepts input pressures up to 4500 psi and outputs pressure within the 200-to-1000-psi range. It is compatible with virtually all markers, mechanical and electronic. It has internally integrated on-off controls, multiple input and output pressure safeties, ambidextrous input/output hose and gauge positioning and on-marker system fractional slide rail adjustments. It is, of course, an approved U.S. Department of Transportation composite-wrapped pressure vessel.

Air America Regulators

The $114.95 Messiah series regulators are engineered to optimize the performance of "high-rate-of-fire" markers. They are designed to maximize low-pressure/high-volume regulated performance, while paying close attention to the confines of the emerging "drop-forward" crowd. The Messiah's overall profile was considerably reduced, producing an economy-sized regulator with professional, tournament-level performance that exceeds the requirements of today's most demanding markers. Messiahs are single-stage regulators capable of accepting input pressures up to 1200 psi. They are machined from a solid block of certified aerospace aluminum. Standard features include the new "stubby" regulator profile, performance styling, massive regulated flow rate and the same high-performance valve combination found in all of the Air America regulators. The Messiah series is designed primarily for on-gun applications as a secondary regulator. It utilizes a standard profile output thread and O-ring shoulder that allows it to be screwed directly into any standard constant-air ASA adapter. The Messiah may be used as a primary regulator for nitrogen and high-pressure air. It may also be used as a second-stage regulator in a dual-regulated nitrogen/high-pressure air system. The regulator's output pressure is fully adjustable from 0 to 500 psi to allow the system to be adjusted to service all markers currently used.

Air America's Unireg Vigilante Regulator comes in a high-pressure version and a low-pressure version. Both of these single-stage, high-tensile-strength aluminum-alloy regulators are $89.95 direct from the manufacturer. The high-pressure version's output pressure is adjustable from 450 to 850 psi, and it will accept inlet pressures up to 1200 psi. The low-pressure version's output pressure is 50 to 450 psi with inlet pressure ability up to 1200 psi. Air America says its advanced "Super Gun" flow volume design outpaces the HPA flow requirements of the most demanding markers.

At $114.95, the Unireg Black Ice is service rated as a secondary regulator for 3000 psi. It is available in two output pressure ranges: standard (an adjustable operational range from 250 to 800 psi) and low pressure (adjustable from 150 to 400 psi). With a standard ASA profile thread and O-ring shoulder, the Black Ice is designed for on-gun applications. Two 1/8 npt access ports are provided for optional accessory flexibility. The user's marker and the modifications made to it will determine the appropriate Black Ice pressure range.

CenterFlag

CenterFlag provides a variety of high-pressure systems for paintball. Dennis Ashley, a long-time paintball player and co-founder of Fox River Games, says his Hyper Flow System "resolves all the existing issues of high-pressure systems."

The single most important element of a high-pressure system (the regulator) is how it handles flow rate or the rate of pressure drop during a rapid-fire string of shots. When you play paintball, you need accurate paint placement and that means you want every shot to be strong and consistent. CenterFlag's Hyper Flow Regulator is designed

Chris Havlock developed the Crossfire adjustable regulators and is one of dozens of paintball designers and manufacturers who travel around to national tournaments to show off the newest, the fastest and the most reliable. Talking to these experts is a wonderful way to learn about your gear and get an overview of your favorite game.

to give you a consistent flow rate. The Hyper Flow has a compact, lightweight and easy-to-adjust design with the fewest possible moving parts (less to go wrong and easier to clean) and is a system that lets you fill directly into the bottle and filter before entering the regulator. The Hyper Flow features a two-way, push-button-type on/off valve with relief of low-pressure gas when you turn it off. This means the line between the regulator and the marker is empty, and that means greater safety.

CenterFlag's 201 series is a 4500-psi stainless steel tank. Its 301 series is a 3000-psi economy tank. You can purchase these tanks or the Hyper Flow (with or without the on/off switch) separately. An 88-cu/in stainless steel 4500-psi tank with a Hyper Flow regulator equipped with an on/off switch is $510.00 from CenterFlag. Without the on/off switch, this setup is only $415.00. Comparable 3000-

AirSource cylinders are full of CO_2 (88 grams) and ready to use right out of the package. Just screw it on your marker and you are back in the game, says Game Face.

psi air systems cost $380.00 and $330.00 respectively.

CenterFlag also has a Hyper InLine Regulator that can be changed from low pressure (90 to 250 psi) to high pressure (200 to 700 psi) with a simple spring replacement. Low pressure with high volume is for markers such as the Matrix and Shocker. The high-pressure kit comes with two springs (purple and orange). The purple spring is medium pressure, and its range is 200 to 450 psi. The orange spring is high pressure with a working range of 400 to 700 psi.

Game Face

AirSource cylinders from parent company Crosman are full of CO_2 and ready to use right out of the package. Just screw on the 88-gram/4-ounce cylinder and you're back in the game. The $12.95 (www.pyramydair.com on 7-29-03) AirSource is pre-filled and disposable. It adapts to any standard air port. Game Face says you can get about 200 shots per tank.

Crosman, the big corporate daddy for Game Face, is one of the world leaders in the production of 12-gram cartridges. They are sold in 15- and 25-count boxes for your backup pump or maybe your BB pistol back home. Game Face even has a 12-gram adapter that allows you, for emergencies (?), to screw a 12-gram CO_2 cartridge onto your marker. That would have to be some emergency.

And just to keep a hand in the higher pool of technology, Game Face has standard aluminum CO_2 tanks in 20-ounce and 12-ounce sizes for $39.04 and $35.19 respectively at www.pyramydair.com on 7-29-03.

JT USA

Of course, JT says your tank needs a padded cover for those "hellacious head-first bunker dives." The 2003 JT tank cover added a feature they called the Skid Fin

A 20-ounce refillable cylinder provides up to 1000 shots per fill in most playing conditions.

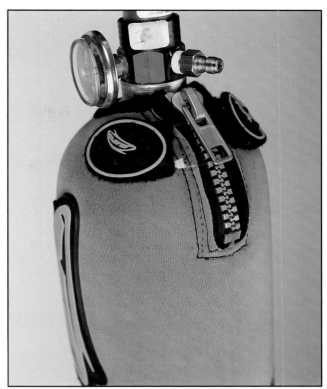

Neoprene tank covers from JT USA come in black, gray, blue and red. The zipper is heavy duty and an extra Velcro fastener holds everything tight. That black bump is the JT "skid fin," designed to keep the tank off the ground during those "hellacious head-first bunker dives!"

to cover their "industrial, man-sized zipper" with a Velcro over-closure. The cover is of neoprene construction with a slip-resistant butt to keep your tank tight against your side and to keep it from frosting you big time. (That's why you have a girlfriend!) It's available in black, gray, blue and red for $24.99 (6-6-03 at *www.paintballgear.com*).

Nitro Duck (Paintball Mania)

Nitro Duck air systems are widely recognized for their unique styling and reliability ... or perhaps for their interesting name and logo. Their new Mega Regulator has a high flow rate and dual-regulated output that eliminates the need for a conventional secondary regulator. It also has a convenient shut-off valve that stops air flowing out of the tank to the regulator so that the tank can be independently removed. This small benefit lets a player take the tank off his marker to get it filled rather than having to lug the entire marker to the fill station.

With a single-regulated air system, Nitro Duck says, the more you shoot, the more your velocity drops. This is because your first regulator was set at a specific tank pressure and as that pressure dropped, your output pressure dropped, too. Single regulators do not compensate for the difference in bottle pressure, so as a result, when output pressure falls, your ball's velocity drops. And this happens consistently throughout the game or as long as you are pulling the trigger.

A dual-regulated system works by keeping a preset pressure, 1000 psi for example, in the first regulator using two, totally separate pistons. The first piston is non-adjustable and takes your pressure down to 1000 psi. The second, adjustable piston allows you to set your output pressure from zero to 1000 psi. This eliminates any worry about pressure spikes, inconsistent regulation and the

need for an expensive, bulky on-marker regulator.

The Nitro Duck Mega-Reg uses what they call "Pressure-Consistent Technology" or PCT. Since all markers operate on a set air pressure, maintaining that pressure is vital to good shooting. A drop in pressure in the bottle during use usually means a drop in output pressure and ball velocity. Low-pressure (high-volume) markers are especially susceptible to this. PCT-equipped regulators are factory calibrated so as bottle pressure drops, your output pressure stays the same.

The adjustable Nitro Duck X-Stream Reg 4500 is CO_2 threaded and guarantees an output from 200 to 900 psi. It will work with any ASA bottom line. It features a large piston and spring pack for consistent high output. This lightweight aluminum regulator weighs only 4.8 ounces and is equipped with mini-gauges for quick pressure checks.

Nitro Duck says its Micro Reg, introduced in 1996, was the first CO_2-threaded preset air system on the market. In 1997, the Mini Reg became the first, true dual-regulated air system to offer self-compensation and full adjustability. Now, the X-Stream Reg features a two-piece adjustable design from 200 to 900 psi. Weight has been reduced from the 4500 preset by using space-age materials. Adjusting the output pressure is easy with the included wrench. For safety and convenience, this regulator offers a bleed-down feature that protects the downstream marker and also allows output adjustment without shoot-down. Internally, the X-Stream incorporates the largest piston in the industry. A large piston allows more air to be moved per shot and keeps the regulator pressure from falling off. The computer-designed and ground main spring keeps pressure almost perfectly consistent.

The X-Stream Reg is available in 45-, 68- and 90-cu/in 4500-psi bottles. "Now there's no need to waste money on a drop-forward bracket," the folks at Nitro Duck say, "the X-Stream will screw into virtually any gun!"

Nitro Duck's lightweight 4500-psi bottle is multi-wrapped. The base is aluminum. This is covered with a carbon-fiber wrap and then coated with Tuff Skin resin. The carbon-fiber wrap is 30 percent stronger than aluminum and allows a 30 percent weight savings by reducing the amount of aluminum needed to structurally contain the high-pressure air. The Tuff Skin coating is very hard, but does not add any weight. It enables you to get down hard and play tough without endangering your tank and air system.

Pure Energy (PMI)

The PMI Pure Energy range of compressed air systems is primarily of the screw-in, preset design. PMI has stepped-up the pressure in their high-end tanks to 5000 psi with a regulator to match that kind of power. The included regulator has a back-checked fill nipple, high-pressure/low-pressure burst disk and a mini-gauge that shows the tank pressure. Output pressure through the included regulator is about 850 psi. Pure Energy believes most blow-back markers (and that is the majority of paintball markers in players' hands) will work fine without the secondary step-down regulator required by a low-pressure marker. This 45-cu/in carbon-fiber-wrapped bottle/regulator costs $315.00 (MSRP) and has a 5-year hydrostatic interval.

Smart Parts

The Max-Flow 4500 system is balanced, temperature compensating and "extremely" high flow. It can be set up either gun mounted or with a remote and with either a 45-, 68-, 88-, or 114-cu/in tank. The high-pressure regulator has a pressure range of 300 to 1000 psi and the low-pressure regulator covers 100 to 240 psi. The regulators are available in black, blue, green, red and purple for $350.00 or $225.00 without the bottle. The $15.00 tank cover upgrade has a rubberized neoprene end cap to keep the tank from shifting.

The $25.00 Tapeworm lets you operate your Impulse marker at a lower pressure and eliminates any related re-cock problems. Normally, the Impulse requires backpressure from the paintball to re-cock properly, but the Tapeworm restricts air from venting from the air chamber, which prevents a drop in the air chamber feeding into the 4-way solenoid.

The 90-cu/in 4500-psi HPA tank from WGP has dual gauges, a dovetail mounting rail and a guard to protect the on/off if you land on it. Aluminum, with a stainless steel or titanium neck, the preset is $225.00 (MSRP) and the aluminum adjustable is $350.00 (MSRP).

WdP

The Angel A.I.R. 4500 is paintball's only electro-pneumatic digital regulator. A.I.R., by the way, stands for Atoms In Rhythm. It features an easy-to-read backlit screen, which is on for 25 seconds with the following information available via a simple, push-button scrolling menu: output pressure, tank pressure and estimated shots remaining (with a $\pm$ 10 percent accuracy, WdP claims). The pressure gauge reads up to 1000 psi and down to 100 psi. The cost for this system is about $525.00.

Worr Games

Bud Orr's people say this high-pressure air system is "the most consistent high flow air system ever made." It features a patent-pending design in a small, lightweight, small-profile regulator with high flow capabilities. The preset is 4500 lbs with 800 lbs output. The adjustable has dual gauges, a dovetail rail and a guard to protect the on/off if you land on it during a game. All are dual-filtered and available in aluminum with a stainless steel or (coming soon) titanium neck. The aluminum adjustable is 70/4500 for $350 MSRP while the aluminum preset is 70/4500 for $225 MSRP.

HYDROSTATIC TESTING

According to Nitro Duck, it is unlawful and unsafe to fill an out-of-date air bottle. All bottles undergo hydrostatic testing to make sure they have enough structural integrity to withstand 3000 psi. All aluminum bottles larger than 12 ounces that do not have any fiber or carbon fiber wrap need to be tested every five years. The date for testing these bottles is usually stamped into the top of the bottle. When your bottle date is due, you can send the bottle to the manufacturer for hydro testing. At Nitro Duck, for instance, this costs $28.00 for the test and $7.00 shipping.

"We do not recommend that people put CO_2 in a fiber or carbon fiber series bottle," Nitro Duck writes, "because of hydro testing. This is not because it is not safe, but because the bottle's chance of passing hydro testing after three years of use is drastically less. CO_2 causes the aluminum shell to shrink ever so slightly. When the shell starts to shrink, it actually pulls the aluminum away from the fiber or carbon fiber wrap. This can happen very unevenly and causes extremely tiny gaps between the two materials. Eventually, it causes the bottle structure to weaken. This can and in practice does decrease the chances of it passing the hydro test. When a bottle fails a hydro test, testers drill a hole in it so it will not be able to hold air again."

A visual inspection alone cannot insure that a tank is safe or will operate correctly, and because it is under high pressure, it could explode. So, hydrostatic pressure testing for leaks and structural flaws by pressurizing them with a liquid is necessary.

First, the valve is removed and the threads and interior of the cylinder are checked for corrosion, pitting or other abnormalities. If it passes the visual inspection, it is placed in a steel chamber, which is then filled with water at normal pressure. A glass burette attached to the side of the steel chamber will read zero, indicating normal or zero pressure of the chamber water. Water is then applied at high pressure to the interior of the cylinder. As the pressure increases, the cylinder will expand and push water from the chamber through a small hole and into the glass burette. After the pressure is released, the cylinder will contract and the water will move from the burette back into the chamber.

Under this testing, a cylinder is normally considered unsafe and will fail if:

1. The water level in the burette continues to rise while the specified pressure is applied. This could be due to a leak from the inside cylinder to the water in the chamber or to a continual expansion of the walls of the cylinder, both of which could be reasonable cause to fail the cylinder.
2. The cylinder stretched and with the pressure released does not return to its original size (or close to it). It would mean the metal of the cylinder is not resilient enough to be considered safe for use. The burette cannot have more than 10 percent of the displaced water remaining after the pressure is released. For example, if the expansion displaced 100 milliliters (ml) of water, after it contracts, it must have a reading of 10 ml or less to pass the test.

CHAPTER 15

PAINT!

According to DraXxus, modern paintballs are made entirely of non-toxic, food-grade ingredients, although oil-based paintballs are still made for foresters and farmers.

To make the hollow shell, manufacturers first pour water into a giant, heated mixing bowl. They then add a secret formula of sweetener, a preservative and a secret combination of food ingredients that companies will not divulge. Next comes the ingredient that gives the shell its resilient shape, gelatin. It is the same kind of stuff that is used in jelly and those chewy gummy bear candies. For about a half hour, the manufacturers melt and mix everything together. Then they filter out any globs that did not completely melt and line it all up for what they refer to as "the drop," transferring the gel from the mixer into a heated vat called the "gel tote."

Once the gel is securely in the tote, they lower in a giant blender and pour in food dye. Then, for the next 20 minutes or so, that big blender mixes everything together.

At other places in the factory, they use virtually the same method to dye what is called "the fill." Fill is the term for the paint that goes inside the shell of the paintball. It's made from polyethylene glycol, the kind of inert liquid used for cough syrup. Then it is thickened with wax. Think of the wax used to make Crayola Crayons. It's about the same as that.

The gel and the fill meet their maker in what is known as the "feed room." There, the vats of gel and fill feed a soft-gel encapsulation machine one floor below. This machine is the same kind used by drug companies to make soft gel-cap medicines. It also can be used to make soft, aromatic bath beads and many other oil-soluble nutritional supplements, such as vitamins A and E, garlic oil, fish oil, lecithin and so on. R.P. Scherer, the world's largest encapsulation company, was the first company to produce paintballs in this manner.

Next, the machine spreads the gel onto a cooled drum to create a continuous, thin sheet called a "gel

Brass Eagle's Afterburner paintballs are sold in 200-round bottles. They have fluorescent orange-green covers and flash-point-orange fill.

ribbon." This cooling cures the gelatin to the point where it can be molded into the hollow shell form of a ball. The machine presses the gel ribbon into a die with half-circle pockets, each forming one half of a paintball shell. Then, it does the next three steps in one shot. First, it aligns two half-shells together to form a hollow ball. Next, it injects the fill, and finally, it seals the two half-shells together.

Newly minted paintballs are still quite soft, and if they are not carefully dried, they lose their shape and even slight imperfections can jam your feed tube or your marker's chamber. So, next, they fall down onto another conveyor belt and roll into a tumble-dryer to be pre-dried while they are still airborne. At last, they are sent to a bakery-style rack until they dry to a specific level. The exact drying "protocol" or formula (how it is done and how long each step takes) is a carefully guarded trade secret.

To make paintballs with two-color outer shells, manufacturers use the exact same process, but feed two colors of gel ribbon into the encapsulation machine, one color for each half of the shell.

Finished paintballs go through an automatic precision counting machine before they are stored or boxed and crated for shipment to stores, fields and wholesalers. According to industry sources, more than 1.5 billion paintballs are produced and sold in the world each year.

Paint comes in a huge number of colors and combinations: balls that glow at night for scenario games; balls with stars printed on them; balls with good old playground names like Spaz! printed right on the yellow cover; red with white paint inside; black with pink inside; two-tone balls; neon colors; tiger stripe black on orange. Really almost anything you can imagine.

But what is a paintball? Well, we all know that paint has evolved and that we no longer shoot an oil-based paint that can only be washed off with turpentine, although that kind of paint is still available. (No fair sneaking a batch of this stuff into your loader, either.) As we mentioned in the story above from DraXxus, inside the molded gel is a mixture of polyethylene glycol, gelatin, glycerin, sorbitol, titanium

dioxide and FD&C-approved food colors. Because of its consistency and the alcohol inside, paintball paint can freeze when it is in the 40s (Fahrenheit), but don't worry about boiling. Its boiling point is practically 400 degrees!

From all of the possibilities that are available at the local field, at mass merchants and online, how do you choose what ball to shoot? (A note on prices shown in this chapter. Unless otherwise noted, all prices quoted were gathered online during the summer of 2003. Prices are for a case lot or 2000 balls and do not include shipping. Usually, these balls will be boxed or bagged in lots of 500 inside the case. The typical sites studied were *www.paintballgear.com, www.xpaintball.com, www. paintballexpress.com, www.paintballsouthwest.com* or *www.paintball-discounters.com*.)

1. Price is one consideration. A case of 2000 balls is around $50.00, but you can buy them for as little as $39.00 (plus shipping) or as much as $75.00. Even though it is not easy to practically evaluate the differences between balls, remember the rule, "You get what you pay for." Cheap factory seconds are probably fine for knocking around in the backyard with a buddy, but if you are practicing for a tournament or serious about developing a competitive team, you will want to spend a little more and get a better ball. You can buy almost anything online these days and there are several dozen Internet sites that feature very price competitive balls. You pay with a credit card and they ship UPS ground. Do you have a credit card? Do you want to wait a week for the balls to arrive? Just some considerations. If you are good at planning, this may be fine, but if you need balls in a hurry, buy local.

2. A local recreational paintball field or scenario game produced at a field will require that you buy paint

Arctic Dusk balls from Game Face are designed for play in cold weather.

Keep a ball sizer in your paintball gear bag to size paintballs when you buy field paint. Depending on the weather and the ball, a slight variation in diameter can cause balls to continually break inside your chamber and barrel. An accurate ball sizer helps you select the right barrel for the paint you will be shooting.

from them. And sure, on the face of it, they rip you off by charging way too much. Often double. But wait. There are a lot of reasons you have to pay more. They prepare the field, hire referees, carry insurance, get a county license, and most of all, they make their living helping you have a good time. So, pay what they need to charge for balls without complaining and chalk it up to an investment in a good, safe experience.

3. What you can buy locally is certainly a consideration, because unless you are buying a case of balls at a mass merchant – in which instance you will probably know more about what you are doing and what you need than the sales people at the store – it may be worth paying a little more and buying at a field or sporting goods retailer, a place where you can take your marker for servicing or which may even have a dedicated service tech who can help you with upgrades. As with any high tech equipment, lots of things can puzzle you and a few can actually break or just "go wrong" with your marker. At that point, it helps to have some local expertise rather than having to send it to the manufacturer UPS and wait for four to six weeks for it to be repaired (you hope) and returned.

4. A third consideration is the kind of image or statement you want to make. If all you care about is putting paint on the enemy, then almost any ball will do. You can get what you need fast and cheap. If, on the other hand, you want to be somebody on the field, if you want to coordinate your team or make a personal statement, let them know who you are, that you're not just any old schmoo running around with a mask on, then make a selection for style. For instance, get everyone on your team to shoot the same color balls or shoot only Yellow Belly Slam balls from PMI that insult the enemy (in a fun and friendly way, of course … not!) while they mark you as a player with serious attitude, somebody to keep an eye on. And that's a good thing.

So, we are going to take a look at some of the popular paintball lines, those you will see at your local field when you go out for a few hours on Saturday and those used by top tournament teams for world-class play. We'll look at the best … and the rest, but first a word about how to take care of the balls after you buy a case.

SIZE MATTERS!

Barrel manufacturers and paint manufacturers disagree. Do you match your barrel to your paint or do you match your paint to your barrel? Since we know that size differences no more than the width of a sheet of paper can make a genuine performance difference, this is a relatively important point.

Since a barrel upgrade costs in the neighborhood of $75.00 (one case of good paint) and you have to buy paint at the field, the question may not make sense. You don't have much control over competition paint and may not always know whether it is a paint labeled "factory seconds" or is the cheapest available. In a tournament, you will probably buy it still in the box or case, so quality will be marked and visible. Plus, every team will be using the same paint. Nevertheless, the best-fit possible is what you are aiming for because an improper size match to your barrel can cause problems.

If your barrel is too small for the paintballs you're

Ball detents such as these from Worr Games keep your balls in place in the chamber before you pull the trigger.

JT USA Maxim 2 Paintballs. "If you don't have the balls to play," JT says, "then use ours!"

shooting, no matter how smoothly honed the inside of the barrel is, the shell will rub against it on the way through, inducing a random spin. You will discover that you are suddenly shooting accidental "curve-balls." A spinning sphere creates lift and, subject to any breeze or torque on the marker while shooting, pulls the ball in various directions.

If your barrel is much too small, the ball will be squeezed and the number of balls breaking in the barrel will increase, leaving a mess that has to be squeegied out and swabbed dry before reasonable accuracy can be restored. Not a good position to be in when you're about to get bunkered!

On the other hand, a barrel that is way too big can be a problem, too, primarily on closed-bolt Autocockers and 'Cocker-clones. With a barrel that's much too big, balls can roll forward as much as a few inches or more before firing, reducing velocity. In extreme cases, the ball may even roll all the way through and drop out the other end! On 'Cockers and 'Cocker-copies, correct barrel fit is absolutely critical to holding the ball in the right position for firing consistently from the same position in the breech every shot.

Correct barrel-to-paintball sizing is a vital key to tight shot groupings, trouble-free marker performance and velocity consistency. (This topic is covered in greater detail in the chapter on barrels.)

"Why Don't the Balls Roll Out the Barrel?"

This is all about the "ball detents" that are built into your marker. Ball detents help feed balls smoothly and one at a time from the feed neck into the chamber for firing, and then they hold the ball in place once it is there. There are several different styles depending on the type marker you have or whether it is an open-bolt or closed-bolt style.

Many open-bolt blow-back markers use a spring to hold the ball detent in place. The detent here is a small plastic or metal ball positioned so that it protrudes just far enough into the breech to hold a ball in place once it drops out of the feed tube. The detent physically prevents the ball from rolling down the barrel. When you pull the trigger, the bolt rushes forward and pushes the ball past the spring-loaded detent into the barrel and instantaneously fires gas at it. This sends it shooting out the barrel and the marker re-cocks.

This system theoretically provides a forgiving solution to a couple of problems. It allows gun manufacturers to use a fairly large breech, which allows fairly large paintballs to pass through, while the ball detent will still hold the smaller paintball sizes preferred in competition. The kinds

of markers with this spring-and-ball detent system include markers at all ends of the price spectrum, from cheap to expensive: the popular Kingman Spyders, PMI Piranhas, National's Rebel, Mongoose, ICON and Silver Bullet, ACI, Indian Creek and most Brass Eagles, not to mention rippin'-fast tournament guns like the Bob Long Intimidator, WDP's Angel and the only non-blow-back model on the list, the spool-valve-powered Matrix, which uses two ball detents.

Tippmann's popular markers use a fiber-type detent that must be changed every few months to compensate for wear if you are shooting a lot. Instead of a spring-loaded ball, a fibrous "flap" protrudes into the breach to do the job. When these detents begin to wear, they may soften and collapse a bit, allowing a few balls to roll down the barrel. Double-feeding and paint breakage in the breech and feed tube can also result from worn fiber detents. Replacement fiber detents are cheap and can be changed in a few seconds. Tippmann shooters will want to carry a couple spare detents in their tool kit.

You may consider ignoring the old rule of thumb that said the ball should "just sit" at the end of the barrel and should not move unless you blow on it hard. That was fine for older pump guns that were all closed-bolt systems without effective ball detents once they were cocked.

Today's open-bolt blow-backs and Matrixes gain great accuracy from a fit where the barrel is just big enough for the ball to just fall right through, but be sure that the detent will hold on to the ball to prevent it from rolling forward into the barrel. On some markers, the amount of detent protrusion can be adjusted a bit to accommodate this setup.

The correct barrel-to-paintball size in a closed-bolt marker is critical, because it is the last resort for ball retention. For instance, Worr Games Autocockers and their many custom-shop derivatives, use a proven closed-bolt system. Once the ball drops into the breach, the bolt moves forward and closes or snugs-up against the ball before firing, placing the ball in front of the ball detent prior to the trigger pull.

In a closed-bolt system, the ball sits momentarily undisturbed in the breach, so that it is stable at the moment of firing. Some people argue this yields enhanced accuracy. In this position, however, with the ball actually in front of the detent, the ball detent system is no longer effective. So, to take full advantage of the closed bolt requires that the ball be held very still by means of the barrel being carefully sized to the average maximum size (measured at the largest place on the ball) of the batch of paintballs that you are firing.

At an event like a scenario game or maybe a tournament where a high volume of paint is being consumed, you may enter the first day shooting one particular batch size of paintballs, only to find yourself in the semi-finals shooting another batch or "lot number" from a different day of production, and then in the finals, yet another batch. No matter what brand or style of paintballs you're using, you are always wise to double-check your barrel-to-paintball size relationship or "fit" before taking the field in order to avoid surprise roll-outs or game-ending barrel bursts.

On closed-bolt systems, which are basically without effective ball detents once they're cocked, you need to carefully size and double-check every time you change paint batches, just to be sure. Remember, gelatin paintball shells can swell several thousandths on a humid day, and there are slight batch variations from every manufacturer. Better safe than totally gakked and fumbling around for your squeegee on the field!

STORING PAINTBALLS

Viewloader says for best performance, store your paintballs between 59 and 86 degrees F (15 to 30 degrees C) and 40 to 50 percent relative humidity. Protect balls from freezing and prolonged exposure to direct sunlight or heating vents.

Nelson Technologies claims that if balls are properly stored, they can be expected to last for several months, so try to buy only what you are going to use within a month or so. Store them in a cool, dry place and keep them in a tightly sealed bag using twist ties or some other means of isolating them from excessive humidity. Never leave your paintballs in the trunk of a car because the heat inside a trunk can be fierce and cause your balls to deteriorate.

There are times, especially in colder climates, when paintballs will show signs of dimpling. "In most cases," Nelson says, "you can open the bag of paintballs, and as you allow them to warm up to room temperature, the dimples will disappear." After the dimples disappear, reseal the bag.

Never leave a ball in your marker's chamber after you quit play or even if you are stopping for an hour for lunch. And it is an excellent idea to store balls in their shipping box or bag, not in your hopper. Empty the hopper and make sure there is no ball lodged in the feed elbow or in the marker's chamber when you quit playing.

Never look down the barrel. After you disconnect your air source, some air can still be in the line. Point your marker well away from anyone or anything close and pull

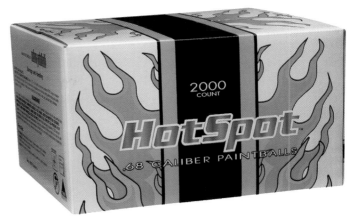

The Nelson HotSpot economy ball.

the trigger a few times to make sure the pressure drops to zero and there are no balls left in the chamber or barrel. If you feel it necessary, take the barrel off to check for paintballs left inside.

How to Restore Brittle Paintballs

First, store the paint at ordinary room temperature for a day or two (70 degrees F/21 degrees C). The brittleness will usually vanish and your balls should perform as expected. If something more is needed, move the balls around with your hand for a moment to re-orient them in the bags and expose them to a few more hours at room temperature. Exercise patience, say the folks at DraXxus.

Another remedy for reviving paintballs that have become brittle due to exposure to cold, dry air is to expose them to the humidity that, in effect, gets stolen during exposure to cold and/or dryness. You can do this by simply opening the bags and leaving them on a bathroom counter while you take a hot shower. Let the balls absorb the moisturized air for about 15 minutes and then stir the balls a time or two. Reseal the bags and return them to room temperature until you're ready to play. The added humidity is absorbed by the gelatin and usually restores performance completely.

If the balls still seem too brittle, let them just sit for a few days or weeks at room temperature. This is generally guaranteed to return them to normal, as the moisture from the fill slowly migrates back into the shell, restoring its resiliency. Reintroducing humidity usually removes the brittleness and also generally ensures there is enough moisture to make the shell resilient so it will "work properly," i.e. travel smoothly and accurately out your barrel and then bust when it hits its intended target. Whether the brittleness disappears completely or not, after these steps, the product should perform as expected.

Dimpled Paintballs

Manufacturers tell us that dimpled paintballs (those with slight indentations or dents in their gelatin skins) will usually fly just as well as those that do not have dimpled surfaces. In fact, they remind us that golf balls are covered

This player is rising over the top of the protective bunker and can expect plenty of paint to fly in his direction. A more protective firing position would be tight against the side in the shadow. Tonight, he'll be washing that shirt.

with dimples for extra-long flight. Of course, golf balls are uniformly dimpled all over and those dimples create multiple points of aerodynamic lift.

Nevertheless, if the dimples concern you, re-hydrate (moisten) the balls. They are dry. The same methods as above for restoring brittle paintballs are recommended. Be patient. Expose them to warm room temperatures and humidity and the dimples should disappear.

GETTING PAINT OUT OF YOUR CLOTHES

DraXxus Paintball says all brands and manufacturers of paintballs use the same general list if fill ingredients. These ingredients are not "paint" at all, but various colorants that are all listed by the U.S. Food and Drug Administration as GRAS (Generally Regarded as Safe). This means they are also used in ordinary household products, including cosmetics, foods and cough/cold remedies. The way to get them out of clothes (left on your clothes, they will stain) is the same as if your toast fell, jelly-side down, into your lap.

1. Cleaning is most successful when performed immediately. As with any spill, the sooner it is removed, the better the expected results.
2. Plain water works in most circumstances, on most fabrics and materials.

3. Ordinary laundry detergent used according to the detergent manufacturer's recommendations will be the final step. For more stubborn cases, you may consider using cold-water bleach while carefully following the bleach manufacturer's instructions.

Dusk by DraXxus is a "premium high quality paintball" manufactured by ProCaps for Game Face.

MEET THE MANUFACTURERS
Brass Eagle

The Afterburner line is Brass Eagle's brand of 68-caliber tournament grade fluorescent paintballs. These balls are available in four convenient quantities: 200-count bottles and boxes of 500, 1000 and 2000. The balls are filled with Brass Eagle's "Dry-Gel" state-of-the-art fill and they are available in four colors: yellow/blue/green with yellow fill, orange/green with orange fill, pink/blue/purple with pink fill and red/blue with red fill. A case of 2000 of these Brass Eagle balls costs about $55.00 or a little more than 2.5 cents per shot.

DraXxus

If you are looking for balls with attitude, National Paintball Supply and Game Face (a division of Crosman) market the DraXxus lines, each with their own special point-of-view.

Dark Legion is the DraXxus glow-in-the-dark ball. Used with a special UV loader, these are great, fun balls for play in low-light situations. There won't be any doubt about whether the bad guys get a face full of paint, even on the darkest night. A case of these special balls costs $79.75 online.

At the opposite end of the line, DraXxus offers a case of seconds for just $31.99.

The standard ball lines like Heat or the high-end Imperial ($78.99) are anchored with a set of medium to medium-small sized balls in the .689 to .691-inch diameter range. Midnight is the standard, economy DraXxus ball at $41.99. Expect a black shell for 300-psi-rated balls. At about $45.00 a case, Blaze is created for fun, no-pressure recreational play and as weekend rec field balls. These are non-staining balls that are easy to clean up. Breaks on target, DraXxus says, but rarely in the marker. Moving up to $54.95, the Inferno is a colorful and slightly heavier ball with "exceptional marking and trajectory." Next in the standard ball line is Hellfire at $67.95 for 2000. Hellfire is the lava brand – orange shell and orange fill. These brittle shells break quickly on target and the intense, heavyweight fills just can't be wiped away by cheaters on the field.

At less than $20 for a case of 2000, the Nel-Splat is Nelson's "bread and butter" ball for recreational shooting.

Game Face SolarFlare paint from DraXxus by ProCaps.

Game Face

DraXxus makes the Game Face brand of balls, SolarFlare, Dusk and Arctic Dusk at the ProCaps facility in Canada. Dusk is their premium, high-quality paintball: two-tone lava/yellow shells with yellow fill, blue/gold with pink fill or ruby/pearl with white fill. Available in quantities of 200, 500, 1000 and 2000 (yellow and pink fill only), a box of 1000 was $29.99 on *www.fogdog.com* on 7-28-03.

Arctic Dusk is a blue/purple ball with glacier-blue fill and is formulated for play in cold weather. It is currently available in 500-count boxes only.

JT USA

The Elite is JT USA's new premium-grade 68-caliber paintball. It is available only in a 2000-count box in bright pink with pink fill or yellow with yellow shell. The economy ball from JT is just $40.00.

JT's 68-caliber tournament-grade Maxim 2 brand comes in two box sizes (1000 and 2000) and two colors: blue/purple with pink fill and orange/red with orange fill. "If you don't have the balls to play," writes JT USA, "then use ours!" Cost is only $50 per case of 2000.

Predator is a JT USA 68-caliber "super premium grade" paintball in brushed red/black. Predator is available in sales sizes of 200, 500, 1000 and 2000. JT USA says this ball has an "exclusive 6-panel design." Cost is $45.00 for a case of 2000.

Nelson

Charles Nelson founded Nelson Technologies in 1940 when he invented a ball of oil-based paint that could be shot out of an air gun. Foresters used his balls to mark hard-to-reach trees. Nelson (*www.nelsonpaintball.com*) claims it was "the original and [it is] still the best."

Anarchy is their "small-bore" tournament-formula paintball. Single-color Anarchy balls are available in four

colors that leave bright marks in purple (called Mayhem with neon-blue fill), blue (called Chaos with neon-yellow fill), gold (called Fury with neon-orange fill) and silver (called Upheaval with neon-pink fill). The suggested retail price for 2000 rounds is $70.00, but online, the price was $49.00 plus shipping.

Challenger is Nelson's premium "Gold Medal Series" paintball. Nelson says this series has tough, durable, two-color shells to decrease breaks inside markers. It "shoots straight and breaks extremely well on target." A case of Challengers is 1000 balls, but, for comparison, two cases or 2000 balls costs $60.00 from Nelson or only $45.00 online. This ball is for "medium-size" bores. The exception to the two-color shells in the Challenger line is the black ball with green fill.

Two fill colors are available for the 68-caliber lower-end ("economical") Nelson Hot Spot ball—yellow and orange—but shell colors vary. Cost is only $35.00 on the Internet.

Nel-Splat is Nelson's standard-grade single-color paintball, but it comes in eight colors with eight different fills. This ball is for "medium bore" sizes. A 2000 count of these balls cost about $50.00 from Nelson ($39 online).

Nelson's mid-range 68-caliber paintball is its Premium and the cost for two 1000-round boxes is about $60.00 ($50.00 from your favorite Internet supplier plus shipping). Two-color Premium balls are only available with green/purple shells and green fill or blue/red and blue fill.

Nitro Duck

Nitro Duck has four grades of paint marketed under its own name:

Professional: The pink or orange glitter fill is super-thick, bright and wipe resistant. The thin shell is AAA high-performance gelatin.

Nitro Duck: This ball is filled with intense, un-wipeable fill, but it is still designed not to cause permanent staining.

The brittle shell is designed to break on impact, not in your marker. It has an interesting and very recognizable zebra-striped shell. Look for this paint in orange, green, white, pink or yellow.

First Choice Competition Grade: This is a mid-line paint, not expensive tournament grade, but still excellent quality. These multi-panel balls, gold panel plus the color of the fill, are filled with highly visible, potent and easy-to-clean fill.

Nitro Ball: This is inexpensive rec and field paint. It is a solid color with a thin shell and bright fill.

PMI

Pursuit Marketing is a big supplier of paintball labels such as Evil and Mercury, all of which are made exclusively for PMI by RP Scherer, the Florida-based paint company that figured out the process for reliable and economical encapsulation. PMI has a big lineup of popular playing balls in dozens of colors for the shell and fill, balls for the highest-level tournament play all the way to shooting at the squirrels in the backyard (when no one is looking…). So, unless otherwise indicated, the price for a 2000-count case was $57.50 during July 2003. This was PMI's MMAP or Manufacturer's Minimum Advertised Price.

The online exception to the above price and listed at $42.00 for a 2000-count case was PMI's Big Ball. When you save the $15.00, you may not get a choice of shell color, however. PMI says these balls are specifically sold for weekend warriors, guys who like to get outside in the woods and really blow their balls!

PMI classes its popular Marballizer as a medium-size ball (.687 to .690). The Marballizer is used by PMI's famous pro team AfterShock and by the All-Americans.

At .689 to .691, the tight production tolerances of the Premium and Premium Gold labels make them both medium balls.

The fragile shell of the All-Star (medium, .688 to .690) is actually printed with tiny black stars.

The PMI Big Ball is listed as a small-medium paintball with diameters from .687 to .691.

Polar Ice is advertised as specifically designed with a slightly thicker shell for play in the winter. Diameters are .689 to .691.

The beautiful El Tigre paintballs are small-medium paintballs with .686 to .689 diameters. They are characteristically painted orange with realistic black tiger striping.

Finally, PMI's outstanding ball called the Slam is yellow with insults printed on it in black. Use these "Yellow Belly" paintballs when you want to call the enemy names like Fool! and Spaz! Ah, it's all in good clean fun … NOT!

TC Paintball

Relatively new in the U.S., TC paint comes in three series:

The Viper Venom series is designed especially for thick wooded areas that most paintballs cannot penetrate. Its shell is formulated to break on impact, but never in the gun or on stray twigs, while tagging your opponent with bright fluorescent Venom fill. It is available in assorted fluorescent colors.

For those players always wanting to shoot something different, the Viper Platinum series is a sharp-looking metallic, tournament-grade ball for a value-oriented price. With bright Venom fills and brittle breaks, it, too, is available in assorted metallic colors.

TC says its Pro series is designed for "everyday hard core players! The same quality but with a fatal Venom fill." The fill is apparently just right for tournament events and to prevent wiping. This is a brittle, quality competition ball with top accuracy that is consistent over the chrono with easy tracking colors. The ball is washable in cold water and is injected with Venom neon pink, yellow and green.

Tippmann

WERKS Premium Paint is Tippmann's brand new line of high-performance 68-caliber tournament grade paint. The balls have a bright, thick and hard-to-wipe-off paint fill and they are available in yellow, gold, orange and pink. A case of 2000 of these balls costs $57.50 online. That's about 2.5 cents per shot.

Viewloader

The I-Balz brand of paintballs belongs to Viewloader, which is now part of the Brass Eagle family of gear

Viewloader's I-Balz – non-toxic, washable, environmentally safe – come in multiple sizes. This is their 900-ball bucket.

manufacturers. Four bright colors are available: red/orange with orange fill, black/purple with purple fill, black/gold with yellow fill and black/red with hot pink fill. Viewloader balls are available in counts of 100, 200, 500, 900, 1500 and 2,000. A case of 2,000 from a good Internet supplier costs $50.00 or 2.5 cents a shot. At that price, you can put serious paint on the enemy castle.

OTHER PAINTBALLS

32 Degrees

Team Colors premium-grade balls are $45.00 and the economy Competition ball is $40.00. The 32 Degrees Crypt-O-Nite is a glow-in-the-dark ball for $50.00.

Empire

Fuel paintballs are "high octane, premium design, precision shelling, victory formulated" and coming soon. "Fuel the fire!"

Great American

Here is a brand of good quality practice paint (.688 to .690-inch diameter) in solid colors for $40.99.

Java Paintballs (Kingman)

Classic balls are available in a variety of colors from black shell with hot pink fill ($64.95 per case MSRP) to blue/orange shells with orange fill ($59.95 per case MSRP) and white/aqua with violet fill ($64.95 per case MSRP). The Supreme brand is Java's tournament ball. It features "high quality gelatin, rounder balls with tighter seams, thick fill which breaks on impact and won't bounce off your opponent." Ball colors are full metallic gold/silver or gold/blue shells with neon yellow fill for $79.95 (MSRP).

Spyder Paintballs

The economical alternative, Point Blank Legends are about $50 a case and are a grade above the Weekend Warrior with thicker fill for better marking. The Weekend Warrior is $43.00 for red/blue shells with white fill for recreational play. ProBall is a yellow or orange small-bore ball (.686 to .688-inch diameter) that costs about $42.99. Steel is specifically designed for low-pressure markers and is priced at $50.00 per case. Then there is Worr Paint (for Bud Orr's Worr Games Products, WGP) with blue/pink shells and pink fill for $44.00.

Severe Paintballs

New to the paintball field, Severe is advertising four qualities of 68-caliber paintballs: Storm (field and rec ball), Hurricane (pro-quality field paint with Severe's "Beach Ball Shell"), Tempest (a high-quality tournament-grade ball with metallic "Vision Shell" for improved accuracy) and Cyclone (a bright, thick fill characterizes this ball).

The Premium is Nelson's mid-range 68-caliber paintball. The cost for a 1000-round box is about $25 online.

Team Colors

Team Colors is a division of 32 Degrees and is marketed through National Paintball Supply. Balls are industry standard 68-caliber size, many with two-tone shells and high-visibility fill. Three brands of balls are marketed by 32 Degrees: Team Colors, Playoff Series and Competition.

Zap Paintballs

Zap's Rainbow is just $28.99 because it mixes and matches all the leftovers from other production runs. Its Seconds are $31.75, but while they usually have blemished surfaces, Zap says there are no other problems with these balls. The 685-caliber Spank is $34.99 with black shells and pink, yellow or white fill in bags of 500. Zap's Primer is $35.99 and the Tork is $39.99 with durable, translucent shells with a variety of fill colors.

"Crank it!" Practice with your .685 gameball, says Zap. Amp is the 685-caliber high end of Zap tournament-grade balls at $46.99. "Power up!" Its specialty is a brittle shell. Chronic is "Pro-circuit proven with addictive performance." Chronic Ultimate has a .687-inch pro-grade brittle gold shell with fluorescent pink fill. The .687 Chronic pro-grade ball has a single-color shell and fill. The "way cool" .680-inch Vapor comes in at an economy price with the same color and fill as Zap's recreation balls.

Zap's unending line includes its "Game on!" ZSX Performance (.685), Sport (.685 with single-color shells and fill) and Recreation (.689 natural shells with blue fill) balls. Zap's .689-inch field balls are called Primer "Load up!"

CHAPTER 16

BALL HAULING

Ahopper is a plastic container that holds paintballs. Plastic is a catchall term for polycarbonate and the formula is roughly the same as for the thermal lenses in your goggles. It fits on top of your marker unless you or the manufacturer modify your set-up with a force-feed arrangement that allows it to mount on the side (in which case, however, it still feeds balls down through the top). A hopper is sometimes referred to as a loader.

Hoppers come in many different sizes and the shapes can be rounded or angular. Viewloader, for instance, makes a basic, roundish two-piece gravity-feed hopper that carries 200 balls, comes in about six colors and costs $3.99 on *www.paintball-discounters.com* (9-10-03). At the other end of the Viewloader product line is the $56.99 Revolution with electronic X-Board that also carries 200 balls, comes in five colors and uses a 12-volt power system to stir the balls, essentially moving them forcefully, but smoothly, into the marker.

Hoppers are available in either gravity-feed or force-feed designs. Gravity-feed hoppers rely on Mother Nature's own mechanics to drop balls down through the feed neck and into the marker. This system works just fine if you are not shooting very fast. If you get up to around 10 balls per second (some would argue five to six balls per second), however, the friction of balls wedging and grinding against each other and along the feed tube throat is going to result in an occasional dry fire or a chopped ball, which is to say a shot without a ball exiting the barrel or a ball breaking in the chamber because it did not fall completely out of the feed tube before the bolt slammed forward.

The upgraded electronic hopper has a battery-powered switchboard to ensure smooth and timely ball feed. Batteries power these small electronic brains to either agitate the balls or push them into and down the throat of the feed tube. This, coupled with an electronic eye that helps regulate ball flow, will virtually eliminate ball breakage in your marker, and an electronic hopper

The Viewloader Quantum Electronic Agitating Feed loader holds 140 balls and operates on one 9-volt battery. The "cat-tail" propeller inside feeds up to eight balls per second into your marker's chamber.

The 200-round gravity-feed Viewloader 200 hopper has a large opening for speed loading. A mounting elbow is included.

The Brass Eagle 50-count pocket hopper is one step up from 10-count feed tubes.

is definitely one of the first upgrades a serious paintball competitor should consider.

Because they are plastic and they attach to your marker by a plastic tube and feed neck, a hopper is easily damaged. On the other hand, they are made from a rugged grade of plastic and will take a little knocking around. The good news is that the basic gravity feed hopper is cheap. The bad news is that if you break one during a game, you are not going to play again until you get a new one. Maybe it's a good idea to have a spare.

Wiping out the inside of your hopper with a clean cloth is usually the only cleaning one needs unless you have an electronic loader like a HALO from Odyssey, in which case you will need to replace the 9-volt batteries every now and then. Non-electronic hoppers sometimes come apart for easy cleaning of the plastic halves, but unless a ball breaks inside the hopper, you will not normally need to clean it.

Don't store balls inside the hopper, though. If one develops a leak or a weak spot, it can be a lot more trouble than is necessary to clean out the dried paint and husk. If you finish a game with paint left, store it in a vacuum-sealed baggie in a cool, dry place.

HOPPERS AND LOADERS
Odyssey

In the past two years, HALO polycarbonate shell loaders have set a new standard for paintball. Ed Walker, head of the service department at Odyssey, which makes the HALO, says, "If you need to shoot fast, this is the solution." HALO, by the way, stands for Highly Advanced Loader Operation.

The Halo B belt-driven electronic loader has been available for two years. This true force-feed loader keeps tension in the ball stack and allows the HALO to actually accelerate balls into the marker via spring tension faster than the gravity limitations other loaders have. It also prevents the marker from disturbing the ball stack with blowback pressure. According to Odyssey, HALO can push 22 balls per second (more than 50 per second in

burst mode) smoothly through the feed tube into your marker's chamber – assuming you can make your fingers go that fast or you are "honking around" on full auto.

This electronic loader notices and reacts to movement, rather than acting on the gap between balls. Odyssey feels that gap-actuation is an inherent design limitation because it means that a hopper requires a gap or a space before it feeds a ball. Odyssey says that one reason for an electronic hopper is so that you don't experience gaps between balls! The HALO operates on six AA batteries, which Odyssey claims is the best configuration for long life. You can shoot 20,000 rounds (10 cases!) before you need a battery change, they say. The Halo B holds 170 balls and costs $150 from the factory (*www.odysseypaintball.com*) or $119.95 from *www.paintball-discounters.com* (on

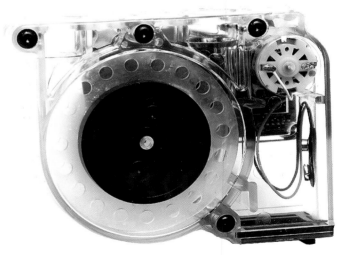

The Warp Feed from Airgun Designs is the world's first pressure-feed system. Instead of relying on gravity to feed your paint, it grips balls and gently pushes them into the breech. A reduction gear allows balls to slip when finished feeding so a ball can't jam or crush. The Warp will feed paint faster than you can pull the trigger; more than 20 balls per second with 12-volt input, says AGD, and with an adjustable, flexible hose, it and your loader are able to be positioned to the side or even to the bottom of your marker. This feature dramatically reduces your silhouette.

The HALO loader has built a name as the top-of-the-line motor-ized loader in paintball. It has three-speed motor operation, and if you can fire it, the HALO can feed it smoothly.

8-28-03). The HALO B is available in blue, black, clear, green, red and smoke.

The new HALO TSA is only $79.00 (MSRP). TSA stands for tilt/sound activation. Inside the hopper, the agitator's electronic switchboard runs the motor when it senses the sound your marker makes firing. If you tilt one way or the other when you shoot, the agitating mechanism pulls balls up toward the feed hole. If you tilt to the right, it spins counter-clockwise. If you tilt to the left, it spins clockwise. Maybe this isn't too important when your hopper is full, but when you are beyond the first air bag or sneaking down a trail toward Aladdin's Castle, this feature will come in handy. Still, it is a gravity-fed loader and 14 balls per second is its top feed rate. The HALO TSA holds 210 balls.

The HALO Backman TSA is $89.00 (MSRP). Yep, lean left and the paddle inside the hopper spins clockwise; lean right, the paddle spins counterclockwise to push balls toward the feed neck. The Backman LCD will give you information on:

1. Set timer
2. Shot counter
3. Motor duration (It has a range of three to 15. The shorter setting is recommended over a longer setting.)
4. Sensitivity threshold (A range of five, which is very sensitive, to 95, which is far less sensitive.)
5. Bolt style selection (Either open-bolt or closed-bolt markers. Since the open bolt starts in the back position, it is already cocked and when you pull the trigger it fires forward sending a ball out the barrel. When you pull the trigger on a closed-bolt marker, the bolt travels back to cock and then forward to fire. You only want the Backman to count this as one ball shot, not two. Hence the reason this selection is important.)
6. Three-speed motor option
7. Timeout adjustment (A range of five to 50; low numbers for high-rate-of-fire markers and high numbers for markers with low shot counts.)
8. A 220-ball capacity

The HALO TSA Backman hopper uses six AA batteries. Odyssey says that the AA battery setting gives nearly twice the active life.

HALO Upgrades

Several HALO hopper upgrades are available. How about different color HALO shells ($30.00) for different types of games? Maybe green for a scenario game or red to match the color of your sponsor's jerseys?

For only $24.95, you can buy a RipDrive Kit and self-install, or for $30.00, you can have a RipDrive installed at the factory. A RipDrive is a manual-feed mechanism that replaces the main shaft and allows manual pre-loading of the drive spring. The RipDrive was originally conceived for tournament players who "have to" be in the game, but it is available for anyone who wants a backup system in case the force-feed system goes down or the batteries go kaput. By manually rotating the RipDrive on the bottom of the loader, you can feed multiple balls into the ball stack at a time. This lets you keep playing at about your full fire rate. Depending on the height of your feed-neck, you can pre-tension as many as 12 to 15 balls for firing.

HALO Z-Code has a new internal jam-detection circuit for the HALO B. It even works on out-of-round paint. The new Z-Code circuit initiates a jam-clearing sequence to attempt to clear a jam – as many as three times – before changing to fail-safe mode to protect the motor and circuitry from being damaged. It costs $15.00 to upgrade to the latest Z-Code for your HALO B.

In fail-safe mode, the HALO rapidly flashes the LED red and green to warn you about a jam. You can then turn the HALO off and clear the jam manually. When battery levels are critically low, the same flashing warning will occur.

This new technology allows an increased rotational force/speed in the HALO without risk of damage. Z-Code includes all the features of past software updates.

HALO loaders manufactured before August 15, 2003, do not have the newest Z-Code. (If you have a HALO and the circuit board has a sticker on the back that has a number followed by the letter Z – e.g., 803Z – then you have the newest Z Code. All loaders with Z-Code have a Z on the back side, too.)

NOTE: The HALO's sensor system works by detecting the motion of the ball stack using infrared technology. Some black-shelled paints are infrared absorbing and HALO loaders have difficulty detecting them. Therefore, Odyssey does not recommend the use of black-shelled paint or even half-black-shell paint with the HALO. All other colors work fine, including blue and dark purple.

To offset your loader to the side so that it is easier to sight along the top of the marker, you can use a clear plastic offset elbow like the universal from Game Face.

Ricochet

If you like angular and fast, you should like an electronic Ricochet loader. Whereas most others have a nicely rounded girly shape, the Ricochet is straight out of Star Wars with a "deflection-styled body."

According to Ricochet, its name-brand loader is capable of a smooth 12 balls per second and holds 185 balls. The electronics are powered by one 9-volt battery that will shoot 5000 balls without needing replacement.

The basic Ricochet loader comes in two 180-ball versions: the 2K, which comes with an LCD screen, and the AK, which does not have a screen. The LCD is mounted directly on the back of the 2K loader so it is in your face with information: game timer, ball counter, low-battery indicator, reset and on/off button.

Both styles of loader, the 2K and AK, come in black and a multitude of colors. The 2K in a color other than black is $99.00 from Ricochet; in black, it is $89.00. The AK costs $69.00 in black or $79.00 in another color.

According to Ennis Rushton, president of Ricochet Development, three new loaders are coming on line now:

1. The 180-ball G2k gravity-feed hopper is made from heavy-duty polycarbonate and carries a $12.00 price tag.
2. At the low end of the mechanized loaders, the 170-ball $29.00 Rhino is designed for budget-minded players. Still, it features an LED and continuous battery-operated ball agitation.
3. At the high end, the new 190-ball Apache-Attack loader is capable of smoothly feeding 17 to 19 balls per second into your marker's chamber. "In testing," the reviewers at *www.warpig.com* said, "the prototype emptied itself very efficiently in 10.0 seconds of its entire capacity, yielding an emptying

rate of 18 balls per second." The Apache is black plastic but has clear diagonal windows on each side for a quick view of the number of balls remaining. The Apache-Attack features a 99-minute, 59-second game timer with 30- and 60-second count-down alarms on its LCD screen. Powered by a 12-volt motor, this electronic loader has a low-battery indicator, but Rushton says Ricochet expects to get 7500 shots per set of two 9-volt batteries. In case the batteries fail, this lightweight, 16-ounce hopper will function in gravity-feed mode! The Apache-Attack costs $129.00 from Ricochet.

The Viewloader Revolution with 12-volt X-Board Agitating Feed Electronic Loader "is the flagship of the Viewloader line." A 200-count hopper, with spring-loaded flip-up cap, feeds 10 to 12 balls per second into the chamber and it is available in several colors.

Viewloader hopper elbows are made from extreme impact plastic and are equipped with integral quick-release thumb-screws. Universal fit for 1-inch and 7/8-inch feed tubes.

Viewloader

The re-engineered VL eVLution II electronic force-feed loader is designed to feed balls smoothly, without interruption or snagging, from the hopper into the chamber as fast as you can shoot, up to 17 balls per second. It features a six-blade propeller and raceway feeder shelf for fast ball flow. The spring-loaded curved door opens down to help you load faster with less spills. The Revolution also includes an LED low-battery indicator, Infrared sensor controlling the on/off propeller actuation and battery-saving circuitry. It uses one 9-volt battery and is available in clear ($79.99 on 6-5-03 from *www.paintballgear.com*) or black ($76.99).

The VL Revolution holds 200 balls and uses "X-Board" circuitry, which means Viewloader patented this electronic, agitating feed circuitry. Viewloader says the new circuit board increases power to the motor by 15 percent. The internal anti-jam mechanism agitates the balls when the feed neck becomes empty and the four-blade propeller is rated to feed 10 to 12 balls per second into the receiver. Two 9-volt batteries are required for operation and the loader is available in black for $49.95 or for just six dollars more, you have a choice of green, clear, purple, red, blue and smoke.

Viewloader's clear plastic VL Quantum ($29.99) is an electronic agitating feed loader with a cat-tail propeller or agitator that moves up to eight balls per second into your receiver. This is fine for a beginner or intermediate player. The Quantum uses a 9-volt battery and holds 140 balls.

The $9.95 VL 200 is an inexpensive 200-count gravity-feed loader that comes apart for a thorough cleaning. Look for it in clear or black.

Viewloader offers two plastic elbows (the VL Bow) to channel balls from the feed tube at the base of the loader into the marker's receiver. Integral thumbscrews are used for tightening and universal fittings allow use on 1-inch and 7/8-inch feed tubes. These black or clear elbows cost between $1.00 and $5.00 depending on the style and attachment mechanism.

This fine harness from Allen lets you carry four extra pods of paint horizontally and either a water bottle or an extra tank of air. It's light and rugged and can keep you in play at critical times when your team is depending on you.

Harnesses with pods to carry extra paintballs like this clear, 100-round plastic pod from Allen are virtually mandatory for tournament play, where you shoot fast and furious, and scenario games, where you can be on the field for hours at a time.

CARRY EXTRA AMMO!

What wise man (or woman) once said that he would rather have 100 too many than just one too few? Well, paintball is like that, especially the higher you rise in competition. So, when you are ready to carry extra paint, take a close look at the harnesses and canisters the pros are wearing. One thing's for sure. These guys never have to surrender because they run out of ammo!

If you are an enthusiastic player, if you just like to shoot a lot of paint or if your team assigns you the job of laying down paint on an enemy position while others sneak around the side, you are going to need to carry a lot of paint into the field for a big game or a scenario event. Most serious players do carry extra paint – a whole lot of it, too – so paintball manufacturers have responded with lots of ways to help.

MEET THE MANUFACTURERS
Allen

You can haul paint in multiple configurations with Allen's V-Gear. Allen says these "tight knit mesh pouches are light, airy and easy to clean" with "Duroplex backing and a Twice-Over Belt for support." The double-wide Velcro closures on the pouches are coupled with grid loops on the hard-to-reach pouches. V-Gear tube carriers fit any 150-round pod or the Allen SNAPP Speed Loaders. Sizes and prices range from the 450-round three-tube model for $39.95 direct from Allen to the large 900-round and one spare tank model for $79.95.

Allen also makes a set of ball-carrying straps and tubes in their Thunderwear line. These are designed to be used with the Allen Lightning 150 tubes. Depending on their carrying capacity, from 600 to 900 rounds, Thunderwear straps and pouches can be ordered direct from Allen for $40.00 to $60.00. A pack of five plastic tubes is $9.95.

Allen makes a speed loading tube that does not require an adapter. Simply pull it out of its pouch, find the alignment bar on the tube with your fingers – you can do this with your eyes closed or while you are on the lookout for a member of the opposition cutting around the air bag – to line it up with the edge of your Allen Ammo Box hopper, push it in and the balls spill out. When you pull it out, the lid automatically snaps shut. This loader tube allows you to "top off your tank" without spilling and wasting balls. The SNAPP carries 150 rounds, but fits in 140-round butt packs. It is made from "extreme impact clear polymer" and available in multiple colors for $6.95 each from Allen.

Ancient Innovations

Unlike standard hopper-based loading systems, the q-loader requires neither gravity nor batteries to silently and reliably load balls at speeds in excess of 30 bps. Using a series of q-pods, q-loader's patent-pending torsion spring system gives you the freedom to maneuver and continuously shoot from any position without regard

The Game Face 5-Tube Deluxe Ammo Pack has a dual waistband adjustment system and holds any size standard paint tubes in a vertical arrangement.

The Six-In-One-Ammo Pack from Game Face holds any tubes of standard size and a replaceable air source. Tubes load horizontally.

to gravity.

The q-loader's mounting flexibility lets you position the q-loader on your marker in the manner that best suits your style or preference. Typical mounting configurations of this tubular-style loader result in a reduced target profile compared with a standard hopper mounting. Each q-pod holds 100 balls and, fully loaded, weighs just less than some empty hopper-based loaders.

The basic q-loader system includes five q-pods that are the same shape and size as standard 140-round paintball pods. The system comes with a reload silo and socket for refilling the q-pods between games and mounting hardware. Additional q-pods may be purchased separately.

Game Face

The Game Face Hinged Pod System (HPS) by DraXxus is a convenient, lightweight belt clip that comes with three 100-round pods – filled, of course! Each pod has a hinged top for quick loading under fire. Refill pods are sold separately. You might need more paint refills than this in a tournament, but your opponents would have to be very slow and very poor shots, indeed.

The star of the Game Face show is its large, Six-In-One Ammo Pack that holds six tubes of paint horizontally, three to a side, and a spare CO_2 tank in the middle.

Their black, five-tube Deluxe Ammo Belt ($20.65 at *www.pyramydair.com* on 7-29-03) holds tubes of any standard size and includes a small pocket for your car keys, money for soft drinks and even a pocketknife. Sewn into the belt are a squeegee clip, padded back support and dual Velcro waist-adjustment system.

The black Game Face belt pouch can be purchased to hold either two 100-round or two 140-round tubes. Game Face offers both 100-count ($8.32) and 140-count ($9.52) empty tubes for guys who like to haul paint and don't like to return to base for a refill.

JT USA's unique neoprene SlamPak SpeedPod harness carries four speed pods in a one-size-fits-(almost)-all harness that doubles as anatomically correct kidney support.

JT USA

The Pro Harness is expandable and reducible in design, holding from one to 20 tubes (more if you absolutely must, JT says) of spare paint. The patent-pending "Stick-n-Go" system allows you to add or remove pod sleeves with a twist of the wrist. Its super-wide elastic flap pulls tight for a secure, comfortable fit even in really demanding and physical games. This pack is jammin' and won't jiggle loose at rush hour.

The JT Slammer System is fresh and different. According to JT you'll "get sideways" over it. It'll carry four Speed Pods in a one-size-fits-almost-all horizontal harness with a low front profile that doubles for "anatomically correct kidney support." (Bet you didn't know you needed that yet.) The soft neoprene pod housing allows easy tube entry or removal from the right or left sides with no Velcro straps. The Slammer has a special pocket so you won't forget or misplace your barrel plug. But we said this was a system, and the other parts are the JT Speed Pods, paint canisters designed for quick fill without spilling because they have an internal baffle to prevent spillage even if the hopper lid stays open. Speed Pods extend your paint capacity from 120 to 150 balls each and are designed to work specifically with Viewloader hoppers.

Finally, the Slammer has a Game-On timer to help you synchronize game times for tactical planning from five to 99 minutes and a one-minute warning beep. It attaches directly to the speed collar for heads-up visibility. Batteries are included.

Major Paintball

The Super Sack from Major Paintball is designed for storage, transport and loading bulk quantity paintballs into individual paintball loader tubes and hoppers. The Super Sack will save time and money, eliminating the

Load up! Three ways to load your hoppers and pods: 1. Grip your marker between your knees. Open the lid of your hopper. Pour balls out of the provided bag. Pick up and blow off all the balls that fell on the ground. 2. Use Brad Vincent's Paintball Rocket ($39.95 MSRP) and never spill a ball. 3. Fill everybody's tubes with a Super Sack from Landon Kissack's Master Mine. Your choice!

"scoop and pour" method or trying to pour balls directly out of a baggie. No paintballs on the ground now! Holds 2000 balls and speed loads directly into tubes. The Super Sack is made from heavy-duty 600-denier nylon with moisture-proof coating, drawstring closure and adjustable shoulder strap. It can be purchased for $29.95 at *www. majorpaintball.com* on 9-3-03.

Mantis

Mantis manufactures a half-dozen harness systems, all with zipper pockets in the back for miscellaneous item storage. The pod tube holders are flexible and will hold 100- or 140-count paint tubes; one size does fit all. Most are available with a flexible black waistband, while the tube holders are accented in red, blue or gray. The $55.00 Pro 3+2 holds five tubes; the $60.00 Pro 4+3 holds seven tubes and the $65.00 Pro 5+4 holds nine pods. In addition, Mantis sells the Hive (five angled pods for quick recovery at $45.00), the Diamond (five pods with an extra wide belt for $35.00) and the only horizontal tube harness in the line, the Horizontal, which holds five pods in an open-ended design for left- or right-handed players ($49.95). All prices are direct from Mantis at www. mantisgear.com.

Raven

Raven has three good-looking paint-hauling harnesses in their OBG Deluxe Pod Pak line. They have secure-hold double-adjustment belt systems made from highly durable Cordura nylon with reinforced stitching that offer a snug fit and open-ended pod pockets with elastic tube holders. You can buy this in two-tone silver on black. It has a removable hook for goggles or gloves when you are off the field. These harnesses are available in either 41-inch (for 28- through 36-inch waistlines) or 49-inch (for 36- through 42-inch waists) lengths. The largest harness is the $59.95 6+5 (11 pods of paint!) and there is a 4+3 for $49.95 (MSRP). The $44.95 (MSRP) 4+4+Remote air slot looks good on players using a remote.

Viewloader's jam-free, force-feed, ball flow system uses a six-blade propeller for fast and uninterrupted ball flow in the eVLution II electronic loader.

Viewloader

For quick refills during a short game, Viewloader offers a heavy-duty Cordura nylon loader pouch with an adjustable web belt. It includes two 100-round tubes. Viewloader also sells 104-round tube loaders, which it calls "Attitubes." Attitude – attitubes – get it?

The Pax Ball Hauler is a heavy-duty Cordura nylon loader pouch with an adjustable web belt. It comes with two 100-count tubes.

This company's "Attitubes" are 104- or 145-count spare tubes for filling your loader in the field or between games. Flip the cap up and pour balls directly into the loader. .

Worr's Nartech line of collapsible harnesses lets you carry as much paint as you can handle around your waist. This is their seven-pod vertical harness. The small Nartech pack will carry up to 11 pods while the large pack will carry a massive 17 pods, more than a case of paint.

The 2-1 Tactical Harness System (THS) from Worr equipped with the drop-down leg strap will feel just right for many players.

Worr Games

WGP's collapsible harness is available in two sizes, a small pack that can carry up to 11 pods or a real monster pack that carries 17 pods (that's a whole case of paint)! Every time you take a pod out of the pack, it snugs up a bit. When you need to finish the game, you don't have to worry about getting shot in a flopping harness. This $65 (MSRP) pack is lightweight, comfortable, provides excellent kidney support and is machine washable.

Worr's THS (Tactical Harness System) is available in 2+1, 3+4, 4+5 and 5+6 configurations. Pods are included. The THS comes with a Velcro release system, adjustable elastic side straps, nylon stitching, and, Worr says, super sizers are available. Two features that will make everybody happy are a concealed, built-in credit card/key pocket and a retractable pod pouch in which you can carry many things besides extra or empty pods. The 2+1 system can be upgraded to a drop leg unit similar to the style of harness rigs that SWAT teams use.

Play Hard and Play Safe

1. Treat every marker as if it were loaded.
2. Never point the marker at anything you don't wish to shoot.
3. Never look down the barrel of a marker.
4. Keep the marker on "Safe" until you are ready to shoot.
5. Always wear eye, face, ear and neck protection that is designed specifically and certified to stop paintballs.
6. Never shoot a person who is not wearing proper protection and never shoot someone at very close range.
7. Keep the barrel plug in the marker's muzzle or the cover over it when not shooting or actively engaged in a game.
8. Always remove the gas source before disassembling your marker. Markers with regulators will hold pressure even after the tank is removed. Shoot your marker several times in a safe direction after the tank is removed to de-gas it completely.
9. Store the marker unloaded and de-gassed in a clean, cool, locked place.
10. Follow the warnings listed on the gas source for handling and storage.
11. Never use paintballs other than those specified for your marker.
12. Never shoot fragile objects such as windows or animals.
13. Paintballs may cause staining on porous objects such as stucco, brick and wood.
14. Always measure your marker's velocity before playing. Never shoot at velocities in excess of 300 fps.

Before you enter the field of play for a tournament, a scenario game or even for recreational play, you will need to shoot your marker over a chronograph to check the speed of your paintballs. A 280-fps speed is typical to prevent injuries.

CHAPTER 17

WHAT TO WEAR

Paintball is not like basketball or bridge. Paintball is something of a cross between blackjack, track and field, and maybe boxing. You need protection from the impact of the speeding balls, especially if someone shoots you at close range or you take a hit in the face. Shooting someone at a distance of a few yards violates the spirit of fair play, but it happens and a hit in the face is relatively common as players stick their heads around obstacles to look for the opposition.

BODY PROTECTION

Get this one! JT USA has a padded chest protector, the eMotion for $42.99, that may offer the ultimate in upper body protection. It's super-hero-styled, too, with bulging pecs and a real six-pack leading to a flat, muscular tummy. It's hot! The puncture resistant Rhino-Hide construction is flexible and vented for comfort and maximum protection. Adjustable elastic Velcro side and shoulder straps make this comfortable without restricting your movement.

The $34.99 (*www.thesportsauthority.com* on 7-29-03) chest protector from Game Face may not look as buff, but it will keep balls from making bruises on your chest, back and sides.

JT also has padded eMotion shin and ankle guards ($44.99 on 6-6-03 on *www.paintballgear.com*) for practically full-body protection. These are constructed with compression-formed and puncture-resistant Rhino-Hyde. Non-slip inner pads will keep you secure by holding these guards in place even when you are running and jumping.

Safety-conscious manufacturers like JT, Raven and Game Face have an item that needs to be in everyone's pack, a real 360-degree neck protector. JT's is high-density neoprene that safely attaches with a flexible Velcro closure. The Raven ($9.99) offers extra trachea protection and slits for venting on the sides. The black Game Face neck protector was $6.99 on *www.fogdog.com* on 7-29-03 and featured an inner lining for extra comfort.

Raven has a set of black protective gear that looks

rough and tough enough for any paintball venue. They identify their gear line as Optimized Bio Gear (OBG) and each of their protective pads and guards comes with a storage bag and reinforced stitching so that they won't bust open the first time you throw your body behind a log or scrape against the ragged side of a log bunker. One size fits all.

The Knee/Shin Guards ($44.95 MSRP) and the Knee Pads ($24.95 MSRP) feature two inches of shock-absorbing memory foam in the knees and an inch of impact-absorbing dense inner foam in the shins. The outer shell is two-mil washable neoprene and they secure around your legs with adjustable Velcro straps. The Elbow Pads ($14.95 MSRP) offer one inch of absorbent, dense inner foam.

An often-overlooked item on every field of play (at least in our experience) is a Throat Protector ($9.95 MSRP). Raven offers 360 degrees of protection from the exposed trachea to the back of your neck. It is washable, adjustable and vented for air flow without loss of protection. Get hit in the throat just one time, and you will swear by one of these forever.

Raven's OBG Slider Shorts ($39.95 MSRP) are breathable, form-fitting lycra/spandex. They have a removable and replaceable soft cup to "protect your valuables" and an elastic waist. Slider Shorts are available in sizes medium, large, extra large and double extra large. If you like a tight fit, like a sense of security or just like "having it all together," these are for you. If you don't like the clingy, pressure feeling of road-bike shorts, you are guaranteed not to like these.

Speaking about protective gear, how about Raven's unique Hydro Pack ($39.95 MSRP)! It is a self-contained drinking pack that straps on your back. The drinking straw can easily be taken out, Raven says, and then tucked away again. It holds 70 fluid ounces in a removable, leak-

Lightweight, flexible body armor for chest, side and back protection from Game Face.

Always wear eye protection specifically designed for paintball!

proof bladder. The outer shell is black nylon with cinch strap and adjustable shoulder straps. So, if a pint is truly a pound the world around, the Hydro Pack is like having a 4.5-pound monkey above your harness on your back. Refs will like this, but although it lays flat, it seems that on a hot day when you would most need the water, it is going to be warm and your back is going to be hot and sweaty. Our guess is, "Nice try, but not quite the answer."

Allen Paintball Products offers a set of one-piece knee/shin guards that are designed for paintball players. Wear these and you can "slide into a bunker without tearing up your legs," Allen says. Knowing the widely mixed sizes of paintball players we have seen, our only question about these lightweight guards is their "one-size-fits-all" design. We recommend you try these (or any other personal item) before buying to be sure they fit your legs. Allen's knee/shin guards come in pairs for $49.95 (*www.allenpaintball. com* on 8-26).

And we would be remiss if we did not mention that special protection for men is available for their private parts. It happens occasionally that a ball fired at close range causes significant pain to the ball zone, the testicular region. Pick up any paintball magazine, and soon enough, you will see a cartoon dealing with this very subject. We have even seen a photo of the region with the telltale bruise on the Internet – and that wasn't a pretty sight!

So, if you are cringing just reading this, you should look into the idea of wearing a protective cup. These gear items have come a long way since your dad played Little League baseball and the coach demanded that the kids wear hard cups and jock straps. Soft cups are available

JT's high-density neoprene neck protector is designed to conform to your anatomy.

Anatomically correct dual-layer JT protection to cushion the smashing those delicate bones in your knees take during an action game.

Oh, baby! If you are into paint – and we mean INTO paint – then you want to take a look at the protection the adjustable JT eMotion chest protector in Rhino-Hyde will give you. Plus, it has the super-hero muscle look, front and back.

that will give you plenty of protection without the grinding, irritating feeling of a strapping a coffee cup over your groin.

A paintball to the groin is one of those sports-related injuries that is kind of funny only when it happens to some other guy...

MASKS, GOGGLES AND LENSES
Dye

Dye says its Invision goggle system is "designed for the art of winning." That sounds good. The body of the goggles is three-stage foam construction with three different foam materials having three distinctive foam densities. Dye says this gives excellent fit and shock absorption. The low-profile frame is modeled from tear-resistant polyurethane and designed for maximum flow-through ventilation. The basic mask is black while the multi-directional vents are available in six colors: red, clear, blue, yellow, smoke and olive. This goggle system comes with a thermal clear lens, integral visor and goggle bag. According to Dye, the lens is the first compound-radius lens ever designed for paintball and it gives you perfect optical clarity. Dye recommends a retail price of $87.95, but it was listed at $64.99 plus shipping at www.paintballgear.com on 9-11-03.

Game Face

Game Face, part of the Crosman airgun family and a partner with ProCaps to market DraXxus balls, offers

The Game Face SKUL mask and goggle system includes anti-scratch and anti-fog lenses.

two highly stylized and recognizable masks, the Skul and the 3D Skul. Game Face says these are not masks, but "goggle systems."

The Skul offers optically correct vision in a one-piece, flexible design. The lens has anti-fog and anti-scratch coatings. The body of the mask features slanted vents and offers complete forehead, face, eyes and ear protection. On 7-29-03, the Skul was just $29.99 on www.pyramydair.com.

In addition to the above Skul features, the body of the 3D Skul has a classy carbon fiber 3D finish and the mirror lens is smoked to cut down on glare. The lens also features anti-fog and scratch-resistant coatings.

JT says its FX-10 is a "dual-density, co-molded, biomorphic mask." JT's Axiom quick-change lens snaps let you change lens tint as the weather changes for the very best view of your playing field. Excellent fog resistance and optical clarity signify JT's lenses.

JT USA

JT USA currently offers several dozen goggles, and their catalog is written by a science fiction writer who just chugged his first beer! It's high test. JT truly has an incredible lineup and any player could browse through their catalog and find something to like that is within their price range. JT divides their goggles into three systems – Axiom, Spectra and Elite – with specific qualities in each.

JT USA Axiom Series: The FX-10 is the new goggle and features a patent-pending quick-change lens-locking system. You have a choice of anti-fog thermal or single lens and the visor is integrated into the face of the goggle. JT describes the mask as dual-density, co-molded and bi-morphic. They say it's "bitchin!" It better be. The FX-10 comes with an integral visor and a goggle bag ($69.99 for thermal lenses, $64.99 for single lenses on 6-5-03 at www.paintballgear.com).

JT USA Spectra Series: The Proteus Sports-Comm Goggle System comes with a built-in audio communication system that plugs in over your right ear. JT says all you have to do is plug it in to your personal FRS recreational two-way radio and you and your team or your manager can talk, give directions … or just hang around and listen

The JT USA Chameleon Series Proteus goggle system, which changes colors when you move, is designed for maximum protection with a minimum target zone.

Replaceable tinted lenses allow you to respond quickly to variations in weather and light for the best possible contrast in your view of the playing field.

to music from your mp3 or CD player (not included). What is included, however, is a thermal lens, integral visor and goggle bag.

The Proteus is also available in a variety of cool Chameleon colors without the communication system – gold/green or cyan/purple – or as the Proteus 2 in clear, steel and smoke. JT says, "Advanced Micro Spectrum Pigments have been created to change colors every time you move." Awesome! The earpiece in the standard Proteus rotates and an inner baffle cushions this goggle around the face. The 260-degree field-of-view thermal Spectra lens is coated to prevent fogging and additionally coated with JT's "Diamond Gloss" finish for an "unbelievable wet look." The visor is integral to the mask and each Proteus comes with a goggle bag. ($79.99 for black goggles and clear Proteus mask 6-5-03 on *www.paintball-discounters. com*. Add $10.00 for Chameleon or other colors and combinations.)

The Brass Eagle Sentry Goggle System was designed by JT USA for maximum airflow and protection. Provides excellent protection at entry-level price.

Lenses for the Flex series are anti-fog thermal, but scratch resistance varies by model. Visors are integral and each sale includes a goggle bag. For JT's Flex series, the goggle is becoming more basic, functional without the frills. It has soft ear protection attached to a rigid upper mask and soft lower to protect the chin and front of the neck. ProFlex ($59.99 on *www.paintball-discounters.com*

6-5-03) goggles are black, blue, red or yellow in a black visor and mask. The Flex 7 ($64.99) combines mask and goggle in a variety of colors: clear/black, black/black, olive/black, blue, graphite or moss yellow.

The economy model goggles in the JT Spectra Series are the nForcer ($42.99 with thermal lens) and ProShield ($39.99 at *www.dickssportinggoods.com* on 6-5-03). Both are available with integral visors and with single lens or a Spectra anti-fog-coated thermal lens. Spring for the thermal lens model and JT includes a goggle bag. The nForcer in black or steel is distinctive because of its clear vent pieces and the hard-plastic ProShield was once JT's top-of-the-line mask.

JT USA Elite System: These are "aggressively styled" entry-level black masks with the Elite 180-degree lens and built-in visors: nVader ($24.99 for the single lens and $34.99 for thermal), Radar and X-Fire ($34.95 for thermal lens and $26.95 for single lens on 6-5-03 at *www. ontoppaintball.com*). "Ideal for beginners to amateurs," JT says.

JT USA offers lenses ($14.99 for a single and $16.99 to $22.99 for thermal on *www.paintballgear.com* 6-6-03) in their Spectra and Elite lines that pass both European and American safety standards, but JT says they also put them to the kind of tests they will be put to in the field. The extreme field! "We shoot them, stomp them, hit them with 1/4-inch steel balls at 400 fps, run over them, and let the dog chew 'em." Poor dog.

The idea behind the JT lens system is that a specific tint can be selected for any weather, sunshine or glare condition. Playing on a wide-open field or at the beach in the summer is going to be a lot different than assaulting a fortress in April in the deep woods. Use the wrong lens in the shade of the woods and you'll think you went through the wardrobe into Narnia. Here is what JT says about lens selection:

Single Lens: Recommended for average, temperate weather conditions where fogging is not a factor.

Single Fog-Resistant Lens: An economical fog-resistant solution for moderate weather conditions where fogging may be a factor.

Thermal Lens: High-performance fog-resistant protection. Recommended for extreme weather conditions where heavy fogging is a factor.

Regardless of lens choice, JT writes, lighting conditions will determine your choice of tint. A tinted lens will not protect your eyes any better or protect the lens itself from scratching or fogging. If you think of how a prism separates sunlight into its constituent colors, you understand the essential reason for any tint. A tint selectively filters out or, in effect, manually changes the angle of some of the light that enters your eyes and this causes you to perceive the world differently. Cool. The different tints are:

Clear: Universally used in all lighting conditions. WYSIWYG—What You See Is What You Get.

Yellow and Amber: Used in low-light conditions to increase contrast for enhanced visibility.

Smoke: The best choice for bright, sunlit days, especially in pen areas like concept fields where the sun is a factor in your game.

Prizm: These lenses are a smoke tint with a titanium color surface coating. They look very cool, but essentially are for bright, open venues. Yes, like the beach.

Gradient: The very best choice for bright, sunlit days, JT claims, on open areas like concept fields. (At *Paintball Digest*, we like the amber lens – makes the world rosy – and the kind the sheriff wore in Paul Newman's movie Cool Hand Luke! Very bad to the bone, indeed.)

If you spend extra for spare lenses to improve your vision under different conditions, you really ought to take a minute to take care of them. It might be like polishing your shoes (your dad does that to his leather Wing Tips, right?), but it stops short of ironing your underwear.

Once you invest in a good mask and several specialty thermal lens systems, you'll want to take care of them with tools like JT's Micro Fiber Cloth and fog-resistant Majik cleaning spray. Lenses scratch easily, so care is needed when removing paint and grit.

JT has four products in its line to help you care for the spare lenses. Sure, you see the macho men spitting on their lenses and wiping them off with their shirtsleeves – right where they blew their noses – but that isn't recommended!

Plexus Plastic Cleaner (7 ounces is $5.77): Protect and polish. This lens cleaner removes paint and has an anti-static agent to repel dust.

Majik Spray (2 ounces is $6.99): Fog-resistant cleaning solution removes the messiest paint and gives the lens good (JT says "superior") fog-resistant properties.

Wizard Cloth: These washable, reusable vegetable-based cloths for cleaning lenses without scratching the surface come 12 per pack.

Micro Fiber Cloth ($3.99): These are for cleaning the inner lens of thermal lenses without scratching the fragile fog-resistant surface and are reusable and washable.

JT's Vortex fan helps circulate air and keeps you cool on those long walks inside the field playing perimeter and while you are waiting for the "GO!" Helps replace stale, humid, CO2-laden inner air with cooler, oxygen-enriched outside air.

JT offers a little-bitty product that can make you happy to grovel in the dirt for the perfect shot in hot, sweaty weather. Really! Believe it or not, they have engineered a fan for your JT mask. The Vortex Fan ($19.95 black and $49.99 clear on 6-6-03 at *www.paintballgear.com* and curiously, the black fan is $39.99 on *www.paintball-discounters.com*) features a high-speed motor to move stale, humid air from inside your goggles and exchanges it with cool, fresh air. The two-way switch either blows air in or draws air out of your goggles. Vortex is built to be shockproof and water resistant with one tiny AAA battery delivering more than 30 hours of operation. JT says it is easy to install and disassemble for cleaning and it fits all JT Elite and Spectra goggle systems. And … a battery is included.

Apparently, after building the Proteus Sports-Comm, the innovators at JT decided it would be cool to make the communication system available for all of their Spectra and Elite goggles. Voila! All you have to do is buy a personal FRS two-way radio, install the communications kit in your goggles and hook up. You can give and take directions on the field as you play: "Left! Left! Your other left!" You can plug in a CD player, too, and listen to Strauss' thunderous "Alzo Sprach Zarathustra" while assaulting a stronghold as the helicopters rise over the horizon or Wagner's "Ride of the Valkyries" to really get pumped!

Kingman - Java

Created for Kingman by its sister company, Raven, the Java goggle line is an economical mask for rec play. The basic, charcoal-gray Java X-Type goggles have a single-pane polycarbonate lens with anti-scratch and anti-fog coatings. These goggles are secured with an adjustable elastic strap and are cushioned against the face with foam padding. The X-Type also offers double-pane thermal lenses in clear and yellow and a goggle bag. The slightly newer V-Type is $29.95(MSRP).

Java's black Guardian Goggles feature a rounder face shield, larger lens viewing area, a visor and larger vent holes. The semi-mirrored thermal lens has an anti-fog coating for $39.95 (MSRP).

Raven

Raven's NVX goggles come with a visor for sun deflection and forehead protection. The goggle base is made from highly flexible, tear-resistant polyurethane. "Soft is in!" Raven says. Venting, like most good masks, is multi-directional to enhance air flow and keep you cool in paintball combat. The foam around the goggles is called "triple density" because according to Raven, it is made from three different materials with different densities for minimal sweat absorption, comfortable wear and a secure fit with enhanced impact absorption. This foam is self-adhesive to the mask and replaceable. In addition, the goggles have a design that inhibits shifting from side to side when you are running and twisting or moving through the brush toward the enemy castle. The basic goggles come in ruby red, silver/clear, gunmetal gray, emerald green and sapphire blue.

New NVX goggles ($79.95 from Raven at *www.kingmanusa.com* in 9-03) come with gray photo-chromatic lenses. These polycarbonate lenses are light-sensitive and change rapidly from clear to dark and back again based on the intensity of the light. They are excellent paintball transition lenses for moving from light to shadow and back. Raven says these are polycarbonate dual-layer thermal lenses, not just lens tints: crystal clear, distortion free, thermal anti-fog and anti-scratch coated with UV protection. Lens options are blue, purple, green, orange and yellow.

VForce

The Morph was VForce's top goggles before the Profiler was introduced at the 2003 World Games. The Morph ($69.95) incorporates the soft mouth and jaw sections that are found on many high-end goggles, plus a sunshade visor. VForce (actually marketed by ProCaps and Diablo) has built in a rugged design and these goggles cover the entire face and ears. Available in blue, smoke or green, this mask is lined with cushy, sweat-absorbing foam. It has a flexible visor and will fit over your glasses.

JT's Spectra nForcer goggle system uses interchangeable vent covers and will accommodate a JT Vortex fan.

The anti-fog lens is scratch resistant and quick-change tinted spherical lenses are available. VForce also offers the Shield at $27.95, which, in black and green, features an extended neck protector and a mask in bright yellow for field referees. The Armor goggles ($19.95) are also available for budget-minded players. Extra lenses (amber, gold, smoke, silver) are available from about $20.00 to $30.00. (Prices on 9-17-03 from *www.thepaintballstore. com.*)

GLOVES

Paintball gloves are of special design because just any old gloves from the basement won't do. A pair of gloves has to be rugged and able to withstand lots of abuse, but still be flexible. You want a supple glove so you can move your fingers and flex your hands without feeling restraint. Something like your dad's and mom's golf gloves, but better, because that extra split second of flexing you need to get your glove to slide forward on the marker might cost you a shot to the head. Paintball gloves have to be tough on the back of the hand to withstand falling and knocking against objects in the field or taking a shot direct to the knuckles. Yet, the grip side has to be sensitive. It's tough to design a glove with all these sometimes opposing features, but there are plenty to choose from. Game Face offers their Half-Finger Gloves ($12.99 at *www.fogdog.com* on 7-29-03) that free the fingertips for perfect sensitivity on your marker's souped-up double trigger. Expect to pay about $15.00 for these style gloves in a store and less (plus shipping) from an Internet site.

JT USA's Pro Series ($36.99 *www.paintballgear.com* 6-6-03) and Premiere Series ($27.75) Gloves ("We've turned the knob up to 11 on innovation!") are designed for touch and tactile sensitivity on the palm side and protection on the back. Made of leather, these gloves feature lycra-mesh double-trigger fingers. A "lens blade" sewn onto the outside of the thumb lets you wipe grit off your lenses and

These black protective gloves from Game Face leave your sensitive fingertips free to SMASH PAINT!

the lycra-stretch zones add flexibility.

Allen offers several styles of playing gloves to help protect your hands when you are running for the flag, perhaps crawling through the woods or sliding carefully along the walls of the enemy castle. The Half-Finger Gloves feature padding on the knuckles and breathable "synthetic leather" on the palms. A pair of these gloves retails for $12.95 (small and medium) or $14.95 (large and extra-large). With more padding, the Half-Finger Armored Gloves are $19.95 for any size and the full-finger Padded Paintball Gloves are $17.95 from Allen.

One of the most interesting paintball gloves available is the Raven Morphion. Now THIS is Hand Armor: "advanced multi-directional attack force absorption and deflection capabilities with sonic welded flexible bio-form protection, breathable spandex, form-fitting airprene wrist support, terry cloth moisture wipes on thumbs, two-tone super-perf mesh knit panels for airflow and adjustable rubberized flex closure with Velcro fastening." Oh, wow! But there's more: "washable synthetic suede, Raven-rubberized pad print logos for a tight grip, gel-fill padded palm protection and pre-curved form for ergonomic fit." And for greater trigger-finger control, the index and middle fingers of the Morphion have cut points that allow you to cut above these lines to remove the tops of these two fingers. The reinforced stitching there prevents the material from fraying after it has been cut. Colors are silver, red, green and blue accented with black and gray and are sized to fit everyone from small to double extra large. After reading the above, you may think this glove costs a couple thou, but it is actually only $28.95 (MSRP).

PROTECT YOUR GEAR

You found something you really like and talked to everyone you know about it. You formed a team and bought equipment. Maybe not everything was as expensive as the marker you're proud of, but all together, it's a bundle. Well, you want to protect that bundle, don't you?

JT USA

JT's Safe Case is specifically designed to keep your equipment safe and sound. Yep. Rhino-Hide. Tough,

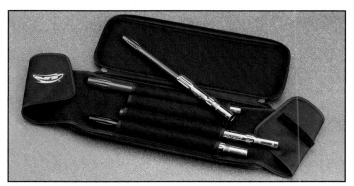

The JT barrel case can handle 4 barrels, each to 16 inches long. Internal dual covers, a tough, JT Rhino-Hyde cover and large grip zippers make this case grand-slam tough.

JT calls their signature line of luggage for paintball players the SUV Series. It includes this large, rolling, soft-sided suitcase with repositionable interior dividers, a top folding garment section, multiple side storage slots and what JT calls "big ass" wheels for tripping through airports.

Here's a great backpack for a day trip to a local field or for schoolbooks and lunch.

compression formed and puncture resistant. For this tough-sided case, JT fused their Rhino-Hide to a laser-cut, open-cell interior and used Velcro fasteners to keep it closed. It features virtually indestructible handles and "man-sized" zippers.

A special Barrel Case by JT is the ultimate protection for your barrels and it can handle any make of barrel up to 16 inches. Features include an internal dual-cover system to envelop your expensive barrels and a Rhino-Hyde outer skin that zips tight.

JT offers a series of five pieces of tournament luggage that will carry everything you need to go from home base advantage to World Champion Triple Crown play: NPPL Series, World Paintball Series and Millennium Series. They call it their SUV Series and it's made up of the following:

CD Case: Its outer cover is made from JT's compression-formed Rhino-Hyde and holds up to 24 CDs.

Medium Soft-Sided Luggage: Constructed with the very highest denier ballistic nylons, it offers a triple storage section, side storage and vented mini-pockets.

Large Rolling Luggage: A massive storage area with repositionable interior dividers, a top folding garment section and multiple side storage slots. JT says this luggage has "big ass" wheels and a locking handle ($139.77 at *www.xpaintball.com* on 6-6-03).

Backpack: Stylish with an interior CD holder with an earphone slot in the top, a multitude of side pockets and an adjustable cell phone holder.

Gear Sack: Patented features make this JT bag cool and useful. It has removable padded marker sleeves and color-coordinated elements with zippers, straps, elastic and buckles.

Hard-sided Gear Case

Rufus Dawg sells a roomy, 21x13x10-inch case to transport and protect your paintball gear. The case's outer shell is tough plastic and is molded with clasps for a padlock (not included). It has a cushioned, removable (10.5x19-inch) marker tray and a small, plastic box buried in the cushioning egg-crate foam for accessories like spare O-rings. This $26.77 case (*www.xpaintball.com* on 8-30-03) is available in red, blue or black.

Mantis Travel Bags

The Thorax is a large rolling duffle bag made from super-strong ballistic nylon measuring 16x34 inches. Its features include ten side pockets for pods, six barrel pockets, cell phone pocket, lots of additional flap pockets for extra storage, padded lower half, heavy-duty aluminum slide-out handle and strong, knobby rubber wheels. It's great for storage or travel. Just fold down the bottom flap and use it as a backpack. Black accented with royal blue, navy blue, red or gray, it costs $149.00 from Mantis.

The Mantis Exoskel Day Pack is a multi-use pack that costs $119.00 in the flyer and $79.00 at *www.mantisgear.*

com. This pack, which has five special tube holders, two nitro bags, two marker bags, a goggle pouch, padded backing and straps, plus extra compartments for tools and a cell phone, is two-tone in red or gray accented with black.

Dye Weekender

Dye says their Weekender is the perfect field bag. It is constructed with five easy-access pockets, a side marker mount envelope and a sports bottle holder. The principal center compartment is easily accessible and large enough to hold all of your essential paintball gear. Handle straps and adjustable shoulder straps are standard. The Weekender is constructed of two-tone heavy-duty nylon with steel D-rings and strap clips. Its dimensions are L24"x W11"x H14" and it carries a price tag of $109.95 (MSRP).

Protective Covers

Redz makes a superior, tight-fitting protective cover for your marker. "Fits like a glove," Redz says. Cost is $24.95 from Redz in red, blue and black. You must specify

Here's what the well-dressed paintball honker is wearing these days. A great looking jersey and matching pants for get-down field play. You don't want any tightness in the arms or legs because you gotta get loose to play with the abandon needed to win. And thanks to Jim Masciale of Rocky Creek Paintball in Gainesville, Florida. "Nice outfit, Jim!"

your marker type for proper fit. You must remove the tank, but not to worry, Redz also offers a series of Performance Bottle Coverz ($16.00 MSRP) made of thick, spongy neoprene in red, blue and black. This keeps the tank from getting scraped and scratched. There's a "sticky panel" on the back, too, so you don't slip with the marker and shoot yourself in the chin. Specify container type and size: 20-ounce CO_2, 48-, 68-, 90- and 114 cu/in.

CLOTHES

And you thought only your girlfriend or your mom needed to make a fashion statement. Not so fast, newbie!

Nelson's top-of-the-line paintball, called Anarchy, costs about $49 per box of 2000. No longer oil-based, this stuff is supposed to come right out, but don't wait to wash your clothes and use plenty of soap.

Let's face it, you gotta wear something and when early paintball studs like Jerry Braun in New York began blasting their buddies just 23 years ago, they were using real paint. A nasty oil-base paint, too.

The difference between those oil-based paintballs and modern paintballs like the Nelson Anarchy is that in the old days you couldn't just wash the stuff off with soap and warm water. In the early '80s, the "binder" in the paint (the chemical that dries and holds the color – called pigment – on the surface) was oil squeezed out of flax seeds (called linseed oil) or out of soybeans (soya oil) or even from the berries from china wood trees (tung oil).

If you talk to one of the older guys in the game, he will probably recall having a "turpentine party" after a match. Players would pass around a rag and a can of turpentine

or mineral spirits and try to dissolve and scrub off the paint. After they scrubbed their hands and face with soap and water, they would still carry around that greasy smell of turpentine. Yuck. No thanks! (At least there wouldn't be any accusations of "wiping" if you used an oil-based paint.)

And what about your clothes splattered with paint? If you played well, you wouldn't be marked too badly and the turpentine would get most of the paint out, although it might take out the color of your shirt and pants, too. But then, you could use the clothes for the next game … or for painting the house. If you were slow or just a bad shot and got thoroughly plastered, you really didn't have much choice except to toss your clothes in the garbage, because the paints were going to dry and stiffen up and those old jeans would not be comfortable to wear again.

God help you, by the way, if you tried to sneak your painted-up jeans into the wash with some of momma's other clothes. If you ever did that, just one time, you might as well hand over all your rights and privileges, because those oil-based paints and the turpentine were going to ruin the other things in the wash and your name was "Mud."

Old Clothes

Great idea. Use the old shirt you wouldn't wear to school or to the office and the old jeans that have a hole in the knee. But hey! How much of this stuff do you really have lying around the house? Okay, probably a lot because your girlfriend says most of what you prefer to wear is pretty awful, but that's just her opinion … just because it didn't come from Sak's … yesterday. Old clothes? Those duds are just getting broken in. To heck with paintball. They're good enough to save for a wedding or a graduation or something!

Camo

The purpose of camouflage is to break up your outline, provide an indistinct human shape and make it hard for other people or big game animals to spot you. Consequently, most camo tries to either mimic the environment (*www.realtree.com*) it will be used in (think of the tan desert camo recently worn by U.S. troops in Iraq) or confuse the eye with irregular patterns that are not found in nature (for instance *www.predatorcamo.com*).

Camo is associated with the military, but hunters have also used some kind of camo for thousands of years, maybe hundreds of thousands of years. Think of the shaggy fur coat the Ice Man wore before he died high in the Alps. Surely these pre-historic hunters put sprigs of grass in their hair and probably understood that a little charcoal on the shiny parts of their foreheads, cheeks and hands helped break up their outline.

Today, most camo is a mixture of earth tones – green, brown, black, gray – and incorporates the shapes of various types of leaves and tree trunks or branches and even rocks and jagged, irregular lines. Good camo is designed to give its wearer clothing with a 3-D or three-

Camo is excellent for rec play and big games. It is readily available, durable and inexpensive. Plus, in the woods it's ... well, camouflaged!

dimensional look. There are specialized patterns for different seasons, too, including a white-based snow camo and, for gun hunters, a blaze orange streaked with black for a hallucinogenic effect that surely gives the deer headaches.

The pioneers of paintball worried that camouflage was going to make paintball seem too militaristic even though the game, as originally envisioned, was a semi-militaristic individual survival game. They were concerned about the image of people shooting at each other in an organized manner, even with balls of brightly colored paint. After all, the very unpopular war in Viet Nam had not been over 10 years when Hayes Noel and Charles Gains began flinging paint at each other. Consequently, camouflage carried something of a negative emotional charge in many areas.

To make wearing camo even more difficult in those days, the anti-hunting and animal-rights movements were becoming more vocal. Hunting, long regarded as a way of life and a fundamental "right" in America found itself on the defensive. Wearing camo in public became unpopular and uncomfortable.

Of course back then, "camo" meant vintage World War II and Korean War woodland patterns and Viet Nam era black and green Tiger Stripe. Curiously, though, at about that time, technological developments in archery changed the shape of the most common kind of bow and participation in hunting with the bow and arrow increased

dramatically. (Although figures are not exact, there may be as many as three million hunting archers today, which is perhaps three to four times as many as there were a quarter century ago. By contrast, the number of hunters with rifle and shotgun is about 16 million.)

The influx of millions of new hunting archers (called bowhunters) allowed a burst in the creative development of equipment and in the design of new camouflage patterns. Virginia's Jim Crumley designed Trebark; within a few years, Bill Jordan in Georgia was promoting Realtree and then Advantage; and in the late '80s, Mississippi's Toxey Haas developed Mossy Oak. Now, you can choose among literally dozens of camo styles and clothing fabrics and textures from these giants and many others.

As a result of the fluorescence of camo patterns (some have called it the camo revolution or the camo boutique movement), camo began showing up at the mall. It became something of a fashion statement when models wore it on the "runways" in New York and even Paris. And when America and its allies twice invaded Iraq successfully, much of the opposition to wearing camo in public gradually declined. Camo may not be appropriate to wear to school or to the office, but it is no longer widely disapproved of by the general public.

So, camouflage clothing might be an excellent choice for paintball ... or it might not. Generally speaking, the pros are:

1. It is designed to give an indistinct pattern to the eye.
2. It is readily available.
3. It has a serious attitude.
4. It is not expensive.
5. It can be used for hunting or fishing or chores around the house or apartment; it's generally pretty durable.
6. It comes in numerous styles, patterns and colors.
7. It is designed to be used outdoors and is made in some very long-lasting fabrics that don't lose their color or patterns quickly.

This means you see a lot of camo on paintball rec fields, if not in tournament play. Of course, if your team decides that members should dress the same – and most teams eventually do – then everyone will want to purchase the same pattern, perhaps one of the more individualized (and more rare) patterns rather than one of the common patterns found in every BigMart, a pattern like SuperFlauge or Skyline or Image Country or Palmetto Country.

Not everyone likes camouflage, however. There are some cons to camo:

1. It has an implied military or hunting or survivalist angle and for a game that is trying to convince the public that it is not violent, this could be a problem.
2. It is questionable whether, at the short ranges that paintballs are typically shot, the camo effect is truly

of any value on an airball or hyperball field. In the woods, of course, it's a different story.

3. As you become more proficient and more invested in high-quality gear, you will probably want to move up to sponsored or gear-specific clothing, which is anything but camouflaged with its neon bright colors.

Speaking of the ultimate camo, Tom Berenger wore a Ghillie (or Shaggie) Suit when he got down to business in the 1992 movie "Sniper." Chances are it was made by Rancho Safari, which sews hundreds of leaf shapes and strips of various soft and absorbent materials such as burlap onto 1/4-inch industrial-strength mesh. A Ghillie suit definitely breaks up your outline, but is going to be a little warm for the summer and is definitely not something in which you will move very quickly.

COOL STUFF FOR HOT SHOTS
Game Face

Game Face is a relative newcomer to paintball, but a natural through its corporate sponsorship by Crosman, one of the world's largest producers of air guns and

Jenn Wang takes a couple for Penn State. Jenn is a front player for her college's paintball team, which means she moves fast, shoots accurately and plays cooperatively with her team and aggressively with the competition … in spite of not having a barrel on her marker!

Half of paintball is how you play and the other half is how you look while you are playing. Here's a stylin' head wrap from www.paintballdaddy.com for $4.99.

accessories. Game Face sponsors a National X Ball League pro team, the Detroit Thunder, and has designed a line of fun looking shirts and hats around the Thunder logo. Look for black, white and red colors with the yellow lightning bolt.

JT USA

If you shoot one of the JT Excellerators, you may want to dress to match. Try their Pro Series Long Sleeve Jersey. It's one of the coolest ("testosterone driven," JT says) shirts imaginable with an angular black and white background overlaid by the JT claw in black and gray, blue, olive, red or yellow. With stretch knit cuffs, V-neck collar, side and under-arm venting, the Premiere Series Jersey features a different design.

JT complements its stylish jerseys with heavy-duty black Tournament Pants and Shorts that have plenty of pocket space, pouches, zippered compartments and Velcro protective spaces to store practically everything you need on the field. Features include "double-reinforced ballistic-nylon-padded knees, rip-resistant stretch crotch, double-snap Velcro fly, adjustable waist straps, stretch mesh lower lumbar zone, ballistic-nylon seat, lycra stretch side panels, drawstring leg closures, rear leg cooling vents and our patent pending JT Paintball Cargo Pockets." They come in black with white accents.

Worr Games

Several styles of colorful new WGP playing jerseys are available. They feature a V-neck, Raglan sleeves and a mesh strip that runs down the side of your trunk, under your arm and to your hand, which keeps you cool and under control. The material is lightweight and made to last. Cost is $40.00 (MSRP).

GET TRACTION!

Tennis shoes. That's the most common footwear on a paintball field. It sure isn't the best, though.

Look at it this way. Aside from getting hit in the eye with a ball and suffering a detached retina, what's the next most possible injury that'll take you out of the action? Okay, running into a fence – lengthwise – is gonna put you down, but you're smart enough to avoid that. (Aren't you?) The next most common game-ending injury is a sprained ankle or a twisted knee.

Now, there are knee and shin pads to help protect the joint of your knee and your kneecap, but what about your feet and ankles? Think those old tennis shoes you usually wear to play paintball will help you? Admit it. You know the ones. The pair your mom won't let you bring into the house any more. The ones you keep in the garage. In a bag. A sealed bag. Yeah, those.

Not good. No traction. No support. Their saving grace is that you have already paid for them.

Magnum USA, a leader in tactical and uniform footwear, sponsors one of America's most outstanding

Scenario game production gang Black Cat Productions wears Magnum USA's black "Stealth" side-zip/lace-up boot exclusively. It gives them support and traction when they are setting up a playing field and designing a production. It also includes three layers of impact-absorbing materials for comfort.

Magnum USA enlisted Blue's Crew, one of America's premier paintball teams, for a trial run of their lace-up Viper boot. Designed for fast action and traction, this soft-sided boot is a favorite with police, firemen and EMTs. An "aggressive," slip-resistant carbon-rubber tread is combined with a molded mid-sole and a contoured, removable insole for a darn good active-game combo.

paintball teams, "Blue's Crew." Led by Michael "Blue" Hanse of New Milford, Pennsylvania, this 30-member scenario-game team is fully sponsored and commands a strong presence at paintball events dressed in their trademarked solid blue outfits.

Magnum *(www.magnumboots.com)* realizes that players, both recreational weekend warriors and scenario professionals, need a proper-fitting, lightweight, durable and supportive boot or athletic shoe. "Well," says Magnum's Cheryl Rebsamen, "that's our specialty."

The Magnum Viper is the boot currently worn by Blue's Crew. It takes what Magnum calls a "progressive approach to affordable tactical footwear." The lace-up Viper is available in 8-inch high-tops ($70.00) and 6-inch low-tops ($65.00) versions. The boot combines a leather/900-denier nylon upper and a unique M-PACT air pad in the heel for extra cushioning when you are running, jumping and screaming your head off. An "aggressive" (there's that word again) slip-resistant carbon-rubber tread is combined with a molded mid-sole and a contoured, removable insole for running. The lining is supposed to

wick moisture away from your foot. It's also a good-looking boot. Kind of hip. Each Viper boot weighs 9.5 ounces and is available in sizes 7 to 15 (up to D widths).

There is a paintball crew that puts on scenario games around the U.S. named Black Cat Productions and Magnum has outfitted this gang with a slightly different boot, something, frankly, more military looking called the Stealth. Black Cat will be giving a number of pairs of these boots away as prizes during their games.

Like the Viper, they are black, too, but they look more like an army jungle boot with a combination of leather and heavy nylon upper, a sturdy side zipper and a slip-resistant outsole (the tread). The lining is supposed to draw or wick moisture away from your foot and ankle while the contoured insole (the layer your foot rests on inside the boot) incorporates three layers of impact-absorbing materials. According to Magnum USA, this $80.00 boot is a popular style for cops, firemen and EMTs. Each Stealth boot weighs 1 pound 11.5 ounces and is available in sizes 7 to 15 and widths to EEE.

Fighting Dehydration

Get Tired. Get Cold. Get Thirsty. It's Okay!

If you enjoy playing paintball, you are going to get hot and tired in the summer, cold and tired in the winter and thirsty practically any season you are running and shooting and going crazy outside. It's healthy and normal. What is normal, but not healthy, is dehydration, sun stroke and hypothermia. And yes, these things can happen to you.

Hot weather is wonderful, but if you are running and gunning with a cap and mask, long-sleeve shirt and long pants with boots, you can over-do it even if you are an athlete in good shape with a low percentage of body fat. Most problems related to being exhausted in warm weather are from dehydration. In the plainest terms, dehydration happens when you lose water and the elements in the water that make you go, faster than you can replace them. We all do this for short bursts, but in an extended play situation, it is very dangerous.

The first sign of drying out is usually feeling thirsty, but we may not want to recognize it because we have things to do and places to go, so we reach for a soft drink. Even though the caffeine in coffee and many soft drinks actually promotes dehydration, as long as we are taking on fluids, and especially the so-called "sports drinks" that are high in sugar and hyped with a lot of national advertising by popular movie actors and professional athletes, we think we are fine. This isn't necessarily true, but those drinks are high in carbohydrates that turn to sugar and then to energy. The result is that we quickly feel better although we may only be treating a symptom and not the real cause. We are only putting off the inevitable unless we pack in the wet stuff.

The first sign of dehydration is often a cramp in your calves and hamstrings, the muscles in the back of your legs that take so much of the strain when you are hunkered down behind a sandbagged bunker or running crouched over for cover. Of course, you will be thinking of the mission first and your own comfort second. (If your personal comfort is such a high priority you would be on the sofa watching television and eating potato chips, right?) So, the tendency is to ignore your thirst because you can always have a drink "in a little bit."

If you get heat cramps, drink as much water as you can hold, go to a cool place and put your feet up. Or just sit down in the shade and drink something non-alcoholic, non-caffeinated and non-carbonated. Do not let some old timer talk you into taking a salt tablet. Absolutely unnecessary.

Take care of yourself when you get a heat cramp or the dehydration that you are experiencing could rapidly lead to heat exhaustion. When you're playing on a hot day and begin feeling dizzy and a wee bit little sick to your stomach and maybe so hot you just can't seem to cool down, you are on the verge of heat exhaustion. It is also called sun stroke. Treat yourself right away. The tendency will be for your buddies to tell you to "Grab a Coke. Shake it off." Do not listen to them. If you get to the point where you begin vomiting, your body may very quickly slide into a position of losing fluids a whole lot faster than you can replace them and a trip to a local hospital emergency room will be necessary. In the hospital, they will do for a lot of money what you could have done for practically nothing in the field. You will lie down, get cool and comfortable, and take on fluids. Of course in the hospital, they will use $75 ice packs and hook you up to a $500 IV, so you better like needles.

If you only sit down in the shade and drink some water out of your canteen, it's better than nothing to alleviate the symptoms of heat and dehydration, but it usually isn't enough. Ignore the symptoms or treat them lightly and Bingo! Heat stroke. Your skin feels warm, but you may not even be sweating. Your temperature will most likely spike up and you could lose consciousness or even have a seizure. Some of your internal organs can quit working. It's beginning to sound serious.

When something like heat stroke happens in the field, call the nearest emergency responders (you have their number handy, right?) and make them take you to a hospital as fast as they can. If you can't get help, lie still in the coolest place possible and drink water, a lot of water. Lie down in the water if you can or even soak your clothing in water from a spare canteen if you have enough, but stay out of the sun.

A couple things to remember. First, as long as you are sweating, you're fine. Sweat shows that heat is escaping from your body. The more humid it is, the harder it is for your body to sweat and lose heat the natural way. Hot and humid days, be careful.

According to *Emedicine.com*, sunburn is "… an acute cutaneous inflammatory reaction that follows excessive exposure of the skin to ultraviolet radiation (UVR). Long-term adverse health effects of repeated exposure to UVR are well described …" and include skin cancer. Emedicine.com recommends an SPF (sun protection factor) cream rated 15 or higher.

On a hot day, you are going to get sunburned on the back of your neck and hands. Use a sunblock. The higher the SPF-number the better. If you put the back of your hand on the side of your marker or the air cylinder and it feels really good, apply a sunblock.

"It's hot out there!" "Drink more fluids than you think you will need" is the rule for running and gunning in hot weather (especially if you are no longer a teenager!), but stay away from alcohol and carbonated beverages. Cold water is best, followed by such electrolyte-replacing and high-sugar beverages like Powerade.

CHAPTER 18

STUFF FOR THE FIELD

TANKS

Matt Steigmeyer at Tippmann Pneumatics says their radical "Hellhound" go-cart is strictly for "promotional purposes," which is suit-talk for FUN. "It's not for sale," he says. Sure. Well, fine. We'll build our own! After all, half the "technicals" battling U.S. troops around the world don't drive anything this cool or, in a paintball kind of way, this deadly.

The Tippmann Hellhound may only be a go-cart built for two – pilot and weapons systems operator – but it's totally rigged:

1. **Grenade Launcher:** Operated by the passenger, the grenade launcher flings a Squadbuster grenade far in front of the Hellhound to clear a path or pop a bunker like a pimple. The launcher is mounted on the back of the Hellhound and carries a half-dozen of the non-explosive grenades that, Tippmann says, will throw paint in a 30-foot diameter.
2. **Ten-barrel cannon:** This is way bad and it is operated by the weapons officer. You don't want to get stuck driving. The rate of fire is adjustable, but at max, it'll spit out 50 rounds per second!
3. **Ceiling-mounted hopper:** You won't need a refill, even if you run into a swarm of gooks and goblins in a scenario game. This baby holds 6000 rounds (three full cases of paint) and balls are fed into the 10-barrel cannon through flexible hoses. Timing-chained agitators in the hopper prevent jamming.
4. **Go-cart:** This baby has a top speed of 45 mph so ain't nobody going to outrun it. Five high-impact storage compartments are mounted on the front and rear with ropes and "stuff" in case the tank gets stuck in the mud, has an unexpected mechanical

Imagine driving these babies onto your next playing field! On the bottom is the Hellhound from Tippmann Pneumatics. It comes complete with a grenade launcher, ten-barrel cannon, 6000 spare rounds and a top speed of 45 mph ... plus a couple fully loaded 98 Customs if all else fails. Oh momma!

failure or the driver needs a sandwich.

5. **Sidearms:** The Hellhound is equipped with two Model 98 Custom Tippmann semi-autos in addition to the cannon and the grenades. It can fire in any direction, any time.

6. **Accessories:** Roll-over protection for sharp turns. Lug tires for GRIP. A power winch in case your girlfriend (or boyfriend!) gets stuck in the port-a-potty. Non-breakable front windshield.

The Squadbuster is a non-explosive paint grenade that Tippmann says has a 30-foot marking zone. It is filled with non-toxic, water-soluble paint. Just pull the pin and toss it in the general direction of the enemy bunker and watch them scatter– too late!

GRENADES
Tippmann Squadbuster

Tippmann makes the granddaddy of all weapons for busting up a bunched-up gaggle of the enemy team or getting your paint on target behind a well-defended bunker. A grenade! And where they are legal, they are truly a bundle of break-bad fury.

The Squadbuster is a non-explosive paint grenade with a 30-foot-plus marking zone. (Yep. Same kind fired by the Hellhound.) It is filled with non-toxic, water-soluble paint, just like your paintballs. All you do is pull the pin and toss one of these mother-of-all-paintballs in the general direction (don't try to aim too precisely) of the enemy and the grenade's patented design causes it to burst (not explode) on impact; and that's when the fun begins. The folks you are fragging won't be able to get out of the way fast enough!

At *www.xtremz.com* it said this grenade paints everything in a 10-foot radius (which we believe is

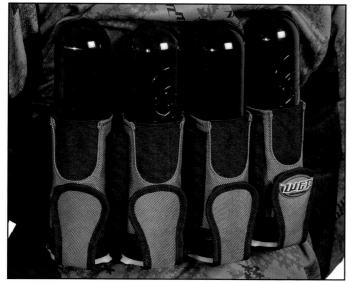

The THS harness system from WGP has a concealed pouch for your credit cards and keys. The system features a low profile, quick-release Velcro closure and a retractable pod pouch for extra gear, maybe even a couple grenades.

wrong) and that the cost was $4.99 each ($3.99 at *www. paintballgear.com* or, for those who want to buy direct from the manufacturer, $5.00 each from Tippmann). The Squadbuster was $5.77 each or 5 for $17.77 from *www. xpaintball.com* (5-19-03).

P&D Assault

The grenade from P&D (Paintball Ordnance) contains a non-toxic, washable magenta paint. When thrown, it hits the ground and sprays in a circle, coating everything within its spray radius. Cost is $2.77 or five for $12.77 from *www.xpaintball.com* (5-19-03). P&D also makes a larger paint grenade called the U-15 ($5.77 or 5 for $17.77).

12-gram BB

Each of these realistic-looking grenades carries 750 12-gram paint BBs, but for one toss, one moment of glory, the price may be a little high. The BB grenade cost $9.99 at *www.xtremz.com*. Seems a little pricey to us, but if you're cornered and in a scenario encounter that allows one of these realistic-looking babies to go off, it can make 'em scatter quick.

Wet Willie

You'll douse your opponent head-to-toe with this $4.99 paint grenade available from *www.paintballgear.com* (5-19-03). The Wet Willie was designed to discharge reliably. After all, you don't want the grenade you just threw to be thrown back at you because it didn't go off! And you don't want it to propel itself in any possible direction, even away from the intended target. Wet Willie claims that with other grenades you could land a perfect throw and still not mark your opponent. Bummer!

Wet Willies incorporate a patent-pending design

called SPSA (Self Propelled Spinning Action), so when a Wet Willie is thrown, the force of the expelling paint (nasty green or blue) combined with its curved, banana-like shape produces a violent spinning action, slinging paint in a circular motion from the center of impact. It's a little like blowing up a balloon and then letting it go. Wet Willie's spinning motion keeps it in the same area of impact during discharge for concentrated and uniform coverage. You won't just get lucky and hit your target with a couple drops of paint. The Wet Willie paints your adversary with each rotation.

Wet Willie paint fill is non-toxic and washable. This grenade comes one per pack and complete with safety clips.

MINES
Major Paintball Master Mine

The Master Mine from Major Paintball is an interesting possibility to add to your field gear (they call it "revolutionary" at *www.paintballgear.com* where it costs $34.95). This compact, reusable mine is powered by a standard 12-gram CO_2 cartridge and sprays 6 ounces of liquid paint, covering an area up to 600 square feet. The Master Mine is an "on-surface" design, meaning you don't need to carry a shovel to the field. Good thing! It sets up in less than a minute and has an ultra-sensitive trigger, allowing you to fasten a light trip cord that can be activated up to 25 feet from the mine's position or even remotely detonated from your hide-out.

The Master Mine uses dual adjustable muzzles to create different spray patterns. Turn them to face outward to cover a wide area, or point them straight ahead for a concentrated "dude drenching" blast. Combine these features with its impressive sound blast and this mine can also double as a superb perimeter warning device. Whatever your strategy, the Master Mine will give enemy players something serious to think about before racing down a trail or trying to sneak up behind your position. You can refill the Master Mine yourself with water-based paint mixes from a Venom Paint Pack, just $3.99 per pack for six refills.

MORTARS

The 62-mm M1A mortar from Tippmann Ordnance in Colorado is CO_2 powered. Think of it as a toy for those radical games where thousands of rabid paintballers storm ashore in Normandy or march on Hanoi in a Viet Nam War scenario game. Including the barrel, base plate and mounting assembly, the M1A weighs 46 pounds so don't expect to run around the field with it.

The M1A is built with a 62-mm diameter barrel, which is what makes it heavy. The barrel is 40 inches long and made from 1/4-inch thick aluminum. Tippmann says it can shoot four rounds per minute as far as 200 yards.

Tippmann says operating their M1A mortar is simple

When people are firing mortars and throwing grenades, a state-of-the-art mask and goggle system such as this one from JT USA is gonna save your newbie butt. It provides full face, chin and ear protection; gives plenty of ventilation; shields your eyes from the sun and has multiple colors and replaceable lens styles.

and set-up is quick and easy. A three-person crew is suggested, but after the M1A is set up, one person can manage it in the field: aim, adjust, load and fire.

This ingenious super-thumper fires a 20-ounce round that produces a kill zone from 50 to 75 feet in diameter. The rounds are supposedly accurate to within 50 feet at more than 150 yards. Constructed of paint, lightweight cardboard and a rubber paint bladder, Tippmann says the round is durable enough to fire out of the mortar, yet fragile enough to burst on its target without causing injury if one lands on top of a player's head. Tippmann says the M1A has a low muzzle velocity and is shipped completely assembled and ready to go. A CO_2 cylinder is not included, but dummy practice rounds are available. Get out your checkbook or credit card, because the cost of this contraption is $1449.95 from Tippmann Ordnance.

OTHER STUFF
12-gram CO_2 Cylinders

Many quality paintball stock pumps, back-up sidearms and even older style single-shot markers like the Sheridan PGP2 from Game Face use these disposable 12-gram CO_2 cylinders. The milled-aluminum Delta 68 paintball assault pistol, for instance, holds 10 rounds and is powered by 12-gram cartridges. The "12-grams" are inexpensive and install quickly, but have a number of drawbacks. They are not refillable. Once you puncture the seal, you either use the propellant or lose it. Even if you shoot just one time,

you can't save the cylinder for much longer than a few hours, because even with a tight, fresh seal, the puncture leaks. A 10-pack of Crosman CO_2 cylinders costs $6.99 or $.70 each from *www.paintballgear.com* (6-4-03). A 25-pack cuts the cost to $13.99 or $.56 each. Because these cartridges are pressurized, they may not be shipped by air.

Universal Marker Sling

Allen makes an adjustable over-the-shoulder sling that will fit any marker. It requires that you use a butt-plate shoulder stock on the back of your air tank, though. Simply drill a half-inch hole in the butt-plate for the sling clip and loop the "non-marking Buna retainer ring over the barrel." Cost is $9.95 from Allen.

If you have a hankering for practice balls to zero your marker, try looking up Rufus Dawg. Chris Rife, business manager at Rufus Dawg, says these hard balls are exactly the same size as .680 balls but are reusable. Caution: It would never be fair to put a handful of these solid balls in your hopper, because at 300 fps, one of them could break the lens in a pair of goggles.

Rocket Loader

Brad Vincent says he has solved the problem of filling tubes fast without spilling balls. "Much like the other great inventions of our time, the Rocket came about when I saw a problem and thought of a way to solve it," he says. "I began playing paintball in December 2001 and one of the first things I noticed was the vast amount of time it took

This Allen butt plate for the back of your air cylinder can give you a steadier position for your marker and that means a more accurate shot.

between games to get ready for the next game. Between games you have to get air, clean your marker and goggles (and anything else covered in paint), get something to drink, check all your equipment and then the most time-consuming task – filling all those empty paint pods."

Brad says that when you are in a hurry to get into the game, every second counts. So, with his plastic Rocket loader, you can fill a tube without having to pour from baggies or even worse, by hand. "The sweat from your hands makes the ball's flight path erratic at best," Brad says. "The Rocket solves this problem. Just place an empty pod in the handle, pull the slide and in one second, you're done. The Rocket loads 140 balls a second and will hold 1000 balls. No assembly is required. It is ready to use when you receive it." The Rocket was $39.99 from www.rocketpaintball.com on 8-30-03.

Check Your Speed

The first time a referee stops you on the field and asks to check your marker's speed, you may think you are doing something wrong. Don't worry about it. The referee is supposed to check everyone to keep markers within safe shooting limits, usually about 280 fps. Faster than that and paintballs hurt like the dickens. A little stinging sensation to let you know you have been hit is one thing, but pain is not a necessary component of paintball play. In paintball, the "no pain, no gain" philosophy is for suckers.

Plus, with field paint, balls traveling super fast may not be as accurate as balls traveling the speed limit. Why? Fast shooting means that a great volume or pressure of air is applied to a soft paintball very rapidly. The greater the force of the air propelling a ball out the barrel, the greater the soft gel ball distorts and the more random friction is involved in the shot.

Chronographs are not perfect. They have margins of error. But Sports Sensors' RadarChron builds a chronograph for paintball that fits in the palm of a referee's hand so they won't need to haul you off the field to check your marker's velocity. And its margin of error, two percent between 150 and 450 feet per second (fps), is acceptable for recreational play.

The RadarChron uses Doppler radar to check speed. It emits a small burst of microwave energy and then detects the change in frequency when those waves of energy bounce off your speeding ball. RadarChron is a one-button, two-digit operator that scrolls the speed in fps on the screen. The Sports Sensors paintball RadarChron sold for $85 on www.roughneck.com on 8-25-03.

Barrel Light

Not a lightweight barrel, but a flashlight that attaches beneath your barrel. "What possible use could that have in paintball?" you ask. Well, how about the nine hours of darkness out of every 24 played in a scenario game? Uh, huh! Well, maybe …

If you have bought into this possibility so far, you may want to take a look at the Tactically Advanced Combat Mount III (TACM) from Diamond Products. Of course, it was initially designed for the police and military.

The TACM is a water-resistant flashlight that mounts in a Delrin plastic bracket and turns on and off with a pressure switch at the end of a cord. Attach the bracket on your barrel, secure the light in the bracket and run the wire with the small pressure switch (choose either 5-inch or 7-inch lengths of wire) along your marker to a position you can easily tap with a fingertip. The pressure pad mounts with self-adhesive Velcro, included.

The TACM III operates on a pair of 3-volt lithium batteries with a xenon bulb. Its reflector is not a chrome-sprayed plastic dish, but a machined aluminum reflector with a super-fine polished surface. The TACM III has a suggested retail price of about $100, which includes a Universal Mount. A red, night lens that illuminates without destroying your night vision is an available extra. If you have a pair of night vision goggles, you may want to spend an extra $35.00 and get the infrared lens.

Viewloader's Talkin' Timer is designed to be attached directly to the Viewloader Revolution hoppers (for IN YOUR FACE game play) or can be worn around your neck on a lanyard.

Two-Way Radios

Commonly thought of as two-way radios, these Family Radio Service (FRS) units eliminate the shouting and confusing gesturing you used to do with your scenario playing buddies, especially if you are critical or desperately signaling your referee for a toilet paper time-out. Hand-held radios can help your team warn you about an enemy approaching from your backside. They can help you coordinate a final assault on a stronghold. And you can certainly use an FRS radio to call for help if you are hurt or in real danger. You may even want to look for a radio with a specific, continuously broadcasting weather channel.

JT's Universal Sportz-Comm – shown here in a JT mask – allows team players to communicate on the field, during the height of the action. Simply plug in your FRS radio, or even an mp3 or CD player! Betcha wish more fields allowed them.

This barrel plug is from Viewloader. They are cheap and easy to misplace so buy some spares.

The advantages of FRS radios are many. They come with 14 channels or public access frequencies and they can be used by anyone … even us paintball players. By simply pressing a button and talking, you can communicate with anyone who is dialed into the channel you are using and within hearing range, i.e. your teammates. These little radios don't require any training or permits or licenses to use and don't rely on any towers to relay the signal. Like beepers, some of them even have a vibration mode that lets you select the call you will take and earphones that allow you to listen in silent mode. You can also plug them into a special communications unit designed for a goggle system like the one from JT USA.

Bet you didn't know these radios work where battery-operated cellular phones are useless. For all of the built-in benefits and possibilities, they are inexpensive and tremendously useful in an emergency.

Some FRS units are made specifically to appeal to active people – cutting down trees, hunting or playing paintball. This suggests that some units are especially lightweight and built especially rugged, but in reality, this may just be packaging and promotion because "lightweight and durable" would describe practically the entire FRS family of radios.

On the other hand, unless you leave the FRS in the car, it is doggone certain to go off with a staticky yelp

Even if you can't use a two-way radio on the field, they are super for keeping up with your buddies on the way to and during team practice sessions.

– "Hey. I just took a hit!" – at just the moment you are leaning out from cover and aiming to take out the enemy executive officer. You're guaranteed to not appreciate it then. All FRS radios are limited to line-of-sight range and work best in open, flat surfaces because a range of two miles is about their max, although this varies with battery strength, the weather and other factors, but – unlike a lot of stuff – spending more money on them doesn't give you stronger communications.

On the disadvantages side, what you say on the air can be heard by anyone listening who is tuned into that channel and, with "atmospheric skip," almost anyone including the opposition will hear what you say if they are tuned to your channel. So, beware! For privacy, look for models that offer channel codes which allow you to engage in communication a little more selectively.

If you or your team is considering using FRS radios, you'll need to practice. Yep, you'll have to have rules about who can talk and when. Otherwise, everyone will be jabbering at once and this great way to give and take directions will fast become aggravating and useless. For most situations, however—certainly including emergencies—you can use FRS radios to excellent team and personal advantage.

Now, do you go to a local BoxMart and buy a set of radios for $20 or do you go high-tech and spend some cash for a couple units that have lots of features. It may surprise you that what we at *Paintball Digest* recommend is that you actually do go to a BoxMart first. Try the cheap set and see if they are right for you and your team. If so, great! If not, spring for units with greater versatility … radios that wear lipstick, make change and predict the weather.

The Garmin Rhino 110 has a GPS (Global Positioning System) unit and two-way radio with 22 channels in one compact unit ($194.27 at *www.garmin.com* 6-6-03). You can talk and transmit your exact position at the same time. It weighs 8 ounces, is water resistant (useful in the rain, but not scuba diving) and has a lot of uses other than rec field time.

Motorola's TalkAbout T6320 has a wide range of

The rigid Combo Squeegee from Brass Eagle will keep your marker shooting straight by cleaning out broken balls.

options such as 38 interference eliminator codes, a scrambler with three settings and a rechargeable battery with drop-in charging unit. This Motorola model has a built-in digital compass, barometer and thermometer, altimeter, clock with alarm and a stopwatch with a lap timer. Like your cell phone, a removable plastic belt clip is available. These small radios come with a one-year warranty. But will it make coffee? ($157.48 at *www.motorola.com* on 6-5-03)

Cobra Electronics offers a relatively inexpensive Micro-Talk series that has auto squelch, backlit LCD screen and water resistance for an affordable price. Just 14 channels for the 104-2, but how many do you need? This model retails for $49.95 at *www.cobra.com* (6-6-03) and that's for two radios!

Paintball on DVD

If you think the madness is over when you get home and clean your marker, you're wrong. You can experience the continuing thrill of running and gunning with DVDs from 1 Shot Productions and other producers. You'll wear out before the thrill of watching Nemesis or Brimstone Smoke face off with the Brass Eagle All Stars at the 2002 Memphis Indoor Challenge wears off.

The beauty of having a DVD of some of the major tournaments, besides the chance to scope out the competition, is that you can learn the airball format and see the moves that work before you get there. Paintball pros play for serious money, and if these videos don't make your motor purr with excitement, nothing will.

For a full range of titles, check out your favorite paintball sites like *www.1shotprod.com*.

Battlepaint!

If you think you've experienced the future, think again. The future may be a cross between ultimate freedom … and ultimate control, especially if Randal Lynch has anything to do with it.

Randal's Battlepaint System is a wireless, computerized system for keeping track of you and your buddies on the field. In its simplest form, you wear a transmitter called an "Informer," which is about the size of a cell phone and a dot that represents you shows up on a computer screen in the field office. At any moment, the field operator (or the people in the grandstand who are watching on a giant screen!) can see where every player is located. At the end of the game, the computer can make a CD for you, and your team can review its progress toward the objective. The Informer can be programmed to keep statistics and transmit information to keep score in real time.

In its more complex form, the transmitter can be coupled with RADD and RefX. RADD is short for Remotely Activated Disabling Device, a tiny mechanical and electronic transmitter situated between your gas source and your marker. RADD gives a field owner the ability to continuously monitor the speed of your balls, and if they exceed the speed limit, he can shut you down. On the spot! RefX works about the same way, giving referees the ability to remotely disable markers if they see or suspect something dangerous.

Randal believes the Battlepaint monitoring system gives the field owner more control, creates a safer environment and can help players have a more realistic and challenging experience. Creating and playing in the "Disneyland of Paintball" is his objective.

GLOSSARY OF PAINTBALL TERMS

Action – As in "the action," a. the mechanical apparatus that operates your marker or b. the combined parts of a marker that determine how it is loaded, discharged and unloaded.

Action, automatic – A marker that loads and fires as long as the trigger is depressed and there are balls available in the loader and feed tube.

Action, pump – A marker that loads and fires each time you complete the cycle of pulling the trigger to fire the loaded paintball and re-cocking manually.

Action, semi-automatic – A marker in which each pull of the trigger results in a complete firing cycle including reloading. It is necessary that the trigger be released and pulled for each cycle. Also called autoloaders, self-loaders or auto-cockers. (An automatic action marker loads, discharges and reloads as long as balls are available and the trigger is depressed. A semi-automatic marker only discharges one ball with each squeeze of the trigger.)

After-market – An add-on to your marker system, not part of the original set-up.

Agitator – Either attached to or included in a hopper, it uses an "impeller" to stir the paintballs in the hopper, aligning them with the feed port at the bottom of the hopper. Paintballs thus fall freely and perfectly aligned into the hopper feed nipple.

Airball – The general term for paintball played on a field with inflatable bunkers for obstacles.

Anti-siphon – A special bulk CO_2 tank designed to keep the marker from sucking liquid.

ASA – Abbreviation for "air source adapter."

Autococker – A marker with a pneumatically operated bolt. A pump opens the chamber on the backstroke so a ball can fall through the feed tube into the chamber. On the forward stroke, the bolt pushes the ball forward and the front edge of the bolt seals the chamber. So when you pull the trigger, the gas or air released goes through the valve and expands behind the ball to push the ball down the barrel. This is a closed-bolt system. In an autococker, the marker is working the same way with pneumatic operation to re-cock the marker for you, instead of you having to pump each time to get a ball to drop into place. The trigger pull releases the air (the first half of the pull) and causes the marker to cycle (the second half of the pull). Thus, the pumping action is "automated." When you release the trigger, the action returns to the starting position. Each trigger pull gives you a shoot-and-re-cock cycle. This is a semi-automatic marker. (Autococker and 'Cocker are trademarks of Worr Games Products.)

Auto (automatic) – The shooting style of a marker that indicates that you do not need to load a new ball each time you shoot one and that the internal design of the marker is such that it self-cocks from a power source that is external to the action.

Full (full automatic) – A marker that fires and reloads to fire again as long as the trigger is held down.

Semi (semi-automatic) – A marker that automatically re-cocks and re-loads the next paintball, but requires squeezing the trigger to fire a single shot.

Auto trigger – A trigger/sear design for pump-action markers. It allows a player to fire each time the pump handle is pulled back – cocking the mechanism – and then forward again. The marker fires automatically each time the pump handle is cycled from front to rear and back as long as the trigger is held down.

Back bottle system – A constant air system design. The marker's ASA adapter is at the rear of the marker, where the constant air tank is attached. The tank is used as the marker's shoulder stock and may or may not have a butt plate attached. Pump markers normally have the ASA adapter in-line with the barrel and cocking mechanism. Semi-automatic markers normally have the ASA adapter in-line with the cocking mechanism.

Back bottle adapter – ASA adapter attached to the rear of a marker that connects the gas supply to the marker.

Barrel plug – Safety device inserted into or over the front end of a marker barrel to prevent a paintball from exiting the barrel if the marker is accidentally fired.

"There! There!" Pros at play

Barrel, rifled (rifled barrel) – A barrel with internal grooves (rifling) down the length of the barrel, either straight or in a spiral, designed to add stability to the paintball in flight.

Blowback – Leakage of CO_2 (or compressed air) between the bolt and the inner barrel wall and/or from the cocking mechanism between the marker's hammer and the inner wall of the housing. Blowback occurs for two reasons. First, and easiest to fix, is that the O-rings on the bolt and/or hammer need to be replaced. The second relates to the positioning of the marker's components when CO_2 is released into the barrel.

Bolt – A marker's bolt typically uses an O-ring at its front end to act as a seal between the bolt and the inner wall of the barrel when the bolt is forward. This is important because a bolt has two functions: it moves a paintball from the point where it loads into the chamber to the bore of the barrel and it helps transfer gas from the marker's valve to the paintball.

Closed-bolt design – When the marker is ready to be fired, the bolt is in the full forward position with the O-ring sealing against the inner wall of the barrel.

Open-bolt design – When the marker is ready to be fired, the bolt is in the full rear position behind the feed nipple port (the port that allows paintballs to flow into the marker).

Venturi bolt design – A bolt with a concave face and multiple holes, known as "thrust ports."

Bore-drop loading – Markers with a bore-drop loading system load paintballs directly into the receiver that is the same size as the barrel or directly into the barrel itself. This keeps the ball from having to load over any large seams or steep angles. (See "breech-drop loading.")

Bottle – The container part of a constant air tank. Slang.

Bottom line – A type of constant air system that positions the ASA adapter/connector (original or after-market) at the bottom of the marker's grip frame. An after-market ASA adapter has a gas line to connect it to the marker that lets gas flow from the tank to the marker. Desired since a bottom line set-up makes shooting a marker with your mask on easier because it repositions it closer to your dominant eye.

Break – The opening moments after a game starts when players are running to their initial bunkers. Also used when a paintball bursts prior to clearing the end of the barrel. Breaks can occur in the barrel and can also be chopped in the breech of the marker.

Breech-drop loading – Markers with a breech-drop loading system load paintballs into an area or device that is larger than the inner diameter of the barrel. A ball is then manually pumped into the barrel. (See "bore-drop loading.")

Breech-lock system – A design that prevents the marker from being pumped twice before it is fired once. Breech-locking markers must be fired before they can be pumped again.

Butt plate – A device that fits on the end of a tank that lets it be used as a shoulder stock.

Bunker – A wall or mound on a paintball field constructed to give one or more players cover while they shoot or look for members of the opposing team. There is no standard field or bunker design. "To bunker" means to charge a fixed position with the intent to lay down paint on the opposition.

CA – Abbreviation for constant air. Allows markers to use bulk CO_2 tanks rather than 12-gram cartridges.

Caliber – The diameter of the bore of a marker or the diameter of a paintball. There are 100 calibers to the inch.

California style – A shooting system consisting of a marker and an L-shaped shoulder stock with a 7- or 10-ounce constant air tank on the bottom. It has a Thermo on/off valve in the shoulder stock's tank holder and a hose that connects the tank to the marker.

Chamber – The part of your marker that accepts the paintball from the feed tube.

Check valve – Allows gas propellant to flow in only one direction.

Chop – When a paintball is broken in the breech of your marker, it is chopped. Not only does paint in the barrel totally destroy any chances of accuracy, but paint shell remains also may prevent your marker from re-cocking.

Chronograph – An electronic device to measure the speed of a paintball directed across it.

CO_2 – Abbreviation for carbon dioxide, a compressed gas used to power your marker.

Cock – To place the striker in position for firing by pulling it back fully.

Constant air – The provision of a prolonged supply of gas at a regulated pressure. Using a constant air system, 300 to 1000 shots are available per tank (depending on size of tank and type of marker). This is opposed to markers using 12-gram CO_2 cartridges that average 15 to 25 shots with variable (usually declining) power per shot.

Cycle rate – The number of cycles (shots) a marker can perform per second.

Dead box – A cordoned-off area where eliminated players go while a game is still in progress. In major tournaments, players in the dead box must sit facing away from the field of play. Also called "player purgatory."

Delrin – A lightweight, but durable and low-wear, low-friction plastic for electronic office equipment, advanced conveyor technology, and applications in fields such as automotive and paintball products. Developed in the '50s by DuPont, it was originally referred to as "synthethic stone."

Detent, ball (ball detent) – Mechanical device that holds a paintball in a stationary position until the bolt pushes the ball into the barrel. This allows only one ball at a time to load into the chamber as the marker executes a cycle. (Also called a ball stop, anti-doubler or a wire nubbin.)

Direct feed – Sends paintballs directly into the chamber or barrel via a feed nipple usually fastened to side of the marker at a 45-degree angle. (Pump-action feed nipples are usually one inch in diameter. Semi-auto feed nipples are usually 7/8 inches.)

Discharge – To cause a marker to fire a paintball.

Disk, rupture (rupture disk) – Small copper disk in the valve of a tank, designed to fail or rupture if the pressure in the tank becomes too great. The rupture disk is usually held in place by a safety plug with vent holes in it.

Double action – Requires only one pull of the trigger to cock and fire.

Dwell – How much air is being passed through the solenoid to fire a marker. Increasing dwell increases ball velocity; decreasing dwell decreases velocity. Dwell should be balanced with a marker's operating pressure, as too high a dwell and too low an operating pressure causes poor efficiency. Too high an operating pressure and too low a dwell causes ball breakage.

Elbow - A hopper adapter. Slang.

Ergonomic – Refers to design that considers or makes concessions to the conformation and mechanics of the human body.

Expansion chamber – A device that "conditions" CO_2 gas by allowing it to expand before it enters the marker's valve system.

Feed apparatus

Feed nipple – A short tube connected to the marker at a 45-degree angle that provides the passageway for balls from the hopper through the hopper adapter (which attaches to the feed nipple) and into the chamber. (Commonly 1-inch diameter for pump markers and 7/8-inch diameter for semi-autos.)

Feed plug – A plug at the bottom of a power feeder that angles balls into the feed port. Turning it stops the balls from feeding into the marker.

Feed tube – Tubular storage container for paintballs usually worn on a belt and used for reloading in the field.

Feeder – A hopper or loader. Slang.

Feeder agitator – An electronic device located at the base of the feeder. The agitator insures that balls feed through the bottom of the feeder and do not jam. Often used on smooth-firing markers like the Angel, AutoMag or Autococker since these markers shake very little. Can also make obsolete a Power Feeder since it insures that a ball will always be available to the gun.

Fill station – A place with a large CO_2 tank (usually 50 to 60 pounds in volume weight) where small tanks can be filled. Consists of a valve, hose and adapter to connect and fill a player's constant air tank.

Firearm – An assembly of a barrel and action from which a projectile is propelled as a result of combustion, which makes it fundamentally different from a marker, from which a projectile is propelled as a result of the release of an inert gas.

Flag station – A team's base camp and the location where the team's flag is kept.

Flaming – Disrespecting someone or their comments in a

The JT USA ProFlex goggle system allows you to change lenses and colors to match your team's image.

paintball Internet chat room. A real no-no. Even newbies have opinions and the only way to learn is sometimes by asking the so-called "stupid" questions.

Flank
As a noun: the far or extreme side as in the left flank of an army in the field.
As a verb: to attack or defend the extreme side (the flank) of a team or bunker.

Fogging up – When breathing and lack of movement cause the goggles to fog over, severely reducing visibility.

Fore grip – Horizontal stabilizing grip located toward the front of a marker. It is usually grasped with the player's "off-hand," the hand not on the trigger.

fps – Abbreviation for feet per second, the standard U.S. measurement of a paintball's speed or velocity.

Freight training (PSP) – Using multiple players who move and act in such a manner so that the lead players, after being marked and eliminated, impede or prevent the timely elimination of other players in the train.

Gas efficiency – The number of shots a marker gets versus the amount of CO_2 it uses, e.g. getting 350 shots from a 7-ounce tank.

Gas pig – A marker and air system that uses more gas than is necessary to spit out a ball at top speed.

Gogged – When a paintball breaks on impact on someone's goggles.

Goggles – Eye protection designed to prevent eye damage. (Paintball goggles are specifically designed for the sport of paintball. They should NOT be substituted with goggles made for any other application.)

Gram – From the metric system, 1000 grams = 1 kg. (kilogram) = 2.2 pounds or 35.27 ounces. Therefore, 3 grams equal approximately 1 ounce. Abbreviated gm.

Gravity – The force of acceleration by which terrestrial objects tend to fall toward the center of the earth.

Grenade – A rubberized shell containing paint and (optional) a paint dispersal mechanism that is useful for attacking bunkers and breaking up pockets of enemy players. Hand thrown, it is NOT an explosive device.

(Not legal on every field or in every tournament. Check with tournament authorities before entering the field with one of these.)

Grip – A component, often replaceable, that fits on the marker's grip frame and provides surface area for the shooter to grip the marker. (Players will want to experiment with styles and materials for comfort and ease of handling.)

Group – A series of shots fired at a target used to adjust the sights or determine the accuracy of a marker.

Worr Games' THS (Tactical Harness System) is available in 2+1, 3+4, 4+5 or large 5+6 configurations. Paint-hauling pods are included in the package.

Hammer terms

Hammer – Part of the marker's action. When released from the cocked position, it strikes the valve assembly, forcing it open and allowing CO_2 to pass through from the gas source to the barrel. Also called "lower bolt" or the "striker."

Hammer down – Pulling the trigger. Putting paint on a target in an intense manner. Showering the target with paint.

Hammer sear – The part of a marker's action holding the hammer in a fixed position, usually under main spring pressure. Pulld by the player's finger, the trigger pushes against the sear. This releases the hammer and allows it to strike the valve assembly.

Harness – Belt, harness and pouches worn by a player to carry extra paintballs, CO_2 cartridges, air tanks, drinking water, a squeegee and other things needed on the field.

High pressure air (HPA) – High pressure compressed air (3000 to 4500 psi) is usually used instead of CO_2 in tournament paintball. HPA requires specialized high-pressure tanks and regulators, which lower the output pressure to what markers can handle.

Hopper – A container, usually on top of a marker, used to hold paintballs before they are fed into the chamber.

Hosing – Constant rapid firing, typically used to pin down an opposing player.

Hydrostatic test – To test a container's wall thickness by measuring its "elastic expansion." This test is required periodically by state Departments of Transportation. The purpose of the test is to assure that the container is safe.

Hyperball – A style of paintball field set-up that uses large black corrugated plastic culverts for bunkers and obstacles. Often, the terms "hyperball" and "speedball" are used either interchangeably or through lack of a clear and accepted definition. Also, a popular arcade game by the same name.

ID – Abbreviation for "inner diameter" or "identification."

In-line configuration – Refers to the manner in which a marker's bolt and hammer are positioned in relation to each other. An in-line configuration indicates that the bolt and hammer are in line with each other, one behind the other.

Jam – A malfunction that prevents the action from operating.

Lands – The uncut surface of the bore of a rifled barrel, as opposed to the grooves.

Lenses, thermal (thermal lenses) – A dual lens system. The outer lens is made from super hard polycarbonate while the inner lens is a different polycarbonate composition that allows anti-fog jell coat to stick to it. The two lenses are attached to each other with a rubber gasket that makes an airtight seal between them. The space between the two lenses becomes a thermal barrier that reduces fogging on the inner lens.

Loader – Feed tube from the hopper to the marker. Or sometimes the hopper itself.

Marker – A mechanical device that is powered by compressed air, nitrogen or CO_2, used to shoot paintballs. (Some consider that the term is the "politically correct" way to refer to a paintball gun.)

MSRP – Abbreviation for Manufacturer's Suggested Retail Price. The price you pay for paintball gear (or a camera or new car or any electronic gear, for instance) will almost certainly be lower than the stated MSRP.

Muppet – A goofy or objectionable person who acts without or before using common sense.

Muzzle – That fore end of a marker's barrel out of which the paintball is propelled.

Muzzle break – A pattern of holes or slots machined into a barrel muzzle that act as exhaust ports. May be either factory-installed or an after-market accessory.

Muzzle velocity – The speed a ball is traveling when it leaves the marker's muzzle.

Nelson-based – Refers to pump-style markers with an in-line bolt and hammer system that were designed based on the original "007."

Nitrogen (N) – A colorless, odorless, essentially non-reactive gas compressed to high densities and used to fill tanks as a paintball propellant. The difference between nitrogen and CO_2 is that nitrogen is measured by pressure while CO_2 is measured by weight. It constitutes about 4/5 of the volume of the atmosphere. Its chemical symbol is "N."

Newbie – A rookie paintball player. Slang.

NPT – A standard for measuring "normal pressure and temperature" set at 14.696 psi and 70 degrees (Fahrenheit).

OD – Abbreviation for "outer diameter."

O-ring – A rubber or neoprene ring used as a gasket.

Offset sight rail – A sight rail mounted at an angle to the marker's vertical axis. It allows a sight to be mounted so that it is un-obstructed by the hopper and feed nipple.

One-for-One – A tournament penalty whereby a judge ejects both the player who committed a penalty as well as another teammate, usually the closest one.

Paintball – A round, lightweight capsule filled with a water-based dye. It is designed to be shot out of a marker, propelled by a compressed gas. It should burst on impact leaving a colorful mark on the target. Balls come in three calibers (sizes): 50, 62 and 68. The most current and popular size, 68 cal., is readily available and offers better range, accuracy and "breakability," perhaps because of its larger size and heavier weight. Also, the popular game of tag used with paintballs.

Paint-check – Time called by a referee or player to check for "splat" marks. It may only be invoked by – and the game restarted afterwards by – a referee. If a player misuses the paint-check rule, he may be removed from the game.

Pattern – The distribution of paintballs fired from a marker.

Pod – A tubular, plastic cylinder that holds paintballs to add to the hopper while a game is in progress.

Viewloader's Proflex pull-through squeegee is made from injection-molded rubber.

Porting – Holes that are symmetrically drilled into a barrel to make the marker quieter and provide for smoother and more accurate flight of the paintball. In theory, the ports allow excessive gas build-up to blow off.

Power feed – A feed nipple design that incorporates the blowback from the marker to increase the rate at which paintballs are fed into the marker. Most power feeds are designed into the marker, but some after-market bolt-on power feeds are available.

Pressure regulator – Regulates the pressure of gas flowing through it, usually stepping it down from a higher pressure to a lower pressure. Some regulators are pre-set to a specific psi and some are adjustable.

psi – The abbreviation for pounds per square inch. Nitro tanks are sold with a psi rating, 3000 psi or 4500 psi, for example, that tells you the maximum pounds per square inch the tank is designed to hold. Filling a tank beyond its psi rating is dangerous.

Pull pin – A pin fastener that can be quickly removed to disassemble a marker.

Pull-through – A type of squeegie used to clear broken paint and shell fragments from a barrel.

Pump action – A marker that needs to be manually cocked before each shot. The pumping sequence is: pull the pump back to cock and load a ball, push the pump forward to chamber the ball and finally, pull the trigger to fire the ball.

Quick changer – Connects to a marker usually via the ASA adapter. Allows rapid loading/unloading of a 12-gram CO_2 cartridge.

Quick disconnect – Used to detach the CO_2 source, especially a remote system, from the marker. Usually made of stainless steel or brass, it is composed of a male fitting and female coupler that connect together to form an airtight connection.

Ram – A double-acting cylinder that helps re-cock a semi-automatic marker.

Rate of fire – Rate of fire is the number of balls shot out the barrel in some measured time frame, but this is actually determined by the setting of the recharge between shots. Often abbreviated as rof.

Rec ball – Short for recreational paintball. Anything non-tournament related is usually referred to as rec ball.

Receiver – Main body of a marker that houses the bolt and hammer. The feed nipple is typically part of the receiver. With sidearms, it is called the frame.

Recoil – The rearward movement of a marker resulting from firing a paintball.

Remote – Power system carried on a player's body, not directly attached to the marker. It consists of a constant air tank, usually in a pouch or fanny pack, and a high-pressure gas line with quick disconnect and all the necessary fittings to connect it to the marker.

Reticle – A system of fine, gradient lines or other pointing aids on the lens of an optical instrument such as a scope or sight to aid in aiming.

Rifling

Internal – Grooves or raised points in the barrel that are either straight or spiral, designed to spin and thereby add in-flight stability to a ball.

External – Spiral hole pattern drilled in the barrel. The ports allow air in front of a paintball to escape as the ball pushes forward. Reduced air resistance allows the ball to fly straighter and farther. Barrel porting also diminishes the noise of a shot. Also known as external porting.

Ringer – A more experienced player hidden in a field of less experienced players.

Round – Either **(1)** spherical like a three dimensional circle or **(2)** one paintball capable of being fired through your marker.

Safety – Device designed to provide protection against accidental or unintentional discharge under normal usage when properly engaged.

Sandbagging – Players or tournament teams dropping back in classification to raise their chances of winning. A mediocre amateur team, for instance, may "sandbag" by dropping down into the Rookie division to play against less-experienced players. This practice is strictly discouraged in most high-level tournament competition.

Scenario game – An organized game with a theme, such as the D-Day Normandy invasion in World War II, an alien invasion or some other factual or fictional situation. These games often run 24 hours and have special rules, story lines and characters.

Semi-automatic – A marker that fires and reloads only once for each pull and release of the trigger.

Sheridan-based – Refers to markers similar to the original Sheridan markers with a "stacked" design, meaning that the hammer and valve system are in the lower section and the bolt in the upper section.

Shot buffering – Electronic action that spaces shots in time no matter how fast or irregularly the trigger is pulled. (Shot buffering does not ignore the trigger pull, but stores the pull in memory.)

Short stroke – Not pulling the trigger far enough to fire and re-cock or sometimes thought of as pulling the trigger faster than your marker can shoot.

Sight rail – Allows mounting of a sighting system to a marker.

Sight rail, raised – A sight rail that is raised up off the body of the marker, thus affording the shooter a better field of view.

Sight, red dot – Battery powered optical sight that produces a red dot reticle or aiming point. (The red dot sights do not project on a target.)

Sight rings – Adapters required to mount your sight to the sight rail. (Sight rings are NOT universal.)

Siphon bottle - A special CO_2 tank designed to suck liquid into the gun.

Skirmish – A fight between small groups of players or any brisk encounter.

Skirmish line – A formation of players in line beside each other and advancing.

Slimed barrel – When a ball breaks in the barrel and coats it with paint. Slimed barrels will not shoot straight. Slang.

Speedball – A game played on small fields with little natural cover. Bunkers usually consist of wooden pallets, tires or other man-made barricades. Speedball fields are designed to allow spectators to see the action. The first speedball field was set up at SC Village in Corona, CA.

Splatter – Residue sprayed or splashed on a player by a paintball when it breaks on a nearby object.

Spring, main – The spring that drives the hammer.

Spring, valve – The spring that closes the valve after it has been opened by the hammer.

Squad – A small group. A team.

Squeegee – An instrument used to clean a marker barrel.

Squid – A new player in paintball, a newbie.

Squid basher – A semi-experienced player who plays very aggressively against new players to the point of ruining their first game.

Stacked configuration – A marker design in which the bolt and hammer are positioned one on top of the other inside the receiver.

Stick feed – A gravity feeder, usually made from PVC material, which holds balls stacked in a line, one on top of another.

Stock – The wood, fiberglass or plastic component to which the barrel and receiver are attached.

Stock "L" – A shoulder stock shaped like an "L" laying on its side. It usually fastens below a marker's grip frame and may have a constant air tank holder attached.

Stock "T" – A shoulder stock shaped like a "T" laying on its side. It usually fastens below a marker's grip frame and may have a constant air tank holder attached.

Suppressing fire – To fire a continuing volley of shots at potential targets, forcing them to take cover while a player or a team member moves through an open space.

Suppressor – A tubular device press fitted into the fore-end of a marker barrel that is designed to reduce the noise of a shot. Also called a silencer.

Sweet spot – Shooting into a spot or lane that has a high likelihood of traffic due to its proximity with a known path to a key bunker. Sweetspotting is done with the hope of striking and eliminating an opponent who runs through this sweet spot area.

Tank

Chilled – A tank that becomes extremely cold due to rapid pressure loss. This may be caused by very rapid firing or by suddenly releasing the remaining gas pressure in a tank. (Note that a tank must be chilled before it can be filled with CO_2.)

Constant air – A container (valve and bottle) for holding gas propellant for a paintball marker.

Anti-siphon – A tank designed to allow only vaporous CO_2 to exit through the valve.

Siphon – A tank designed to draw liquid CO_2 from the bottom of the tank. This is accomplished with a gas line attached to the back of the tank valve. The other end of the line is weighted so that it remains located in the bottom of the tank.

Tapeline – The left and right field boundaries of a field. Also called "the wire."

Teflon – DuPont began developing this plastic in the '30s and it is still listed in the Guinness Book of World Records as the slipperiest material in the world, with the lowest coefficient of static and dynamic friction of any solid. This measurement is the equivalent of the surface of wet ice rubbing against wet ice!

Thread saver – A protective cap that screws onto a tank valve to keep its threads from being damaged when not in use.

Three-way (3-Way) – The job of the 3-Way is to transfer regulated air from the regulator to the front and rear of the ram.

Timing - The time between the firing of the marker and the re-cocking. On most good quality markers, this is an adjustable interval.

Tool, velocity adjusting – A tool used to adjust the velocity of a marker.

Tournament cap – A cover over a marker's velocity adjuster so that it cannot be changed during a game. Normally required for tournaments.

Trajectory – The ball's path to its target. At very short distances, the trajectory will be nearly flat, but at longer distances, the trajectory of a ball follows a curved path.

Trigger, hair – A slang term for a trigger requiring very low force to actuate. Note: Hair triggers are frequently desired in competition or tournaments. The reduced force needed to pull the trigger allows the shooter's arm and marker to remain steady.

Trigger pull – The average force that must be applied to the trigger to cause the marker to fire. Note: Typically, non-competition-mode markers have a minimum of 3 to 4 pounds pull.

Trigger shoe – After-market product that fits on the trigger to provide more trigger surface area and a more comfortable feel.

Tube, paintball (paintball tube) – A small, cigar-shaped tube that carries 10 paintballs. Tube is also occasionally applied to "pod" although a refill pod carries 100 or 140 balls and is used to refill a loader in the middle of a game.

To squeegee or not to squeegee … flexible quad-disk-design squeegee from Game Face.

Tunnel vision – Refers to a player who focuses so intently in one direction that he loses his peripheral vision and thereby is not aware of players moving on his sides.

Turpentine – Turpentine is a unique "paint thinner," which means it re-hydrates the binder oils in oil-based paints and allows you to wash paint off your skin and even out of your clothes. (Turpentine is used in some medicines, too, if you can believe that!) It is derived from the sap (also called the gum) of conifers like the pine tree.

Velocity adjuster – Normally a set screw on a marker that is designed to turn and thereby increase or decrease the marker's muzzle velocity.

Valve – A device for controlling flow of a gas or liquid.

Valve porting – Enlarging holes or drilling additional holes in a valve body so that more gas will be released when the valve is opened.

System – A marker's internal parts that control the flow of propellant.

Walk-on – A recreational player who brings their own equipment to a field.

Wipe – The most heinous act of smearing paint from one's person or gear with the intention of NOT getting called out. In tournament play, the penalty for wiping is the ejection of the offending player from the game in addition to three (3) teammates.

Wrench, Allen – Hexagonal tool in various sizes that is used to turn screw fasteners such as hex head or button head screws. Also used to turn anything with a hexagonal hole. Used to adjust a marker's velocity as well as disassemble it.

X-Ball – Slang for the NXL, national professional league, or play in the fast, confrontational style of play of that top competitive league.

PAINTBALL INTERNET DIRECTORY

MANUFACTURERS

1 Shot Productions
www.1shotprod.com

32 Degrees
www.32degrees.com
and www.32ice.com

Action Markers
www.actionmarkers.com

Action Sports Paintball
www.actionsports-paintball.com

Adrenaline Games
www.supairball.com and
www.adrenalinegames.com

AKA
www.akalmp.com

Air America
www.airamerica.com

Air Concepts Industries (ACI)
www.acisports.com

Alien Paintball
www.alienpb.com

Allen Paintball
www.allenpaintball.com

Ancient Innovations
www.qloader.com

Armotec
www.armotech.com

Atomic Ordinance
www.atomicordnance.com

Ballistic Sports
www.ballisticsports.com

Battlepaint
www.battlepaint.com

Bob Long
www.boblong.com

Brimstone
www.brimstonepaintball.com

CenterFlag
www.centerflagproducts.com

Cobra
www.cobrapaintball.com

Custom Sports Gear
www.customsportsgear.com

Dark Horizon
www.darkhorizoncorp.com

Dye
www.dyeprecision.com

Equation Design
www.equationUSA.com

Empire
www.empirepaintball.com

Evil
www.evil-paintball.com

Free Flow Technology
www.4freeflow.com

Game Face Paintball
www.gamefacepaintball.com

Great American Paintballs and Inflatable Bunkers
www.greatamericanpaintballs.com

Hammerhead
www.hammerheadpaintball.com

Indian Creek Design
www.icdpaintball.com and
www.icdproducts.com

JJ Performance
www.jjperformance.com

Jet City Specialties (Blackpoint Engineering)
www.bp-usa.com

JT USA
www.jtusa.com

Kick Ass Products
www.kickasspaintball.com

Kingman
www.kingmanUSA.com

Lapco Paintball
www.lapcopaintball.com www.lapco.net

Major Paintball
www.majorpaintball.net

Mantis
www.mantisgear.com

Nelson Paintballs
www.nelsonpaintballs.com

Next Level
www.nextlevelproducts.com

o2 Sports
www.3a-paintball.com

Odyssey Paintball Products
www.odysseypaintball.com

Paint Check – The Game
www.paintcheckthegame.com

Paintball Junkies
www.paintballjunkies.com

Paintball Magazine
www.paintballmag.com

Paintball Mania (Nitro Duck)
www.nitroduck.com

Palmers Pursuit Shop
www.palmer-pursuit.com

PMI
www.flashpaintballs.com and
www.pminetwork.com

Powerball
www.powerball.co.up

PowerLyte
www.powerlyte.com

Professional Paintball
www.professionalpaintball.com

Pro-Team Products
www.proteamdirect.com

Psychoballistics
www.psychoballistics.com

Raven USA
www.ravenUSA.com

Redz Comfort Gear
www.redzcomfort.com

Ricochet Development
www.ricochet2k.com

Rocket Paintball
www.rocketpaintball.com

RP Scherer
www.rps-paintball.com

Rufus Dawg
www.rufusdawg.com

Scott USA
www.scottusa.com

Severe Paintball
www.severepaintball.com

Shannon Outdoors
www.shannonoutdoors.com
and www.bugtamer.com

Smart Parts
www.smartparts.com

Sports Sensors
www.sportssensors.com

System X Paintball
www.xenterprises.info

TC Paintballs
www.tcpaintballs.com

Tippmann
www.tippmann.com

Tippmann Ordnance
www.tippmannordnance.com

Topstitch
www.topstitch.net

Unogun Industrial
www.kalloyuno.com

VForce
www.vforcepaintball.com

Viewloader
www.viewloader.com

WdP (Angel)
www.wdp-paintball.com

Wicked Air Sport
www.wickedairsportz.com

Worr Game Products
www.worr.com and www.budorr.com

Zap Paintball
www.zappaintball.com

DISTRIBUTORS

National Paintball Supply
www.npbs.com

Pursuit Marketing International
www.pminetwork.com

CLUBS AND ORGANIZATIONS

Collegiate Paintball League
www.collegepaintball.com

Future Paintball
www.futureball.com

International Assn. for the Leisure & Entertainment Industry
www.ialei.org

IAO (International Amateur Open)
www.teameffortevents.com

Maine Recreational Paintball League
www.mrpl.org

National Collegiate Paintball Association
www.college-paintball.com

National Professional Paintball League
www.nppl.tv

Newfoundland-Labrador Paintball Association
www.infonet.st-johns.nf.ca

Paintball Sports Promotions
www.pspevents.com

PanAm Circuit
www.panamcircuit.com

Ronn Stern Paintball Camps
www.paintballcamps.com

Society of Paintball Players and Teams
www.spplat.com

DIRECT SALES

3A-Paintball.Com
www.3a-paintball.com

BargainPaintball.Com
www.bargainpaintball.com

Bulldog Paintball
www.bulldogpaintball.com

Cobra
www.cobrapaintball.com

Discount Paintball
www.discount-paintball.com

First Call
www.firstcallpaintball.com

I&I Sports Wholesale
www.iisports.com

Paintball Ballistix
www.paintballistix.com

Paintball Discounters
www.paintball-discounters.com

Paintball Daddy.com
www.paintballdaddy.com

Paintball Express.Com
www.paintballexpress.com

Paintball Gateway
www.paintballgateway.com

Paintball Nation
www.paintballnation.com

Paintball Sniper Supplies
www.paintballsnipersupplies.com
and www.pbsnipersupplies.com

Paintball Store
www.thepaintballstore.com

Paintball Supply
www.paintballsupplyusa.com

Paintball Wizard
www.paintballwizard.com

Planet Eclipse
www.planeteclipse.com

PMI
www.buypmi.com

Ronin Gear
www.roningear.com

Roughneck Paintball
www.roughneckpaintball.com

ShockTech
www.shocktechusa.com

Skanline Sports
www.skanline.com

Tactical Markers
www.tacticalmarkers.com

Warped Sportz
www.warpedsportz.com

MAGAZINES AND COMMUNICATIONS

Action Pursuit Games
www.actionpursuitgames.com

Crossfire Paintball Magazine
www.crossfiremag.com

Facefull
www.face-full.com

Force of Nature
www.forceofnature.com

P8NT Magazine
www.p8nt.com

PaintMagazine.Com
www.paintmagazine.com

PaintBall.com
www.paintball.com

Paintball 2Xtremes
www.pb2x.com and
www.paintball2xtremes.com

Paintball Channel
www.paintballchannel.com

Paintball City
www.paintballcity.com

Paintball Games International
www.p8ntballer.com

Paintball Nation
www.pbnation.com

Paintball News
www.paintballnews.com

Paintball Sports International
www.paintballsportsinc.com

Paintball Tips
www.paintballtips.itgo.com

Paintball Zone
www.paintballzone.com

Paintball Review
www.pbreview.com

Pod Bitch
www.podbitch.com

Scenario News
www.scenarionews.com

Scenario Paintball Calendar
www.scenariopaintballcalendar.com

Scenario Paintball Games
www.scenariopaintballgames.com

World And Regional Paintball Information Guide
www.warpig.com

INSURANCE

American Paintball League
www.paintball-apl.com
and www.paintball.net

Paintball Business Assn.
www.paintballinsurance.com

PAINTBALL MANUFACTURER LISTING

PRIMARILY MARKERS

32 Degrees (NPS)
570 Mantua Blvd
Sewell, NJ 08080
(800) 346-5615
www.32degrees.com
or www.32ice.com

Action Markers
3908 Fourier Dr.
Ft. Wayne, IN 46818
(866) 478-2255
www.actionmarkers.com

Airgun Designs,
804 Seton Ct.
Wheeling, IL 60090
(847) 520-7507
www.airgun.com

Alien Paintball
9006 Wimbley Ct.
Elk Grove, CA 95624
(916) 868-8686
www.alienpb.com

ANS Xtreme
3885 Cochran
Unit R, Simi Valley, CA 93063
(805) 527-5661
www.ansxtreme.com

Bob Long (NPS)
570 Mantua Blvd.
Sewell, NJ 08080
(800) 346-5615
www.npbs.com or
www.boblong.com

Brass Eagle
P.O. Box 1956
Rogers, AR 72757
(800) 861-6095/(479) 464-8700
www.brasseagle.com

Component Concepts
530 S Springbrook Rd.
Newberg, OR 97132
(503) 554-809
www.phantomonline.com

Game Face Paintball
Routes 5 & 20
East Bloomfield, NY 14443
(585) 657-3085
www.gamefacepaintball.com

Evil (PMI)
55 Howard Ave.
Des Plaines, IL 60018
(800) 334-0502
www.evil-paintball.com or
www.pminetwork.com

Free Flow Technology
160 School St.
Victor, NY 14564
(585) 924-9930
www.4freeflow.com

Indian Creek Design
1019 First St.N
Nampa, ID 83687
(208) 468-0446
www.icdpaintball.com or
www.icdproducts.com

Kick Ass Paintball Products
57 W. Barham Ave.
Santa Rosa, CA 95407
(707) 571-8068
www.kapp1.com or www.
kickasspaintball.com

Kingman USA
14010 Live Oak Ave.
Baldwin Park, CA 91706
(877) 467-2836
www.kingmanusa.com

National Paintball Supply (NPS)
570 Mantua Blvd.
Sewell, NJ 08080
(800) 346-5615
www.npbs.com

o2 Sports, Inc.
1038 E Bastanchury Rd. #193
Fullerton, CA 92835
(714) 964-7322
www.3a-paintball.com

Palmers Pursuit Shop
3951 Development Dr.
Sacramento, CA 95838
(916) 923-9676
www.palmers-pursuit.com

Powerball Units 7-8
Elliott Industrial Park, Eastern Rd.
Aldershot, Hampshire
GU12 4TF, United Kingdom 01252
408 550
www.powerball.co.uk

Psychoballistics
570 Mantua Blvd.
Sewell, NJ 08080
(800) 346-5615
www.psychoballistics.com

Pursuit Marketing International (PMI)
55 Howard Ave.
Des Plaines, IL 60018
(800) 334-0502
www.pminetwork.com

Raven USA
14010 Live Oak Ave.
Baldwin Park, CA 91706
(877) 467-2836
www.ravenusa.com

Smart Parts
East: Loyalhanna Business Complex
100 Station St., Latrobe, PA 15661
West: 950 Spice Island Dr.,Sparks, NV 89431
(800) 992-2147
www.smartparts.com

System X Paintball
330 S Harbor Blvd.
Santa Ana, CA 92704
(800) 974-3355
www.xenterprises.info

Tippmann Pneumatics
3518 Adams Center Rd.
Fort Wayne, IN 46806
(260) 749-6022 [West Coast (310) 328-7625]
www.tippmann.com

Toxic Performance
956 S Second St.,
Ronkonkoma, NY 11722
(631) 580-4375
www.toxicperformance.com

WdP (Angel)
417 Main St. #201,
Huntington Beach, CA 92648
(714) 536-9011

Metro Triangle
Nechells, Birmingham,
B75QT, England
+44 (0) 1213282228
www.wdp-paintball.com

Worr Game Products
252 Granite St.
Corona, CA 92879
(800) 755-5061/(909) 520-9969
www.worr.com or www.budorr.com

Zap Paintballs
720 Wright St.,
Strathroy, Ontario, Canada,
N7G 3H8
(800) 265-6555
www.zappaintball.com

PAINTBALLS

Draxxus Paintballs/ Pro Caps
6000 Kieran, Ville St.
Laurent, Quebec, Canada, H4S 2B5
(514) 337-1779
www.draxxus.com

Nelson Paint
One Nelson Dr.
PO Box 2040, Kingsford, MI 49802
(800) 236-9278
www.nelsonpaintballs.com

RP Scherer Recreational Products
11399 47th St. N,
Clearwater, FL 33762
(727) 572-4000
www.rps-paintball.com

Severe Paintball
www.severepaintball.com

TC Paintballs
Homestead Sports Complex,
Miami, FL
(786) 293-7444
www.tcpaintballs.com

Zap Paintballs
720 Wright St.,
Strathroy, Ontario, Canada,
N7G 3H8
(800) 265-6555
www.zappaintball.com

ACCESSORIES

Action Sports Paintball
229 North Main,
Cheboygan, MI 49721
(616) 627-3474
www.actionsports-paintball.com

Adrenaline Games USA
100 Station St.,
Loyalhanna, PA 15661
www.supairball.com or www.adrenalinegames.com

Air America
2240 Elmhurst Rd.,
Elk Grove Village, IL 60007
(847) 545-9999
www.airamerica.com

Air Concepts Industries (ACI)
701 Auto Center Dr.,
Ontario, CA (877) 832-6224
www.acisports.com

[Also: 954 Manufacturers Rd., Dayton, TN]

AKA
PO Box 441186
Indianapolis, IN 46244
(317) 631-7200
www.akalmp.com

Allen Paintball Products
34 W Interstate Rd.,
Bedford, OH 44146
(440) 439-3222
www.allenpaintball.com

Ancient Innovations
PO Box 2999
Weaverville, CA 96093
(800) 910-4522
www.qloader.com

Armotech
2794 Locker Ave. W,
Carlabad, CA 92008
(760) 268-0735
www.armotech.com

Atomic Ordinance
1156 W Broadway,
Forest Lake, MN 55025
(651) 982-9546
www.atomicordnance.com

Ballistic Sports
PO Box 226,
Osceola, IN 46561
(574) 254-1200
www.ballisticsports.com

Battlepaint
2018 Woven Tr.,
Lewisville, TX 75067
(214) 724-7015
www.battlepaint.com

Bauer Compressors
1328 Azalea Garden Rd.,
Norfolk, VA 23502
(757) 857-1041
www.bauer-kompressoren.de/en/index.htm

Brimstone Enterprises
1695 Centerpoint Rd.
Oak Hill, OH 45656
(740) 682-6232/(450) 424-6572
www.brimstonepaintball.com

Camouflage Systems,
11271 Ventura B1 #297
Studio City, CA 91604
(877) 810-9614
www.bushrag.com

CenterFlag
102 E Schoolhouse Rd.
Yorkville, IL 60560
(630) 553-2611
www.centerflagproducts.com

Custom Sports Gear
162 Penn-Adamsburg Rd
Jeannette, PA 15644
(724) 522-1505
www.customsportsgear.com

Dark Horizon,
17 Steeple Dr.
Robesonia, PA 19551
www.darkhorizoncorp.com

Dead on Paintball
2817 E. Jackson,
Muncie, IN 47303
(765) 286-9725

Dye
10637 Scripps Summit Ct.
San Diego, CA 92131
(858) 536-5183
www.dyeprecision.com

Empire (NPS)
www.empirepaintball.com

Equation Design & Manufacturing
6503 E. Frye Rd. Ste. #12,
Chandler, AZ 85226
(480) 705-7390
www.equationusa.com

Evil (NPS)
www.evil-paintball.com

Free Flow Technology
160 School St.,
Victor, NY 14564
(585) 924-9930
www.4freeflow.com

Game Face Paintball
East Bloomfield, NY 14443
(585) 657-3085
www.gamefacepaintball.com

Great American Paintballs & Inflatable Bunkers
[Soft GelCaps West], 10121 Hwy. 50 E,
Carson City, NV 89706 (775) 246-2111
www.greatamericanpaintballs.com

Hammerhead
8300 Gaylord Parkway #16
Frisco, TX 75034
(800) 908-9060
www.hammerheadpaintball.com

Jet City Specialties
Blackpoint Engineering, LLC,
65695 US 33
Goshen, IN 46526 (800) 518-2200
www.bp-usa.com

JJ Performance
410 E Wood St.
Shreve, OH 44676
(330) 567-2455
www.jjperformance.com

JT USA
515 Main St., Chula Vista, CA 91911
(619) 421-2660
www.jtusa.com

Kick Ass Paintball Products
57 W. Barham Ave.,
Santa Rosa, CA 95407
(707) 571-8068
www.kapp1.com or www.kickasspaintball.com

Lapco Paintball
9528 Miramar Rd. #217
San Diego, CA 92126
(858) 693-0068
www.lapco.net

Lloyd Enterprises,
PO Box 681644,
San Antonio, TX 78268
www.paintballsnipersupplies.com

Magnum USA
4801 Stoddard Rd.
Modesto, CA 95356
(800) 521-1698
www.magnumboots.com

Major Paintball
Rt. 2, Box 2155, Oak Valley Rd.,
Toccoa, GA 30577
(706) 282-5041
www.majorpaintball.net

Mantis
9275 E M-36,
Whitmore Lake, MI 48189
(810) 691-4308
www.mantisgear.com

National Paintball Supply (NPS)
570 Mantua Blvd.
Sewell, NJ 08080
(800) 346-5615
www.npbs.com

Nexed
99 Wood Ave. S, Suite 805
Iselin, NJ 08830
(732) 321-4040
www.nexed.com

Odyssey Paintball
3850 Marquis Dr.
Garland, TX 75042
(972) 494-2500
www.odysseypaintball.com

Paintball Junkies,
1151 N Kraemer Pl.
Anaheim, CA 92806
(714) 632-9616
www.paintballjunkies.com

Paintball Mania (Nitro Duck)
4951 Sean Dr.
Imperial, MO 63052
(636) 296-0964
www.nitroduck.com

PowerLyte
5811 McHines Pl. #105,
Raleigh, NC 27616
(919) 713-4317
www.powerlyte.com

Professional Paintball
10 Railroad St.
Victor, NY 14564
(585) 924-9910
www.professionalpaintball.com

Pro-Team Products
PO Box 1555,
Flagler Beach, FL 32136
(386) 437-3375
www.proteamdirect.com

Pursuit Marketing International (PMI)
55 Howard Ave
Des Plaines, IL 60018
(800) 334-0502
www.pminetwork.com

Rancho Safari
PO Box 691,
Ramona, CA 92065
(800) 240-2094
www.ranchosafari.com

Raven USA,
14010 Live Oak Ave.
Baldwin Park, CA 91706
(877) 467-2836
www.ravenusa.com

Redz Comfort Gear
3 Reeves Station Rd.,
Medford, NJ 08055
(877) 873-3432
www.redzcomfort.com

RhinoTech USA
19528 Ventura #328,
Tarzana, CA 91356
(818) 387-0554 www.
rhinotechusa.com

Ricochet Development
8552 N Dysart Rd. #200C
El Mirage, AZ 85335
(877) 613-0623
www.ricochet2k.com

Rocket Paintball
104 Springfield Rd.,
Elizabethtown, KY 42701
(866) 762-5384
www.rocketpaintball.com

Ronn Stern Gear & Paintball Camps
5910 Meadowood Ln.,
Richmond, VA 23237
(804) 751-0352
www.paintballcamps.com or www.
ronnstern.com

Rufus Dawg
PO Box 13719
Dayton, OH 45413
(937) 898-3287
www.rufusdawg.com

Safe Play (AtomixTurf)
1020 Decker Rd.
Walled Lake, MI 48390
(248) 926-9980

Scott USA
PO Box 2030
Sun Valley, ID 83353
(208) 622-1000
www.scottusa.com

Skull Sock
500 Plaza Circle, Suite K
Clinton, SC 29325
(866) 348-7266
www.skullsock.com

Sports Sensors, Inc.
PO Box 46198
Cincinnati, OH 45246-0198
(800) 589-3805
www.sportssensors.com

Tippmann Ordnance
Loveland, CO
(970) 613-2051
www.tippmannordnance.com

Topstitch
632 N Market St.
Redding, CA 96003
(530) 244-2220
www.topstitch.net

VForce
6000 Kieran, Ville St
Laurent, Quebec, Canada, H4S 2B5
(514) 337-1779
www.vforcepaintball.com

Viewloader
P.O. Box 1956,
Rogers, AR 72757
(800) 861-6095/(479) 464-8700
www.viewloader.com

Wicked Air Sportz
3269 Maricopa Ave. #114-511
Lake Havasu City, AZ 86406
www.wickedairsportz.com

Worr Game Products
252 Granite St.
Corona, CA 92879
(909) 520-9969
www.worr.com

MAGAZINES AND VIDEOS

1 Shot Productions
6329 S. 115th E. Place,
Broken Arrow, OK 74012
(918) 250-8786
www.1shotprod.com

Action Pursuit Games
CFW Enterprises, Inc., 4201
Vanowen Pl., Burbank, CA 9150
(818) 845-2656
[Subscriptions (800) 877-5528]
www.actionpursuitgames.com

Crossfire Paintball Magazine (NPS)
PO Box 690, Sewell, NJ 08080
(888) 834-6026
www.crossfiremag.com

Facefull Magazine
Edited by Adrenaline Editions
1 Rue Borda 75003 Paris, FR
+33 142 781 949
www.face-full.com

P8NT Magazine
4047 N Sheridan Rd. #4,
Chicago, IL 60613
(773) 929-2811
www.p8nt.com

Paintball 2Xtremes (NPS)
PO Box 690
Sewell, NJ 08080
(888) 834-6026
www.pb2x.com or www.
paintball2xtremes.com

Paintball Games International
Maze Media (2000), 89 East Hill
Colchester, Essex
CO1 2QN England 44 (0)1206
797541
www.p8ntballer.com

Paintball Magazine
CFW Enterprises, Inc., 4201
Vanowen Pl.,
Burbank, CA 91506
(818) 845-2656 [Subscriptions
(800) 877-5528]
www.paintballmag.com

Paintball News
P.O. Box 1608,
Hillsboro, NH 03244
(603) 464-6080
www.paintballnews.com

Paintball Sports International,
59 E Main St.,
Mt. Kisco, NY 10549
(914) 241-7400
www.paintballsportsinc.com

Scenario News
PO Box 1036
Spring, TX 77383
(281) 288-5523
www.scenarionews.com

CLOTHING

Advantage Camouflage,
390 Box Circle
Columbus, GA 31907
(800) 992-9968
www.advantagecamo.com

Mossy Oak Camouflage
3330 Cumberland Blvd.
Atlanta, GA 30339
(800) 331-5624
www.mossyoak.com

Predator Camouflage Clothing
2605 Coulee Ave.
LaCrosse, WI 54601
(608) 787-0500
www.predatorcamo.com

Realtree Camouflage
1390 Box Circle
Columbus, GA 31907
(800) 992-9968
www.realtree.com

Sabatini Enterprises
721 Nevada St. #306,
Redlands, CA 92373
(909) 793-4471
www.paintballdaddy.com

Shaggie 3-D Cover Systems
Rancho Safari, PO Box 691
Ramona, Ca 92065
(800) 240-2094
www.ranchosafari.com

Shannon Outdoors
PO Box 444
Louisville, GA 30434
(800) 852-8058
www.bugtamer.com or www.
shannonoutdoors.com

SCENARIO GAME & TOURNAMENT PRODUCERS

American Paintball League
PO Box 3561 CRS
Johnson City, TN 37602
(800) 541-9169 (423) 282-6834
www.paintball.net

Black Cat Paintball Productions
PO Box 127
High Rolls, NM 88325
(505) 682-7921
www.blackcat-productions.com

MackZ Xtreme Sportz
PO Box 936
Sugar Land, TX 77478
(281) 565-9381
www.mxsportz.com

Millennium Paintball Productions
670 Country Club Dr.
Crystal River, FL 34429
(352) 795-0691
www.mppgames.com

National Professional Paintball League
417 Main St. Ste. 201,
Huntington Beach, CA
92648 (714) 536-9261
www.nppl.tv

Nocer Paintball Productions
PO Box 23422,
Jacksonville, FL 32241
(904) 591-4020/434-4238
www.nocerproductions.com

Paintball Sports Promotions
1229 Mystic Dr.
Loganville, GA 30052
(770) 466-5558
www.pspevents.com

Team Effort Events
251 Westvue Rd.
Wexford, PA 15090
(724) 775-8299
www.teameffortevents.com

Viper Enterprises

2743 Triway Ln.
Houston, TX 77043
(713) 690-4311/(281) 844-4572
www.viperpaintball.com

Wayne Dollack Scenario Games

4841 S Pine St.
Ocala, FL 34474
(352) 401-1801
www.waynes-world.com

WHOLESALERS

National Paintball Supply

570 Mantua Blvd.
Sewell, NJ 08080
(800) 346-5615
www.npbs.com

NPS Midwest

545 Busse Rd.
Elk Grove Village, IL 60007 (877) 776-2277

NPS SE

771 Fentress Blvd. #8
Daytona Beach, FL 32114 (386) 274-2282

NPS South

2010 Century Center Blvd. #S
Irving, TX 75062 (972) 871-9156

NPS SW

14101 Rosecrans Ave.
La Mirada, CA 90638 (562) 404-1390

NPS NW

1454 McDonald St. NE
Salem, OR 97303 (503) 362-4999

Pursuit Marketing International

55 Howard Ave.
Des Plaines, IL 60018
(800) 334-0502
www.pminetwork.com

PMI NE

4650 Wedgewood Blvd., #108, Frederick, MD 21701 (800) 344-4633

PMI SE

7935 N Armenia Ave., Tampa, FL 33604 (800) 761-9600

PMI South Central

1101 Royal Pkwy., #117, Euless, TX (800) 318-4916

PMI SW

12507 East Florence, Santa Fe Springs, CA 90670 (562) 941-0999

PMI NW

18711 SW 65th Ave., Lake Oswego, OR 97035 (503) 682-8450

PMI

Canada, 98 Bessemer Ct. Unit 9, London, Ontario N6E 1KG

OTHER

American Paintball League

1212 W. Mountainview Rd.,
Johnson City, TN 37604
(800) 541-9169
www.paintball-apl.com and
www.paintball.net

American Society for Testing and Materials (ASTM)

100 Barr Harbor Dr.
West Conshohocken, PA 19428
(610) 832-9500
www.astm.org

Cleo Fogal & Company [Sport & Event Photography]

HC2, Box 2245, Rt. 903
Jim Thorpe, PA 18229 (570) 325-9935
www.skirmishphotos.com

Collegiate Paintball League

537 Newark Ave.,
Newark, NJ 07306
(201) 656-2900
www.collegiatepaintball.com

International Assn for the Leisure & Entertainment Industry

33 Henniker St.
Hillsboro, NH 03244
(603) 464-6498
www.ialei.org

National Collegiate Paintball Assn.

1133 Industrial Blvd. #3,
Chippewa Falls, WI 54729
(715) 720-9131
www.college-paintball.com

Newfoundland-Labrador Paintball Assn.

c/o Neil Coombs, 20a Weymouth St, St. Johns, NF, Canada A1B 2B6
www.infonet.st-johns.nf.ca

Ted D'Ottavio Photography

517 Third Ave., Store #1
Brooklyn, NY 11215 (718) 788-6631
http://209.15.34.242/

Paintball Business Association,

155 Verdin Rd.
Greenville, SC 29607(864) 297-9727
www.paintballinsurance.com

Paintball Operators of America

(Field Insurance)
(417) 869-4263

Society of Paintball Players and Teams

www.spplat.com

Springfield Paintball (Paintball Netting)

(417) 869-4263

Sterling & Sterling (Paintball Insurance)

(603) 464-6498

WHERE TO PLAY: IN EVERY STATE & AROUND THE WORLD

STATE DIRECTORY
Paintball Retail Outlet and Playing Field Listing

The following listing was prepared from many sources during the 2003 development of *Paintball Digest*. However, we know that operating a successful small business in the U.S. or around the world, for that matter, is a dynamic and challenging enterprise. Styles change, the field falls victim to a lawsuit or government over-regulation, or an expensive and widely publicized tournament is rained out. Things happen. Therefore, before relying absolutely upon entries in this list, the publisher recommends that you telephone or check the Internet for the most up-to-date information.

ALABAMA

Auburn
Area 51 Paintball, 1007 Rustic Ridge Rd 36830 (970) 824-2474
Birmingham
Advanced Alabama Adventures, 7880 Bear Creek Rd 35147 (205) 672-2860
Paint Wars, 1827 Otis Rd. 35235 (205) 856-2179/841-2255
Centre
Centre Martial Arts Academy, 1260 W Main St. 35960 (256) 927-8453
Cordova
Cordova Paintball Planet (205) 483-1429
Cullman
High Adventure, 410 3rd Ave. SE 35056 (256) 734-3374
Foley
Eternity's Image Paintball Adrenaline, 720 Orange Ct 36535 (251) 979-8699
Paintball Paradise, 14809 Hwy 59 N 36535 (251) 943-2355
McCalla
Paintball Quest, 8651 Serene Dr. 35111 (205) 477-9922
www.paintballquest.com
Huntsville
Splat Alley, 705 McKinley Ave 35801 (205) 539-5959
Montgomery
Alabama Silverhawks Paintball Club [Private] (334) 538-5961
Slocomb
Dothan Survival Games (334) 793-8202
Sterrett
Advanced Alabama Adventures, 7880 Bear Creek Rd 35243 (205) 672-2860

ALASKA

Elendor
Sector 7G Paintball, 4046 Blake Ave. Unit A 99506 (907) 753-0431
Fairbanks
OK Lumber/Ace Hardware, 272 Illinois St. 99701 (800) 478-6270

ARIZONA

Cottonwood
Xtreme Paintball, 590 N Main St. 86326 (928) 684-7700
Lake Havasu City
South Coast Paintball, 296 London Bridge Rd. #B 86403 (928)680-1151
Mesa
Phoenix Gremics/Crosscheck, 745 W Baseline Rd., #15 85210 (480) 632-6634
Phoenix
The Command Post, 4139 W Bell Rd., Ste #2 85023 (602) 863-2569
Exxtreme Paintball, 1932 W Aster 85029 (602) 707-7227
Family Scuba & Paintball, 3927 E Indian School Rd. 85018 (602) 840-8333
The Paintball Store, 1601 E Bell Rd. #A5 85022 (602) 923-7585
Phoenix Gremics/Crosscheck, 4139 N 19th Ave. 85015 (602) 636-0168
ReneGade Paintball Supply, 8126 W Hilton Ave. 85043 (623) 478-7988
www.renegadepaintball.net
Survival & Army Surplus, 15231 N Cave Creek Rd. 85032 (602) 482-6663
Westworld Paintball Adventure, 2920 W Thomas Rd. 85017 (602) 447-8200

Prescott
Assault Force Paintball Supply, 234 S Montezuma 86301 (928) 776-9214
Prescott Valley
Northern Arizona Paintball, 8056 E Hwy. 69 86314 (928) 772-3486
Tempe
The Command Post, 1432 N Scottsdale Rd. 85281 (602) 970-6329
Tucson
Desert Fox Paintball, 9651 S Houghton 85747 (520) 574-9232
Paintball Headquarters, 1097 W Prince Rd. 85712 (520) 293-5850
Paintball Unlimited AZ, 6540 E 22nd St. 85710 (520) 790-7995
Tucson Bob's Crossfire, 7702 N John Ha, Tucson, AZ 85741

ARKANSAS

Arkadelphia
First Assault, Rt. 51 71923 (501) 245-3549
Benton
Motion Sports, 16838 Hwy. I-30 72015 (501) 316-900 www.motionsports.net
Scuba Dreams, 17680 I-30 #2 72015 (501) 316-1021
Ft. Smith
B&E Paintball, 7320 Rogers Ave. #15 72903 (501) 452-8863
Jacksonville
T-Square Paintball, 5327 Old Hwy 67 72076 (501) 985-7729
Mayflower
Paintball Arkansas 72106 (501) 470-4400
Siloam
Wild World Paintball, 2025 E Main St. 72761 (501) 524-8676

CALIFORNIA

Alameda
Bay Area Paintball Supply, 1205 B Lincoln Ave. 94501 (510) 814-1809
Alpine
Weekend Warriors, 25 Browns Rd. 91901 (619) 445-1217
Anaheim
Strategic Game Supply, 10680 Katella Ave. 92804 (714) 772-6422
Unique Paintball Pro Gear, 10680 Katella Ave. 92804 (714) 772-6422
Antioch
Schwinn City Sports Center, 814 A St. 94509 (925) 757-0664
Arroyo
Big Boy Toys, 1544 W Branch St. 93420 (805) 481-1476/0873
Central Coast Paintball Park, 1554 W Beach St. 93420 (805) 481-1476
Azusa
B&M Paintball, 605 N Azusa Ave. 91702 (818) 334-0498
Bakersfield
City Splatter Zone, 4621 White Ln. 93309 (661) 834-4198
www.citysplatterzone.com
Gorilla Paintball, 614 18th St. 93301 (661) 323-1066/1022
Valley Gun Shop, 2728 Chester Ave. 93301 (805) 325-9468
Bellflower
Hollywood Sports Park, 9030 Somerset 90706 (562) 867-9600
www.hollywoodsports.com
Bloomington
Hobby World, 18575 Valley Blvd. 92316 (714) 824-1747
Bonita
Velocity Paintball, 4248 Bonita Rd. #B 91902 (619) 470-3533
Campbell
ABC Paintball, 535 Salmar Ave., Unit B 95008 (408) 866-9222
Extreme Adventure, 2931 S Winn Dixie Blvd. 95008 (408) 871-3111
Capitola
Outdoor World, 1440 41st Ave. 95010 (408) 4779-1501
Carson
I&I Sports South Bay Mega Store, 19751 S. Figueroa St. 90745 (800) 898-2042
Chico
Paintball Games by Dean, 2751 Mariposa Ave. 95973 (530) 345-0832
Chino
Turner's Outdoorsman, 12615 Colony St. 91710 (909) 590-7425
City of Industry
I&I Sports – Puente Hills, 18232 E Gale Ave. 91748 (626) 810-5523
Clear Lake
Element X Paintball, 14404 Lakeshore Dr. 95422 (707) 994-9785

Concord
Ballseye Paintball, 3375 Clayton Rd. 94519 (925) 691-4700
Delta Archery's Splat Div., 1820 D Arnold Industrial Hwy. 94520 (510) 685-7141
Corona
SC Village, River Rd. & Hellman St. 91720 (949) 489-9000
www.scvillage.com
Tombstone Paintball Park, 2388 Pomona Rincon St. 92880 (909) 737-0899
Costa Mesa
Skan-Line Game Supply, 1677 Superior Ave., Unit H 92627 (714) 645-5463
Cucamonga
Tagline, 9077 Arrow Route 100 91730 (909) 481-7753
Eagle Rock
PSH Paintball, 1613 Colorado Blvd. 90041 (323) 254-7300
El Cajon
Spotcha Paintball, 828 N 2nd St. 92021
Elk Grove
Sinister Sports #1, 8531 Elk Grove Blvd. 95624 (916) 714-3688
www.sinister-sports.com
Escondido
Action Paintball, 240 N Broadway 92027 (760) 738-1097
Mr. Paintball, 525 N Andreason #C 92029 (760) 737-8870
Fair Oaks
Survival Sports, 4800 Minnesota Ave. 95628 (916) 965-1770
Fallbrook
Sperling Weaponry & Collectibles, 1215 S. Mission 92028 (760) 723-4155
Fresno
Maximum Paintball Supply, 4741 N Blackstone Ave. 93726 (559) 222-3814
Gardena
I&I Sports – Gardena, 1524 W 178th St. 90248 (310) 715-6800
Indoor Speedball, 15000 Avalon 90248 (213) 323-1021
Goleta
Check Yourself Paintball, 5708C Hollister Ave. 93117 (805) 967-6190
Grand Terrace
Extreme Performance Paintball, 12210 Michigan Ave. #3 92313 (909) 825-0101
Grass Valley
JF Paintball, 1253 E Main St. 95945 (530) 273-3582
Hayward
Operation Paintball, 1932 West Winton Ave #1 94545 (888) 553-4443
www.diggthis.com
Hemet
Bryson Paintball Repair & Supply, 209 E Florida Ave. 92543 (909) 658-3777
Hollister
BCT Hobby, 125 Forth St B 95023 (831) 636-7550
Indio
JW's Paintball Armory, RJ Paintball Park, 45-114 Smurr St. 92201 (760) 775-2222 www.jwspaintballarmory.com
Inglewood
Brigade 3234, 11014 S LaCie 90304 (818) 701-5228
Laguna Hills
SC Village, 23501 Ridge Route Dr., Suite E 92653 (949) 489-9000
La Mirada
Paintball Player's Club, 14525 E Firestone Blvd. 90638 (714) 690-7747/(877) 938-7747
Lake Forest
Paintball Player's Club, 24296 Swartz Dr. 92630 (949) 951-7771
Lancaster
Fun Times, 44756 Shadow Creek 93536 (661) 949-3764
Littlerock
Field of Fury, 9817 East Ave. 93543
Loomis
Foothill Paintball, PO Box 1757 95650 (916) 652-4700
Los Angeles
Warped Sportz, 11919 W Pico Blvd. 90064 (310) 914-9222
Los Gatos
I&I Sports – Los Gatos Pro Shop, 15349-A Los Gatos Blvd. 95032 (408) 358-9774
Mammoth Lakes
King of the Hill Paintball, 45 Hill St. 93546 (760) 937-4363
Milpitas
Bear Creek Pursuit, 584 Cestaric Dr. 95035 (408) 946-7676
Modesto
Crescent Paintball Supply, 801 Eight St. 95354 (209) 529-3490
Monterey
Outdoor World, 222 N Fremont St. 93940 (408) 373-3615
Moss Landing
J&S Surplus, Hwy. 1 & Struve Rd. 95039 (408) 724-0588
Newhall
Paintball USA, 22400 The Old Rd. 81321 (800) 919-9237 www.paintballusa.org
Norco
Gramps & Grizzly's Paintball, 2085 River Rd. – B 92860 (909) 278-0173
North Hills
X Park Indoor Paintball, 8345 Hayvenhurst Pl. 91343 (818) 895-0808
North Hollywood
X-Creations, 6006 Vantage Ave. 91606 (818) 769-8060
Oakdale
P.8ball Outlet, 1617 S Yosemite Ave. 95361 (209) 847-8118
Ontario
Iron Horse, 931 W Holt Blvd. 91762 (909) 984-5878/3179
Paramount
National Paintball, 15950 Downey Ave. 90723 (800) 628-5641

Pacoima
Wypers Paintball, 10741 San Fernando Rd. 91331 (818) 686-0068/0058
Palmdale
Nicols Specialty Merchandise, 38712 La Mancha 93550 (661) 810-5603
Pleasanton
Outdoor World, 3903 Santa Rita Rd. 94566 (510) 463-3221
Porterville
Paintball Supplies, 770 S Main St. 93257 (559) 784-2112
Poway
Velocity Paintball, 12643 Poway Rd. 92064 (619) 513-2778
Redding
Topstitch, 632 N Market St. 96003 (530) 244-2220 www.topstitch.net
Redlands
Ditto Paintball, 721 Nevada St. #306 92373 (909) 739-4471
www.paintballdaddy.com
Outlaw Paintball Supply, 419 East State St. 92373 (909) 335-8841
www.outlawpaintball.com
Reseda
Skirmish Inc., 7361 Reseda 91335 (818) 705-6322
Riverside
Action Paintball Supply, 6682 Magnolia Ave. 92506 (909) 684-2200
Gramps Grizzly Outpost, 7203 Arlington Ave. Unit F 92503 (909) 359-4859
Rocklin
Sinister Sports #2, 6839 Five Star Blvd., Suite C 95677 (916) 630-9029
info@Sinister-Sports.com
Rosemead
General Joe's Paintball, 9433 Valley Blvd. 91770 (626) 443-0854 (626) 443-0854
Running Springs
Paintball Adventures, 30778 Hwy. 18 92382 (909) 867-5743
Sacramento
Action Paintball Games, PO Box 278593 95827 (916) 366-6212
www.actionpaintballsac.com
Palmer's Pursuit Shop, 3951 Development Dr. 95838 (916) 923-9676
www.palmers-pursuit.com
Surplus City, 4106 Franklin Blvd. 95820 (916) 485-1120
Wild Adventures Paintball (916) 396-7435 www.wildadventurepaintball.com
San Clemente
Paintball Player's Club, 415 Avenida Pico Ste. H 92672 (949) 369-6969
San Francisco
Paintball Paradise, 260 Shotwell St. 94110 (415) 552-5335
San Jose
Adventure Game, 3604 Ross Ave. 95124 (408) 723-1455
Cambrian Surplus, 2059 Woodard Rd. 95124 (408) 377-6953
I&I Sports – San Jose, 5637 Cottle Rd. 95123 (408) 224-6800
San Juan
SC Village, 27132 A Paseo Espada #403 92375 (949) 489-9000
San Marcos
North County Paintball 92069 (619) 440-5944
Santa Clarita
Close Encounters, 26413 Kalb Ct. 91321
Santa Fe
Springs Bud Orr's Pro Shop, 13517 Alondra Blvd. 90670 (310) 407-2898
Worr Games Products, 13517 ½ Alondo 90670 (562) 407-2898
Santa Margarita
Central Coast Paintball Park, 4765 Santa Margarita Lk. 93453 (805) 481-1476
Santa Maria
Auction Surplus, 512 S Blosser Rd. 93454 (805) 928-7408
Santa Paula
Reality Paintball, 410 Willard Rd. 93060 www.realitypaintball.com
Santa Rosa
Kapp Xtreme Sports, 65 Brookwood Ave. Ste. #2 95405 (707) 571-1077/0868
Pacific Paintball Supply, 3181 Cleveland Ave. #C 95403 (707) 571-1077
Saugus
Field of Fire, 28515 Sugar Pin 91350 (805) 297-7948
Simi Valley
ANS Extreme, 3885 Cochran St., Unit R
Sonoma
A.C.P. Paintball, 19655 Arnold Dr. 95476 (707) 939-8550
Stockton
Someplace Special, 8807 Thornton Rd. 95209 (209) 235-3389
Temecula
Head Hunter Paintball, 27715 Jefferson Suite 111 92590 (909) 676-1360
Tracy
Van's Ace Hardware, 2695 N Tracy Blvd. 95376 (209) 835-8286
Upland
Extreme Sports, 323 #B North Mountain Ave. 91786 (909) 949-3937
Mountain View Paintball, 780 E Foothill Blvd. D-3 91786 (909) 946-5323
Vallejo
Paintball Jungle, PO Box 5694 94591 (707) 552-2426
www.paintballjungle.com
Valley Center
Eagle's Nest, PO Box 1788 92082 (619) 749-0281
Van Nuys
Adventure Game Supply, 17618 Sherman Way 91405 (818) 708-3384
Ventura
Battlefield Adventures, 47 S Oak St. 93001 (805) 643-4190
Victorville
Bring It On Paintball Supplies, 15319 Palmdale Rd. Ste A 92392 (760) 241-9097

Visalia
Jungle Supply, 2840 E College 93292 (209) 636-3128
Visalia Paintball Supply, 210 Cotta Ct. 93292 (559) 627-8771
West Covina
Paintball Player's Club, 2237 E Garvey N 91791 (626) 966-6665
West Los Angeles
I&I Sports – West L.A., 2957 S Sepulveda Blvd. 90064 (310) 715-6800/444-9988

COLORADO
Arvida
The Paint Pellet Game, 9538 W 58th Ave. 80002 (303) 422-6025
www.paintpelletgame.com
Aurora
Bike Path 80011 (303) 363-8800
Colorado Springs
Adventure Games, 425 Thames Dr. 80906 (303) 893-4263
Dragon Man's Paintball Park, 1225 Dragon Man Dr. 80929 (719) 683-2200
Rocky Mountain Paintball, 430 W. Fillmore St. 80907 (719) 473-3725
Splat Master's Paintball, 6855 Constitution Ave. 80915 (719) 574-7004
Craig
Area 51 Paintball, 2605 E US Hwy. 40 81625 (970) 824-2474
Denver
Z Warzone, 835 E 50th Ave. 80216 (303) 292-0818
Englewood
Paintball Adventures, 1500 W Hampden 80110 (303) 762-6160
www.paintballadv.com
Warped Sportz, 3970 S Broadway 80110 (303) 806-9721
Ft. Collins
Jax, Inc., 1200 N College 80524 (970) 221-0544
Gunnison
All Sports Replay, 115 W Georgia 81230 (970) 641-1893
Greeley
Action Pursuit Paintball, 2017 9th St. 80631 (970) 395-0664
www.actionpursuitpaintball.com
Littleton
Pro-Star Sports, PO Box 1280 80160 (303) 972-4113
Rocky Mountain Paintball, 7500 S University #110 80122 (303) 689-7608
Loveland
Tippmann Ordnance, 418 8th St. #82 80537 (970) 613-2051
www.tippmannordnance.com
Silver Cliff
Spurfect, 113 Mill 81252 (719) 783-3240

CONNECTICUT
Branford
Eastern Paintball Supplies, 223 E Main St. 06405 (203) 488-5721
www.easternpaintball.com
Bridgeport
Paintball Addicts, 3073 Main St. 06606 (203) 371-4216
Danbury
Paintball Plus, 5 Padanaram Rd. 06811 (203) 730-8850
East Windsor
Xtreme Paintball, 122 Prospect Hill Rd. Rt. 5 06088 (860) 627-6666
Groton
Supply Depot, 441 Long Hill Rd. (Lighthouse Sq.) 06340 (800) 871-8479
Old Lime
Eastern Paintball (#2), 19 Hall St. Rt. 1 06371 (860) 434-4089
Meriden
Hogan's Alley, 998 N Colony Rd. 06450 (203) 238-2875
www.hogansalleypaintball.com
Milford
Splatter Zone, 394 New Haven Ave. # 4 06460 (203) 878-0693
Naugatuck
Bullzeye Paintball, 399 N Main St. 06770 (203) 723-0634
New Haven
Hogan's Alley, 59 State St. 06473 (203) 234-1972
www.hogansalleypaintball.com
Newington
Hoffman's, 2208 Berlin Tpk. 06111 (860) 666-8827
Newport
Land Air & Sea Surplus, 1733 Monmouth St. 41071 (859) 291-7770
New London
Viper Paintball Sales, 280 Connecticut Ave. 06320 (860) 437-1150
North Haven
Hogan's Alley Paintball, 445 State St. 06473 (203) 288-2746
Shelton
Paintball Unlimited, 273 Canal St. 06484
Stratford
K-5 Arms Exchange, 2505 Main St. 06615 (203) 380-2783
Terryville
AJ's Car Audio, 163 Main St. 06786 (860) 589-0445
Thompson
The Gun Rack, 240A Rt. 21, County Home Rd. 06277 (203) 928-1511
Tolland
Splattown USA, 223 Merrow Rd. Rt. 195 06084 (860) 870-9737

DELAWARE
Dover
DNR Paintball, 3833 N DuPont Hwy. 19901 (302) 730-8664
Paintball Adventures, 1438 Woodmill Dr. 19904 (302) 736-5777
Georgetown
JBR Sales Paintball & More, 608 E Market St. 19947 (302) 856-9474/3365
www.jbrpaintball.com
Newport
ECX Action Sports, 21 W Market St. 19804 (302) 998-1009
www.ecxactionsports.com

FLORIDA
Allandale
GI Jeff's, 5257 S Ridgewood Ave. 32123 (904) 767-2131
Alta Monte Springs
Al's Army Store, 1440 E Hwy. 436 32701 (704) 834-2000
Crestview
Black Angel Paintball (S), Superflea Flea-Market near I-10 and SR85 32536 (850) 974-7332 www.blackangelpaintball.com
Bradenton
Hi-Tec Paintball Park, PO Box 301 34206 (941) 746-5866
Dade City, 13951 7th St. #10 33525 (352) 567-7116
Edgewater
Elite Forces Field, Cowcreek Rd. (904) 767-2131
Ft. Myers
Extreme Rage, 3598 Fowler St. 33901 (941) 939-0911/(888) 880-0911
Paintball Park, 8240 Durrance Rd. (941) 939-0911/598-1015
Gainesville
Rocky Creek Paintball, 10614 SW Archer Rd. 32608 (352) 371-2092
Hialeah
Paintball Experts, 70 W 49th St. 33012 (305) 823-6892
Paintball R Us, 3639 West 16 Ave. 33012 (305) 827-5656
Homestead
American Paintballs, 27201 S Dixie Hwy. 33032 (305) 246-3731
www.americanpaintbals.com
Jacksonville
First Coast Paintball, 8159 Arlington Expy., Suite 7 32211 (904) 725-8303
Warped Sportz, 2294-12 Mayport Rd. 32233 (904) 242-0012
Jupiter
Jerry Leslie's Sports, 750 S Old D. Bay 11 33458 (561) 744-7332
Kissimmee
Osceola Extreme Sports, 3431 W Vine St., Osceola Square Mall 34741 (407) 933-7785
Lake City
Stone Serious Paintballs & Accessories, SW Domino's Way (behind Dominos Pizza on US 90 W) (386) 755-5600
Largo
Florida Paintball Center, 8440 Ulmerton,#500 34641 (813) 538-9946
Lynn Haven
RKS Paintball, 305 Ohio Ave. 32444 (850) 271-8884
Melbourne
Action Gun Outfitters, 2787 Aurora Rd. 32935 (321) 242-1114
Miami
Combat Zone, 14450 SW 208th Ave. 33196 (786) 293-2102
Ruff & Tuff Sports, 7232 SW 8th St. 33144 (305) 267-1122
Sharp Shooters (Dolphin Mall, Unit RMU45) 33175 (305) 406-557
South Florida Paintball, 7232 SW 8th St. Suite 2 33144 (305) 267-1122
Splat Attack, 10129 SW 72nd St. 33173 (305) 412-9991
Splatt Force, 15771 SW 106th Terrace #102 33196 (305) 382-3345
www.splatforce.com
Tropic Trades, 9696 SW 40th St. 33165 (305) 221-1371
Naples
Extreme Paint, 3832 Exchange Ave. 34104 (941) 261-1588
Southwest Military Surplus, 2347 E Tamiami 34112 (941) 732-5831
Newberry
First Strike Paintball, 5619 SE CR 337 32669 (352) 338-8408/870-1199
www.firststrikepaintball.com
Oakland Park
Xtreme Paintball, 3561 NW 9th Ave. 33309 (305) 564-5451
Ocala
Wayne's World, 4841 S. Pine Ave. 34480 (352) 401-1801
www.waynes-world.com
Orlando
Al's Army Store, 23 N Orange Blossom Tr. 32805 (407) 425-4932
Orlando Outdoors, 6525 East Colonial 32807 (407) 381-7977
www.orlandooutdoors.net
Orlando Paintball, 7215 Rose Ave. 32810 (407) 294-0694
Xtreme Assault, 9916 E Colonial Dr. 32817 (407) 737-1355
Pursuit Paintball Games, 5132 Conroy Rd. #918 32811 (407) 843-3456
Paintball World, 3445 Vineland Rd. 32811 (407) 648-8404
Palatka
Palatka Army Navy, 3721 Reid St. 32117 (904) 328-8127
Pembroke Pines
G&H Sterling, 8362 Pines Blvd. #290 33024 (305) 438-7571
South Florida Indoor Paintball, 2801 SW 31st Ave. 33009 (954) 893-8284
Palm Coast
Pro-Team Products, 2334 E Rt. 100, Suite 7-B 32164 (904) 437-3375
Panama City
Panhandle Paintball, 2305 Sherman Ave. 32405 (850) 785-2030
www.panhandlepaintball.net
WMW Paintball Supply, 402 Dogwood Way 32404 (850) 871-5673
www.wmwpaintball.com

Pensacola
Paint Station Paintball Supply, 8622 Pensacola Blvd. 32534 (850) 475-8883
Sports World, 1090 W Michigan 32505 (850) 439-3145
Plant City
Herndon's Battle Zone, 4416 ½ N Cooper Rd. 33565 (813) 986-8812
Punta Gorda
Guerrilla Games, 111 W. Olympia Ave. 33950 (813) 627-8865
Survival City, 111 W Olympia Ave. 33950 (813) 639-1100
Riviera
USA Performance Products, 8125 Monetary Dr. 33404 (561) 841-7622
Royal Palm Beach
Mike's Paintball, 10307 Southern Blvd. 33411 (561) 790-0755
www.mikespaintball.com
Sanford
Al's Army Store, 1401 S French Ave. 32771 (02) 322-5791
Stuart
Hangin' Loose Paintball, B&A Flea Market, 2201SE Indian St., F-25 34996
(772) 223-7133 www.hanginloosepb.com
Sunrise
Sunny's at Sunset 33322 (305) 741-2070
Tallahassee
Spy Shop, 2418 N Monroe #250 32303 (850) 385-4467
Tampa
Headquarters Military, 1450 Skipper Rd. 33613 (813) 971-8805
PMI Southeast, 7935 N Armenia 33604 (813) 915-1912
Titusville
Space Coast, 3600 Garden St. 32796 (321) 264-4484
Venice
B&D Army, Navy & Paintball, 1231 US 41 By. 34292 (941) 493-7011
Winter Haven
Holly Army Navy, 3440 Ave. G NW 33880 (813) 967-5920

GEORGIA

Atlanta
Wildfire Paintball, 7301 Campbellton Rd. 30331 (770) 493-8978
Augusta
Bay's Paintball, 501 Eve St. 30904 (706) 733-1055
Calhoun
A-1 Paintball Forest & Supply, W Pine Chapel Rd. 30701 (706) 625-0072
Conyers
Crosshairs Paintball, 2051 Hwy. 138 NE 30012 (770) 602-2912
Dacula
Wildfire Paintball, 2191 Rabbit Hill Cr. 30211 (770) 493-8978
Dalton
Appalachian Paintball, 1116 S Thornton Ave. 30720 (706) 226-1765
Forest Park
Indoor Paint Games, 285A Lake Mirror Rd. 30050 (404) 361-6740
Ft. Oglethorpe
Insane Paintball, 986 Battlefield Pkwy. 30742 (706) 866-2121
Grayson
Backwoods Paintball, 2355 Chandler Rd. 30017 (678) 878-9895
Hiram
Action Paintball, 1818 Hiram Doug. #C 30141 (770) 439-8555
Hortense
Guerilla Mike's, Rt. 32, Box 200-C 31543 (912) 473-2881
Lawrenceville
Wild Bill's Paintball Emporium, 280 Arnold Rd. 30044 (770) 963-0400
www.wildbillspaintball.com
Lookout Mountain
Mountain Adventure Games, 123 S Campus Rd. 30750 (706) 820-4419
Madison
Wildfire Paintball, 2641 Hesterton Rd. (770) 493-8978
Marietta
Georgia Paintball, 1289 Roswell Rd. 30620 (770) 971-8040
Martin
Pirate Paintball, 236 B Bobby Jo 30907 (706) 228-3779
Milledgeville
Baynes Army Store, 18 S Wayne St. 31061 (912) 452-2384
Newnan
Powers Paintball, 467 Charlie B. Johnston Rd. 30263 (770) 502-9981
Norcross
Splat Zone Indoor, 5050 Jimmy Carter Blvd. 30093 (404) 441-9333
Rome
Outer Limits, 220 Holbrook Dr. SW 30165 (706) 234-9896
Roswell
Country Heritage, 11210 W Rd. 30075 (770) 998-5490
Paintball Atlanta, 700 Holcomb Bridge #300 30076 (770) 594-0912
Snellville
Al's Army Navy, 3334 Hwy. 78 30078 (770) 972-1224
Wildfire Paintball, 3725 Stone Mountain 30078 (770) 493-8978
Tucker
Wildfire Paintball, 1989 Tucker Ind. Rd. 30084 (770) 493-8978
Vidalia
Rapid Fire Paintball Supply, 207 E Third St. 30474 (912) 537-8330
Villa R.
VR Paintball Games, 481 Little Vine 30180 (770) 214-2091
Warner Robbins
Chuck's Bait & Tackle, 603 Watson Blvd. 31093 (478) 922-9851
Waycross
Advanced Tronics, 508 City Blvd. 31501 (912) 285-4060
www.advancedtronics.com

Winder
Dynamic Games (Paintball Arena), 223 Pickle Simon Rd. 30680 (770) 868-5630
Winston
Sureshot Paintball, 7470 Bankhead Hwy. 30187 (770) 949-9304

HAWAII

Ewa Beach
Xlent services, PO Box 2271 96706 (808) 671-1110
Kailua
I&I Sports – Honolulu, 602 Kailua Rd. #101 96734 (808) 261-7743/230-2326
Pearl City
Xtreme Paintball Supply, 98-718 Moanalua Rd. 96782 (808) 484-2772
www.ballisticeirsoft.cc

IDAHO

Boise
Walter Middy's MMOV, 6759 Supply Way 83705 (208) 429-1276
Burley
Kerb's Oil Co., 1715 E. Main 83318 (208) 878-3831
Caldwell
Idaho Paintball Supplies, 1410-1/2 Albany St. 83605 (208) 761-5303/455-3462 www.all3cal@juno.com
Idaho Falls
G&H Reflections, 2344 Briarcliff 83404 (208) 529-8630
Iona
Winders, 5515 E Iona Rd. 83427 (208) 523-2475
Meridia
Aktion Zone Paintball, 37 E Broadway 83642 (208) 887-1634
Priest River
4 Paws, 4799 Hwy. 2 83856 (208) 448-1113

ILLINOIS

Algonquin
Dream Tactics Paintball, 102 S Main St. 60102 (847) 658-3107
Aurora
Challenge Games, 2256 Fox Valley Ctr. D21A 60504 (630) 499-1025
Fox River Games, 1891 N Farnsworth 60505 (630) 585-5651
Bartlett
Pursuit Adventure, 956 S Bartlett Rd. #282 60103 (630) 736-9107/9132
Benton
Depot Surplus, 320 S Main St. 62812 (618) 438-5037
Carlinville
Cheap Trax, North University 62626 (217) 825-9339
Chicago Ridge
Aggressive Sport Shop, 10343 Southwest Hwy. 60415 (708) 581-2555/389-0135
Chillicothe
Chilli Paintball Pits, 21324 N Benedict 61523 (309) 274-5251
Des Plaines
Air America, 2275 S Mt. Prospect Rd. 60018 (847) 545-9999
Your Supply Depot, 632 W Algonquin Rd. 60016 (847) 640-7774
Dundee
GAT Guns, 14 N 915 Rt. 25 60118 (847) 428-4867
Elk Grove
Air America, 2240 Elmhurst Rd. 60007 (847) 545-9999
PaintballGear.com, 1728 Elmhurst Rd. 60007 (847) 437-5510
Frankfort
LJ's T-Shirt & More, 47 E Lincoln Hwy. 60423 (815) 464-2148
www.frankfortpages.com
Glenview
Strange Ordnance, 914 Greenwood Ave. 60025 (708) 998-8312
Hampshire
Operation Paintball, 15N850 Brier Hill Rd. 60140 (630) 736-9107
Huntley
Video Smideo, 10408 Rte. 47 60142 (847) 669-3225
Johnston City
Top Outfitter's Army, Rt. 37 S 62951 (618) 983-6971
Lansing
Bad Boyz Toyz, 17913 S Torrence Ave. 60438 (708) 418-8888
www.shocktechusa.com
Machesney Park
Rockford Paintball Games, 7821 N Second St. 61115 (815) 282-2992
Wyld Side Sports, 8750 N Second St. D3 61115 (815) 636-9970
Mackinaw
Area 52, 30166 Tyrell Rd. 61755 (309) 447-6809
McLeansboro
Larry's Gun Shop, Hwy. 142 S 62859 (618) 643-2170
Naperville
Bad Boyz Toyz, 888 S Rt. 59 #104 60565 (630) 355-8808
www.shocktechusa.com
Orland Park
Bad Boyz Toyz, 15160 LaGrange Rd. 60462 (708) 460-1122
www.shocktechusa.com
Peoria
Paint N Place, 736 S Washington 61601 (309) 637-0466
Rodhouse
Paintball To Go Pro Shop, RR 3 Box 135 62082 (217) 589-5673
www.paintballtogo.com

Schiller Park
P.M.I., 5035 River Rd. 60176 (847) 233-9900
Skokie
Bad Boyz Toyz, 7135 Central Ave. 60077 (847) 679-9125
Sterling
Sinnissippi Paintball Mania, 23181 Moline Rd. 61081 (815) 625-9650
Vernon Hills
Bad Boyz Toyz, 700 N Milwaukee Ave. #126 60061 (847) 362-4848
www.shocktechusa.com
Waukegan
Military Supply, 2110 Grand Ave. 60085
West Dundee
Fox Paintball, 737 S Rt. 31 60118 (847) 426-1061

INDIANA

Angola
Apocalypse Games, 302 W Gilmore 46703 (260) 668-1022
Arttica
Paintball Barn, 5800 North 820 East 47918 (765) 572-2352
www.paintballbarn.com
Aurora
Gotcha Covered Paintball, 120 Main St. 47001 (812) 926-6013
Bloomington
Bent Arrow Caving & Paintball, 7888 W Eller Rd. 47403 (812) 825-2283
Bluffton
Frank's Sports Shop, 6171 E State Rd. 124 46714 (219) 565-3277
In Your Sights Paintball, PO Box 382 46714 (219) 824-7844
Brazil
Predator Creek Paintball, 9155 N Eppert 47834 (812) 448-3093
Corydon
Paintball Fun, 2690 Breckenridge Rd. 47112 (800) 952-3580
www.paintballfun.com
Denver
Fantasy Fields Paintball, PO Box 194 46926 (765) 985-3068
Evansville
Duffy's Paintball, 1800 Stringtown 47711 (812) 422-3488
Paintball Players MD, 1326 N Weinbac #E 47711 (812) 471-7911
Fishers
Adventure Zone, 8641 E 116th St. 46038
Ft. Wayne
Paintball Sports, 821 W Coliseum Blvd. 46808 (260) 471-4334
Paintball USA, 506 Edgerton 46808 (219) 422-8801
Greenfield
Word Movers Painting, 1106 W 4th St. 46140 (317) 462-9432
Harlan
Yurferae (DBA), 15135 Scipio Rd. 46743 (219) 652-5031
Hobart
Blast Camp, 608 Third St. 46342 (219) 947-7733
Indianapolis
Dark Armies, 2525 N Shadelands Ave. 46219 (317) 353-1987
Gator Joe's Paintball, 1223 S Girl's School Rd. 46231 (317) 247-0410
Indianapolis Army & Navy, 6032 E 21st 46219 (317) 356-0858
Indy Extreme, 9508 Haver Way 46240 (317) 566-9115
Jasper
Audio World, 701 W 6th St. 47546 (812) 482-1155
Kokomo
Blast Factory, 100 E North St. 46901 (765) 457-3227
Bullseye Boats & Guns, 148 Creekside Dr. 46901 (765) 459-0077
Lafayette
Midwest Paintball Warehouse, 626 N Earl Ave. 47904 (765) 447-2012
Logansport
Chuck's Bait Shop, 4316 Pottawatami Rd. 46947 (574) 722-4517
Madison
Lee Army Surplus, 2800 Clifty Dr. 47250 (812) 273-5081
Marion
Paintball Splat Attack, 5435 N Hunting 46952 (765) 651-0750
Merrillville
Bad Boyz Toyz, 415 W 81st Ave. 46410 (219) 736-5952
www.shocktechusa.com
Warped Sportz, 1515 W. 81st. Ave. 46410 (219) 736-6111
Michigan City
Blast Camp, 109 9th St. 46360 (219) 947-7733
Muncie
Wizard's Keep, 416 N Martin St. 47303 (770) 923-1746
Richmond
H&H Paintball, 921 E Main St. 47374 (765) 965-9300
South Bend
Michiana Paintball Club, Scottsdale Mall (219) 291-2540
Paintball Outfitters, 60981US Hwy. 31 S, Suite 5 46614 (219) 299-5303/0901
PPD On-line, 61920 Scott St. 46614 (219) 291-0272
Psycho Ballistics, 21999 Kern Rd. 46614 (219) 299-0901
Sullivan
Treehugger's Paintball, 1418 N Co. Rd. 450 W 47882 (812) 382-4419
Summit
Fire Base Tango, 3646 W 1850 N 46070 (765) 948-3209
Warsaw
Northeast Paintball, 3699 N 175 E, Lott 55 46582 (219) 267-2101
Rat City Outdoor Paintball, 5585 S Country Club Rd. 46580 (219) 566-3320
West Harrison
Harrison Paintball Supply, 27755 Daugherty Ln. 47060 (812) 637-6999

Wooburn
Splat Ya, 18122 Ehle Rd. 46797 (219) 632-9571
Yorktown
River Valley Paintball, 10013 W River 47396 (765) 759-7123
www.gostevens.com

IOWA

Burlington
Joker's Wild Paintball, 12457 Y Camp Rd. 52601 (319) 753-5497
Cedar Falls
College Square Scheels, 6301 University Ave. 50613 (319) 277-3033
Clear Lake
North Iowa Arms, 810 N 8th St. 50428 (515) 357-3545
www.northiowaarms.com
Coralville
Iowa City Scheels, 1461 Coral Ridge Ave. 52241 (319) 625-9959
Velocity Paintball, 1324 5th St. 52241 (319) 351-4245 www.velocityiowa.com
Davenport
Duck's Blind, 328 W Central Park 52803 (319) 579-4077
Total Paintball, 324 E 4th St. 52801 (319) 324-0276
Des Moines
ICU Paintball Worgamz, 4489 NW 2nd Ave. #10 50313 (515) 282-9089
Dubuque
Best Shot Paintball, 2250 Washington St. 52001 (319) 588-1077
Iowa City
Team Products, 1102 E Davenport 52245 (319) 337-3629
Sioux City
Sioux City Scheels, Market Place 2829 Hamilton Blvd. 51104 (712) 252-1551
Spring Valley
The Edge, 203 Broadway 52336 (319) 854-6474
Tracy
Frog Holler, 1932 185th Place 50256 (515) 842-2984
Waterloo
Waterloo Scheels, 2060 Crossroads Blvd. #126 50702 (319) 234-7534

KANSAS

Clay Center
The Paintball Garage, 934 Dexter St. 67432 (785) 632-2793
Emporia
Paintball Trader/Vaporworks, 1117 Commercial 66801 (800) 639-4339
www.vaporworks.net
Garden City
Paintball Mania Kansas, 218 N Main St. 67846 (620) 276-4455
Lawrence
Drop Zone Extreme Sports, 811 E 23rd St. 66044
www.dropzonepaintball.com
Lenexa
Victory Paintball, 95th & Renner Blvd. 66212 (913) 397-0966
Olathe
Drop Zone Extreme Sports, 409 S Parker 66062 (913) 768-0200/(785) 841-1884 www.dropzonepaintball.com
Quenemo
Tornado Alley Paintball, 6341 E 268 Hwy. 66528 (785) 746-8856
www.kansaspaintball.com
Topeka
Drop Zone Extreme Sports, 5849 SW 21st St. 66604 (785) 228-9200
www.dropzonepaintball.com
Wichita
Blasters, 1931 S Water 67213 (316) 264-5443
Relentless Pursuit Paintball, 1603 W Douglas 67213 (316) 264-5455/5255

KENTUCKY

Bowling Green
N-Tense Sports, 110 Vanderbilt Ct. 42104 (270) 976-4120
www.ntensesports.com
Cynthia
Dryden's Sporting Goods, 344 S Church 41031 (606) 234-0785
Danville
Chubby's Paintball Supply, 725 S Second St. 40422 (859) 936-9449
Elizabethtown
Conder's Pro Paintball, 813 Hawkins Dr. 42701 (270) 765-4517
Elsmere
Crossfire Paintball, 4111 Dixie Hwy. 41018 (606) 342-9386
Florence
American Paintball Games, 8471 US 42 Box #6 41042 (888) 440-1088
Crossfire Paintball, 7381 Empire Dr. 41402 (859) 342-9386
Fordsville
Hometown Paintball Supply, 61 E Main 42343 (502) 276-3339
Gravel Switch
Jimmy Elliott Firearms, Box 156 Poorhouse Rd. 40328 (606) 332-7728
Greenup
R&R Paintball, 310 Vine St. 41144 (606) 473-9818
Hagerhill
Tri-State Paintball, 1172 Middlefork Rd. 41222 (606) 197-6283
Horse Cave
Rebel Ridge Paintball Park, 795 London Pace Sink Rd. MUB 13 42749 (270) 786-4991
Junction
War Zone Paintball, 497 S Lucas St. 40440 (859) 621-1480

Latonia
Die Hard Paintball, 3906 Winston Ave. 41015 (859) 261-4273
Leitchfield
Buddy Ringo Paintball, 335 Winn Dr. 42754 (270) 259-5828
Louisville
Paintball Headquarters, 4746 Bardstown 40218
Pape's Archery, PO Box 19889 (502) 955-8118
Turtle's Toybox, 5043 Preston Hwy. 40213 (502) 961-6116
Milford
Crossfire Paintball, 128 Mill St. Rte. 50 45150 (513) 576-1112
Paris
B&H Paintball, 1236 Brentsville 40361 (859) 987-7701
Pendleton
J. Long's, 3971 Patton's Creek Rd. 40055 (502) 222-9703
Radcliff
US Cavalry, 2855 Centennial 40160 (502) 351-1164
Richmond
Foley's Outdoor, 1424 E Main 40475 (859) 626-0008
Whitesburg
Double R Sporting Goods, 61 Orchard Rd. 41858 (606) 633-3257
www.rrsportinggoods.homestead.com
Winchester
Custom Cylinders, 1220 Enterprise Dr. 40391 (859) 744-5544
www.customcylindersintinc.com

LOUISIANA

Elm Grove
Off Limits Extreme Sports, 608 Robinson Rd. 71051 (318) 987-2696
Houma
Shell Shocked Paintball, 1407 W Tunnel Blvd. 70360 (504) 223-1700
Lafayette
MA Paintball, 2415 Verot School Rd. 70508 (318) 984-6014
Metairie
Rock-It Games, 3409 Metairie Rd. 70001 (504) 828-8008
Shreveport
Kiddie Mia's Fun Center, 1119 Shreveport Barksdale Hwy. 71105 (318) 869-3566 www.kiddiemias.com
Slidell
Maratell's Paintball, 707 Old Spanish Tr. 70458 (985) 649-3255

MAINE

Belgrade
Brookside Paintball, RR1, Box 189D 04917
Berwick
Berwick Paintball, Office (#3 Old Pine Hill Rd.), Field (#38, Rt. 236) 03901 (207) 698-1392
Brewer
Maine Military Supply, 733 Wilson St. 04412 (877) 608-0179
www.mainemilitary.com
Calais
The Outdoor Company, 296 North St. 04619 (207) 454-3666
East Lebanon
Van Houten Army/Navy, Lower Cross Rd Box 130 04027 (207) 457-1224
Woodland Warriors, PO Box 130 04027 (207) 457-1224
Fort Fairfield
Triple T Paintball, 521 Dorsey Rd. 04742 (207) 473-9370
Guilford
Flying Dutchman, Box 73 Sebec Shores Rd. 04443 (207) 564-3369
Lebanon
PG's Adrenaline Sports Park, 40 Skydive Ln. 04027 (603) 765-3984
Manchester
202 Paintball, 918 Western Ave. 04351 (207) 623-9960 www.paintgirls.com
Mexico
Crossfire Paintball Adventures, 452 River Rd. 04257
Newport
Maine Military Supply, 80 Moosehead Tr. 04953 (207) 368-5460
www.mainemilitary.com
Oxford
New England Paintball Supply, 734 Main St. 04270 (207) 539-8473
Saco
Blast'em Paintball, 54 New Country Rd. 04072 (207) 284-8205
Standish
Maine Recreational Paintball League, PO Box 80 04084 www.mrpl.org
Rogue Paintball, 190 Northeast Rd. 04084 (207) 642-7648

MARYLAND

Annapolis
The Company Store, 2303-K E Forest Dr. 21401 (410) 571-1156
Arbutus
Outdoor Adventures, 1642 Sulphur Spring Rd. 21227 (410) 737-0800
Baltimore
Action Zone Indoor, 4401 O'Donnell #I-2 21224 (410) 522-2255
Outdoor Adventure, 1642 Sulphur Spring Rd. 21227 (410) 737-0800 www.oapaintball.com
Outdoor Sportsman, 807 Eastern Blvd. 21221 (410) 391-0222
Bel Air
JC's Indoor Paintball Field & Pro Shop, 112 N Tollgate Rd. 21014 (410) 420-2070
Robin Hood Paintball, 2310 Churchville Rd. 21015 (410) 273-1555
Easton
S&S Paintball, 8266 Ocean Gate Way 21601 (410) 822-1103

Elkton
Absolute Paintball & Skateboarding, 104 W. Main St. 21921 (866) 398-0052
Ellicott City
Paintball Discounters, 10176 Baltimore Nat'l Pike #215 21042 (410) 750-1502
Frederick
Paintball Wholesalers, 205 C Bucheimer Rd. 21701 (301) 624-4399
RKH Specialty Merchandise, 10418 Old Liberty Rd. 21701 (301) 898-0070
Germantown
The Company Store, 13015 Wisteria Dr. 20874 (301) 515-2680
Hancock
Timber Ridge Paintball Club, 14432 Tollgate Ridge 21750 (301) 678-5451
Henderson
Art's Paintball & Supply, 25050 Beetree Rd. 21640 (410) 482-6335
Hunt Valley
Warped Sportz, 118 Shawan Rd. #281 21031 (410) 527-1522
Lexington Park
The Tackle Box, 22035 Three Notch 20653 (301) 863-8151
Ocean City
Ocean City Paintball, 12605 Ocean Gateway 21842 (410) 213-2500/845-0065
Parkville
Maryland Paintball, 8507 Harford Rd. 21234 (301) 937-6101
Prince Frederick
Matteson Supply, 1800 Solomon's Island Road S 20678 (410) 535-0552
Rockville
Pev's Paintball Pro Shop, Edmonston Crossing, 1044 Rockville Pike 20852 (301) 738-3200 www.pevs.com
Salisbury
Delmarva Paintball, 1922 N Salisbury Blvd. 21801 (443) 260-0959
www.delmarvapaintball.com
Silver Spring
Extreme Paintball, 704 Cloverly St. 20905 (301) 388-2255
Taneytown
Paintball Wholesalers, 2400 Bear Run Rd. 21787 (410) 756-1006
Westminster
Paintball Wholesalers, 38 W Main St. 21157 (410) 840-8669
www.paintballwholesalers.com
White Plains
Maryland Surplus & Outdoor, Rt. 301 & Mermarr Rd. 20695 (301) 645-0077

MASSACHUSETTS

Agawam
Madman's Realm, 369 Main St. 01001 (413) 599-1448
Auburn
X-Fire Paintball, 850 Southbridge St. 01501 (508) 721-0003
www.xfirepaintball.com
Avon
P&L Paintball, 491 W Main St. 02322 (508) 897-0022 www.pnlpaintball.net
Bellingham
J&M Paintball, 15 N Main St., Bellingham Commons Plaza 02019 (508) 966-4700
Boston
Boston Paintball Supply, 131 Beverly St. 02114 (617) 742-6612
Bourne
Cape Cod Paintball, 173 Claypond Rd. 02532 (508) 759-5130
Bridgewater
Paintball Heaven, 1221 Bedford St. 02324 (508) 697-5808
Brockton
P&L Indoor Paintball, 45 Emerson Ave. 02301 (508) 897-0022
Danvers
D&D Paintball, 159 Elliott St. 01923 (978) 777-6323
East Templeton
Fire-Pro-Tech NE, 131 Patriots Rd. 01438 (978) 632-3808
East Wareham
Gateway Paintball, 3152 Cranberry Hwy. 02538
Easton
P&L Paintball, Bay Rd. (508) 238-1365
Framingham
Boston Paintball Supply W, 50-60 Worcester Rd #9E 01701 (508) 879-6621
Hadley
Amherst Drop Zone, 227 Russell St. 01035 (413) 585-0783
Holbrook
Apache/P&L Paintball, End of Spring Lane (508) 897-0022 www.pnlpaintball.com
P&L Paintball/Apache, Spring Lane 02343 (508) 897-0022
Marlboro
Metro-West Paintball and Dart, 110 Pleasant St. #301 (508) 481-3791
Methuen
Canobie Paintball, Raymer's Express 41 Danton Dr. 01844 (603) 893-1863
North Easton
P&L Paintball, 159 Bay Rd. 02356 (508) 238-1365
Plainville
PW Paintball, 150 South St. 02762 (508) 643-7406
Randolph
Randolph Paintball & Skateboards, 410 South St. 02368 (781) 986-2255
www.randolphpaintball.com
Saugus
Ultimate Adventure, 7 Sweetwater St. 01906 (617) 231-0114
South Attleboro
Clear Shot/P&L Paintball, 946 Washington St. 02703 (508) 399-1111
www.pnlpaintball.net
Taunton
P&L New England Indoor Paintball, 391 W Water St. 02780 (508) 822-7788
www.pnlpaintball.net

Tewksbury
Paintball Wizard, 2235 Main St. 01876 (978) 988-5657
www.paintballwizard.com
Pointblank Paintball, 677 W Field St. 01089 (413) 732-8026
Tewsbury
Action Games 01876 (508) 459-8699
Townsend
Paintball Paradise, 256 Main St. 01469 (978) 597-3501
www.119paintball.com
Upton
Fox 4 Paintball, 159 Milford Rd. (Rte. 140) (508) 529-3694
www.fox4paintball.com
West Springfield
Point Blank Paintball, 677 Westfield St. (Rt. 20) 01089 (800) 215-3027
Westport
Torpedo Paintball, 1105 State Rd. 02790 (508) 730-2602
Wilbraham
Madman's Corner, 33 Delmore Ave. 01095 (413) 599-1449
Woburn
ADCO Sales, 4 Draper St. 01801
West Springfield
Point Blank Paintball, 683 Westfield St. #2 01089 (413)788-7352

MICHIGAN

Allendale
Crossfire Paintball Arena, 11233 68th 49401 (616) 895-5777
Ann Arbor
Harry's Army Surplus, 201 E Washington 48104 (313) 994-3572
Battle Creek
Chaos Paintball, 409 Upton 49015 (616) 968-6399
Excalibur Paintball, 10580 N Dr. 49014 (616) 963-3925
NuWave Sports, 10580 N Dr. North 49014 (616) 963-3925
www.nuwavepaintball.com
Belding
Woodland Paintball Games, 5590 Belding Rd. (M-44) 48809 (616) 794-1941
www.woodlandpaintball.com
Bellevue
The Ruins Paintball, 8883 Sand Rd. 49021 (616) 763-0304
Brighton
Wade Frank, 10414 Green Bridge 48114 (802) 205-7740
Burton
Rocky's Great Outdoors, 4014 S Saginaw 48529 (810) 742-5420
Canton
Battle Grounds, 42118 Ford Rd. 48187 (734) 981-2255
Cedar Springs
West Michigan Paintball, 12040 Hoskins Ave. 49319 (616) 863-0869
Cheboygan
Action Sports Paintball, 710 S Main 49721 (616) 627-3474
Chesaning
Bio Shield, 9982 E Peet 48616 (517) 845-6099
Chesterfield
Falcon Paintball Unltd., 48075 Forbes 48047 (586) 246-0110
www.falconpaintball.com
Clare
Jay's Sporting Goods, 8800 S Clare Ave. 48617 (989) 386-3475
www.jayssportinggoods.com
Coldwater
Big Time Sports, 261/2 S Moroe St. 49036 (517) 278-2770
Davison
R.J. Performance, 8392 Potter Rd. 48423 (810) 658-5274
Eastpointe
Wild Side Paintball, 22109 Gratiot Ave. 48021 (810) 771-2889
Eaton Rapids
Arrowhead Archery, 2252 S Waverly 48827 (517) 663-6422
Escanaba
Land'N Lakes, 845 N Lincoln 49829 (906) 786-5263
Flint
Outsiders Paintball, 2341 S Dort Hwy. 48529 (810) 742-5057
Fremont
Colors Firld, 12874 N Maple Island 49412 (616) 924-6561
Gaylord
T.C. Paintball, 132 W Main St. 49635 (517) 705-7288 www.tcpaintball.com
Gladstone
Splat-U-Later, 8547 O Lane 49837 (906) 428-9599
Grand Rapids
Bullseye Army Surplus, 4907 S Division 49548 (616) 530-2080
T.C. Paintball, 734 W. 36th St. 49509 (616) 261-3435 www.tcpaintball.com
Grandville
Action Pursuit Games, 2437 Palm Dale 49418 (616) 261-5664
Hancock
Northwoods Trading Post, 120 Quincy St. 49930 (906) 482-5210
Harrison Township
Ultimate Paintball Challenge, 41300 Production Dr. 48045 (586) 463-8801
www.upcindoor.com
Hastings
True Value Hardware, 111 E State St. 49058 (616) 945-2003
Holland
M-40 Paintball, 1890 Ottawa Beach 49424 (616) 738-3866
The Perimeter, 180 W Lakewood 49424 (616) 392-5252

Ionia
R&R Paintball, 710 Euclid 48846 (616) 527-5514
Jackson
Action Outdoors, 1622 E Michigan (517) 783-4434
Jackson Paintball, 929 Lansing Ave. 49202 (517) 788-5477
Kalamazoo
Hole in the Wall, 6423 Stadium Dr. 49009 (616) 637-8749
R&S Paintball Supply, 516 Piccadilly Rd. 49006 (616) 553-6896
Young's Army-Navy, 3416 Westnedge St. 49008 (616) 382-1900
Lansing
American Eagle Paintball, 901 N Larch 48906 (517) 482-3765
www.bigwholesale.com
Outpost Paintball Supplies, 340 Morgan Ln. 48912 (517) 332-1332
Lapeer
Michigan Paintball Outlet, 111 W Genesee St. 48446 (810) 245-1914
www.mipaintball.com
Livonia
Action Paintball, 34383 Plymouth 48150 (734) 425-2545
Futureball Paintball Fortress, Livonia Mall, 7 miles & Middle Belt Rd. 48150 (248) 471-1800 www.futureballpaintball.com
Killer Paintball, 19590 Middlebelt Rd. 48334 (248) 615-0000
Madison Heights
P&P Paintball, 30909 Dequindre Rd. 48071 (248) 589-2739
Midland
Ace Hardware & Sports, 419 E Main St. 48640 (989) 832-8829
RG&J Paintball, 2922 Riggie St. 48640 (517) 631-8025
Monroe
S&I Paintball Supply, 3525 N Dixie Hwy. 48162 (734) 289-1960
Napoleon
Napoleon Paintball, 140 Nottawasepe 49261
Orion
Gingerville Ace Hardware, 3970 Baldwin Rd. 48359 (248) 391-2280
Pinckney
Exotic Sportz, 125 Pearl St 48169 (734) 878-2002/(888) Exotic-1
www.exoticsportz.com
Hell Survivors, Paintball Playfield, 619 Pearl St. 48169 (734) 878-5656/878-6540
Port Huron
Crossfire Creek, 3735 LaPeer Rd. #F 48060 (810) 987-7528
VF Sports, 4136 LaPeer Rd. 48060 (810) 985-7733
Rose City
American Paintball, 301 S Bennett 48654 (989) 685-8244
Saginaw
Swan Creek Paintball, 9550 Swan Creek 48609 (517) 781-1416
South Haven
Hole in the Wall, 68111 16th Ave. 49090 (616) 637-8749
Sturgis
Paintball Express, 305 N Nottawa 49091 (616) 651-2667
Taylor
Exotic Sportz, 23944 Eureka Rd. 48180 (734) 287-6460
Traverse City
America's Army Navy, 1421 Airport Rd. 49686
T.C. Paintball, 1218 Garfield Ave. 49686 (231) 933-0171
www.tcpaintball.com
Utica
Lone Wolf Creek Paintball, 45129 Cass Ave. 48317 (313) 739-1790
Walled Lake
Atomix Paintball, 1020 Decker Rd. 48390 (248) 926-9980
Warren
Paintball World, 24220 Mound Rd. #B 48091 (810) 757-8000
Waterford
Exotic Sportz, 5312 Highland 48327 (888) Exotic-1 [396-8421]
www.exoticsportz.com
Y2K Extreme Sports, 315 N Telegraph/Summit Place Mall 48328 (248) 682-1403
Whitemore Lake
Futureball Paintball Park, 9269 East M-36 48189 (248) 446-0772
www.futureballpaintball.com
West Branch
Ogemaw Joe's Paintball, 3008 Rifle River Tr. 48661 (989) 873-4207
Wyoming
Holiday Fine Guns, 4107 S Div. 49548 (616) 531-7304

MINNESOTA

Arden Hills
Adventures in Paintball, 1847 Todd Dr. 55112 (651) 639-9364
Brainerd
Have Guns Will Travel, 717 SW 6th St. 56401
Burnsville
Adventure Zone, 13700 Nicollet Ave. S 55337 (612) 683-1180/(952) 890-7961
Blaine
Splat You're Out, 10980 Central Ave. NE 55434 (763) 754-8620
Grand Prairie
Paintball Encounters, 9301 Ryden Rd. 55605 (807) 683-7071
Iron Mountain
It's A Blast Paintball, 5190 Co. Rd. #457 55768 (218) 258-2215
www.paintballmn.com
Mankato
River Hills Scheels, River Hills Mall, 1850 Adams St. #404 56001 (507) 386-7767

Mapleton
Sgt. Steve's Paintball, 15440 599th Ave. 56065 (507) 524-3299
Millville
Zumbro Valley Paintball, Rt. 1 Box 29A 55957
Minneapolis
Jaycor, 1759 16th Ave. 55448 (612) 767-7064
Splatball, 2412 University Ave. SE 55414 (612) 378-0385 www.splatball.org
Moorhead
Moorhead Downtown Scheels, 505 Center Ave. 56560 (218) 233-2751
Morris
MP's Army Surplus, 118 Division 55052
Staples
Team Special Forces Paintball Park, 31350 Timberlane Rd. 56479 (218) 330-0179 www.teamspecialforcespaintball.com
St. Cloud
Crossfire Paintball, PO Box 2255 56302 (320) 253-3630
St. Cloud Scheels, 4201 W Division St., Crossroads Center #109 56301 (320) 252-9494
St. Paul
Splat Tag, 854 Rice St. 55117 (651) 488-7700
White Bear Beach
Combat Zone, 4775 Banning Ave. 55110

MISSISSIPPI
Brandon
Redneck Rampage Paintball, 1093 Hwy. 471 39042 (601) 209-7860
Jackson
Hobbytown USA, 6380-D Ridgewood Ct. 39211 (601) 957-9900
Long Beach
Primal Assault Paintball, 5527 Beatline Rd. 39560 (228) 865-9162
Ocean Spring
Warped Sportz, 2752 Bienville Blvd. 39564 (877) 927-7331
Southhaven
Army Surplus Outlet, 8520 Hwy. 51 38671 (662) 393-7486
West Point
Brass Eagle Retail Store, Mossy Oak Outlet Center, 1239 Hwy. 45 Alt. S 39773 (601) 494-4500

MISSOURI
Arnold
Paintball Mania Supplies, PO Box 528 63010 (314) 296-0964
Wacky Warriors, PO Box 414 63010 (314) 296-0964
Eureka
Fearless Fighters, 1747 W 5th St. 63025 (636) 938-5559
Forest Fighters, 6848 Twin 63025 (636) 938-5002
Festus
Express Paintball Supply, 3656 Hwy. 61 S 63028 (314) 937-4321
Gladstone
Drop Zone Extreme Sports, 7711 N Oak Trafficway 64118 (816) 436-9994 www.dropzonepaintball.com
Gravois
Mills Dragon Arms Paintball, 30845 Copperfield Rd. 65037 (573) 372-2409
High Ridge
GI JO Outfitters, 5660 B State Rd. 63049
House Springs
The Paintball Store, 5645 Old Hwy. 21 63051 (636) 942-4422
Imperia
Paintball Mania, 4951 Sean Dr. 63052 (636) 296-0964
Independence
Green Dragon Martial Arts, 1325 S Noland Rd. 64055 (816) 833-3507
Jefferson City
Cole County Adventure, 1821 Rolling Hill 65109 (573) 690-1328
Meadow Ridge Paintball, 5824 Meadow Ridge Dr. 65101 (573) 395-4910
Joplin
Paintball Ridge, 3483 Coyote Dr. 64804 (417) 781-7703
Kansas City
Irish Brigade Paintball Store, 512 W 103rd St. 64114 (816) 942-9696
Jaeger's Subsurface Paintball, 9300 NE Underground Dr. 64162 (816) 452-6600 www.jaegers.com
National Pro Shop, 11142 Lindbergh Business 63123 (314) 845-7079
Warped Sportz K.C., 512 W 103rd St. 64114 (816) 942-9696 www.warpedsportzkc.com
Kingdom City
Battle Creek Paintball, 3643 CR 221 65262 (573) 642-7246
Leasburg
Saranac Springs, 1079 Springs Ln. 65535 (573) 245-6620
Ozark
Adult/Youth Paintball, PO Box 701 65721 (417) 485-6205
St. Louis
Paintball Outfitters, 5519 S Lindberg 63128 (314) 842-9938
St. Peters
Missouri Extreme Paintball, 418 Mid Rivers Mall Dr. 63376 (636) 278-2250
Springfield
Owens Outpost, 1939 E Florida 65803 (417) 443-6201
Paint Games Plus, 1411 W Kearn 65803 (417) 866-8862
Springfield Paintball, 601 N National 65802 (417) 869-4263
Warrensburg
Owens Outpost, Hwy. 50 64063 (816) 850-6338

MONTANA
Billings
Rimrock-Scheels, 300 S 24th St. W 59102 (406) 656-9220
Great Falls
Holiday Village-Scheels, #3 Holiday Village 59405 (406) 453-7666
Kalispell
Renegade Paintball Supply, 315 E Center Suite B 59901 (406) 755-8834
Livingston
Jam, Inc., 323 S 8th 59047 (406) 220-3198

NEBRASKA
Arlington
Big Dawg Paintball, 14062 Co. Rd. 7 68002 (402) 456-7795
Grande Island
Wayne's Pawn Shop, 203 W. 3rd St. 68801 (800) 903-4173
Kearney
Warped Sportz, 108 E 11th St 68848 (308) 234-9277
Lincoln
Lincoln Scheels, 2960 Pine Lake Rd., Suite B 68516 (402) 420-9000

NEVADA
Fallon
Mad Paint, 165 S Main St. 89406 (775) 867-2905
Fernley
Herbie's Paintball Games, Hwy 95 S Alt 89408 (775) 575-6946 www.herbiespaintball.com
Henderson
Textonx Paintball, 149 N Gibson Suite C 89014 (702) 567-6850
Las Vegas
House of Paintball, 5220 Steptoe St. 89112 (702) 617-0531 www.vegaspaintball.com
I&I Sports, 7680 Las Vegas Blvd. S Suite 208 89123 (702) 269-5964
Pneumi Cube, 9939 Antelope C 89147 (702) 254-9861
Wild Card Paintball ProShop, 1903 E Charleston 89104 (702) 471-7418
Reno
Desert Dawg's Paintball, 11505 Decodar Way 89506 (775) 971-9434
Sparks
National Paintball Supply West, #102 – 750 Freeport Blvd. 89431 (803) 458-7722/(609) 464-1068

NEW HAMPSHIRE
Dover
PG Xtreme, 256 Central Ave. 03820 (603) 742-3456
Keene
PG Xtreme west, 140 Main St. (866) 749-8736
Laconia
Beauia's Army/Navy, 24 Canal St. 03246 (603) 524-1018
Lincoln
Charlie's Gun & Sports, Rt. 112 03251 (603) 745-6112
Long Branch
MI Paintball, 604 Second Ave. #2 07740 (732) 222-1900
Manchester
Adventure Games Paintball Supply Outlet, 297 S Willow St. 03103 (603) 647-2255 www.agpaintball.com
Nashua
X-Fire Paintball, 295 Daniel Webster Hwy. (Sun Plaza) 03060 (603) 891-8300 www.xfirepaintball.com
Plaisto
Gordon's Army/Navy, 134 Newton Rd. 03865 (603) 382-1122
Portsmouth
Portsmouth Paintball, 250 State St. 03801 (603) 436-5511
Salem
Boston Paintball Supply North, 101 Main St. 03079 (603) 894-6359
Weare
Adventure Games, Rt. 149, 158 Deering Center Rd. 03281 (603) 529-3524 www.agpaintball.com
Windham
Canobie Paintball, 47 Roulston Rd. 03087 (603) 893-1863

NEW JERSEY
Absecon
Ben Franklin Variety, 150 New Jersey Ave. 08201 (609) 641-6934
Atco
Manhunt Paintball, 1000 Jackson Rd. 08004 (856) 768-2220
Brick
MI Paintball, 2060 Rt. 88 08724 (732) 714-2000
Carteret
Westwood Auto Supply, 60 Roosevelt Ave. 07008 (732) 969-3636 www.westwoodautoandpaintball.com
Cherry Hill
South Jersey Paintball, 1939 Rt. 70 E, Suite 250 08003 (609) 772-2878
Collingswood
Collingswood Hardware, 726 Haddon Ave. 08108 (856) 858-2662 www.collingswoodhardware.com
Columbus
Hector's Outdoor Haven, Columbus Farmer's Market, Rt. 206 08022 (609) 267-0119
Outdoor Haven Sporting Goods, Rt. 206 08022 (609) 267-0119

Cream Ridge
Top Gun Paintball, 567 Monmouth Rd. 08514 (732) 928-2810 www.topgunpaintball.com
Edison
Impact Paintball, 2037 Woodbridge Ave. 08817 (732) 339-0820
Englishtown
East Coast Paintball 1, Englishtown Rd. 07726 (732) 446-5606
Garfield
ET Paintball, 15 Madonna Pl. 07026 (973) 772-3866 www.etpaintball.com
Hackettstown
Paintball Depot, 1551 Rt. 57, 3 miles west (908) 684-4220 www.paintballdepot.com
Hewitt
ABC Paintball Supply & Field 1745 Greenwood Lake Tpk. 07421 (973) 728-1762
Greenwood Lake Sport Center, 1754 Greenwood Lake Tpk. 07421 (973) 728-1000
Howell
East Coast Paintball 3, Roseland Shopping Center 4326 Rt. 9 S 07731 (732) 901-1180
Pro Shot Paintball, Collingwood Auction Hwy. 33 & 34 07731 (732) 919-0175 www.proshotpaintball.com
Jersey City
Paintball Stix Ent., 537 Newark Ave. 07306 (201) 656-2900
Keyport
MI Paintball, 50 W Front St. 07734 (732) 739-1141
Ledgewood
Paintball Depot 1451 Rt. 46 07852 (973) 584-2220 www.paintballdepot.com
Lindenwold
On-Target Sports Paintball Supply, 505 N White Horse Pike 08021 (856) 784-9130
Long Branch
M.I. Paintball, 604 2nd Ave. Suite 2 07740 (732) 222-1900 www.murderincpaintball.com
Mantua
Gino's Golf & Paintball Center, 669 Rt. 45 Bridgeton Pike 08051 (856) 468-1643 www.ginosgolfandpaintball.com
National Paintball Supply East, 670 Rt. 45 08051 (609) 464-1068
South Jersey Paintball, 675 Rt. 45 07461 (888) 834-6026
Manville
Midstate Paintball, 247 S. Main St. 08835 (908) 722-9798
Marlboro
East Coast Paintball 2, 415 Rt. 9 S 07726 (732) 617-9942 www.bigmonsterpaintball.com
East Coast Paintball, 415 Rt. 9 S 07726 (732) 901-1180 www.eastcoastpaintball.com
Millville
Cumberland County Paintball, 5378 Rt. 49 08332 www.countypaintball.com
Monmouth
On Top Paintball, 45 Richard Rd. 08852 (732) 355-9450
Newark
North Eastern Paintball, 177 Jefferson St. 07105 (973) 344-4501
North Field
Drop Zone Army-Navy, 801 Tilton Rd. (World's Gym Plaza) 08225 (609) 484-2577
North Hanover
Fireball Mountain, 281 Meany Rd. 08562 (609) 758-0855 www.fireballmountain.com
Paramus
Ramsey Outdoor Stores, 226 Rt. 17 07652 (201) 261-5000
Pedricktown
Del Hobbies, 322 Artillery Ave. 08067 (856) 299-6000 www.delhobbies.com
Pennsauken
Pennsauken Mart Army & Navy, Rt. 130 Haddonfield 08110 (856) 665-2044
Piscataway
Rutgers College Rec., 656 Bartholomew Rd. 08854 (732) 445-0462
Ramsey
ABC Paintball Supply & Field 1216 Rt. 17 N 07446 (201) 327-6600
USA Nitro, 1216 Rt. 17 N 07446 (201) 760-9108
Roselle
Park Panther Equipment & Supplies, 19 E Westfield Ave. 07204 (908) 245-4399 www.pantherpaintball.biz
Sewell
National Paintball Supply, 570 Mantua Blvd. 08080 (800) 346-5615 www.nationalpaintball.com
Sussex
Radio Shack, 205 St. Hwy 23, Ames Plaza 07461 (973) 702-7717 www.sussexpaintballclub.com
Tom's River
One Shot Paintball Supplies, 1594 Rt. 9 08757 (732) 914-8430
Shore Paintball, 1184 Fischer Blvd. 08753 (732) 831-0400
Up Sad River
Indoor Paintball Planet 107, Pleasant Ave. & Rt. 17N 07458 (201) 934-1100
West Milford
Knightbreed Paintball, 625 Macopin Rd. 07480 (973) 697-5712 www.knightbreedpaintball.com
Winslow Township
Paintball Invasion, 192 S Rt. 73 08037 (609) 704-7787
Wrightstown
Fireball Mountain, 281 Meany Rd. 08562 (609) 758-0855
Yardville
Harry's Army Navy, 691 Rt. 130 08691 (800) 486-7872

NEW MEXICO

Albuquerque
Genesis Paintball, 7200 Menaul NE 87110 (505) 888-2025 www.genesispaintball.com
Paintball Action Games, 1331 Juan Tabo #2B 87112 (505) 332-3310
Paintball Guns-N-Stuff, 6303 4th St. NW 87107 (505) 345-6870
SC Village, 12931 Indian School Rd NE 87111 (505) 299-3100
Artesia
Valley Diesel Paintball Store, 2101 N Roselawn 88210 (505) 746-9530
Carlsbad
Desert Wave Paintball, 6202 Tidwell Rd. 88220 (505) 236-6182
Las Cruces
Genesis Paintball, 1675 E Lohman 88005 (505) 524-2251 www.genesispaintball.com
Los Alamos
Air-Tipps, 2149 A 34th St. #A 87544 (505) 667-6144
Peralta
Paintball Service, 3581 Hwy. 47 87942 (505) 865-6241

NEW YORK

Albany
First Prize Paintball, 1219 Central Ave. 12205 (518) 449-2255
Ancramdale
Hornet's Nest, 746 Roche Ln. 12503 (518) 329-3101
Bay Shore
High Velocity Paintball, 235 S Fehrway 11706 (631) 242-2096 www.highvelocitypaintball.com
Belfast
GRC Paintball, VanAllen Rd. 14711 (716) 365-2470
Brewste
Omega Ent., 1610 Rt. 22 10509 (914) 242-0800
Broadalbin
L&L Paintball Supply, 224 Co. Hwy. 138 12025 (518) 883-8315
Bronx
Crazy Paint, 2956 Jerome Ave. 10468
Brooklyn
NYC Paintball Supply, 37 Ave. T 11223 (718) 714-0575
Operation Stingray Pro Shop, 762 Grand St. 11211 (718) 384-1280
Paintball Survival Game HQ, 945 Coney Island Ave. 11230 (718) 462-9731
Walt's Hobbie Shop, 7909 Fifth Ave. 11209 (718) 745-4991
Cheektowaga
Army Navy Surplus, 1158 George Urban Blvd. 14225 (716) 684-8728
Cicero
Play to Win Paintball, 8116 Brewerton Rd. 13039 (315) 699-4640
Constantina
AAA Paintball Park, 303 Co. Rt. 23 (315) 472-9988 www.aaapaintballpark.com
Deer Park
Cousins, 1776 Deer Park Ave. 11729 (631) 243-1100 www.playpaintball.com
East Rochester
Paintball Game Supplies, 160 Dispatch Dr. 14445 (716) 383-5662
Elma
Outdoors Cain, 3211 Transit Rd. 14059 (716) 656-9944
Farmington
Splatball – The Game, P.O. Box 25351 14425 (716) 742-1486
Franklin Square
Cousins, 1157 Hempstead Tpk. 11010 (516) 616-0520
Glovers
Lennon's Adirondack Supply, 429 St. Hwy. 12078 (518) 773-7175
Harriman
Major Paintball Supply, 186 Rt. 17 M 10926 (845) 783-6053
Haverstraw
Matt's Sporting Goods, 57 Rt. 9W 10927 (845) 429-3254
Hicksville
Paintball Garage, 122 New South Rd. 11801 (516) 932-5200 www.paintballgarage.com
Hilton
Millennium Paintball, 20 East Ave. 14468 (585) 392-4899
Huntington Station
Island Paintball Supplies, 770 E Jericho Turnpike 11746 (631) 423-9086 www.islandpaintballsupply.com
Keeseville
Tiger Stripe Paintball, 1117 Rt. 9N 12944 (518) 834-5226
Kingston
Hudson Valley Paintball, 33 Broadway 12401 (845) 331-6777/(631)692-7668
Lake George
3 Guys Games & Paintball, 175 Canada St. 12845
Mahopac
Mac Mac's, 903 S Lake Blvd. Rt. 6N 10541 (845) 628-3488
Medford
Cousins, 2900 Rt. 112 11763 (631) 698-3657 www.playpaintball.com
Paintball Long Island, 2900 Rt. 112 11763 (631) 698-6230
Middletown
Mark's Cycle Corner, 154 Wickham Ave. 10940 (914) 343-4480
Mid Hudson Hobbies, 2 North St. 10940 (914) 342-8697
Mohegan
Crazy Paint Paintball, 1949 E Main 10547 (914) 526-0806
Montgomery
Montgomery Sporting Goods & Paintball, 32 Union St. 12549 (845/914) 457-4678 www.montgomerypaintball.150m.com
Mooers Forks
Jeux Arnold Paintball, 4431 Rt. 11 12959

Mt. Kisco
Cousins, 159 E Main St. 10549 (914) 241-3294
Palenville
Palenville Paintball Games, Rt. 23A 12463 (800) 362-9695
Patterson
Liberty Paintball, Rt. 22 and Birchill Rd. 12563 (845) 878-6300
Pine Valley
Red's Paintball, 27 Clair St. 14872 (607) 795-0411
Plattekill
Survival New York, Sunset Camp Road (914) 241-0020
Plattsburgh
3 Guys Games & Paintball, 331 Cornelia St. #2A 12901 (518) 561-6607
Poland
D&D Paintball Supply, 132 Tanner Rd. 13431 (315) 845-8410
Potters
Word of Life, 4200 Glendale Rd. 12860 (518) 532-7687
Poughkeepsie
Champion Paintball, 43 Vassar Rd. 12603 (845) 462-9292
www.championpaintball.com
Dragon's Den Comics, Poughkeepsie Plaza, 2600 South Rd. 12601 (845) 471-1401
Queens
American Paintball, 23 June Dr. 12804
Queensbury
Adironodack Paintball Games, PO Box 4550 12804 (518) 792-8845
3 Guys Games & Paintball, 968 Rt. 9 12804 (518) 793-4587
www.3guysgames.com
Rensselaer
Recon Challenge, 390 Columbia Tpk. 12144 (518) 477-7156
Rochester
Joshua's Paintball Jungle, 1039 N Greece Rd. 14626 (716) 225-3493
Upstate Hobby Supply, 45 Whitby Rd. 14609 (585) 482-8630
Rock Hill
Paintball Madness, 998 Wolf Lake Rd., Rt. 17E (845) 794-9365
www.paintballny.com
Rome
HeadRush Paintball, SR 49 13440 www.headrushpaintball.com
The War Club, 7624 Watson Hollow Rd. 13440 (315) 337-6259
www.thewarclub.com
Schenectady
KB Paintball, (800) 575-5272 www.kbpaintball.com
Mohawk Army Navy, 3514 State St. 12304 (518) 382-0001
Staten Island
Staten Island Paintball Center, 2727 Arthur Kill Rd. 10309 (718) 317-0101/227-1400 www.sipaintball.com
Syracuse
HeadRush Paintball, 6255 E Taft Rd. 13212 (315) 725-7874
Tonawanda
Sports Replay, 1614 Niagara Falls Blvd. 14150 (716) 834-6595
Victor
Pro Paintball, 10 Railroad St. 14564 (716) 924-9930
West Babylon
Paintball Arena, 400 Patton Ave. 11704 (631) 694-2707
Wolcott
Paintball Adventure, 10865 Wilson Rd. 14590 (315) 587-4995

NORTH CAROLINA

Angier
Black River Paintball, Rt. 2, Box 82-M 27501 (910) 897-5093
Ashevill
Wolverine Paintball Adventures, 441 N Louisiana #T 28806 (828) 254-4371
Belmont
World of Paintball, 6422 Wilkinson Blvd. 28012 (704) 825-5444
Burlington
Paintball Central, 2602 Eric Ln. 27215 (336) 228-3800
Charlotte
Sports Warehouse, Extremes Sports Park, 10930 Granite St. 28273 (704) 583-1444 www.extremes-usa.com
Concord
Boss Paintball Pro Shop, 5356 Zion Church Rd. 28025 (704) 784-4365
www.bossproshop.com
Cornelius
CJ's Paintball, 18505-A05 Statesville Rd. 28031 (704) 987-5053
www.cjpaintball.com
Durham
Amazing Castles, 4350 Garrett Rd. 27707 (919) 493-8973
Fayetteville
Force of Nature, 6243 Yadkin Rd. 28303 (910) 860-4469
www.forceofnature.com
Forest City
Danny's Paintball Supply, 436 Flack Rd. 28018 (828) 247-1070
Garner
Action Tagg Paintball, 514 Village Ct. 27529 (919) 661-8244
Gates
Sandy Point Paintball, 49 Sandy Point Ln. 27935 (252) 209-4491
www.sandypointpaintball.com
Granite
Castle Sports Unlimited, 2741 Connelly Springs Rd. 28630 (828) 728-9113
Greensboro
North Carolina Paintball Supply, 1702 Spring Garden St. 27407 (336) 292-1102 www.ncpbonline.com
Paintball Central, 1814 Spring Garden St. 27403 (336) 274-4002

Greenville
S&R Distribution, 102 Hungate Dr. 27858 (252) 756-9565
Hendersonville
Wolverine Paintball, 500 Brookside Camp Rd. (just off Exit 13, I 26) 28792
(828) 696-4371 www.wolvpb.com
High Point
Shoot 'Em Up Paintball, 3205 E Kivett Dr. 27260 (336) 689-2215/454-4317
Horse Shoe
Line of Fire Paintfields, 923 Gilreath Loop Rd. 28742 (828) 891-2399
www.lofpb.com
Jacksonville
Milty's, 3521 New Bern Hwy. 28546 (910) 938-0099
Turbo Paintball, PO Box 12294 28546 (910) 324-6862
Kannapolis
DC Paintball, 2969 N Cannon Blvd. 28083 (704) 737-7250
Lewisville
X-tremist Paintball, 330 Dorse Rd. 27023
Lexington
Wicked Sports, 970 S Main St. 27292 (336) 238-6080
Marshville
Paintball Kingdom, 2407 Ansonville Rd. 28103 (704) 624-4115
Matthews
CJ's Paintball, 1600H Matthews Mint Hill Rd. 28105 (704) 814-7393
www.cjpaintball.com
North Wilkesboro
Cook's, 1402 Willow Ln. 28659 (336) 667-4121
Raleigh
Gotcha Paintball, 4339-C Falls of the Neuse 27609 (919) 501-7770
Rockingham
Idol's Adventure Sport 28379
Sedalia
Paintball Central, 6106 Burlington Rd. (336) 274-4002
Statesville
Action Quest, 3208 Taylorsville 28625 (704) 878-6880
Winston-Salem
North Carolina Paintball/Midway, Hwy. 52 S at Hickory Tree 27284 (910) 764-2701
Youngsville
Gotcha Parts Paintball, 176 Darius Pearce Rd. (919) 271-3367

NORTH DAKOTA

Bismarck
Paintballer's Paradise, 216 E Main Ave. 58501 (701) 255-7126
Kirkwood Scheels, 802 Kirkwood Mall 58504 (701) 255-7255
Fargo
Scheels All Sports, 3202 13th Ave. S 58103 (701) 298-2918
Grand Forks
Grand Forks Scheels, Med Park Mall 1375 A, S Columbia Rd. 58201 (701) 780-9424
Kindred
Sherwood Forest Year 2, 16449 54th St. SE 58501 (701) 281-6592
Minot
Dakota Square Scheels, Minot Dakota Square 58701 (701) 298-2918
Pingree
Manley Paintball (701) 320-3762
Wahpeto
Hidden Valley Adventure, 822 3rd Ave. N 58075 (701) 642-1252

OHIO

Akron
Indian Springs Paintball, 2849 Summit Rd. 44321 (330) 745-5722
Alliance
3-D Sports Specialties, 13500 Union Ave. 44601 (330) 821-5666
Ashland
Fin-Feather-Fur Outfitters, 652 Rt. 250 44805 (419) 281-2557
PB Supply, 1403 St. Rt. 89 44805
Ashtabula
DT Paintball, 2367 Dewey Rd. 44004 (440) 224-0604
Ridgeline Firearms, 5998 Bldg. C State Rd. 44004 (440) 998-1241
Bedford
Allen Paintball, 34 W Interstate 44146
Belle Center
Paintball Games Coliseum, 3621 St. Rt. 273 43310 (513) 464-4480
Bellevue
Great Lakes Paintball, 11903 Dining Rd. 44811 (419) 483-7800
Bethel
Edge Paintball, 2860 SR 125 45106 (513) 734-4777
www.edgepaintball.cjb.net
Bowerston
Edie's Paintball, 9022 Derry Rd. 44695 (740) 269-9046
Bowling Green
R&B Games 178 S Main St. 43402 (419) 353-2176
Caledon
Olentangy Paintball, 2694 Caledonia-Northern Rd. 43314 (419) 845-3472
Canal Fulton
Splat-Paintball, 333a Lafayette Dr. 44614 (330) 323-7706
Chardon
Pinnacle Woods, 10241 Old State Rd. 44024 (440) 286-6167
www.pinnaclewoodspaintball.com
Tech/Mark, 9301 Brown Rd. 44024

Cincinnati
Desert Storm, 493 Old St. Rd. 45244 (513) 528-317
FuzGunz.com, 568 Old 74 45244 (513) 528-3173
Ringler Rentals, 6700 Clough Pike 45244 (513) 231-6868
www.ringlerrentals.com
Cleves
Miami Valley Paintball, 208 S Miami Ave. 45002 (513) 467-0087
Cleveland
North East Survival Games, 4197 Pearl Rd. 44109 (216) 749-2868
Columbus
paintball-discounters.com 43224 (800) 536-1104/(614) 784-1104
www.paintball-discounters.com
Paintball Field of Fun (614) 784-1104
Central Ohio Paintball Pro Shop, 3069 Silver Dr. 43224 (800) 536-1104/(614)
784-1104 www.copaintball.com
Surplus World, 4200 W Broad St. 43228 (614) 351-1211
Surplus World, 2590 Morse Rd. 43231 (614) 475-1111
Cuyahoga Falls
Erie Outdoors, 1407 Main St. 44221 (800) 500-5311
Underground Sports, 3480 Hudson Dr. 44221 (330) 923-8916
Dayton
Splatland Paintball, Wrightway Rd. N (513) 293-5560
Euclid
Paintball City, 20001 Euclid Ave. 44117 (216) 404-0400 www.pbcity.com
Fairfield
Queen City Paintball, 5961 #4 Boymel Dr. 45014 (513) 942-2255
Findlay
R&B Games 528 S Main St. 45840 (419) 427-2176 www.rbgames.com
Fostoria
R&B Games, 113 E North St. 44830 (419) 435-4225
Galion
.68 Caliber Paintball, SR 288 44833 (419) 468-4300
Geneva
KGB Paintball, 1337 Harpersfield Rd. 44041 (440) 415-0945
Hamersville
Red Dragon Paintball, 2726 Lucas Rd. 45130 (937) 379-1448
Jeromesville
Mohawk Paintball Field, 453 Co. Rd. 2000 44840 (419) 368-4089
Knoxville
Buckeye Paintball, 6232 Cloverleaf 45871 (419) 753-3231
Lima
The Paintball Company, 1910 W Robb Ave. 45805 (419) 222-8892
Logan
Paintball Wars of the World, 9014 Voris Rd. 43138 (740) 385-7720
Lorraine
Adrenaline Zone, 810 W 13th St. 44052 (216) 681-4445
Mansfield
Mass Paintball, 515 Park Ave. E 44905 (419) 522-3080
Richland Paintball, 888 Laver Rd. 44905 (419) 589-5577
www.richlandpaintball.com
Marietta
J&J Sporting Goods Paintball Park, Rt. 9, Box 89A 45750 (740) 374-3719
www.jjpaintball.com
Marysville
Marysville Paintball, 843 East Fifth St. 43040 (937) 642-3345
Mason
Mason Paintball, 126 W Main St. 45040 (513) 573-9742
www.masonpaintball.com
Massillon
JP's Paintball, 7928 Hill-N-Dale's Rd. NW 44646
Mentor
Pinnacle Woods, 8752 East Ave. 44060 (440) 974-0077
www.pinnaclewoodspaintball.com
Miamisburg
Jungle Jim's Paintball, 152 S Main St. 45342 (513) 859-0916
Middleport
Combat Adventures, 295 S Second 45760 (614) 388-8601
Middletown
Beacon Hill Paintball, 2008 Wilbraham 45042
Moraine
Xtreme Paintball Sports, 3081 Dryden Rd. 45439 (937) 298-5138
Mt. Gilead
Splatterpark Paintball Games, 5560 CR 109 43338 (800) 536-1104/(419)
946-4964
Newark
Ground Zero Paintball, 1860 Hebron Rd. 43055 (740) 788-8220
New Bremen
J&D Paintball, 9 N Herman St. 45869 (419) 629-3942
New Paris
JONT Enterprises, 1396 New Garden Rd. 45347 (513) 437-7195
North Canton
Intense-Paintball, 5677 Nimishille Church Rd. 44721 (330) 877-3647
North Ridgeville
Bulk-N-Bushel, 33146 Center Ridge 44039 (440) 888-5611
Oak Hill
Shiloh Fields Paintball, 1695 Centerpoint Rd. 45656 (740) 682-6232
Parma
Central Ohio Paintball Pro Shop, 5755 Ridge Rd. 44219 (440) 842-8035
Friendly Fire, 5399 Pearl Rd. 44129 (440) 887-0066
Pataskala
General Merchandise, 13690 Broad St. 43062 (740) 927-3586

Portage
Bull Creek Paintball Park, 9703 Greensburg Park 43451 (419) 266-4799
Richwood
Deer Run Paintball, 17124 Harmon-Patrick Rd. 43344
Shelby
Sportsman's Den, 48 Mansfield Ave. 44875 (419) 347-3007
Sidney
Carty's Bike Shop, 412 S Brooklyn Ave. 45365 (937) 492-4562
Springfield
Alternative Sports Supply, Valley Loop Rd. 45503 (937) 399-2403
Strongsville
Pinnacle Woods, 13500 Pearl Rd. 44136 (440) 846-0441
www.pinnaclewoodspaintball.com
Sydney
Cutter's Paintball, 1881 Miami 45365 (513) 492-6548
Sylvania
Steve's Hobbies, 5834 Monroe St. #S 43560 (419) 824-9925
Tiffin
Combat Zone, 7060 S Twp. Rd. #131 44883 (419) 447-8424
Gase Enterprises, 146 N Washington St. 44883 (419) 447-2712
Tipp City
DJ's Paintball, 9800 St. Rd. 20 45371 (937) 667-7576
Toledo
Action Enterprises, 5860 Lewis Ave. 43612 (800) 552-3089
Action Enterprises, 709 N Reynolds Rd. 43615 (419) 534-2634
Team Sith Lords, 1140 Hamilton 43607 (419) 241-1872
Toledo Indoor Paintball, 5860 Lewis Ave. 43612 (419) 478-2221
www.toledoindoorpaintball.com
Uniontown
TPA Paintball, 13075 Cleveland Ave. NW 44685 (330) 699-5057
Urbana
For the Love of Sports, 719 Miami St. 43078 (937) 484-4142
Vandalia
Miami Valley Shooting, 7771 S Cassel Rd. 45377 (513) 890-1291
Wadsworth
Rainbow Fields, 296 Johnson Rd. 44281
Westlake
Five Alarm Paintball, 28979 Bassett Rd. 44145 (440) 336-5911
Whitehouse
All Star Paintball, 6807 Providence St. 43571 (419) 877-4704
Wooster
Buckeye Paintball, 1130 E Bowman St. 44691 (330) 264-9277
Youngstown
Miller Rod & Gun, 5140 Youngstown – Poland Rd. 44514 (330) 755-3451
www.propaintball.com
The Paintball Sphere, 7178 West Blvd. 44512 (330) 549-3400

OKLAHOMA

Anadark
Oakridge Christian Camp, Rt. 3 Box 233 73005 (405) 247-5433
Blackwell
Hit & Run Paintball, 106 W Coolidge Ave. 74631 (580) 363-2422
Henryetta
Cedar Ridge Paintball Games, 306 N 1st 74437 (918) 652-8891
McAlester
H.L. Guns & Pawn, 1232 S Main St. 74501 (918) 426-1146
Moore
Splatter Paintball Supply, 2600 N Moore Ave. 73160 (405) 912-0405
Norman
Adrenaline Paintball Supply, 1280 Interstate Dr. 73972 (405) 579-3500
Oklahoma City
Dodge City Paintball Field, 9601 NE 63rd St. (405) 771-5229
Shaggy Brothers Paintball, 5575 NW Expy. #B 73132 (405) 720-2432/(800)
320-7277
Sapulpa
Paintball Adventure Games, 10242 S 49th W Ave. 74066
(918) 224-1055 www.pbadventuregames.com
Sand Springs
Top-Of-The-Line Paintball, 212 E Broadway 74063 (918) 245-8686/(888)
288-8685
Stillwater
Boot Hill Paintball Field, 1 mi. N ½ mi. E Fairgrounds (405) 669-2723
Sulphur Springs
Heath Fire & Safety, 1602 W Broadway 73086 (580) 622-2146
Tulsa
All American Paintball, 3716 East 51st 74135 (918) 293-2269
Paintball of Tulsa, 6390-H E 31st St. 74135 (918) 665-7856
SportPaint, 5014 S Quincy Ave. 74105 (918) 744-4488

OREGON

Albany
Splat Paintball Sports, 2880 Ferry SW 97321 (541) 928-0957
Aloha
Armory, 751 SW 185th 97006 (503) 259-8596
Eugene
Paintball Games, 1820 W 7th Ave. 97402 (541) 465-4766
Forest Grove
Armory, 2541 23rd Ave. 97116 (503) 359-5434
Gresham
The Game Pad/Oregon Paintball, 140 NW Miller St. 97030 (503) 666-7930

Keno
Whack'm & Splak'm, PO Box 58 97627 (503) 884-8942
LaGrande
Fireball Paintball Supply, 2211 First St. 97850 (541) 663-9808
Warpaint Paintball Supply, 2304 E Adams Ave. 97850 (503) 963-6947
Lebanon
Hosking Supply, 2495 S Santiam Hwy. 97355 (541) 258-3232
Medford
Splatt Paintball, 3454 N Pacific Hwy. 97501 (541) 770-3232
www.splattpaintball.com
Portland
Adrenaline – Sportz, 9921 SE Stark 97216 (503) 251-0065
Ollie Damon's, 236 SE Grand Ave. 97214 (503) 232-3193
www.olliedamon.com
Seaside
Edge Of The Earth Paintball, 2950 Hwy. 101 N 97138 (503) 738-5900
Tigard
Paintball Online, 15717 SW 74th #400 97224 (503) 697-9476
Vale
MB&L Welding, 949 A St. W 97918 (541) 473-2273
Wilson
PMI, 27350 SW 95th A #3016 97070 (503) 682-8450

PENNSYLVANIA

Allentown
Kuba's Surplus Sales, 231 W 7th St. 18102 (215) 433-3877
Aston
Capt'n Carl's Paintball, 1-A Rosalie Ln. 19014 (610) 364-9666
www.captncarls.com
Bedford
68 Caliber Paintball, 203 E Pitt St. 15522 (814) 624-0668
Berwick
Fuzzy Grub Tackle Shop, 216 Martzville Rd.
Bluebell
Data Nation, 1 Sentry Pkwy. 19422 (610) 825-7720
Butler
Boyd's Front Line, 420 Butler Mall 16001 (724) 285-8740
J&J Rogerson Paintball, 153 Freeport Rd. 16002 (724) 285-1500
Conestoga
Ambush, 700 Sickman's Mill Rd. 17516 (717) 871-8632
Dillsburg
Wanna-Play Paintball, 725 N Route 15 17019 (717) 432-7997
Dunmore
Xtreme Depot, 1213 Wheeler Ave. 18512 (570) 344-1773
Eagleville
Poco Loco Paintball, PO Box 61 19408 (877) 529-4373
East Stroudsburg
K&B Amusements, 11 Shawnee Valley 18301
Easton
USA Paintball, 240 Folk St. 18042 (610) 438-1344
www.usapaintballsupplies.com
Erie
Charlie's Custom Archery & Paintball, 1126 W 26th St. 16508 (814) 454-1428
Fairless
Hills Triage Paintball, 225 Lincoln Hwy. 19030 (215) 949-4600
Fairview
Pentagon Paintball, 7250 Avonia Rd. 16415 (814) 474-5580
Freedom
Three Rivers Paintball, 284 Rochester Rd. 15042 (724) 775-6232
www.trpaintball.com
Greensburg
Statler's Fun Center, RD 7, Box 261-B 15601 (724) 539-7805
Jim Thorpe
Skirmish, SR 903 HC-2, Box 2245 18229 (800) SKIRMISH
www.skirmish.com
Kennett Square
Paintball Adventure, 327 E State St. 19348 (610) 444-9293
www.paintsplat.com
Lancaster
Kelly's Paintball, 201 Greenfield Rd. 17601 (717) 291-1060
Lansdale
Cobra Command, 20 N Cannon 19446 (215) 855-7252
LeMoyne
Sgt. York's, 900 Market St. 17043 (717) 761-3819
Lewisberr
Revolution Paintball @ Ski Round Top, 925 Round Top Rd. 17339 (717) 432-9631 www.skiroundtop.com
Loyalhanna
Punishers Paintball, 100 Station St. 15661 (724) 537-7246
Smart Parts, 100 Station St. 15661
Meyersdale
Paint Crusades, 146 Center St. 15552 (814) 634-1951
Milford
Action Outfitters, 546 Rt. 6/209 18337 (570) 796-6657
Montgomery
Montgomery Army Navy, Old Schoolhouse Bldg. Rt. 309 & 463 18936 (215) 362-0879
Moscow
Bill's True Value Hardware, RR 6, Box 6220 18444 (570) 842-7645
Natalie
Paintball Thunder Action Park, Rt. 54 17851 (570) 339-4810
www.paintballthunder.com

New Milford
Big Boys Toys, RR 3, Box 23 18834 (570) 465-2051
E.M.R. Paintball Park, PO Box 728, Rt. 706 & 601 18834 (570) 465-9622
www.emrpaintball.com
Phoenixville
French Creek Outfitter, 270 Schuylkill Rd. (Valley Forge Mall) 19460 (610) 933-7200
Pittsburgh
Action Fanatics, 8 Clairton Blvd. 15236 (412) 655-2121 www.pbfanatics.com
Paintball Sports Arena, 1600 SmallMan St. #300 15222 (412) 434-6900
Punishers Paintball, 1319 Washington Blvd. 15206 (412) 362-7246
Uwchland
Gordon's Sports Supply, 129 Pottstown Pike/PO Box 700 19480 (610) 458-5153
Waynesburg
Gadget Paintball Pro Shop, 439 Haines Hollow Rd. 15370 (724) 627-7933
White Haven
Roadrunner Paintball, 402 Erie St. 18661 (570) 443-0976 www.rrpball.com
Wilkes-Barre
Command Post, 238 Kidder St. 18702 (570) 829-3818

RHODE ISLAND

Coventer
Capital Paintball, 853 Tiogue Ave. 02816 (401) 823-5402
Cranston
Atwood Paintball, 471 Atwood Ave. 02920 (401) 942-9955
www.atwoodpaintbal.com
Johnston
Boston Paintball Supply North, 1428 Hartford Ave. 02919 (401) 351-2255
Pawtucket
Paintball Wizards of NE, 682 Broadway 02860 (401) 724-3751
Providence
Indoor Paintball, 95 Hathaway St. #H46 02907 (401) 467-2815
Westerly
Gun & Dive Shop, 140 Main St. 02891 (401) 596-4469
Woonsocket
J&M Paintball, 272 Main St. (251 Bernon St.) 02895 (401) 765-8828

SOUTH CAROLINA

Aiken
Adrenaline Heaven Paintball, 1310 Whiskey Rd. 29801 (803) 643-8199
Charleston
Camo Bunker, 5627 Rivers Ave. 29406 (843) 566-9573
www.camobunker.com
Florence
Defender Firearms Training, PO Box 7377 29502 (843) 317-9969
Greenville
Paintball, Inc., 155 Verdin Rd. 29607 (864) 458-7221
Pro Fox Paintball, 1200 Woodruff Rd. 29607 (803) 458-7221
Xtreme Sports Outlet, 205 Cedar Lane Rd. 29611 (864) 250-0050/(877) 907-7528 www.shop4paintball.com
Greer
Badlands Paintball, 1421 W Wade Hampton 29650 (864) 877-9558
Hartsville
Crazy Dave's, 125 Darlington Ave. 29550 (843) 857-4450
Lake View
Ground Zero Paintball, 2078 Bermuda Rd. 29563 (888) 759-2578
www.gzpaintball.com
Lexington
Ace Hardwarehouse, 300 W Main 29072 (803) 975-9300
Ballbusters Paintball, 4952 Sunset Blvd. 29072 (803) 957-5822
www.ballbusters-paintball.com
Mount Pleasant
Henry's Sporting Goods, 1662 Hwy. 17 N 29464 (843) 881-0465
Paintball Charleston, 473 Shipping Ln. 29464 (843) 747-0660
Newberry
Clarence T Summer, 1207 Boyce St. 29108 (803) 276-2778
North Charleston
The Paintball Store, 5131 Dorcester #14 29418 (843) 458-7221
Rock Hill
College Cycles, 361 W Oakland Ave. 29730 (803) 329-0992
www.paintball-adventures.com
JC Robinson's Attic, 2742 Celanese 29732 (803) 366-3809 www.jcattic.com
Summerville
Paintball Charleston, 178 Irby Dr. 29483 (843) 819-7070
Psycho Paintball, 908 Bacon's Bridge Rd. 29485 (843) 821-2337
West Columbia
Trigger Tyme Paintball, 2860 Oakwood Dr. 29169 (803) 786-4539

SOUTH DAKOTA

Rapid City
Rapid City Scheels, 480 Rushmore Mall 2200 N Maple 57701 (605) 342-9033
Rapid City Winnelson, 1525 C Samco Rd. (800) 898-6470
Sioux Falls
41st St. Scheels, 501 W 41st St. 57105 (605) 334-7767
ABN Army Surplus, 1520 W 3rd St. 57104 (605) 357-8855
Empire Scheels, 1650 Empire Mall 4001 41st St. 57106 (605) 361-6839
Sioux River Adventure, 2029 South Dakota 57105 (888) 775-2823
Spearfish
Big Jim's Feud Ranch, HRC30, Box 17 57783 (605) 578-1808

Watertown
Paintball World, 10 S. Broadway 57201 (605) 886-7208

TENNESSEE
Blountville
The Alternative Sport, 409 Overhill Dr. 37617 (423) 279-7787
Chattanooga
Adventures in Paintball, 5600 Brainerd Rd. C-18 37411 (423) 485-9077
Cordova
Challenge Park – Memphis, 1345 N Germantown Pkwy. 38018 (901) 754-4205
The Paintball Store, 1345 N Germantown Pkwy. 38018 (901) 754-4205
Gallatin
Wolf Hill Paintball, 670 S Water Ave. 37066 (615) 451-7600
www.wolfhillpaintball.net
Harrison
Chapman's LT Plus, 6918 Barter Dr. 37341 (423) 344-4918
www.chapmansltplus.com
Hixson
River City Pool & Spa, 7319 Dayton Pike 37343 (423) 842-5151
Jasper
R&R Bait & Tackle, 8333 Hwy. 41 37347 (423) 942-5276
Joelton
Academy of Self-Preservation, 7236 White's Creek Pike 37080 (615) 876-3010
Johnson City
Albert's Paintball, 104 W Market St. 37604
Kingsport
J&P Splatterball, 1102 Lomax St. 37660 (423) 247-2460
Knoxville
In Line Skate Center, 6541 Chapman Hwy. 37920 (865) 577-3103
Knoxville Paintball Sports, 6673 Maynardville Hwy. 37918 (865) 925-2766
R&T Coal Co., 11852 Kingston 37922 (865) 966-0877
Splat 1 Adventures, 2627 Sutherland Ave. 37919
Lakeland
EZ Paiontball, 9160 Hwy. 64 Ste. #7 38002 (901) 384-7200
Lakeland
Paintball Park Memphis, 9640 Davie Plantation E 38002 (901) 372-3383/385-4851
Lake Oneida
Major Splatter (423) 569-4342
Maryville
Airborne-6 Paintball, 4850 Sevierville Rd. 37804 (865) 982-4205
Foothills Paintball Games, 2725 US Hwy. 411 S 37801 (865) 983-2189
Springfield
Extreme Paintballers, 300 N Walnut St. 37172 (615) 382-9858

TEXAS
Abilene
Paintball Magic, 1257 S Danville 79605 (915) 695-2727
Alvin
Ultimate Paintball of Texas, 1802 Algoa-Friendswood Rd. 77511 (409) 316-2000 www.ultimatepaintballoftexas.com
Amarillo
Bryan's House of Paintball, 1941 S. Seminole 79103 (806) 374-1706
www.paintslingers.com
Power Sports, 6513 Storage Dr. 79110 (800) 732-6085/(806) 467-0277/1653
www.thepaintballstore.com
Aransas Pass
Outpost Paintball Field, 2341 Murdine Rd. 78336 (512) 758-2181
Arlington
Diablo Direct West, 2500 E Randall Mill #200 76011 (817) 633-6400
Austin
Constant Action, 1701 W Ben White #120 78704 (512) 326-1109/837-3787
www.constantactionpaintball.com
Olympic Paintball Sports, 3601 Parmer Ln. 78727 (512) 834-9290
Paintball Mart, 12129 Ranch Rd. Suite 420 78750 (512) 258-0795
www.paintball/mart.net
Bandera
Pipe Creek Paintball, 910 Cypress Ark Ln. 78003 (210) 896-7166
Chandler
The Paintball Shack, 101 Cedar Ln. 75758 (903) 849-6293
Commerce
Adventure Expeditions, 1308 Chestnut St. 75248 (903) 886-7691
Dallas
C.M. Support/ViewLoader, 4921 Olson Dr. 75227 (214) 381-3075
Paintball Doctor, 3136 Route St., #105 75201 (214) 720-0292/0276
www.paintballdoctor.com
Unicam, 2624 Elm St. 75226 (214) 651-1350
Conroe
Paintball Challenge, 619 Brook Hollow 77385
Del Valle
Olympic Paintball Sports, 15010 Fagerquist Rd.
El Paso
Genesis Paintball www.genesispaintball.biz
East, 2000 Lee Trevino, Suite T 79936 (915) 629-0655
West, 6600 N Mesa, #603 79912 (915) 585-8545
Euless
Awful Ventures Paintball & More, 4309 W Pipeline 76040 (817) 282-3636
Paintball & More, 4309 W Pipeline Rd. 76040 (817) 282-3636
Paintball Game Supply of Texas, 1101 Royal Pkwy. #117 76040 (817) 571-1177

Flower Mound
DFW Adventure Park, PO Box 270007 75027 (972) 539-6682
Forney
Official Paintball Games of Texas, 17437 Adams Tr. 75126 (972) 203-0014
www.officialpaintball.com
Fort Worth
Fun on the Run, 4224 Karen Ln. 76135 (817) 237-0299
Mad Ivan's, 1813 W Bowie 76110 (817) 923-6422 www.madivan.com
Paintball Player's Supply, 7024 Jacksboro Hwy. 76135 (817) 237-0299
Garland
Survival Games of Dallas/Ft. Worth, 105 Waits Cir. 75048 (817) 267-3048
Gun Barrel
Carry Right Gun Shop, 248 N Gun Barrel Ln. 75147 (903) 887-4867
Harlingen
South Texas Paintball, 2307 Louis Pl. 78550 (956) 245-9550
Houston
Adventure Village Strategy Games, 8311 FM 1960 Bypass 77338 (281) 548-3386
Choo Choo's Family Fun Center, 1430 Wallisville Rd. 77049 (713) 451-3010
Command Post, 8635 Long Point 77055 (713) 827-7301
www.armysurplususa.com
Command Post, 10607 I-10 East 77029 (713) 675-3221
Houston Rookie League, 8215 Lugary Dr. 77074 (713) 862-5555
www.houstonrookieleague.com
Paintball Bonanza, S Main at Chimney Rock 77035 (713) 935-0552
Paintball Gear, 7979 N Eldridge #3018 77041 (281) 897-8678
Paintball Gear, 12121 NW Fwy. 77092 (713) 935-0552
Paintball Store, 9220 FM 1960 W 77070 (281) 469-9777
Paintball Maxx, 5829 W Sam Houston Pky. N #601 77041 (713) 983-9190
www.paintballmaxx.com
Paintball Zone, 2811 Dixie Farm Rd. 77089 (281) 660-0663
www.paintballzone.net
Survival Game of Texas, 2309 Aldine Meadows 77032 (713) 370-4263
Humble
Adventure Village, 8311 FM 1960 Bypass 77338 (281) 548-3386
www.adventurevillage.com
Huntsville
Comics & Games, PO Box 323, Elkins Ln. 77340 (936) 295-7541
Iola
Boondocks Recreation, 10658 CR 175 77861 (979) 777-1241
www.boondocksreckranch.com
Irving
National Paintball of Texas, 2010 Century Center Blvd., Suite S 75062 (800) 346-5615 www.nationalpaintball.com
Paintball Games of Dallas, 3305 E John Carpenter Fwy. 75062 (214) 554-1937
Kempner
The Bunkers, 3699 FM 2657 76539 (254) 518-3279
Killeen
Centrex Paintball, Rt. 7, Box 192 76542 (817) 628-7076
Laredo
Army Corp., 1310 Grant St. #F 78040
La Favorita, 1215 Zaragoza 78040 (956) 724-7280
Lewisville
Paintball Supply of Lewisville, 1081 W. Main St. #107B 75067 (972) 221-9036
Longview
D.A.M. Games of East Texas, PO Box 5270 75608 (214) 297-2075
Lubbock
Challenge Games, S. Plains Mall, 6002 Slide Rd. M-10 79410 (806) 792-4551
West Texas Paintball, 2235 19th 79401 (806) 744-4000
Magnolia
Lone Star Paintball, 23214 Baneberry 77355 (713) 356-2158
Mansfield
Hit & Run Paintball Park, Rt. 2, Box 156 D 76063 (817) 453-8914
McAllen
Green Beret, 2213 N 10th St. 78501 (956) 687-1147
McAllen Paintball, 4220 N Bicentennial, Suite F 78504 (956) 630-0901
Midland
Dave's Custom Firearms, 3808 Monty 79703 (915) 262-5313
Multiple Enterprises, 4811 W Illinois 79703 (915) 262-5507
Odessa
Just 4 Fun, 410 E 8th 79761 (915) 580-0200
Pasadena
Command Post 2843 SE Beltway 8 77503 (281) 998-3233
Pottsboro
A Ray Zipper, 261 Ranger Rd. 75076 (903) 786-3254/2251
Ransom Canyon
West World Paintball, 55 E Canyon Village 79366 (806) 767-0945
Rhome
Paintball Paradise, 3523 E Hwy. 114 76078 (940) 433-5447
Roanoke
DFW Adventure Park, 13055 Cleveland Gibbs Rd. 76262 (817) 854-0085
www.dfwap.com
San Antonio
Paintball Mart, 15737 San Pedro 78232 (210) 491-0506
www.paintball-mart.net
Temple
Olympic Paintball Sports, 712 N 31st 76504 (254) 791-5050
Olympic Paintball Sports, 36 White Flint Park Rd. 76510
Texas City
Calico Welding & Paintball, 119 29th St. S 77590 (800) 767-3171
Tomball
Paintball-For-Less, 28155 Tomball Pkwy. #6A 77377 (281) 351-9880

Tyler
 Crossfire Paintball, 6611 S Broadway – Red Barn Square 75703 (903) 939-3255
 Wild Side Sports, 4703 Troup Hwy. 7573 (903) 561-7565
Waco
 .The Gizmo Guru, 3206 Ferndale Dr. 76706 (254) 662-1896/1199
 www.gurupaintball.com
 Guru Paintball Park, 2234 E Tinsley 76706 (254) 662-1896
 Heart of Texas Paintball, 4301 Meyers Ln. 76705 (254) 799-9699
Waxahachie
 Paintball of Waxahachie, 507 N Hwy. 77 #614 75165 (972) 937-2468
Wichita Falls
 Field of Honor, 2317 Hampton Rd. 76305 (940) 761-5566
Wolfe City
 Wolfe City War Games, Rt. 2 Box 267 75496 (903) 450-1006

UTAH

American Fork
 The Bike Peddler, 24 E Main St. 84003 (801) 756-5014
Bountiful
 Ops Gear, 1067 S 1550 E 84010 (801) 295-4237
Mt. Carmel
 Zion Ponderosa Resort, PO Box 5547 84755 (435) 648-2700
Ogden
 Straight Shooter Paintball, 3940 Washington Blvd. 84403 (903) 450-1006
Richfield
 Jorgensen's, 980 S Main St. 84701 (435) 896-6408
Salt Lake City
 CCS 1Air Assault, 175 E 400 St. #1000 84111 (801) 350-9102
Sandy
 Paintball Planet, 8700 S Sandy Pkwy. 84070 (801) 562-1400
Springville
 Paintball X-Press, 981 S 400 E 84663 (801) 491-6278
St. George
 Paintball Outpost II, Red Cliffs Mall 84709 (435) 652-1243
 www.paintballoutpost.com
 Preparedness Mart, 1090 E Tabernacle 84770 (435) 673-0437
West Valley City
 PT Enterprises, 1422 W 3500 S 84119 (801) 886-0919

VERMONT

Rutland
 3 Guys Games & Paintball, 1236 Rt. 4 E 05701 (802) 775-1548
 Mike's Hobbies, 162 N Main St. 05701 (802) 775-0059
West Dover
 First Downhill 05356 (802) 464-7743

VIRGINIA

Ashland
 BCBG Paintball, 11501 Washington Hwy. 23005 (804) 798-1551
 www.bcbg-paintball.com
Camelia
 Just For Fun Sporting 8330 Daybreak Dr. 23002 (804) 561-5575
Chantilly
 Check It Paintball, 14511 F Lee Jackson Hwy. 20151 (703) 378-1150
 Powerhouse Paintball, 15214 Sovereign Pl. 20151 (703) 802-8179
Charlottesville
 Splathouse, 946 Grady Ave. Ste. 8 22901 (804) 977-5287
Chesapeake
 Action Town Sports, 501 Kempsville Rd. 23320 (757) 548-6368
Chesterfield
 SplatBrothers Paintball, 16910 Hull St. Rd. 23120 (804) 739-7590
 www.splatbrotherspaintball.com
Collinsville
 Extreme Paintball, 2009 Daniels Creek Rd. 24078 (276) 647-5985
 www.checkyourselves.tripod.com/paintball
Culpepper
 Hobby Town of Virginia, 1218 Blue Ridge Ave. 22701 (703) 825-8729
 Soggie Bottom Paintball, 219 Southgate Shopping Ctr. 22701
 (540) 829-6203
 www.soggiebottompaintball.com
Doswell
 BCBG Paintball, 10134 Kings Dominion Blvd. 23047 (804) 755-4388
 www.bcbg-paintball.com
Fairfax
 Pev's Paintball, 11204 Lee Highway A-1 22030 (703) 273-7732
 www.pevs.com
Fredericksburg
 Corky's, 921 Caroline St. 22401 (540) 373-4984 www.corkysdowntown.com
Ft. Eustis
 Action Town Sports, 876 Lee Blvd. 23606 (757) 878-5822
Gloucester
 Paintball Ally, 4145 George Washington Hwy. 23061 (877) 552-4582
 www.paintball-ally.com
Harrisonburg
 Valley Surplus, 1084 Virginia Ave. 22802 (540) 564-0002
 www.valleysurplus.com
Hayes
 Paintball Alley, 4145 George Washington Mem. Hwy. 23072 (804) 684-2183

Hopewell
 SplatBrothers PaintBall, 13908 James River Dr. 23860 (804) 452-2566
 www.splatbrotherspaintball.com
King George
 EF Action Sports, 10083 Kings Hwy. 22485 (540) 775-4343
Lanexa
 Shogun, 14375 Marine Corps Dr. 23089
Leesburg
 Hogback Mountain Paintball (703) 777-0057
Lynchburg
 Painted Forrest Adventure Games, 14307 Wards Rd. 24502 (804) 237-8774
 www.paintedforrest.com
Moseley
 SplatBrothers PaintBall, 16901 Hull Street Rd. 23120 (804) 739-7590
 www.splatbrotherspaintball.com
Portsmouth
 Ka-Splat Paintball, 4015 Cedar Ln. 23703 (757) 483-5870
Richmond
 BCBG Paintball, 7540 W Broad St. 23294 (804) 755-4388
 www.bcbg-paintball.com
 Paintball Authority, 11101 Midlothian Tpk. 23235 (804) 897-9030
 www.pbauthority.com
Roanoke
 Holsters & More, 2205 Williamson 24012 (540) 265-8810
Stafford
 Pev's Paintball, 556 Garrisonville Rd. 22554 (540) 720-1319 www.pevs.com
Sterling
 Pev's Paintball Pro Shop, 50-A Pigeon Hill Dr. 20165 (703) 709-7387
 www.pevs.com
Strasburg
 Skyline Paintball, 363 Radio Station Rd. 22657 (540) 465-9537
 www.skylinepaintball.com
Suffolk
 ActionTown Sports, 2109 Holland Rd. 23434 (757) 539-3756
Virginia Beach
 Beach Paintball, 2955 Virginia Beach Blvd. 23452 (757) 340-7318
 www.beachpaintball.com
Warrenton & Colonial Beach
 Rankin's Hardware & Sports (804) 224-8996/(504) 347-2499
Winchester
 Eagle Military Outfitters, 1810 S London St. 22601 (540) 667-6947
Woodbridge
 Pev's Paintball, 2594 Hanco Center Dr. 22191 (703) 897-0989
 www.pevs.com
 Pev's Paintball, 13932 Jeff Davis Hwy. 22191 (703) 491-6505
 www.pevs.com
Yorktown
 Virginia Sports-South 51, 1215 G George Washington Hwy. 23693 (757) 595-2694

WASHINGTON

Bellingham
 Semper Fi Paintball Supply, 5373 Guide Meridian #E-3 98226 (360) 398-8081
Bothell
 AWOL/Splat Mountain, 7018 NE Bothell Way 98011 (206) 487-9158
Burlington
 Mobile Tactics Paintball, 1829 Hwy. 20 Unit E 98233 (360) 755-9020
Chehalis
 The Outdoor Sports Shop, 1970-B S Market Blvd. 98532 (360) 740-6219
 www.outdoorsportsshop.com
Everett
 Doodle Bug Extreme Sportz, 5626 Evergreen Way 98203 (425) 238-7625
 www.doodlebugsportz.com
 Doodle Bug Sportz, 3813 Rucker Ave. #12 98201 (425) 257-9800
 West-Side Paintball Supply, 6325 Evergreen Way #3 98203 (425) 513-6211
Kennewick
 Western Paintball, 419 B West Entiat Ave. 99336 (509) 585-8353/585-9695
Kent
 Hole-In-The-Wall Paint, 14902 SE 274th St. 98042 (253) 639-3099
 Splat Attack Paintball Supplies, 23 809 104th Ave. SE 98031 (253) 852-8561
 www.splat-attack.com
Monroe
 Spalt 'Em Sports, 18600 Hwy. 2 98272 (360) 863-1020
Renton
 Shadow Lake Paintball, 2237 196th Ave SE 98058 (206) 852-7105
Richland
 Tri-City Paintball, 288 Williams Blvd. 99352 (509) 946-6141
Seattle
 AWOL Sporting Supply, PO Box 44398 98155
 The Jolly Soldier, 902A NE 65th St. 98115 (208) 524-2266
Shoreline
 AWOL, 1124 NE 170 St. 98155 (206) 368-5500
Silverdale
 Kitsap Sports, 10516 Silverdale Way #110 98383 www.kitsapsports.com
Snohomish
 West-Side Paintball Field, 17305 Old Mill Rd. 98290 (425) 513-6211
Spokane
 Army Surplus #4, 12218 Sprague Ave. 99206 (509) 928-4460
 Boomer's Paintball, 3807 E Sanson 99207 (509) 483-1879
 Camokaze Paintball, N 3209 Monroe St. 99205 (509) 324-0750
Woodinville
 AMS, 18144 Woodinville-Snohomish Rd. 98072 (425) 483-8855

Vancouver
Pacific Paintball Supply, 4219-F NE St. Johns Rd. 98661 (360) 750-1000
Vaughn
Paintball Sports, 5110 Lackey Rd. 98394 (253) 884-5293
www.aaapaintballsales.com
Yakima
Paintball Products NW, 205 S 4th Ave. 98902 (509) 453-4963

WEST VIRGINIA

Branchland
AC Enterprises, Rt. 3, Box 76 25506 (304) 778-3981
Elkins
Tom's Army Surplus, 400 ½ Randolph Ave. 26241 (304) 637-2769
Friendly
HM Strudwick Enterprises, 2875 S St. Rt. 2 26146 (304) 652-1773
Mineral Wells
Phillips Paintball Arena, PO Box 787 26150 (304) 863-3174
Scott Depot
Scary Creek Paintball, 434 Scary Creek Rd. 25560 (304) 755-5973

WISCONSIN

Appleton
Appleton Scheels, Fox River Mall 4301 W Wisconsin Ave. 54913 (920) 830-2977
Betyton
Bass Masters Paintball, 25936 Penny Benton Rd. 53803 (608) 965-3126
Big Bend
Fickau Service Center, 8880 W 229 Clark St. 53103 (262) 662-3301
Brookfield
Casanova's Outdoor Adventure Store, 13735 W. Capitol Dr. 53005 (262) 783-6456 www.casanovasadventures.com or www.adventurezones.com
Eau Claire
Eau Claire Scheels, 4710 Golf Rd. 54701 (715) 833-1886
First Strike, 1025 Sheridan Rd. 54703 (715) 833-1686
Elk Mound
Bubba's Paintball, E 7275 Cty. Rd. J 54739 (715) 664-8393
Ellsworth
Traynor Paintball, N4700 710th St. 54011 (715) 273-4100
Germantown
Milwaukee Paintball Center, N113 W18750 Carnegie Dr. 53022 (262) 532-2666 www.milwaukeepaintball.com
Grafton
On The Move Paintballs, 1309A Wisconsin Ave. 53024 (262) 376-0726
Helenville
Jungle Cat Paintball, W 2513 Bakertown Rd. 53137
Janesville
The Edge Paintball, 5946 S Hwy. 51 S 53545 (608) 743-0533
www.needguns.com
Goepfert's Paintball, 1621 N Washington St. 53545 (608) 755-1640
Kennan
Hillcrest Paintball, N 5605 Woodlawn Rd. 54537 (715) 474-3359
www.hillcrestpaintball.com
Kenosha
Kenosha's Paintball Supply, 1552-22 Ave. 53140
Lyndon Station
Stalker Paintball, W1923 Bass Lake Ln. 53944 (608) 666-2400
www.paintballwi.com
Mequon
Brush Fire Games, 11138 N Cedarburg Rd. 53092 (262) 238-8870
Virtual Magic.Net Cyber Centre, 11138 N Cedarburg Rd. 53092 (262) 238 8870 www.brushfiregames.com
Milwaukee
Paintball Dave's, 203 N Broadway 53202 (414) 271-3004
Monroe
Klines Arrowsmithing, N2153 Steiner Rd. 53566 (608) 329-7989
Neenah
Outdoor Adventure's I, 929 Zemlock Ave. 54956
Oshkosh
TechToys, 716 Ohio St. 54902 (920) 233-9007 www.techtoysonline.com
Poynette
Apocalypse Paintball, W 9496 City Hwy CS 53955 (608) 635-7324
Racine
Paintball Sam's, Hwy. K 53185 (414) 534-3197
Racine Paintball, 1813 16th St. 53403 (262) 939-8984
Raymond
Paintball Sam's, Hwy. K
St. Germain
JD Paintball Supplies, 7045 Hwy. 70E 54558 (715) 479-5838
Tomahawk
Zinger's Paintball, W5594 Muskelung Lake Rd. 54487 (715) 453-8792
Trevor
Promised Land Paintball, 29039 Hwy. C 53179 (262) 694-1540
www.promisedland.com
West Allis
War Game Room, 6780 W Lincoln 53219

WYOMING

Douglas
Attic Air Guns, 115 S 2nd St. 82633 (307) 358-3039

Gillette
Darts & Stuff, 402 E 2nd St. #D 82716 (307) 687-7384
Rock Springs
Dv8 Paintball, 1006 Wyoming St. 82901 (307) 382-4034

CANADA

ALBERTA

Calgary
Paintball Adventure World, 1912 Mackay Rd. NW T3B 1C7 (403) 289-8887
Edmonton
Alan Kerr/Ty Cale Security Equipment, 10769 99th St. T5H 4H6 (403) 424-8851
AllSports Replay, 8315 Argyll Rd. T6C 4R2 (780) 440-4835
www.allsportsreplay.com
Edmonton Survival Game, 4968 98th Ave. T6B 2Y7 (403) 469-4263
Pursuit Supplies Int'l, 5809 118th Ave. T5W 1E5 (403) 477-9252
T.A.G. Paintball Games, 5011 RR 180 T0B-4A0 (780) 663-2362
www.tagpaintballgames.com
Unique Outdoor Supplies, 4968 98th Ave. T6B 2Y7 (403) 627-7644
Red Deer
AllSports Replay, 5237 54th Ave. T4N 5K5 (403) 346-0700
www.allsportsreplay.com
Tactical Adventure Game, Box 344 T4N 5E9 (403) 347-4444
Olds
Weekend Warriors, RR #20 T4H 1P3 (403) 269-7025

BRITISH COLUMBIA

Brentwood Bay
GTO Paintball Canada, 7105-F West Saanich Rd. V8M-1P7 (250) 652-3231
www.gto-paintball.com
Langley
Panther Paintball, #4 5734 Production Way V3A-4N4 (604) 533-0890
www.pantherpaintball.com
Prince Rupert
Adrenaline Sports, 1050 Saskatoon Ave. V8J 4P1 (604) 627-7644
Surrey
BC Elite Adventure Sports, 16492 104th Ave. V4N 1Y5 (604) 951-0988
Frontline Paintball Supply, 13377 72nd Ave. V3W 2N5 (604) 501-0903

MANITOBA

St. Laurent
Paintball Paradise (204) 338-1535

NOVA SCOTIA

Dartmouth
Banshee Paintball, 122 Portland St. B2Y 1H8 (902) 469-6926
North Glasgow
Wizard Paintball, 11 Riverside St. B2H 3S1 (902) 755-9904
Sackville
L&M Surplus, 1823 Sackville Dr., Mid. B4C 2S7 (902) 865-6794
Truro
Spike's Action Games, 416 Robie St. B2N 1L8 (902) 893-8377/897-7700

ONTARIO

Brooklin
RLD Games, 350 Brawley Rd. W L0B 1C0 (800) 668-5809
Colborne
Triangle Computer & Hobby, 6 George St., Pt. L3K 3S1 (905) 834-4341
Hamilton
CD Paintball Supply, 6 Brucedale Ave W L9C 1C2 (416) 383-9614
Soldiers of Fortune Paintball, 6320 English Church Rd. L0R-1W0 (905) 679-8303 www.sofpaintball.com
Kleinburg
Ultimate Adventures, 76 Cardish St. L0J 1C0 (905) 893-1815
Lansdowne
Flag-Grab Paintball, PO Box 30 RR #1 K0E 1L0 (613) 659-4145
Mississauga
Champion's Paintball Supply, 7050 A Bramalea Rd. #17 L5S-1T1 (905) 671-3056 www.championspaintballsupply.com
Sault Ste. Marie
Superior Paintball, 94 Megginson Dr. P6A 6A9 (705) 946-8773
Scarborough
Premium Paintball Products, 371 Old Kingston Rd. #2 M1C 1B7 (888) 236-6090
Stratford
Outer Limits Paintball, RR #1 Nswhamboro N0B 2G0 (519) 625-8306
www.outer-limitspaintball.com
Wasaga Beach
Wasaga Beach Paintball, 396 River Rd. W L0L 2P0 (705) 429-5065

QUEBEC

Hemmingford
Arnold Paintball, 474 Chemin Covey Hill (514) 949-0873
Iberville
Le Jeu Survival (514) 346-2709
LaSalle
PBL/PMI Canada East, 8136 Jean Brillon H8N 2J5 (514) 595-5993

Mansonville
Le Jeu Survival (514) 295-2706
McMasterville
Adventure Division, 860 Bernard Pilon J3G 5W8 (514) 441-1129/464-5639
Quebec
Quebec Paintball, 800 Chemin de la Canardiere G1J 1B7 (418) 623-4496

SASKATCHEWAN

Lloydminster
Adventure Company Paintball, 2713 45th A Ave. S9V 1A6 (306) 825-7902
Maidstone
Moosehorn Paintball Games, PO Box 278 S0M 1M0 (306) 329-4290
Asquith
Paintball Action Games, PO Box 454 S0K 0J0 (306) 329-4290

CARIBBEAN

Bad Boyz Toyz, Caracasbaaiweg #164, Esther Blds. Unit 8, Curacao, Netherlands Antilles 5999-4656402
Caribbean Water Craft, 1747 Central Ave., Rio Piedras, PR 00920 (809) 790-8345
Extreme Toys, Rd. #2 Casablanca Shops, Hormidueros 00660 (787) 849-1419
Hunter's Paintball Field, O St. #129 Ramey Base, Aguadilla, PR 00604 (787) 890-2064
King's Jewelers, Munoz Riviera #105, Fajardo, PR 00648 (809) 863-0909
Seven Seas Bike Shop, 53 Union, Fajardo, PR 09648 (809) 863-8981
TBT, PO Box 1557, Luquillo, PR 00673 (809) 889-3685

AUSTRALIA

Adventure Quest Games, 19 Sommerset St., Epping, Sydney, NSW 2121 02-876-6382
Aussie Paintball Game, 201 Canterbury, Bankstown, NSW 2200 02-790-1401
Hamsta Where? Action Apparel, 18 Brunker Rd., Greenacre, NSW 2190 02-796-8536
Hot Shot Paintball, 226 Yarra St., South Geelong, VC 3220 011 613-52232-1931 www.paintballskirmish.com
Impact Paintball, 102 The Esplanade, Ettalong Beach, NSW 2257 02-43-413-829
Paintball Australia Pty., Gold Coast War Museum, Springbrook Rd., Mudgeeraba Gold
Coast, QD 4213 07-5-305222
Paintball Skirmish Games, 1175 High St., Armdale, VC 3143 03 822 1100
Phantom Zone, 93A Argyle St., Parramatta, NSW 2150 01-891-1848
Samford Skirmish, Samford Rd., Samford, QD 4520 07-289-1820
Skirmish, Mary St., Unley, SA 5061 08-371-0776
Skirmish Adventures
Greenacre, NSW, Level 2, 18 Brunker Rd. 2190 02-796-7955/8397
Gunning, NSW, Pinch Hill Hume Hwy. 2581 1-800-63-62-61
Helensburgh, Sydney, NSW, Lawrence Hargreave Dr. 2190 1-800-63-62-61
Townesville, QD, Bowhunter's Rd. 4810 01-796-2671
Skirmish Sunshine Coast, Ettamogah Pub Aussie Village, Bruce Hwy, Palmview, Sunshine Coast, QD 07-4-94-5566
Skirmish Survival Games, 35 Spring St., Sandringham, VC 3191 018-370-390
Top Gun Paintball Fields
Peperra, QD, Glengarry Rd. 4054 07-392-002
Mt. Tamborine, QD, Cedar Creek Lodge, Thunderbird Park 07-392-0022

BRAZIL

Mercenarios Paintball Supply, Shopping Center Lapa-Rua Catao, 72-k-18, Sao Paulo, SP 05049-901 www.mercenarios.com.br
Wargames Paintball, Target Emp. Com. Field & Supply, Av. Brig. Luis Antonio 478 5o and Sao Paulo 01426 01155-11 232-5470

CZECH REPUBLIC

Survival Games Bohemia, Jana Masaryka 26 Praha 2, Czech Republic 120 00 042-2-691-0843

DENMARK

Action Pursuit Centre, Nybrovej 304 C5, DK-2800, Lyngby 8781211 31535511
Arms Gallary City, Nybrogade 26, 1203 Kobenhaven K 33-118-338
Danish Paintball, Osterbro 37 A, 9000 Aalborg, 98 124277
Danish Paintball, Frederiksgade 72 Kld, 8000 Aarhus C 86 98937

Proline Scandinavia A/S, Yderlandsvej 25, Kobenhavn S 2300 45 3154 2045
Shoot To Thrill, Amagerbrogade 220 B, DK-2300 Copenhagen S 45 32 97 44 04

FRANCE

CAMP, 64 rue des marhurins, 75008 Paris, France 01.42.68.10.00
F.L.A.G., 1 rue du Rocher, 78610 St-Leger-En-Yvelines, France 34.86.33.14
Skirmish France, Domaine de Bousserain, 71320 Toulon, Sur Arroux, France 40-279-45-65

GERMANY

Brass Eagle Germany, Rainer Ehrig-Braun, Siegfried-Leopoldstrasse 5, 5300 Bonn-Beuel 0228-473205
Doc's Paintball Shop, Myhler Strasse 19, 27711Osterholz-Scharmbeck 04791-89-136
Farbdschungel Furth Paintball Gear, Elsternstrasse 3a, Tuch-enbach 90587 0911-7568-212
HarBur Marketing, Auf der Pick 5, D-66849 Landstuhl 49 06371 60291
BM SchieB-Sport-Bedarf, Postfach 5843, D-8700, Wurzburg 09302-846
Kaiserslautern Rod & Gun Club, 86 SVS SVBH, Unit 3240, Box 535, APO AE 09094 49-631-57484
Kotte & Zeller, Industristrasse, 415 65, W-95365 Rugendorf 092-21-84034
OPM Paintball Supplies, Ronsdorferstr 143, Tor 11 40233, Dusseldorf 02111-733-3155
Paintball Consortium, Holderlinsallee 6, 2000 Hamburg 60 40-279-45-65
Paintball Special Sports, PO Box 6532, D 4400, Munster 0251-55503
Paintball Sports Germany, Kleine Pfaffengrasse 3, 67346 Speyer 06232 / 620571
Venom, The Toxic Toys, Lohbecker Berg 18, 45470 Muhleim an der Ruhr 0208-380280

GREECE

Voyager Adventure Games, 25 Sigala St., 542 48 Thessaloniki 30-31 325833

ISRAEL

The Bazelet Paintball Site, K.Ayelet-Hashahaur Upper Galil 12200 9972-4-6932721 www.bazelet.com
Israel Paintball Games, PO Box 53052, Tel Aviv 61530 972-3-482653

IRELAND

Dscarmouche Paintball, Belfast 327500, SimulateD ActivitieS, Cork 150-4624
Skirmish Ireland Cranwell, Rockville Crescent, Blackrock, Dublin 010353 12819009

ITALY

Associazione Giochi Sopravvivenza, PO Box 38, 21020 Casciqago-VA
Survival Game Sport Adventures, F.I.G.P., Via Strada del Trombone, 14, 44013 Consandolo FE

JAPAN

International Paintball Game Federation Japan1024 Kamikasuya Isehara, Kanagawa 11-11 81-463-87-5895
J.P.P.L., 7-1 Yama Iwadecho Nagagun, Wakayama 649-62 81-736-61-6322

KOREA

Asia Pacific Int'l, Keoyang Bldg. Rm. 202, #51-8, Susongdong, Chongno Gu, Seoul 110-140, 82-2-734-9130

MEXICO

Chango's Army, Aeropuerto Atizapan, Distrito Federal 525-519-0303
Snyper Pro Shop, Blvd. Agua Calienten #1300-215, Tiajuana, BC 22420 www.snyperpro.com

NETHERLANDS

ASCO Sports, Hoefblad 12, 1911 PA Uitgeest 0-2513-14870
ASCO Paintball Games, 1e Middellandstraat 104b, 3021 BH Rotterdam 010-4778979
Euro Paintball Adventures, Marimbastraat 6, 5802 LW Venray 04780-87087
Jobs Paintball Shop, William De Zwijgerlaan 71-73, 1056-JG, Amsterdam 020-850-700
The Old Man Hardware, Damstraat 16, Amsterdam 1012 2M 020-627-0043
Realistic Fantasies Paintball, Erasmusgracht 5, 1056BB, Amsterdam 020-683-6474
Splat Attack, Schenkkade 293-294, 2595 AX'-Gravenhage 31-0-70-385-6699
Stichting Paintball Limburg, Dwarsstraat 27, 6361 XM, Limburg 31-45-244385

NEW ZEALAND

Super Splatz, 241 Dlenheim Rd./PO Box 22662, Christchurch 64 03 343-3055

NICARAGUA

Telerpustos, Col. Los Robles 3Ra, Etapa #196, Managua 011-505-278-0706

NORWAY

IB Paintball, Vogts Gate 39, 0444 Oslo 4 47-22-718102
Paintball Centre, Ostrifaret 10, 1476 Rasta 47-2-700-130

PANAMA

Sports International, Via Brasil, Building #38, Local #24, 6-9425 El Dorado 265-0625

PHILIPPINES

Gotcha, 291 P. Guevarra Ave., San Juan Metro Manila 011-63-2-70-64-47

ROMANIA

Mercenars Club, B-dul 1 mai nr. 29, B.PF9 ScB. Ap. 35, Constanta cod 8700 004041587592

RUSSIA

Action Paintball Games, Panfilova 20-2, Moscow 125080 +7-095-7851738 www.paintball.ru
Borodino Paintball, Moscow Region, Mytischensky District "Klyasminskoe Vodohranilische" pansion +7-095-3901880
Labyrinth Indoor, Vyatskaya 27, Moscow 103055 +7-095-2854935
Paintland Paintball Sports Club, Kalashny pereulok 10, Moscow 095-918-4580, 291-2259
Russian National Paintball Association, 5 Kozuhovskaia, Moscow 22-1-60, 095-277-7424, 166-6200
Top Gun Paintball, Krasnooktyabrskaya 40, Bolshevo-2, Pervomaisky +7-095-7822144 www.topgun.rr

SLOVENIA

Soberl d.o.o., Rosinova 3, Maribor 62 000 62-413-946

SOUTH AFRICA

IMEXO, PO Box 7216, Roggebaal, Cape Town 8001 021-701-5941
Indoor Paintball City, 7 Du Preez St., Knights 1413 Johannesburg 011-828-7583
Paintball Supplies, PO Box 3090, Symridge 1420 Johannesburg 011-828-7583

SWEDEN

Paintball Sports, Bismotalagaten 7, 591 30 Motala 0141-55550
Tradition Sturegallerian
114 46 Stockholm 08-611-45-35
411 06 Goteborg 031-15-03-66

THAILAND

International Paintball Club, 437-118 Soi Yodsak, Pattaya (66) 01-919-2635

UNITED KINGDOM

ENGLAND

Activ 8 Paintball, 62-63, Worcester St., Wolver Hampton W, Midlands WV2 4LQ 1901 835444, 1902 835442
Adventure Sports, Wedgenock Rifle Range, Wedgenock Ln., Warnick, Warwickshire CV35 7PX 01926-491-948
Ashcombe Valley Centre, Ashcombe, Dawlish, Devon EX7 0QD 01626-866766
Belsales, 60 Peabody Rd., N. Camp Farnborough, Hants GU14 6HA 01252-376827
Bridgehouse Survival, 51 Caldervale Ave., Charlton-Cum-Hardy, Manchester M21 7PN 0161-445-8804
CCS Leisure, 20 Griffith St., Rushden, Northampton NN10 0RL 01933-314805
Cheltenham Paintball, Unit 3, The Vineyards, Glouchester Rd., Cheltenham, Clouchestershire 01242-245504
Global Leisure, 95a Nutwick Rd., Havant, Hamshire PO9 2UQ 01705-499-494
Grizzley Sports, 11 St. Margaret's Crescent, Putney, London SW15 6HL 0181-780-0480
Hook Gun Co., 399 Hook Rd., Chessington, Surrey KT9 1EL
Lodge Bushes Paintball, 49 Salisbury Grove, Giffard Park, Milton Keynes, B'hamshire
MK14 5QA 01908-618-386

L.S.E., 20 Mt. Vernon Rd., Barnsley, S. Yorkshire S70 4DJ
London Paintball Co., 3 Kirkdale Close, Chatham, Kent DA1 5BH 01634-864-173
Marksmann Paintball, 22 HorseCroft Place, The Pinnacles, Harlow, Essex CM19 5BX 01279-626135
Mayhem Megastore, Pryor's Farm, Patch Park, Abridge, Essex 014028-424/014028-517
Mayhem Paintball Power Games, The Power House Lewes Rd., Blackboys Nr. Uckfield, East Sussex TN22 5LG 01825-890-033
Mayhem Paintball, Midlands, 172 Argyle St., Cuckoo Bridge Ind'l Estate, Nechells,
Bham B7 5TE 01435-866-189
Operation Paintball, Unit 23C, Hagh Ln. Ind. East, Hexham, N. Cumberland NE46 3PU
Paintball Experience, 27 Sidmouth St., Devizes, Wiltshire SN10 1LD 01380-728-982
Paintball Planet, 251 Deansgate, Manchester M34EN 44 (0) 161 839 2789
Paintball Planet, Unit 11 Millside Trdest., Lawson Rd., Dartford, Kent DA1 5BH 44 (0) 1322 222270
Paintball Sports, 291 Deansgate, Manchester M3 4EW 0161-839-8493
Paintcheck Epsom, 16 Beaconsfield Pl., Epsom, Surrey KT17 4BD 01372-726-224
Pidley Paintball, 49 Craitherne Way, North Arbury, Cambridgeshire CB4 2LZ 01223-67665
Predator Paintball, 14-16 Holbeach Rd., Catford, London BR2 9NY 0181-690-7717
Pro-Line, 8a Midas Bus. Ctr., Wantz Rd., Dagenham, Essex RM10 8PS 0181-595-7771
QED Leisure, 166 Lynne Rd., Downham Market, Norfolk PE38 9QG 01366-384-778
Sheffield Paintball Centre, Unit C4, Main St., Hakenthorpe, Sheffield S12 4LB
Skirmish-Kent, The Holt, Church Ln. Chelsham, Surrey, CR6 9PG 01883-627376
Skirmish-Nottingham, Unit 1, Wellbeck Ind. Est., Alfred Close, Nottingham NG3 1AD 01602 410 454
Survival Game, Canterbury 52 Swale Ave., Rushenden, Isle of Sheppey, Kent ME11 5JX 01795-583-303
Survival Game/Frome, 14 Arcacia Dr., Frome, Sommerset BA11 2TS 01373-471-035
Survival Game (Staffs), Painley Hill Farm, Bramshall, Uttoxeter, Staffordshire ST14 8SQ 01889-502-508
Survival Game (SW), Southdown Farm, Yarnscombe nr. Barnstable, N. Devon EX31 3LZ 01271-858-279
Survival Game West Midlands, C/O Dystate, Newcastle St., Stone Staffordshire ST15 8JU 01785-819-609
Survival Game (Yorks) Moore Farm, Elsham near Brigg, S. Humberside 01652-688-912
Wigan Birds & Pewts, 80 Ormskirk Rd., Newtown, Wigan WN5 9EA WDP
Unit 5, Metro Triangle, 221 Mount St., Nechells, Birmingham B7 5QT 0121-328-2228

SCOTLAND

Aberdeen Profields, Cullerlie By Skene, Aberdeenshire AB3 6XA 0133-08414
Alternative Leisure, East Woods Bus. Ctr., Green Hill Ave., Glasgow G46 6OX01416 382-811
Edinburgh Pro Fields, 136A St. John's Rd., Edinburgh EH12 7SB 0131-316-4004
Maxamillion Events, Overton Cottage, Kirknewton, Midlothian EH27 8DD 01506-884-088
Mayhem – Edinburgh, 14 Ochiltree Ct., Mid Clader Livingstone, W. Lothian EH53 0RU
SimulateD ActivitieS, 4 Lochrin Pl., Tollcross, Edinburgh EH3 9QY 0131-229987

WALES

Leisure Pursuits, Langrove Country Club, Fairwood Common, Swansea, S. Wales 0144-128-2410
Paintball Cosortium, 53 Station Rd., Deeside, Clwyd, N. Wales 01244-821490
SimulateD ActivitieS, 19 Seymour St., Aberdare, Mid Glamorgan CF44 7BL 01685-875-633

VENEZUELA

Estrategia, C.C. Multicentro 1er Piso, Local 26 Cagua, Aragua, 2122044-960455, 044-99577970
Sport de Paintball, Venezuela Ave., Francisco di Miranda, Centro Plaza, Niveo Jardin,
Local CC-322-A, Los Palos Grandes, Caracas 582-286-4483
Survival Games Club, CA, Calle Baruta con Los Cerritos, Res. Paso Real #18, Caracas